ISBN-13:
978-1507529102

Library of Congress Control Number : 2015900582
Publisher: CreateSpace Independent Publishing Platform, North Charleston, SC

Dedication

To my wife, Gisela Janders Harkins; my daughter, Dr. Suzanne Andrea Harkins; my sister, Deborah Faith Harkins and my twin brother, Peter Schubert Harkins

CONTENTS

Preface

My primary purpose in this book is to illustrate and document what I believe is the immediate future environment of corporate computing from the perspective of the corporate executive, not the future of computer architecture or hardware. That future is the virtual elimination of the corporate in-house computer, in-house programming staffs and in-house computing operational staffs, replaced by cloud computing, cloud managed services, sophisticated application software, cognitive computing, real-time predictive autonomic computing, and a new universe of computing capability.

Pervasive implementation of real-time program auditing of executing computer programs is the crucial advancement necessary for real-time predictive autonomic computing, and is an important basis for the virtual elimination of almost all corporate programmers. Real-time program auditing provides a permanent video camera like recording and instant availability of all statements executed and data processed inside the computer, and is as useful as the now almost universal worldwide implementation of the security camera and all video recording.

Imagine law enforcement, or the National Football League, without any recorded video review and replay capability, or the television industry without any video recording or video streaming playback capability, and that is where the corporate computing industry is today. Imagine the airline industry without the "black boxes' used to record real-time flight information for disaster analysis.

The computing industry is employing and utilizing far too many programmers using the same archaic methods, such as guessing what is happening or did happen inside the executing program, as it did sixty years ago, with disastrous cost, low productivity, and low capability, while enabling criminal fraud such as the Bernard Madoff case. This will all soon change, enabled by the real-time program auditing revolutionary computing advancement as is illustrated in Appendix B The Power of Traceability

The driving forces behind this immediate transformation from corporate in-house computing to cloud computing are overwhelming economic, productivity, capability and competitive benefits. A detailed review by senior corporate executives of the corporate in-house computing budget, by line item, over a period of years and a comparison with superior cloud computing costs and capability is the crucial first step in that transition. A crucial second step by senior corporate executives is the stark and realistic assessment of how competitive the corporation is now, where it wants to be, and how best to get there.

That future includes a direct and interactive dialogue and user interface (UI) between the ultimate user and the computer without programming as we know it today, utilizing extensions of cognitive computing and real-time predictive autonomic computing (true self-healing computing). This book provides the corporate executive with a better understanding of corporate computing, including costs and opportunities, and the capability to better implement and utilize corporate computing throughout the enterprise. Thus the book title and first chapter: The Future of Corporate Computing.

I have been directly and continuously involved in corporate computing from virtually the beginning of corporate computers and corporate programming starting in 1960 until now. Corporate computing and programming caused the end or death of the Herman Hollerith 1890 Unit Record (punched card) 70 year era and directly ended the careers of virtually all the Unit Record board wirers and accounting machine operators in less than a decade.

Today the current 60 year era of the **immensely expensive, ineffective, and unproductive in-house computer programmer** (including developer) and computer datacenter operator and corporate IT environment as we know it is rapidly ending, replaced by mature and sophisticated vendor supplied and managed application software, and the processing cloud.

The end of the in-house corporate computer, and possibly the end of corporate computer programming as we know it today, is just another significant innovation in a long line of innovations mandated by competition and economics since the beginning of corporate computers, this time in software rather than in hardware. Thus the second chapter: **The End of the Corporate In-house Programmer**

More than five decades of direct involvement and observation and worldwide consulting with many CEOs, COOs, CFOs and CIOs demonstrates to me that corporate executive management really does not understand and cannot effectively manage and coordinate the crucial function of corporate computing (or Information Technology), and is in real danger of failure and is far behind in moving towards the future. All of these C level executives including the CIO, are really managers who should be focused on utilizing corporate computing as a major tool and asset for accomplishing the corporate objectives, and not be mesmerized by the "black box' of computing.

Change is always most cruel to those who are displaced. The Chief Information Officer (CIO) of a corporate in-house computing system can either embrace change or reject change, but cannot long stop it. Thus the third chapter: **Corporate Executive Migration Path to Cloud Computing**

Ever wonder how and why, in the past, so many CEOs and corporate executives rose from the mailroom and the lowest jobs to the pinnacle of corporate and financial success, while most other people languish in the same dead-end job? The primary reason is that the mailroom was traditionally the focal point of information coming into and leaving the company, and for information flowing among departments within the company.

An observant, interested and ambitious mailroom person could literally observe exactly how the company worked and could also directly communicate with key people in every department of the company. That mailroom focal point of information flow and opportunity to observe and learn exactly how a company works is now performed by the corporate computing department.

Today, a Drexel University co-op student interning in the corporate computing department of a corporation has an incredible opportunity to learn and understand exactly how the entire company works, and has the opportunity to interface directly with executive management. And, my focus is on Drexel University as that is my university and cooperative education experience, although I believe this focus applies to all university education.

CEOs and executive management have also discovered that the corporate computing department is perhaps the best opportunity for their children to intern in the business during at least one summer, on their probable way up at the company at graduation. Drexel University has a new and huge opportunity to replace the traditional lower level disappearing manufacturing co-op jobs with many high tech and high paying co-op opportunities around the world, and to greatly expand the number and value of their relationships with many more companies wanting to utilize co-op interns.

I address these opportunities in chapter topics **What to do with the CEO's son or daughter this summer?, and What should the Drexel co-op do in the corporate computing department to be the most valuable?, and the most important questions What must Drexel do to best prepare its co-op students to be most valuable now and in their careers?, and What must Drexel Co-op students require of Drexel to be the most valuable now and in their careers?** Thus the fourth chapter: **Mailroom or Intern or Co-op to CEO in Today's Corporation**

Champion contestants on the TV show *Jeopardy!* are made financially successful by demonstrating their superior and instantly expressed knowledge of a large spectrum of subjects—and doing it faster than their competitors. Their success, like the success of most other people, results from a series of positive actions to gain knowledge and skill to be competitive and their ambition to get on the *Jeopardy!* Show.

IBM's Watson computer demonstrated that a powerful corporate computer and sophisticated software can beat the most accomplished humans in information storage and instantaneous retrieval. This chapter illustrates several examples of how corporate computing in most corporations holds and distributes valuable information and knowledge critical to success in all areas in the company and provides access and interaction to all levels of corporate management, and provides unexpected opportunity to those who will take it. Thus the fifth chapter: **The Road to Singapore**

The Bernard L. Madoff Ponzi Scheme was the largest financial Ponzi scheme in history, with investors being defrauded out of more than 17 billion dollars of investments. The fraud was never uncovered by the Securities and Exchange Commission or other regulators over the many decades the fraud was taking place. I reference detailed public record documents and voluminous sworn testimony produced during the government trials in the Madoff case, which show exactly how this fraud was accomplished without ever any investments being actually made by Madoff, together with many books authored by defrauded investors illustrating how this fraud ruined their lives.

I believe that this type of fraud is continuing largely undetected today as the auditing, detection, and enforcement systems have not been significantly enhanced to stop these frauds from happening, and I can offer my proven patented solution for preventing this kind of fraud from ever happening again. Thus the sixth chapter: **The Bernie Madoff Case - The Forensic Accounting Investigation**

When I joined IBM full-time in 1962 out of college for my dream career as an IBM Systems Engineer, IBM was one of the most admired, respected and profitable companies and certainly by far the largest and most successful computer company in the world.

Today IBM is a diminishing shell of what it was during my twenty one plus years at IBM. IBM is relying on its vast but shrinking store hundreds of thousands of installed customers for diminishing revenue, while floundering against competition. SAP is succeeding and growing and is poised, I believe, to overtake IBM. My revolutionary strategy is crucial to the future success and significant growth of both IBM and SAP.

And, I believe that IBM's vision, definition and implementation of Autonomic Computing and of Big Data are seriously deficient and do not provide for the capability and implementation of (true) real-time predictive autonomic computing and for really big data that is crucial to the future of corporate computing.

I have been directly but fruitlessly communicating to IBM executive management a strategy for succeeding and growing, a strategy I illustrate in this seventh chapter: **How IBM and SAP Can Succeed and Grow: A Revolutionary Strategy.**

The future of corporate computing is now unfolding upon us, and it is bringing revolutionary and almost totally unknown changes in how corporate computing is achieved. These revolutionary changes will virtually eliminate in-house programming and programmers and programming languages as we know them today, while providing almost total transparency, visibility, instant auditability and universal understanding of all computing processing. Thus chapter eight: **My Conclusions (and my Opinion)**

The book **appendixes** include several copyrighted and published articles illustrating the future of corporate computing (actually already evolving corporate computing), the Real-Time Program Audit (RTPA) active U.S. patent that is fundamental to future corporate computing, and bibliographical background information. Specific references are provided including Internet addresses for virtually all reference material.

This book is my honest and expert opinion, as expert as any opinion formed and refined over my active observation and participation in hundreds of companies worldwide, of the automation of America and now the world from 1960 to today.

The book is not and I am not against programmers or IBM or the Government or education or anyone else.

It is now time to move on from the technology and world of the 1960s to the world of today, and to prepare for tomorrow. It is also past time to identify and address the selfish, self-serving, incredibly harmful, costly resistance to change and the failure to embrace available change, such as in the Bernie Madoff Ponzi scheme that have caused needless grief and loss, including suicides, to so many innocent people and immediate risk to so many others who are at the same risk today.

I include a few of my corporate computing experiences to document what it was actually like to work all alone at new customers far away from any IBM support as the only IBM on-site representative and with total responsibility for success, and for weeks at a time, and to provide a perspective for my opinions and thinking about the future of corporate computing.

There was no collaborating with multiple on-site team members and no cell phones and no one back at the IBM branch office to help you. You just did what you thought was best, and figured out the problems yourself, and worked directly with every level of management and staff and made every decision yourself, as long as the customer went "on rent" and paid for the IBM equipment when it first arrived and kept paying for it. The customer wanted and needed the new computing capability and made surprising and bold sacrifices to implement it.

My personal computing experiences and extensive reference material of past critical times for IBM and corporate computing within my active working career are to some perhaps trips down memory lane. But, they cover almost the entire period of the most profound changes to corporate computing from the first corporate computers through today, as is illustrated in the book **The Innovators - By Walter Isaacson.**

My five decades long career personal observations, experiences, and direct participations in corporate computing perhaps focus on IBM, as it was the largest company in corporate computing and my employer for decades, and provide a unique contemporaneous record not from press releases but from what actually happened for the those who follow to critique as desired.

All of our knowledge today of human history and events over millennia is from contemporaneous records which someone took the time and effort to record and provide context and perspective, and which survived for someone later to observe and analyze and benefit from. Those records started with drawings on walls, then with letters in early language on scrolls and paper, then with signs, then with the Guttenberg press, then with the photograph and video, and now largely with the computer.

Incredibly, all of the records and information in human history until that stored inside the computer were essentially human readable, visible to the eye. These records could be simply and immediately viewed as made available and literally grasped by the hands of anyone and independently analyzed by anyone and everyone, except now for information stored inside the computer and processed by the computer.

Computer programmers are the modern day priests and scribes of the middle ages who literally controlled vital information and how it was stored and presented and interpreted to the masses and to royalty, until the invention of the Guttenberg press provided access and visibility of information to all in the common language understood by the public.

Getreidegasse

Priests and scribes wrote in Latin on scrolls buried away from the public, and periodically interpreted the meaning and significance of that information as they desired or was to their advantage. Modern day computer programmers write in arcane and cryptic programming languages and store information inside the computer, including critical processing steps how the corporation works, and periodically interpret the meaning and significance of that information to the corporation and to corporate executives.

A modern and liberating equivalent to the Guttenberg press today is to provide authorized real-time access and visibility and transparency of computer information to all. That is by permanently automatically recording as in a video recording of all computer stored **and computer generated** information, including program data and the data being processed, and making it immediately available to all in the common language understood by the public, without the need for computer programmers.

So, although the modern day corporate computer can process information perhaps a million times faster than manual systems, and perhaps store a million times more information than manual systems, that information is obscured from the view of corporate executives and of Government regulators and the public with often horrific and tragic consequences.

The cover of this book "The Future of Corporate Computing" illustrates a fork in the road, and I have experienced several crucial forks in in the road towards my working career, starting with the decision to go to Drexel as a co-op engineering student, rather than to become a history teacher, and my Drexel co-op jobs which lead to my dream career at IBM. I relate my most crucial fork in the road experience at Drexel and I hope it helps all Drexel co-op future students.

Every fork in the road I took that was different from my peers and conventional thinking was a leap into the challenge of the unknown for me, and was ultimately successful for me.

The Road Not Taken

Two roads diverged in a yellow wood,
And sorry I could not travel both
And be one traveler, long I stood
And looked down one as far as I could
To where it bent in the undergrowth;

Then took the other, as just as fair,
And having perhaps the better claim
Because it was grassy and wanted wear,
Though as for that the passing there
Had worn them really about the same,

And both that morning equally lay
In leaves no step had trodden black.
Oh, I kept the first for another day!
Yet knowing how way leads on to way
I doubted if I should ever come back.

I shall be telling this with a sigh
Somewhere ages and ages hence:
Two roads diverged in a wood, and I,
I took the one less traveled by,
And that has made all the difference.

Robert Frost 1920
(Public domain)

I hope you enjoy and benefit from this perspective and match it with your own.

Paul Houston Harkins

1 The Future of Corporate Computing

The immediate future of corporate computing is a consumer friendly utility providing all users with transparency and visibility to real-time information, without corporate in-house computers, in-house computer operations staffs or in-house programming staffs.

That future is the virtual elimination of the corporate in-house computer, in-house programming staffs and in-house computing operational staffs, replaced by cloud computing, cloud managed services, and sophisticated vendor supplied application software, cognitive computing, and real-time predictive autonomic computing and analytics. It includes direct and interactive dialogue between the ultimate user and the computer without programming as we know it today utilizing extensions of cognitive computing including real-time predictive autonomic computing.

Computer languages from the dawn of computers, such as **COBOL** (Common Business Oriented Language) developed by Dr. Grace Hopper, to **BASIC** (Beginners All-purpose Symbolic Instruction Code), to interactive cognitive computing, strive to interact with the computer in nearly the native language of the user, rather than the arcane and cryptic assembler like programming languages popular today, such as the **C programming language**..

The COBOL Programming Language
http://www.engin.umd.umich.edu/CIS/course.des/cis400/cobol/cobol.html

BASIC
http://en.wikipedia.org/wiki/BASIC

C (programming language)
http://en.wikipedia.org/wiki/C_(programming_language)

The consumer includes corporations, executives, businesses, households and individuals who will utilize mobile and Internet technology, as in smartphones, tablets and PCs to access and process all computer business related information, and all of corporate computing. Only the very largest corporations will be able to possibly justify in-house business computing capability and computer staffs, and that will be far different than today.

- How is this future without in-house corporate computers and in-house programmers possible and better and economically desirable, and when?
- Why are there so many expensive corporate programmers now after so many years of corporate computers and applications development and computer advancements?
- Exactly what are the enormous costs of corporate computing versus alternatives?
- Why has not someone focused on eliminating very expensive and primitive and unproductive computer programming, development and support technology?

- How can corporate executives immediately regain control and understanding and costs of corporate computing and fulfill their fiduciary duty of care responsibilities?
- How can corporate executives immediately become more competitive and successful and reduce risk with better corporate computing?
- Why is it that Government and corporation executives and others are not able to adequately manage and audit and understand corporate computing, as in the Bernie Madoff Ponzi scheme, and at what economic and social cost

These and a host of related important questions and their relevant answers have not been previously raised or answered, although the fundamental reason is incredibly simple and obvious and the solutions are simple and available.

The reasons for Computer programmers
The invention of the corporate electronic computer in about 1946 brought about a fundamental and dramatic change from all prior methods, over millennia, in how information was stored, processed, analyzed and was then made available to all end users, including corporate management.

Corporate electronic processing dramatically increased the speed and capabilities of information processing, but it for the first time hid or obscured the information from the end user, and it hid or obscured the exact processing from the end use. This may sound unimportant, but for the first time in history, nobody in the corporation could access computer related information without passing the gatekeeper of corporate computing and sometimes the computer programmer as the information was invisible inside the computer.

With computers, the end user lost independent and immediate independent visibility to information, which was previously stored in traditional paper accounting ledgers and paper files, or in unit record punched cards, and of course in books and in pictures. The manual documents stored information and processes, such as bank ledgers and bank accounting could not be accessed by the bank president or a teller or a clerk, or a customer without being retrieved from the computer and made available in a user readable form. Also the computer programmer was required to write or maintain computer source programs to input the user information, to process the computer information and to create output reports or analysis of the stored and otherwise hidden information.

Even in previous Herman Hollerith unit record punched card corporate installations the individual punched cards could be read by users without data processing help as the cards were normally available in file cabinets in between being processed for statements or reports, and the processing steps were simple and easily understood.

Sounds simple and obvious and a problem that command and control of corporate computing was put in the hands of a new group of computer programmers, who programmed (or wired control boards) in arcane and cryptic languages and could not and still do not understand what is happening inside the computer as their programs execute with the customer information. Worse is that the corporate executives and often corporate computing management still do not know what the programmers do or what the programs do today.

Thus the Bernie Madoff Ponzi scheme, where the Security Exchange Commission agents were and are dumbfounded at computer fraud, partly because they apparently still do not have a clue of what the computer programs are doing, while billions of dollars are stolen from innocent investors.

The obvious and practical solution to this kind of corporate computer programming and computer management, and Government auditing management is to dramatically streamline it or even eliminate it, and replace it with an incredibly better alternative solution, and the appendixes in this book illustrate exactly how to do so.

The future of corporate computing (sometimes referred to as Information Technology or IT and in the old days Data Processing), and indeed computing itself, is inexorably following the path of virtually every other successful major invention, innovation and adaption throughout recorded history.

That path of identification of a need or objective, search for viable solutions, simplification of use, economic advantage, trial and error of possible solutions, selection of a viable solution (as in a patent), justification (economic or other), development and marketing and implementation of the solution, resistance to change, competition, changing environments, and ultimate success are universal for all productive change.

Harold Evans book **"They Made America: From the Steam Engine to the Search Engine: Two Centuries of Innovators"** wonderfully illustrates how this same path of innovation applies to virtually all important and successful innovation, including computers.

What none of the inventors or innovators profiled in Harold Evans book including Thomas Edison, inventor or the light bulb and phonograph, Alexander Graham Bell, inventor of the telephone, Karl Benz, inventor of the gasoline powered automobile, and John Eckert and John Mauchly, inventors of the ENIAC computer could have realized is how pervasively their inventions were being used 60 years or a century later, how much they had changed, and why.

While the idea and invention and need had been proven and accepted and virtually universally adopted, the passage of time brings ever changing economic, social, and political, enhancements and competition to obsolete the original innovation and replace it with simply better implementations.

Thomas Edison's brilliant invention of the incandescent light bulb in 1879 using DC power is obsolete, replaced by LED technology and AC power, as is his phonograph, replaced with streaming video and sound.

Alexander Graham Bell's invention of the telephone in 1876 required telephone lines and switchboard operators to connect calls, and is largely obsolete, replaced by billions of wireless cellphones and smartphones and the Internet with fully automatic routing of telephone calls. Economics, enhancements and the impossibility of having perhaps millions of telephone switchboard operator **drove that transformation to a virtually totally automatic system.**

Karl Benz's invention of the gasoline powered automobile in 1885 required hand crank starting (with risk of a broken arm), a mechanics tool kit and skills and an adventurers spirit, Replaced today by about **260 million cars and motorcycles in the USA**, with push button starting, self-parking cars that are interchangeably drivable by any 16 year old of either sex. Oh, and if there is an issue, the *car* can automatically call OnStar (worldwide remote assistance), locate itself with GPS and the *car* will diagnose the issue, and even stop in an emergency.

U.S. motorcycle registrations in 2012, by state (in 1,000 units)

http://www.statista.com/statistics/191002/number-of-registered-motorcycles-in-the-us-by-state/

There are more than 4 million U.S. registered motorcycles in 2012, which are part of about 260 million U.S. registered automobiles and motorcycles in 2012. These 260 million automobiles and motorcycles are serviced today by only **700,000 mechanics,** with about one mechanic, earning only about twice the minimum wage, for every 400 automobiles in 2012, This is **down by a factor of perhaps 100 times from early days of the automobile.**

Economics, enhancements, standardization, demand, computer diagnostics and the impossibility of having perhaps many millions of rarely needed mechanics drove that transformation.

The **U.S. Bureau of Labor Statistics Occupational Outlook Handbook** provides important annual statistics including hundreds of occupations including total number people employed and the average annual compensation and hourly rate of pay.

NOTE – I have included the latest available detailed Bureau of Labor Statistics descriptions of all of the type of corporate computing jobs as defined by the U.S. Government, including the job description and annual compensation. Corporate executives who spend perhaps ten minutes reviewing this information will be able to better understand corporate computing, and to analyze their own corporate computing environments, costs, budgets and capability.

The occupations of mechanic and computer related occupations are illustrated for in-depth analysis, while the occupations of the telephone switchboard operator and many others have simply disappeared over time.

Note that the Bureau of Labor Statistics median pay does not include fringe costs, such as holiday pay, vacation pay, sick pay, health coverage, social security matching contribution, possible matching retirement contribution, etc. Fringe costs are normally about one-third of the direct median U.S. Bureau of Labor Statistics median pay costs.

Note that the Bureau of Labor Statistics occupational categories such as mechanic or computer programmer are rather broad. One skilled person may be able to and need to do several of the job categories in a small company, while several skilled people may share areas of expertise in an occupational category in a large company.

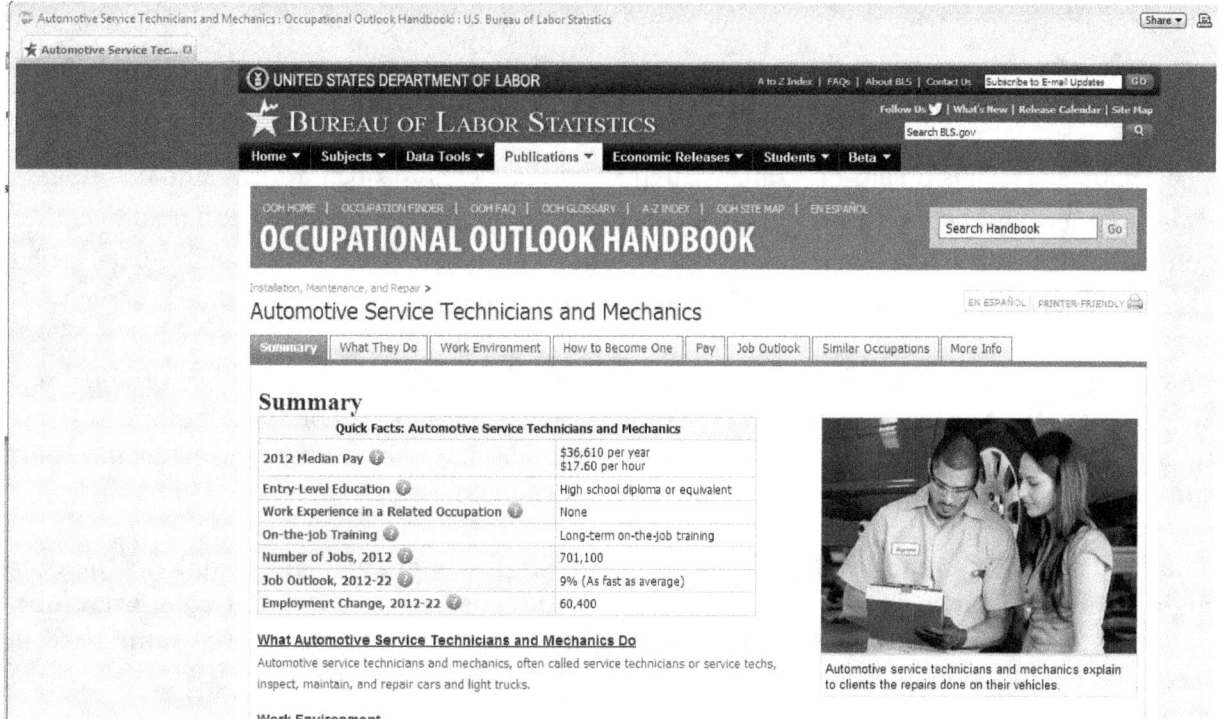

http://www.bls.gov/ooh/installation-maintenance-and-repair/automotive-service-technicians-and-mechanics.htm

What Automotive Service Technicians and Mechanics Do

Automotive service technicians and mechanics, often called service technicians or service techs, inspect, maintain, and repair cars and light trucks.

Quick Facts: Automotive Service Technicians and Mechanics	
2012 Median Pay	$36,610 per year $17.60 per hour
Entry-Level Education	High school diploma or equivalent
Work Experience in a Related Occupation	None
On-the-job Training	Long-term on-the-job training
Number of Jobs, 2012	701,100
Job Outlook, 2012-22	9% (As fast as average)
Employment Change, 2012-22	60,400

Note that the automotive mechanic hourly median pay was only slightly more than **two times** the U.S. minimum wage of $7.25 per hour in 2012, and that more than 50,000 gas stations have closed in the last two decades as the need for automobile mechanics steeply declined, and automobile fuel economy has improved.

The primary reasons why the mechanics wage is so low is that so very many people can do the mechanic job, that computer diagnostics largely identify the problem and solution, and automobiles need far less maintenance.

The 1950s and 1960s dream of so many high school students to open a local automobile garage and pump gas and be a mechanic has virtually disappeared as the need and technology and economics demanded. Similar opportunities of telephone switchboard operators and secretaries have also essentially disappeared because of technology including Microsoft Office Word.

The automobile repair and maintenance industry is a mature industry that has been refined into a very cost-efficient and effective industry. While the mechanics job is not easily exported offshore, it has a low paid and relatively shrinking labor force that may shrink much further as the internal combustion engine is replaced with electric powered vehicles.

The 1960s and 1970s and 1980s dream of so many high school and college students to become highly-paid corporate computer programmers and analysts and related computer jobs is about to follow the same path of steep decline as the mechanic, and for the same need and technology and economic reasons.

The huge and expensive ENIAC computer invention in 1946 is obsolete, replaced by hundreds of thousands of corporate computers that are millions of times more powerful, incredibly inexpensive computer hardware, and incredibly powerful although expensive and complex software and support.

Today, these hundreds of thousands of corporate computers, or computers processing the functions of an entire company as in corporate computing rather than an as individual computing, are supported by literally millions of expensive, and I believe, un-productive computer related in-house staff doing computer related functions including; programming, analysis, operations and related activities.

Major software and operations related corporate computing jobs found in many companies are illustrated below including:

Quick Facts: Computer Systems Analysts	
2012 Median Pay	$79,680 per year $38.31 per hour

Quick Facts: Software Developers	
2012 Median Pay	$93,350 per year $44.88 per hour

Quick Facts: Computer Programmers	
2012 Median Pay	$74,280 per year $35.71 per hour

Quick Facts: Computer Support Specialists	
2012 Median Pay	$48,900 per year $23.51 per hour

Quick Facts: Web Developers	
2012 Median Pay	$62,500 per year $30.05 per hour

Quick Facts: Network and Computer Systems Administrators	
2012 Median Pay	$72,560 per year $34.88 per hour

Other computer related jobs not necessarily related directly to corporate computing at most mid-size companies are illustrated below including:

Quick Facts: Computer and Information Research Scientists	
2012 Median Pay	$102,190 per year $49.13 per hour

Quick Facts: Computer Network Architects	
2012 Median Pay	$91,000 per year $43.75 per hour

Quick Facts: Database Administrators	
2012 Median Pay	$77,080 per year $37.06 per hour

Quick Facts: Information Security Analysts	
2012 Median Pay	$86,170 per year $41.43 per hour

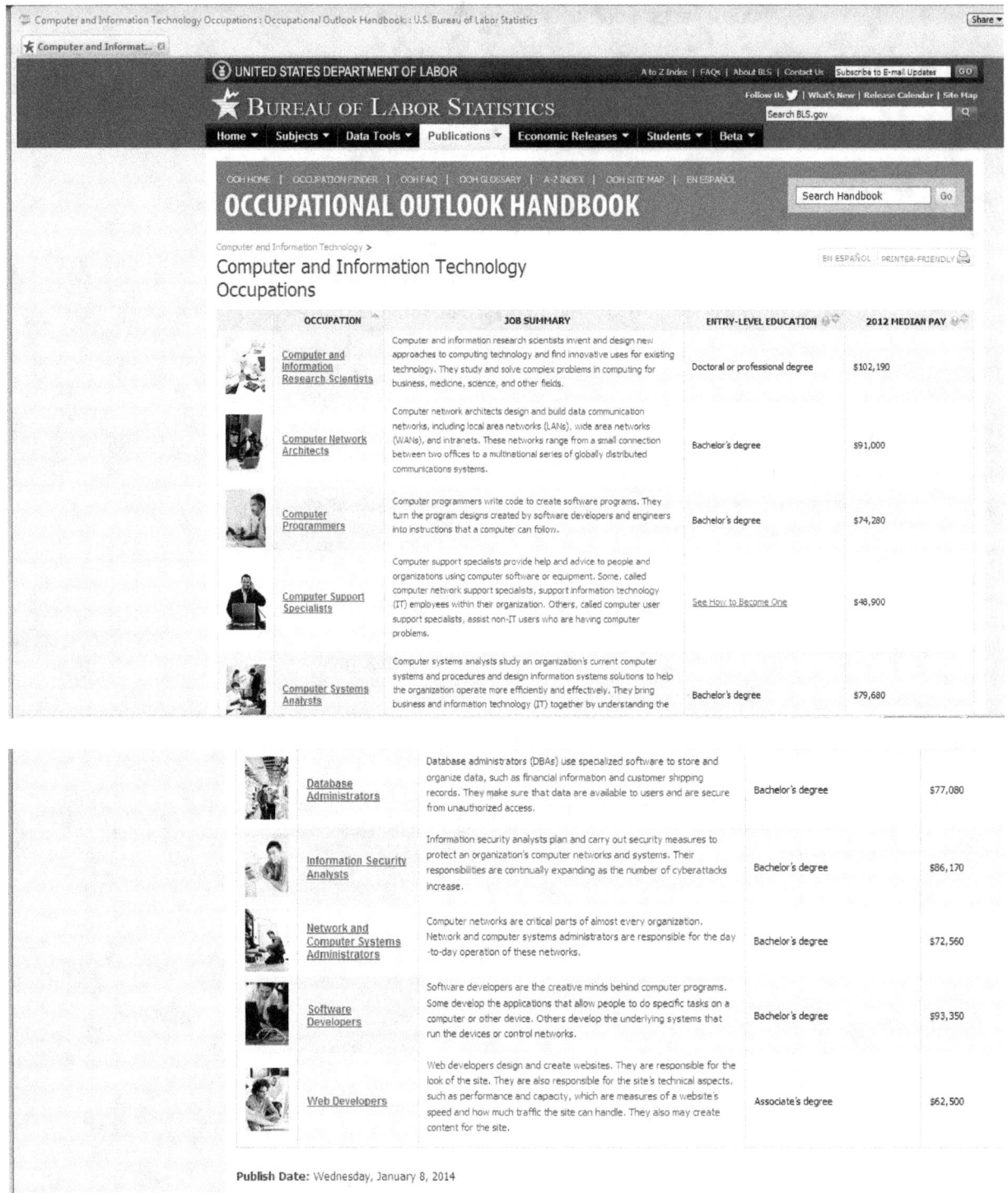

Computer and Information Technology >

Computer and Information Technology Occupations

EN ESPAÑOL | PRINTER-FRIENDLY

OCCUPATION	JOB SUMMARY	ENTRY-LEVEL EDUCATION	2012 MEDIAN PAY
Computer and Information Research Scientists	Computer and information research scientists invent and design new approaches to computing technology and find innovative uses for existing technology. They study and solve complex problems in computing for business, medicine, science, and other fields.	Doctoral or professional degree	$102,190
Computer Network Architects	Computer network architects design and build data communication networks, including local area networks (LANs), wide area networks (WANs), and intranets. These networks range from a small connection between two offices to a multinational series of globally distributed communications systems.	Bachelor's degree	$91,000
Computer Programmers	Computer programmers write code to create software programs. They turn the program designs created by software developers and engineers into instructions that a computer can follow.	Bachelor's degree	$74,280
Computer Support Specialists	Computer support specialists provide help and advice to people and organizations using computer software or equipment. Some, called computer network support specialists, support information technology (IT) employees within their organization. Others, called computer user support specialists, assist non-IT users who are having computer problems.	See How to Become One	$48,900
Computer Systems Analysts	Computer systems analysts study an organization's current computer systems and procedures and design information systems solutions to help the organization operate more efficiently and effectively. They bring business and information technology (IT) together by understanding the	Bachelor's degree	$79,680
Database Administrators	Database administrators (DBAs) use specialized software to store and organize data, such as financial information and customer shipping records. They make sure that data are available to users and are secure from unauthorized access.	Bachelor's degree	$77,080
Information Security Analysts	Information security analysts plan and carry out security measures to protect an organization's computer networks and systems. Their responsibilities are continually expanding as the number of cyberattacks increase.	Bachelor's degree	$86,170
Network and Computer Systems Administrators	Computer networks are critical parts of almost every organization. Network and computer systems administrators are responsible for the day-to-day operation of these networks.	Bachelor's degree	$72,560
Software Developers	Software developers are the creative minds behind computer programs. Some develop the applications that allow people to do specific tasks on a computer or other device. Others develop the underlying systems that run the devices or control networks.	Bachelor's degree	$93,350
Web Developers	Web developers design and create websites. They are responsible for the look of the site. They are also responsible for the site's technical aspects, such as performance and capacity, which are measures of a website's speed and how much traffic the site can handle. They also may create content for the site.	Associate's degree	$62,500

Publish Date: Wednesday, January 8, 2014

http://www.bls.gov/ooh/computer-and-information-technology/home.htm

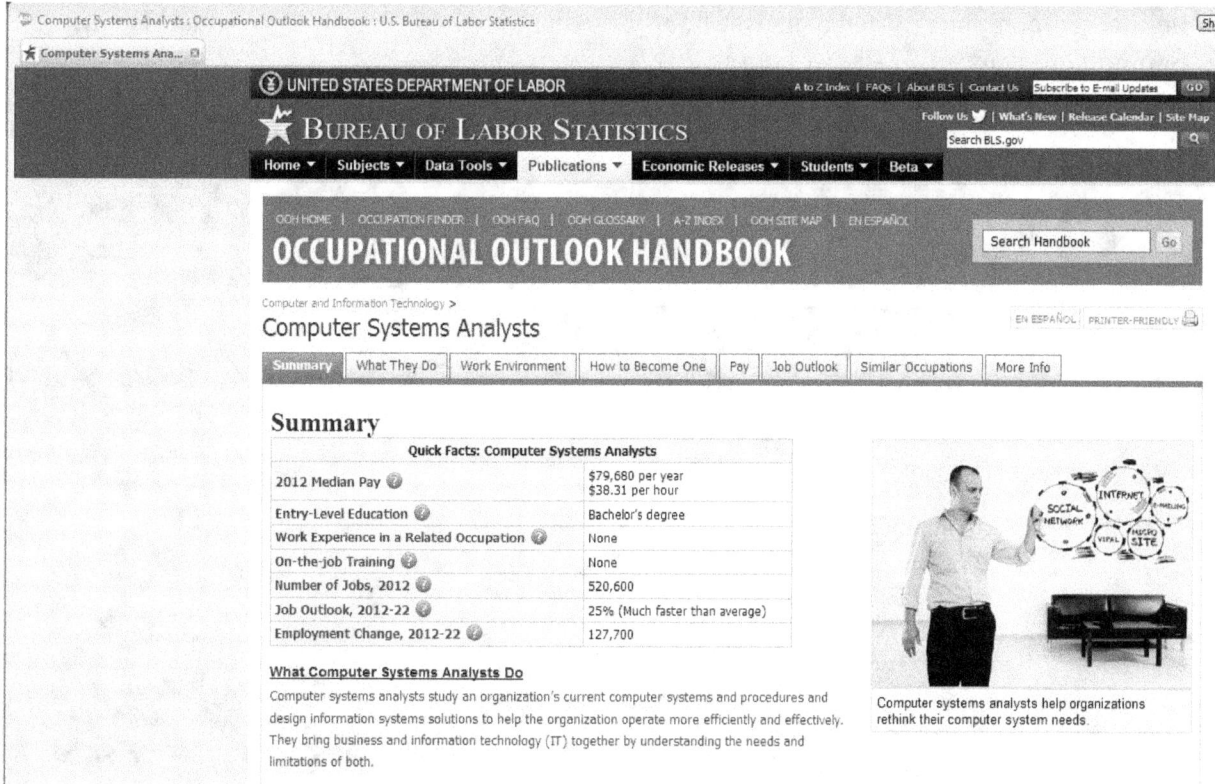

http://www.bls.gov/ooh/computer-and-information-technology/computer-systems-analysts.htm

What Computer Systems Analysts Do

Computer systems analysts study an organization's current computer systems and procedures and design information systems solutions to help the organization operate more efficiently and effectively. They bring business and information technology (IT) together by understanding the needs and limitations

Quick Facts: Computer Systems Analysts	
2012 Median Pay ❓	$79,680 per year $38.31 per hour
Entry-Level Education ❓	Bachelor's degree
Work Experience in a Related Occupation ❓	None
On-the-job Training ❓	None
Number of Jobs, 2012 ❓	520,600
Job Outlook, 2012-22 ❓	25% (Much faster than average)
Employment Change, 2012-22 ❓	127,700

Note that the computer systems analyst hourly median pay was slightly more than **five times** the U.S. minimum wage of $7.25 per hour in 2012.

http://www.bls.gov/ooh/computer-and-information-technology/software-developers.htm

What Software Developers Do

Software developers are the creative minds behind computer programs. Some develop the applications that allow people to do specific tasks on a computer or other device. Others develop the underlying systems that run the devices or control networks.

Quick Facts: Software Developers	
2012 Median Pay	$93,350 per year $44.88 per hour
Entry-Level Education	Bachelor's degree
Work Experience in a Related Occupation	None
On-the-job Training	None
Number of Jobs, 2012	1,018,000
Job Outlook, 2012-22	22% (Much faster than average)
Employment Change, 2012-22	222,600

Note that the computer software developer hourly median pay was slightly more than **six times** the U.S. minimum wage of $7.25 per hour in 2012.

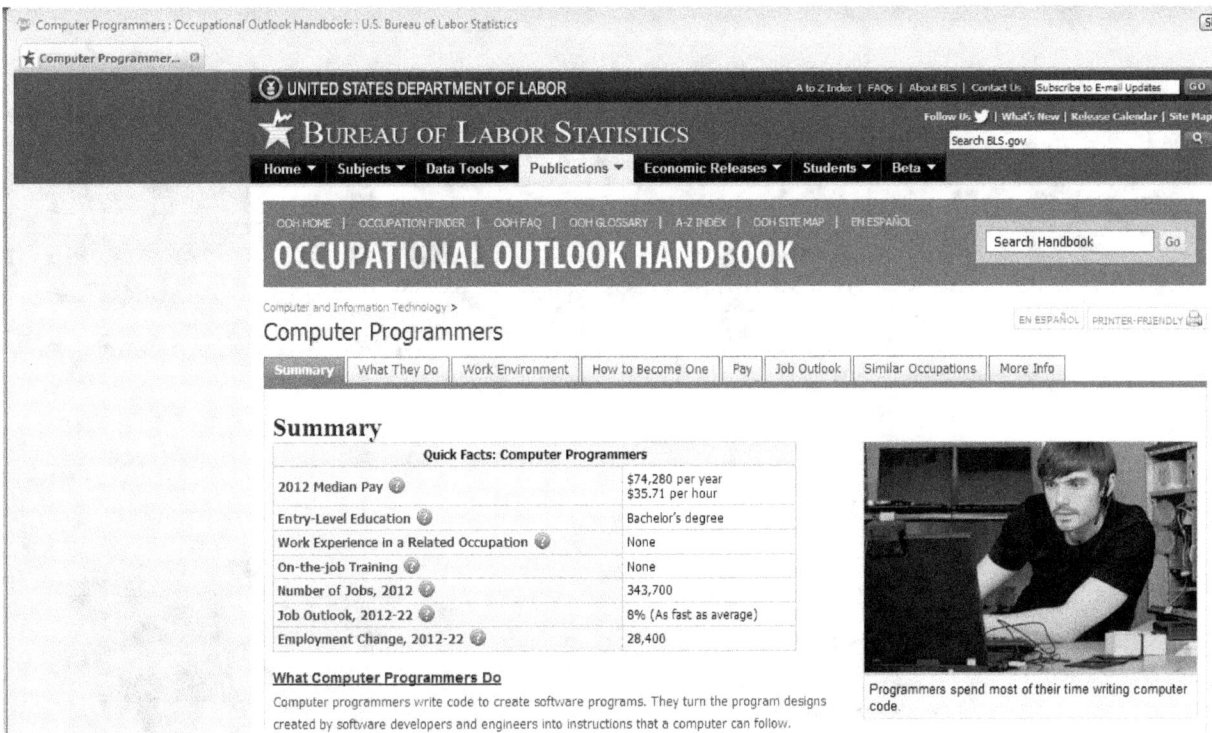

http://www.bls.gov/ooh/computer-and-information-technology/computer-programmers.htm

What Computer Programmers Do

Computer programmers write code to create software programs. They turn the program designs created by software developers and engineers into instructions that a computer can follow.

Quick Facts: Computer Programmers	
2012 Median Pay ⓘ	$74,280 per year $35.71 per hour
Entry-Level Education ⓘ	Bachelor's degree
Work Experience in a Related Occupation ⓘ	None
On-the-job Training ⓘ	None
Number of Jobs, 2012 ⓘ	343,700
Job Outlook, 2012-22 ⓘ	8% (As fast as average)
Employment Change, 2012-22 ⓘ	28,400

Note that the computer programmer hourly median pay was about **five times** the U.S. minimum wage of $7.25 per hour in 2012.

http://www.bls.gov/ooh/computer-and-information-technology/computer-support-specialists.htm

What Computer Support Specialists Do

Computer support specialists provide help and advice to people and organizations using computer software or equipment. Some, called computer network support specialists, support information technology (IT) employees within their organization. Others, called computer user support specialists, assist non-IT users who are having computer problems.

Quick Facts: Computer Support Specialists	
2012 Median Pay	$48,900 per year $23.51 per hour
Entry-Level Education	See How to Become One
Work Experience in a Related Occupation	None
On-the-job Training	See How to Become One
Number of Jobs, 2012	722,400
Job Outlook, 2012-22	17% (Faster than average)
Employment Change, 2012-22	123,000

Note that the computer support specialist hourly median pay was slightly more than **three times** the U.S. minimum wage of $7.25 per hour in 2012.

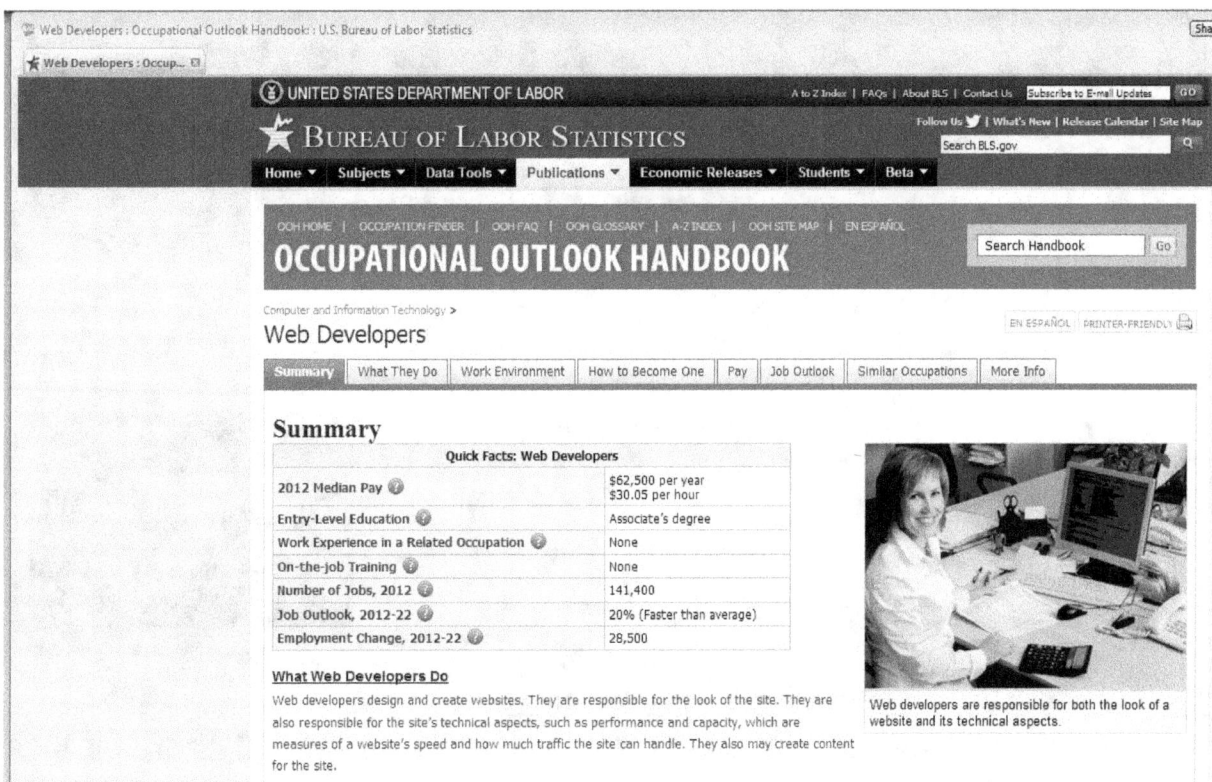

http://www.bls.gov/ooh/computer-and-information-technology/web-developers.htm

What Web Developers Do

Web developers design and create websites. They are responsible for the look of the site. They are also responsible for the site's technical aspects, such as performance and capacity, which are measures of a website's speed and how much traffic the site can handle. They also may create content for the site.

Quick Facts: Web Developers	
2012 Median Pay ⍰	$62,500 per year $30.05 per hour
Entry-Level Education ⍰	Associate's degree
Work Experience in a Related Occupation ⍰	None
On-the-job Training ⍰	None
Number of Jobs, 2012 ⍰	141,400
Job Outlook, 2012-22 ⍰	20% (Faster than average)
Employment Change, 2012-22 ⍰	28,500

Note that the Web developer's hourly median pay was slightly more than **four times** the U.S. minimum wage of $7.25 per hour in 2012.

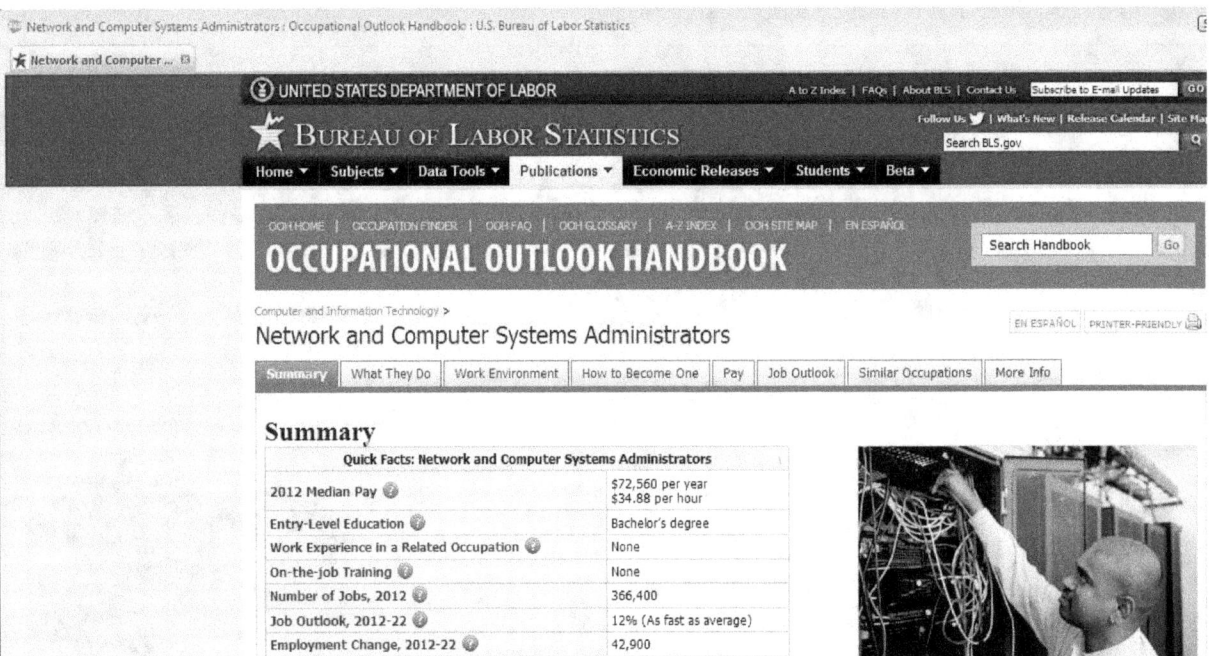

What Network and Computer Systems Administrators Do

Computer networks are critical parts of almost every organization. Network and computer systems administrators are responsible for the day-to-day operation of these networks.

Quick Facts: Network and Computer Systems Administrators	
2012 Median Pay ⓘ	$72,560 per year $34.88 per hour
Entry-Level Education ⓘ	Bachelor's degree
Work Experience in a Related Occupation ⓘ	None
On-the-job Training ⓘ	None
Number of Jobs, 2012 ⓘ	366,400
Job Outlook, 2012-22 ⓘ	12% (As fast as average)
Employment Change, 2012-22 ⓘ	42,900

Note that the Network and computer systems administrator hourly median pay was slightly less than **five times** the U.S. minimum wage of $7.25 per hour in 2012.

U.S. Computer Related Jobs Occupational Summary

The U.S. Bureau of Labor Statistics clearly illustrates that there are literally **millions of highly paid** people in the United States occupied in mostly corporate computer related jobs, and the job outlook is largely for faster than average job growth in the next ten years.

These U.S. computer related jobs pay from about three times the U.S. minimum wage to about eight times U.S. minimum wage, compared to the mechanics pay of slightly more than two times the U.S. minimum wage.

Additionally, and perhaps not tracked by the U.S. Bureau of Labor Statistics Occupational survey, there are perhaps millions of overseas and non-corporate people vying for computer related jobs in the United States, normally as consultants or contractors, via the Internet or through computer vendors offering global services and software support, such as IBM, SAP, Oracle and others.

These non-corporate in-house computer related services are offered at an incredible range of costs and capabilities, from ten dollars per hour, or slightly more than **the minimum wage** for offshore Java language programmers, to IBM Global Services and software services at from **thirty to forty times** the U.S minimum wage contract cost (note- The person in the USA performing the contract may be paid **seven to ten times** the U.S. minimum wage.)

The fundamental reasons for this huge range of computer related job pay, from about the **minimum wage to perhaps forty times the minimum pay** for the services of possibly a person of very similar mental capability, training, and education, and even the need for those services at all is a major subject of this book, and is explored in depth in several later chapters.

Apple has sold and is selling billions of very sophisticated phones and computer devices worldwide, while having only a relatively few computer software development staff, perhaps one person for a million phone users. The Apple phone user can immediately utilize the device and select desired applications from a menu of available applications, without actually programming anything.

Corporate computing is rapidly evolving towards the elimination of in-house programming and operations staffs and to cloud hosted hardware as in the Apple model in spite of fierce resistance to change and decades of the entrenched ability to control desirable and economically needed change.

Worldwide Computer Related Jobs Occupational Summary

Worldwide, there are almost certainly several times the number of corporate computers as in the United States, and several times the millions of U.S. computer related jobs tracked by the U.S. Bureau of Labor Statistics.

Computer related jobs and computing itself are more and more easily exported overseas, or performed overseas, via the Internet and the computing Cloud, as the relentless economic search for lower cost and more productive computing follows the relentless economic search for lower cost and productivity in the manufacturing and other industries, and as better solutions are developed and implemented.

The rapidly evolving future of corporate computing

The corporate computer industry is still a relatively young and rapidly changing industry, with some of the early adapters, like me, still active today and observing profound changes like cloud computing shaking the foundations of traditional corporate computing.

These profound changes today in the corporate computing industry will, I believe, dramatically change the job outlook for most computing jobs in the United States, and corporate computing itself, and very soon.

All of the important and life changing inventions and innovations in Harold Evan's book, and a never ending torrent of new inventions are based on useful and practical and economic solutions to real needs and provide universal simplification and ease-of-use and productivity to the end user or consumer.

While the invention itself and its enhancements may be seemingly complex and sophisticated to the public, virtually all inventions, including the computer, provide the public or consumer or user with a greatly simplified and productive environment and allow virtually universal implementation.

Thus the operator of a **16 row head John Deere combine** can sit in a half-million dollar machine in air conditioned comfort and observe the GPS steering the combine while more quickly and efficiently doing the work of hundreds of laborers with scythes. All thanks to modern enhancements to the combine invention of Hiram Moore in 1836.

John Deere S690 Combine with 616C 16 Row Corn Head ...
https://www.youtube.com/watch?v=uePjX09U7_c

Free market (excluding government and quasi-government) competition, innovation, the pursuit of market share, profit, economics, and the ability to enter and compete in a market have always been the most important factors in the ongoing enhancement, simplification, productivity and use of almost all inventions, as is evidenced in all of the above inventions, **except for programming and support of corporate computers.**

That is because virtually all inventions and innovations start with a revolutionary idea and implementation and cost structure, like the telephone, electric light, automobile, and combine, and then evolve over many years of complementary if seemingly minor enhancements like the stock ticker tape and the electric starter for the automobile.

Thus, the major cost of the automobile has remained the automobile itself, not the gasoline or insurance, and mass production and distribution has dramatically dropped the real cost of the automobile to within almost universal reach. This allows shopping for price among brands and outlets for an essentially well-known and predictable performing product.

Even the cell phone or smart phone cost for the phone itself is a major cost and there is some competition among communication carriers with competing plans and prices for relatively known and similar and standard services. Also, the consumer or customer is not required or even normally allowed to program or modify the environment beyond selecting applications to be accessed.

Contrast this normal invention and innovation enhancement scenario over time for most innovations with the corporate computing environment over the 60 plus years from the original ENIAC computer in 1946, which cost six million dollars (in today's dollars) and had hardware but no software, as the ENIAC was not a stored programmed computer. ENIAC programs were accomplished with electric plug board wires similar to the Herman Hollerith IBM Unit Record punched card machines.

Today in corporate computing the computer hardware is essentially free (not a significant cost) and it is almost infinitely powerful and reliable, while the computer systems (vendor supplied) software to utilize the hardware is expensive, as in the charts below.

However, the huge and continuing costs of vendor supplied application software packages and in-house programming and operations staff costs and in-house programming staff costs normally dwarf all other corporate computing costs. These huge costs are largely the result of the use today of essentially the same or similar primitive and ancient and, I believe, severely deficient computer languages and software technology, which was used at the dawn of corporate computing in the 1960s.

Thus, corporate computing economics are essentially totally different now than in the early days of computing when there were no application packages and programmers wrote and maintained all the applications at little or no cost (IBM programmers, like me, were **free** to IBM customers), and IBM hardware was incredibly expensive, as in the charts below.

.

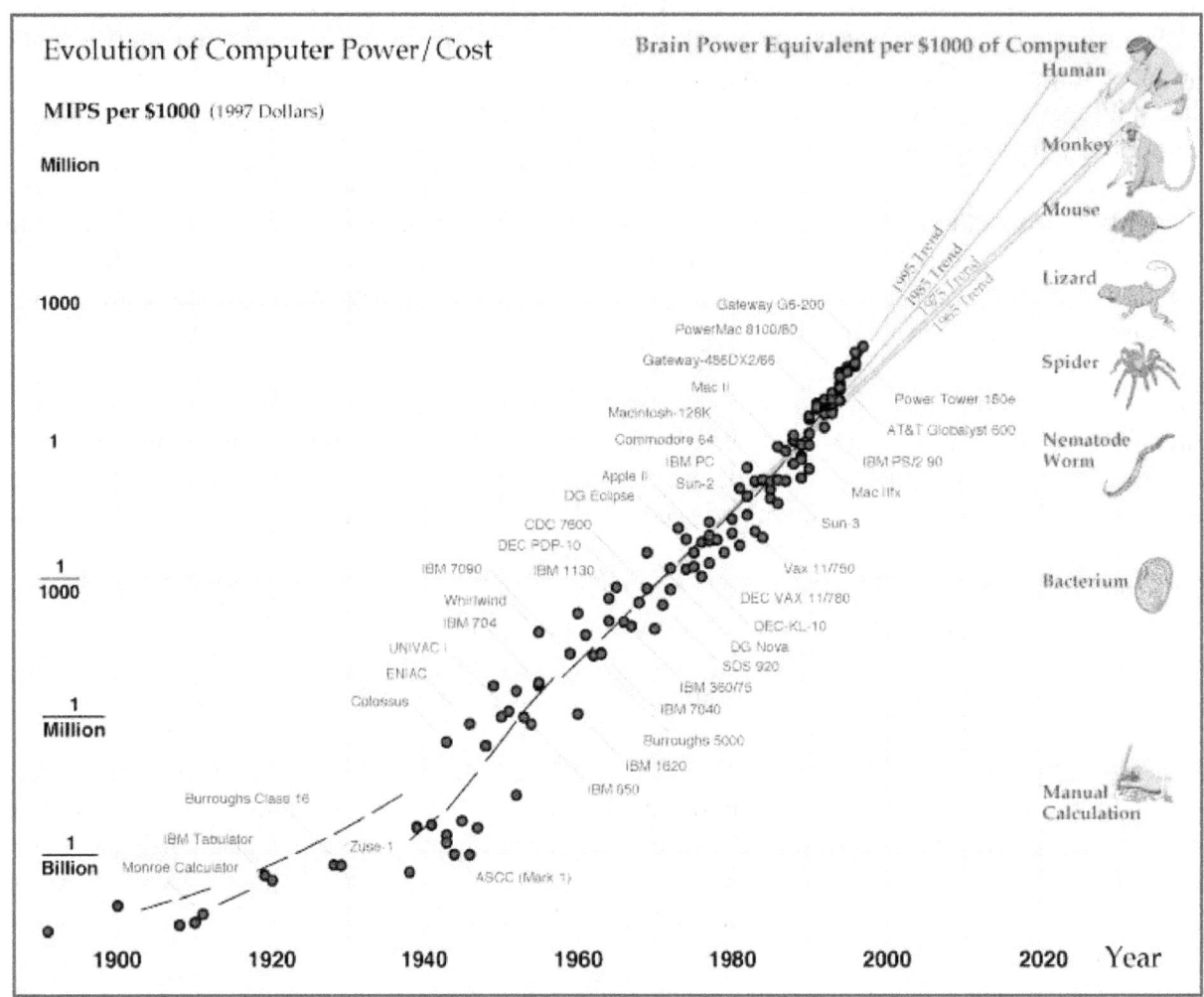

http://www.transhumanist.com/volume1/moravec.htm

Today a small or midsize corporation can **purchase** brand new business computer hardware capable of running virtually all of its business applications, such as an IBM i Power8 computer for about the annual salary of a single and expensive in-house application programmer (whose compensation is about 6 times the effective minimum wage of ten dollars per hour) . The small or midsize corporation can **lease** annually the same brand- new IBM i computer and all the required IBM system software, in-house or in the cloud, for about the same annual salary of a single and expensive in-house application programmer.

The obvious and crucial questions include:
- Do we need or want an in-house corporate business computer?
- How can executive management gain full understanding and control of IT?
- Is our corporation competitive and cost effective and current in corporate computing?
- Is executive management actually exercising its required fiduciary responsibility?
- Why do we need expensive in-house applications programmers or developers at all?
- What is a better alternative to in-house programmers or developers?

- How can we double or triple the productivity of in-house programmers or developers?
- How can the corporation quickly achieve its ideal corporate computing environment?
- How can the corporation quickly reduce corporate computing costs and complexity while increasing corporate computing capability and gain competitive advantage?
- What are the realistic disaster recovery time, cost, plan and consequences if our in-house computing system fails?
- What happens if our in-house computer system disaster recovery fails?
- What happens when our key in-house corporate computing staff leaves?

Counting The Cost Of Power8 Systems

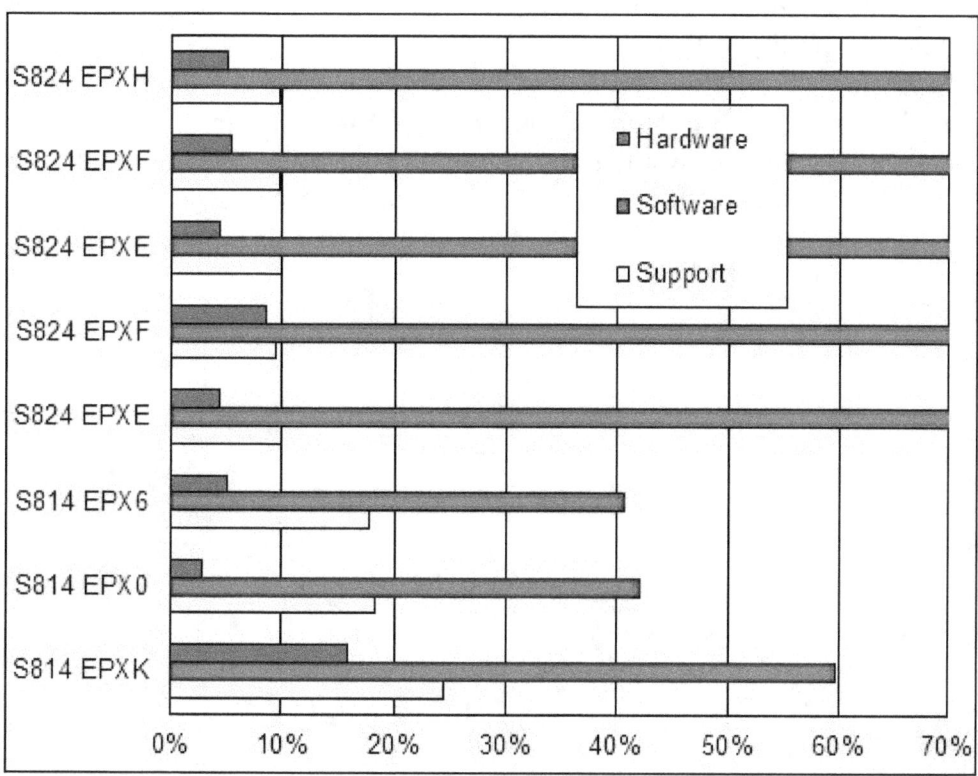

The above chart is courtesy of www. ITJungle.com, and illustrates the relative costs of the newest IBM i Power8 processors among hardware, systems (IBM) supplied software including program language compilers, and support or IBM maintenance.

Additional corporate computing costs would include significant vendor application package costs, and very significant operations and programming staff costs.

My analogy is that the corporate in-house operation staffs and in-house programming and developer staffs are like the mechanics of the early automotive days; originally very necessary on almost every road trip, and now not needed and certainly not economically justifiable with automobiles having first scheduled major maintenance at 100,000 miles.

Moving corporate computing to the cloud eliminates the in-house operations staff and probably the in-house programming staff and provides executive management with a far better understanding and control of corporate applications and procedures. Additionally, it provides far more secure and reliable disaster recovery capability, transforming in-house corporate programming and development from career employment jobs at low productivity to focused and productive project activity only when needed by corporate executive management.

In summary, the future of corporate computing is already here, with corporations essentially utilizing cloud computing as a utility with state-of-the art applications capability and with required programming and computer operations expertise not in-house and used only when needed. Chapter three **Corporate Executive Migration Steps to the Cloud** illustrates this transition process in detail and hopefully also demystifies the corporate computing function while returning control and understanding of corporate computing to the executive suite.

2 The End of the Corporate In-house Programmer

The end of the corporate in-house (resident) programmer era is happening now and will accelerate simply because it is no longer economically justifiable, is no longer needed, and is no longer competitive with current technology.

Every existing technology in every industry is constantly evolving over time as innovations are made, as conditions change, and as economics change. A review of the revolutionary Herman Hollerith punched card computing implementation and its eventual swift replacement by corporate in-house computers illustrates how rapid and pervasive is massive change, especially in technology.

The fundamental reasons for the change from manual tabulating to Herman Hollerith punched card tabulating were economics, capability, and productivity and in 1890 the requirement to complete the U.S. census tabulation within ten years. These reasons are exactly the same with the addition and availability of sophisticated vendor supplied applications software, which allows the change from in-house corporate computing to cloud computing and managed services. This change will be equally swift as the transformation from Herman Hollerith Unit Record electric- mechanical processing to the stored program computer. In-house corporate computing skeptics are at risk of ignoring the obvious and being among those displaced instead of embracing new opportunity in an ever changing world. Corporations such as IBM who hang on to the old and resist change, for possibly self-serving reasons or inertia are equally at risk.

The millions of U.S. expensive in-house corporate programmers, analysts, developers, operations support specialists and related occupations illustrated in the U/.S. Bureau of Labor Statistics Occupational handbook in chapter one will quickly disappear and are already disappearing from residence in corporations.

They will disappear from corporations now almost as quickly as did virtually all of the previous computing generation of Herman Hollerith unit record punched card equipment and personnel did in the 1960s when the first corporate computers swept them away in a decade with primitive computers like the IBM 1401 tape computer. Note- punched cards were used exclusively as the means to store information in the Herman Hollerith unit record systems as the unit-of-record, and punched cards made the transition to the stored program computer for some time, as there was no disk storage capability or any visual display terminals, or PCs available for the early computers.

I know because I was a direct witness to and a participant in that 1960s transformation, where virtually the entire data processing staff including control panel wirers and of operators of unit record machines including sorters, collators, and accounting machines, simply vanished as they were replaced by the stored program computer.

The 1960s transformation from unit record punched cards to the early stored program computer, with programs written in assembler language like IBM Autocoder, was sudden and dramatic. A single corporate computer could literally replace scores of unit record machines and scores of unit record operators in a large space with only a very few people in a tiny space and do much more productive work.

I witnessed this 1960s data processing transformation to computers at the Gulf Oil Credit Card Processing Center on City Line Avenue in Bala Cynwyd PA and at the Esso Oil Processing Center at Monument Avenue and City Line Avenue. I was wiring IBM 407 Accounting Machine control panels as a moonlighting job while finishing my last semester at **Drexel** Institute of Technology, prior to my career job at IBM.

Cooperative Education | Drexel University

http://catalog.drexel.edu/undergraduate/coop/

Each of the many IBM 407 control panels in a customer installation were hand wired or programmed to print a specific report, such as a customer credit card statement, and each of the completed panels might have had about 500 wires, although some boards had over 1000 wires. Each wire carried an electric current from one function like the card input area to another function such as counters or to the print area.

If this uniquely wired one-of-a-kind wired panel looks like spaghetti, imagine an in-house corporate computing source program of some 10,000 statements (originally five boxes of punched cards) uniquely written by one or more programmers in an arcane programming language and perhaps changed over time by a dozen other programmers. And, as in the worlds of literature, artistic painting, and music, each of the board wirers and programmers wired or programmed in his or her unique style. The little plastic connectors or splitters on the wired board split the electric current of one wire into two or more wires, with resulting issues of possible electric back circuits and the reset red light.

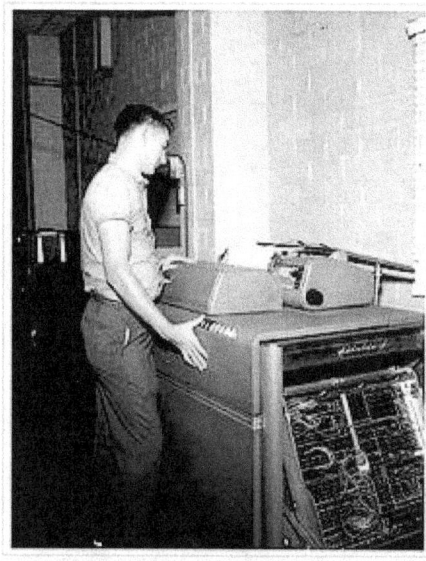

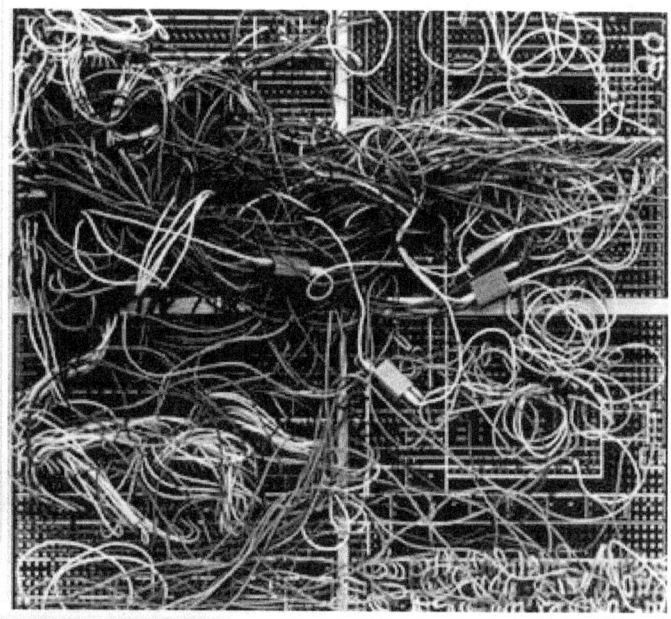

An IBM 407 Accounting Machine at
US Army's Redstone Arsenal in 1961.

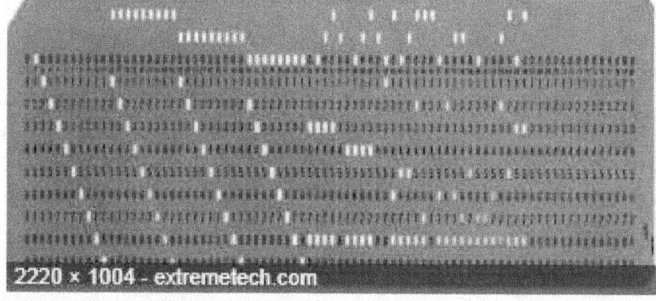

Unit record equipment
http://en.wikipedia.org/wiki/Unit_record_equipment

Plugboards and petaflops
http://www-03.ibm.com/ibm/history/witexhibit/wit_definitions.html

ibm 80-column punched card

https://www.google.com/search?q=ibm+80-col-umn+punched+card&biw=1464&bih=796&tbm=isch&tbo=u&source=univ&sa=X&ei=Gt2uVIe_I4b7sAT1tYGIAQ&ved=0CC0QsAQ#tbm=isch&q=ibm+80-column+punched+card

A public domain example of a popular modern day programming language, the C programming language, illustrates how a programmer accomplishees a very simple step in a C language source program of concatenating two fields together. Note – programmers often do not include the comment statements (/* prefix) describing what the following source statements are intended to accomplish. Thus, making it much more difficult for anyone else to understand the program, and makes the program even more arcane. Some would say that also provides perceived job security for the programmer.

C Programming/Strings

This function is used to attach one string to the end of another string. It is imperative that the first string (s1) have the space needed to store both strings.

Example:

```
#include <stdio.h>
#include <string.h>
...
static const char *colors[] = {"Red","Orange","Yellow","Green","Blue","Purple" };
static const char *widths[] = {"Thin","Medium","Thick","Bold" };
...
char penText[20];
...
int penColor = 3, penThickness = 2;
strcpy(penText, colors[penColor]);
strcat(penText, widths[penThickness]);
printf("My pen is %s\n", penText); // prints 'My pen is GreenThick'
```

Before calling `strcat()`, the destination must currently contain a null terminated string or the first character must have been initialized with the null character (e.g. `penText[0] = '\0';`).

The following is a public-domain implementation of `strcat`:

```
#include <string.h>
/* strcat */
char *(strcat)(char *restrict s1, const char *restrict s2)
{
    char *s = s1;
    /* Move s so that it points to the end of s1. */
    while (*s != '\0')
        s++;
    /* Copy the contents of s2 into the space at the end of s1. */
    strcpy(s, s2);
    return s1;
}
```

The Gulf Oil processing center employed dozens of huge IBM unit record accounting machines and related sorters, collators, interpreters, reproducers, calculators and key punches and several hundred unit record employees to operate them.

One day workers built a small glass enclosed room, with air conditioning, at the end of the huge room, and Gulf Oil installed an IBM 1401 tape (no disk) computer, which soon replaced the entire unit record operations and displaced the hundreds of unit record employees with only a very few people.

The strange part to me was that the mass displaced skilled unit record operators virtually all just gave up and many went back to driving oil delivery trucks rather than even attempt to learn the new world of stored program computers. The unit record employees had no power to slow or stop the rapid transition to the computer and no skills needed in the new environment.

IBM even developed manuals "From Control Panel to Stored Program" to ease the transition from unit record machines to stored program computers, as the early IBM 1401 computer (with 4 THOUSAND characters of memory) was designed to somewhat simulate the unit record machine control panel layout with fixed read and print core storage memory locations.

A crucial point is that there was **virtually no resistance** to this change to computers by the entire corporate unit record operations staff even as they were quickly mass displaced, as they had no power or ability or apparently desire to stop the clearly beneficial and economically better implementation of computers.

Also crucial is the point that unit record processing required many steps in processing an application, such as credit card billing, and required many skilled people and machines such as key punching, sorting, collating, perhaps calculating, reproducing and printing on the accounting machine (at 100 or 150 lines per minute). Each of these steps could be easily learned and understood, even how the accounting machine control panels were wired, so the unit record operators had **virtually no leverage or control or important and unique understanding** of what was the application process, unlike in corporate computing today.

IBM unit record punched card processing was punched cards and electro-mechanical machines and control panels with wires and many visible and easily understood physical steps, unlike the stored program computer programs written in arcane cryptic programming languages and executing mysteriously and without audit capability inside the black box of a computer.

In a pinch in the unit record processing days, data processing management and even I sometimes had to step in and run production jobs that had no written documentation, sometimes having to trace and change (as in date change) the electric wires in a control panel in production if an operator had left or was sick

Today in the stored program "black box" corporate computing world, computer programmers or developers work in essentially the very same environment as in the 1960s and use essentially the same primitive, ancient and I believe, severely deficient arcane and cryptic programming languages, very much as they did in the 1960s, and with, unfortunately, similar poor results.

The programmers, and certainly management, cannot see what is happening inside the computer as the programs execute with data, and they have no comprehensive or full audit of what the program and data actually processed, as in a video camera of the entire program execution from start to completion. Thus, the programmers, and management, **must guess at what is or actually did happen**, including in program abnormal execution scenarios and error conditions.

Only the computer programmer or developer can actually write (source code), change, enhance or correct vital corporate in-house written or modified application programs that run the business of the corporation, certainly not executive management or even information technology management. And, because corporate application in-house written programs are unique and written in the cryptic style of the individual programmer and are running (sometimes wild) inside the computer without any audit of exact program execution, the **programmer today has tremendous leverage and control and a unique understanding of vital corporate computing.**

The words **"Did he happen to mention source code?"** in an old cartoon have been essentially repeated many times in my presence and in desperation, including in Singapore last summer.

"This may be an awkward time, but did he happen to mention source code?"

https://books.google.com/books?id=mXEbp4U3AT8C&pg=PA3&lpg=PA3&dq=%22This+may+be+an+awkward+time,+but+did+he+happen+to+mention+source+code?&source=bl&ots=DjPD0Z-x1_&sig=s_dcQN0Y6FgK9qKA42EmJk-IPiM&hl=en&sa=X&ei=g2GbVOCnHY2_sQSugoCYAg&ved=0CCEQ6AEwAQ#v=onepage&q=%22This%20may%20be%20an%20awkward%20time%2C%20but%20did%20he%20happen%20to%20mention%20source%20code%3F&f=false

Corporations still employing in-house corporate computers, programming and development staffs, and computer operations staffs, instead of moving these functions out-of-house to the Cloud or managed service, **incur huge economic costs for highly paid computer related jobs, and incur huge risks of failure, making those jobs essentially career long employment.**

Rosetta Stone

The discovery of the Rosetta stone in France in 1799 provided important new capability in translating among three ancient languages. Today there are literally dozens of computer languages in wide use in corporate computing, with each of the languages written in unique the style of the individual programmer. This makes it very difficult for another programmer to easily understand the actual functioning of the program as it processes specific data and follows different paths of executing program statements based on the data actually processed.

There is no other known capability to record and audit and potentially translate real-time executing programs of different programming languages to a common understandable English like language, and perform real-time analytics, other than the Real-Time Program Audit (RTPA) software illustrated in Appendix H **and** Appendix D On-Demand Forensic Accounting Universal Program Auditing Language.

.

Rosetta Stone

The Rosetta Stone

Material	Granodiorite
Size	114.4 × 72.3 × 27.93 cm (45 x 28.5 x 11 in)
Writing	Ancient Egyptian hieroglyphs, Demotic script, and Greek script
Created	196 BC
Discovered	1799
Present location	British Museum

http://en.wikipedia.org/wiki/Rosetta_Stone

Even though a single computer programmer or developer can write and support only a tiny fraction of the millions of lines of source code of the application software used by a company, perhaps one percent in a working career, the resident in-house programmer may have the best and possibly the only chance "keep the place going" as they apparently know something about the application programs, as management alone surely cannot and does not know much about the unique in-house developed application programs.

That is a crucial difference from the unit record days when the unit record operators were essentially an interchangeable commodity, and for automobile mechanics, which are essentially an interchangeable and inexpensive commodity today.

The conventional wisdom that the computer programmer must utilize his or her years of expertise and knowledge and understanding of the computer source code to understand, and in my opinion to guess what is happening as the program and data are executing is simply not true.

My U.S. patented Real-Time Program Audit software provides a video camera like audit of exactly what the programmer is futilely attempting to guess, thus perpetuating the mystique of the almighty programmer and allowing the resisting of necessary change

Computer programmers and developers have an incredibly wide range of abilities and performance, with one superior programmer or developer being able to out produce several or many less superior or average programmers. This is true because computer programming is like all other occupations requiring more than just physical commodity skills.

It is obvious and observable and true that in all occupations including artists, musicians, cooks, writers, basketball players, and even mechanics, that all are not equally talented or capable, physically or mentally, or worth the same. One star basketball player can easily consistently score five times the points as some of the other players under the exact same conditions and that is true in corporate computing also.

The obvious and observable huge differences in ability and performance and output so visible in most occupations and particularly in skilled occupations, as in sports where quarterbacks are a highly skilled position, are not nearly as obvious or observable to corporate executive management in in-house corporate computing and particularly relating to corporate programmers and in-house corporate operations. That is because of the corporate executives do not understand the arcane programming world and the largely unaudited corporate operations world, and cannot effectively audit computing productivity.

Specifically, both public and private corporate executives including the CEO, CFO and the board of directors have well defined fiduciary responsibilities which include timely and accurate financial reporting, and the fiduciary duty of care. Yet, few CEOs and CFOs in my experience have a clue about the existence of an effective corporate computer disaster recovery plan, if there is one, and how the corporation could or would quickly recover from a corporate computing disaster or major outage.

That corporate computing disaster recovery plan is all too often somewhere in the heads of the CIO or programmers and operations staff, and is a powerful leverage to job security and longevity, until the staff leaves and the disaster recovery plan with it, or until there is a corporate computing disaster.

Corporations still employing corporate in-house programming staffs and in house operations staffs and in-house corporate computers are simply not nearly as competitive, agile, secure, productive or cost effective as those corporations not burdened by these ancient and obsolete methods and costs.

This is illustrated by the rapid and accelerating increase in Cloud computing and the rapid decline of in-house corporate computing

Corporate executives are expert and proficient in virtually all aspects of the often cut-throat and cost-competitive environments in their industry relating to their products or services, but in my experience and observation, they are often totally befuddled about the enormous cost, complexity, unknowns , lack of security, best use and mystery of in-house corporate computing.

So, what is a corporation with expensive and un-productive in-house corporate computing to do, and how?

Simply take action to understand and appreciate and research the technologies and realities and costs and capabilities of today, including the economic and competitive realities, and then take action to implement efficient and effective and competitive corporate computing, and do it now.

Realize that the some sixty years of stored program application development and competition has resulted in the availability of sophisticated applications software in virtually every imaginable industry. That sophisticated applications software is available as the basis or foundation for virtually all corporate computing, as it is for personal computing. Virtually everyone uses the Windows Word product, and most probably use a tax product like TurboTax and personal accounting software like QuickBooks without any programming required.

Comprehensive and sophisticated corporate computing applications software is available from huge corporations such as SAP and Oracle and a host of other corporations that replaces in-house programmers with analysts and programmers, where virtually all development and programming is performed by the software vendor. The days where a unit record control panel was uniquely wired for a task at a single customer and where an in-house corporate programmer programs a unique task at a single customer are over, at least economically.

In the long gone glory days of IBM in the 1960s and 1970s, when corporations were installing new IBM computers and new and productive applications, and when IBM still had systems engineers, like me, active for months in customer accounts to make it all happen, we always did the following to ensure success:

- Review, document, report and discuss what the customer was currently doing (Document brochure, and probably Standard Operating Procedures).   Time required about 1 week.
- Review, document, report and discuss what the customer wanted to do with the enhanced capability.   Time required about 1 week
- Review, document, report and discuss how and when and with whom to best accomplish what the customer wants to do, and at what cost and effort. Time required about 1 week.
- Do it, even if the IBM systems engineer had to do it all (The IBM systems engineer is now probably a top independent consultant)

Corporate executives today would be wise and successful to utilize a similar strategy today and not wait as they become less competitive and burdened with unnecessary and un-productive expense.

The following illustrations illustrate the need for corporate executive action now to become competitive and take advantage of current technology and move in-house corporate computing to the processing cloud. All of these illustrations and implementations utilize sophisticated programming, but that programming is hidden from the user.

1. **Google's driverless car is now "fully functional"**

2. **Audi, Mercedes Benz debut driverless cars**

Now not only is the mechanic obsolete, but so is the automobile driver

3. **BNSF moves toward allowing trains with 1 crew member ...**

Now only the train engineer is needed, and plans are to eliminate the engineer also.

4. **WordPress is web software you can use to create a beautiful website or blog**

Many non-technical people can quickly and easily design and implement a new web site and focus on content, and implement other important web technologies such as GoToMeeting conferencing, without wanting or needing to learn programming languages like HTML and PHP.

An obvious and possible strategy of corporations with in-house corporate computers and in-house programmers would be to implement needed productivity and economic enhancements and become much more viable as a long-term computing solution. This also applies to vendors such as IBM which provides much of the computer middleware such as programming language compilers used in in-house programming and in-house developed applications.

However, a fierce resistance to change by both the middleware vendors and in-house programmers and a fierce determination to hold on for as long as possible, has crippled and delayed needed change and only fueled the move to the cloud. IBM wants to keep its revenue stream going and the in-house programmers want to keep their jobs until they retire in spite of the economic and competitive costs to the corporation.

Simply put, the era of in-house corporate programming, and in-house computer operations, has passed, as did the era of an on-board automobile mechanic for virtually every automobile, and the eras of so many other no longer economically viable or productive occupations before.

The Bureau of Labor Statistics is not going to accurately anticipate or recognize fundamental changes in technology and economics any more than are universities in updating their course offerings and teaching you what you need to know for your success. The BLS and universities, and corporations are primarily focused on the past and the immediate present and on their own agendas, not yours. Only you are ultimately responsible for your current and future success and ultimately only you will strive for your long-term success.

If you are an in-house corporate programmer now, then you are at significant risk now, and the decisions that you make now will determine your success in the world of cloud computing.

A stunning real-life illustration of how corporate programming, development, and support could transform itself from being economically unproductive and inefficient and on the decline into an incredibly economically valuable and powerful and productive position is illustrated below.

A single and seemingly simple innovation, the metal shipping container, literally flipped the economics and power and productivity equation of ship cargo handling from a largely manual and low paid job of using nets to load and unload ships to secure metal and stackable containers. Malcolm Mclean turned a low skilled and low paid hard and non-productive job into a technologically advanced and crucial job for those who would do it, with annual compensation including benefits of some $200,000 annually, with an $80,000 annual pension, far above programmer's compensation, and the change happened almost overnight.

In 1956, Malcom McLean developed the metal shipping container and revolutionized the method, productivity and economics of dry goods shipping from the cargo nets used from Roman times.

On the Waterfront - Wikipedia, the free encyclopedia

http://en.wikipedia.org/wiki/On_the_Waterfront

https://www.flickr.com/search/?q=dock+cargo+net&ct=0&mt=all&adv=1

(Source: Flickr)

$147,000 A Year Just For Sitting On The Dock Of The Bay

http://news.investors.com/ibd-editorials/020615-738418-dock-workers-union-demands-hurt-consumers.htm

https://www.flickr.com/search/?q=Container+ships&ct=0&mt=all&adv=1

(Source: Flickr)

How and why Malcom Mclean was able to singlehandedly revolutionize a vital industry by simply doing the now obvious, how he became wealthy because of his invention and how perhaps inadvertently he made today's dock workers wealthy and so powerful and so visibly critically needed is perhaps a lesson for today's unproductive and expensive corporate programmers to ponder and solve.

In 1948, Edwin Land introduced the Polaroid Instant Camera, which enabled film photographs to be viewed virtually instantly after being taken instead of days or weeks later, all because his young daughter in 1943 has asked the question "Why can't I see these pictures right now? I don't want to wait".

A Triumph of Genius

https://www.google.com/?gws_rd=ssl#q=A+triumph+of+Genius

Poloroid Land camera inside with film
Saffanna

Today I ask the simple but profoundly important question "Why can't we see and record and use in real-time what is happening inside the computer?"

I asked that simple question in the 1960s, and now the answer is that we can, and it opens a whole new universe of computing and productivity.

Unlike the 1960s displaced Herman Hollerith unit record operators who went back to driving oil delivery trucks, the displaced corporate computing in-house programmers and developers can succeed.

They have the skills to transform themselves into the new world of cloud computing, if they will.

3 Corporate Executive Migration Path to Cloud computing

There are several types of cloud computing including cloud services and cloud management as illustrated below.

What is most important for corporate executives with in-house corporate computers, programming and development staffs and computer operational staffs is to understand why cloud computing is so much better than in-house corporate computing and the necessity for change. The next steps include how to select and implement a strategy and a vendor to move essentially all the in-house corporate business and network computer functions to a secure and cost effective off-site environment.

The actual migration to the cloud typically takes several months including installation of communication lines depending on the complexity of the migration and is normally almost entirely accomplished by the cloud vendor. Securing communication lines is often the responsibility of the customer migrating to the cloud, and can be a very lengthy process unless jointly managed and constantly audited by executive management.

Corporate executives should next investigate and seriously consider the economic, strategic, and competitive advantages of replacing in-house developed and supported computer applications with appropriate and comprehensive externally developed application software.

The in-house corporate computing or cloud computing decision is ultimately a make or buy decision, and virtually all of the considerations, costs and trends now heavily favor the buy decision.

The brutal reality in the in-house corporate computing make or buy decision is that the in-house programming, development and operations staff capability, cost, reliability and competence is almost never as competitive or actually as expert or secure and reliable as that of multiple available external cloud and application software vendors. Crucially important is that the virtually guaranteed 24 hour a day, 7 day a week availability and timely disaster recovery of co-located remote cloud datacenters, and 24 by 7 help desk and available external programming support which protects against the unexpected loss of critical in-house corporate computing staff.

In my experience, **there is a very wide difference in the quoted costs for essentially the same implementation** of moving from in-house corporate computing to the cloud among available cloud options and vendors. As in auditing and accounting, the big name vendors, such as the Big Four Auditing firms, may have a forty percent or more premiums for essentially the same service above a regional or local provider. Cloud processing vendor **costs may vary by several times** for national cloud vendors over regional vendors.

Again in my experience, the total monthly costs for migrating from in-house corporate computing to the processing cloud, including both IBM processors like the IBM AS/400 computer and networked processors, and including 24 by 7 availability and 24 hour help desk support is much less than might be expected when compared with the costs of in-house corporate computing and support. One time migration costs are also much less that might be expected, especially when compared to the on-going costs of in-house corporate computing and in-house support.

These kinds of crucial executive questions and issues were addressed by IBM long ago and in my time at IBM, except that instead of Cloud computing the issue was, and is, corporate computing and corporate computers and software and corporate performance.

Here is how IBM worked directly with and directly influenced and directly cooperated with corporate CEOs and the executive committee.

In the glory days of IBM, when I worked as an IBM Systems Engineer (SE), IBM customers were ordering from their local IBM marketing representatives (salesmen) and installing tens of thousands of new and expensive computers like the IBM System/360 and the IBM System/34 (an early predecessor to the IBM AS/400 and current IBM i).

My IBM job was to make sure the new IBM customers could immediately utilize their expensive new computers and accept the computers and would immediately pay for them. The customers at first used mostly custom written in-house business application (which the **free** IBM Systems Engineers often designed and authored on-site at the customer), and later used proven customer industry sophisticated business applications packages licensed directly from IBM, such as the **IBM Apparel Business System/34 Installed User Program (IUP),** which I authored for IBM.

https://books.google.com/books?id=Wz-oh7ZQo8MC&pg=PA54&lpg=PA54&dq=IBM+Apparel+Business+System&source=bl&ots=6Gm-deCNSw&sig=ABBGven-79lhAnFbAqlM9dzeK4k&hl=en&sa=X&ei=NU3zVL60GI3esATnxYGABA&ved=0CEoQ6AEwCA#v=onepage&q=IBM%20Apparel%20Business%20System&f=false

The local IBM branch office marketing representative (salesman) had a sales territory of perhaps twenty installed IBM customers and perhaps twenty other companies who were prospects for new IBM computers, as prospects for the coveted "new account" business, and who were part of the salesman's annual sales quota.

The local IBM marketing representative normally called on the customer at the level of office manager, or data processing manager, but rarely at the executive management level, perhaps because that would be a too obvious selling session.

The often near resident IBM systems engineer often worked directly with all levels of management and operations in the company, including executive management, but was usually not in direct "sales" mode as was the marketing representative. Instead, the IBM SE worked diligently to improve the customer's use of the corporate computing systems and thus to have the customer really need more computing capability. The local systems engineer was also all too often too much like **Dilbert** in the cartoon, and not entirely welcome in executive meetings where the IBM marketing representative was in direct selling mode.

http://dilbert.com/

The result was that IBM local marketing support was most often not in direct marketing contact corporate executive management, at least not without calling in IBM executive management direct support.

Thus, IBM very effectively developed and utilized world-wide (including Dr. Joseph Orlicky), national, regional and sometimes local account executives, which were often recognized industry experts and who could very effectively mingle with, smooze, and directly relate with corporate executives, and who did not have a sales annual quota. IBM also had IBM **Executive Briefing Centers** , including golfing at the **IBM Country Club in Poughkeepsie New York**.

http://www-03.ibm.com/systems/services/briefingcenter/rochester/

http://www.forbes.com/sites/work-in-progress/2010/12/13/mourning-the-ibm-country-club-and-end-of-the-corporate-family/

A Manufacturing Revolution (excerpt)

Enter MRP. This was introduced in the US in 1960 by Dr. Joseph Orlicky[2], a Czech-American engineer working with IBM.

http://h2g2.com/approved_entry/A3488646

I presented one the five IBM program products that I authored, The IBM Apparel Business System/370 IUP at the IBM Arthur K Watson International Education Center in La Hulpe Belgium, in 1977 with simultaneous translation in five languages and headphones, in a setting very much like the United Nations.

IBM Arthur K Watson International Education Center

https://www.linkedin.com/groups/IBM-Arthur-K-Watson-International-40109.S.129997089

And, dinner afterwards in nearby Brussels Belgium with top customer executives from several countries was equally memorable, as was the wine and ambiance.

That IBM La Hulpe international executive education center and many of the IBM executive briefing centers and IBM county clubs are today long gone, along with the IBM industry account executives, and expert IBM industry expertise, and IBM industry application software products.

That was the result of IBMs becoming the "low-cost producer", together with a boatload of lost profits and growing business and growing customers for IBM.

When the local IBM marketing representative or his marketing manager wanted to present a customer CEO with a proposal or recommendation for significant new business, an IBM account executive, or even a world-wide industry executive was often asked to hold a formal planning session with the corporate CEO and executive management.

The IBM executive planning session or the first of several planning sessions, at least on the local level on-site at the customer, was essentially a "brain-storming" session, sometime over several days, where many important and timely questions were asked, where ideas were expressed, and later when possible solutions or possible opportunities were encouraged. In those old days flip charts and magic markers were used and the flip chart pages were taped to the walls of the conference room for later discussion and possible action, and if the executive briefings were at the IBM country club, social activities were included.

The executive briefing crucial sequence of topics then is the same as it should be today for corporate executives considering migrating to the Cloud. Several of these topics include"

- **What are we doing now, why, at what cost, are we competitive and profitable?**
- **What should we, could we, must we do for the same reasons?**
- **How do we compete now and in the future?**
- **What are we going to do?**
- **How are we going to do it, including an implementation plan, costs, schedule, and benefits?**
- **How to track and audit implementation, costs, benefits, and adjustments?**

In summary:

- **What are we doing?**
- **What do we want to do?**
- **What should we do?**
- **What are we going to do?**
- **What are the costs, benefits, effort and resources required?**
- **How are we doing it?**
- **How did we do?**
- **How do we adjust?**

The IBM executive planning sessions and executive briefings resulted in semi-formal documented objectives, plans, budgets, schedules, and benefits which are essentially the same as corporate executive management must accomplish today

With whom from IBM corporate executive management today collaborates on a regular basis, and with what success is to me unknown, but it is almost certainly not as successful and productive as in my time at IBM.

Cloud computing

From Wikipedia, the free encyclopedia

Cloud computing is computing in which large groups of remote servers are networked to allow centralized data storage and online access to computer services or resources. Clouds can be classified as public, private or hybrid.[1][2]

http://en.wikipedia.org/wiki/Cloud_computing

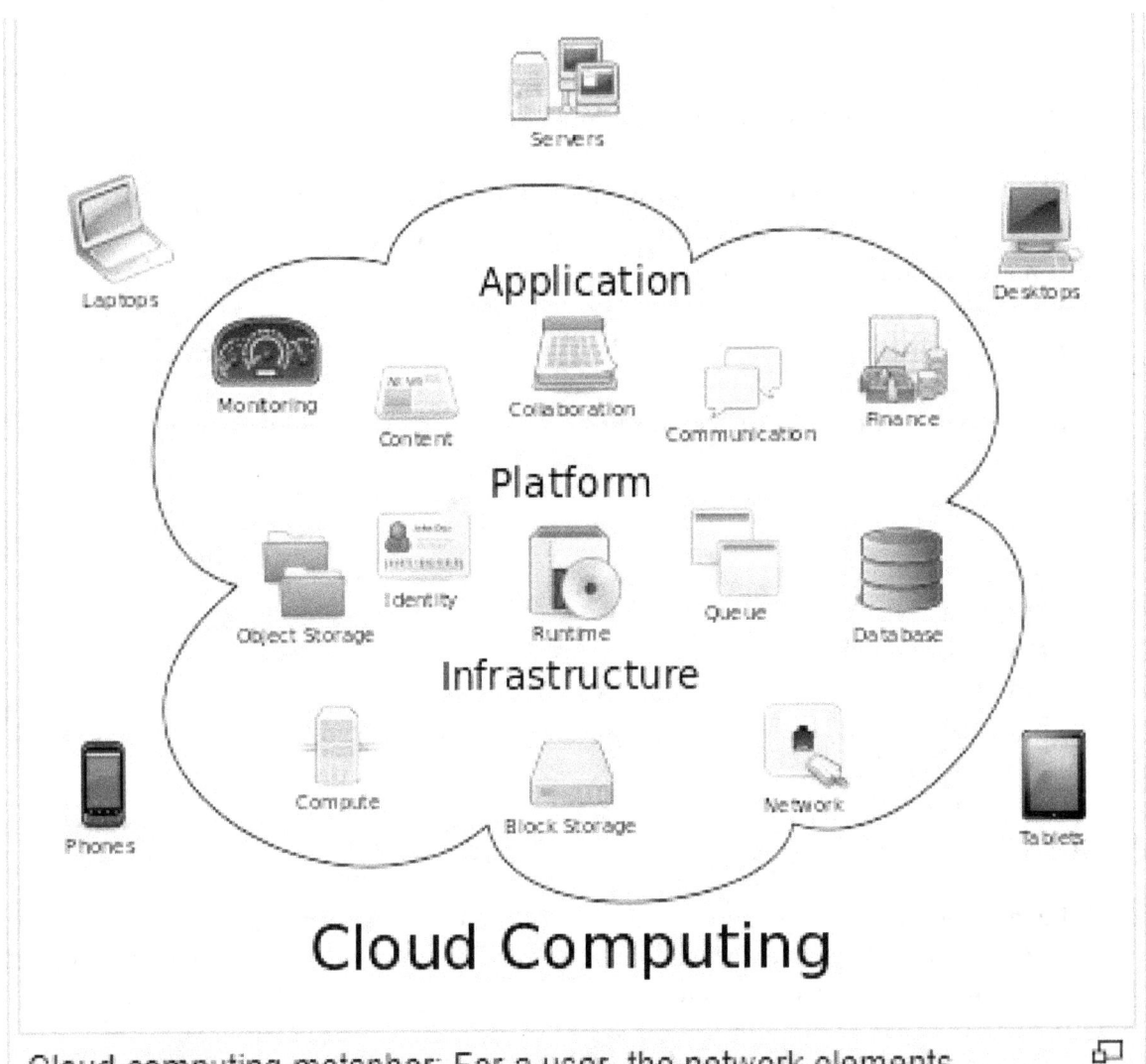

Cloud computing metaphor: For a user, the network elements representing the provider-rendered services are invisible, as if obscured by a cloud.

http://en.wikipedia.org/wiki/Cloud computing

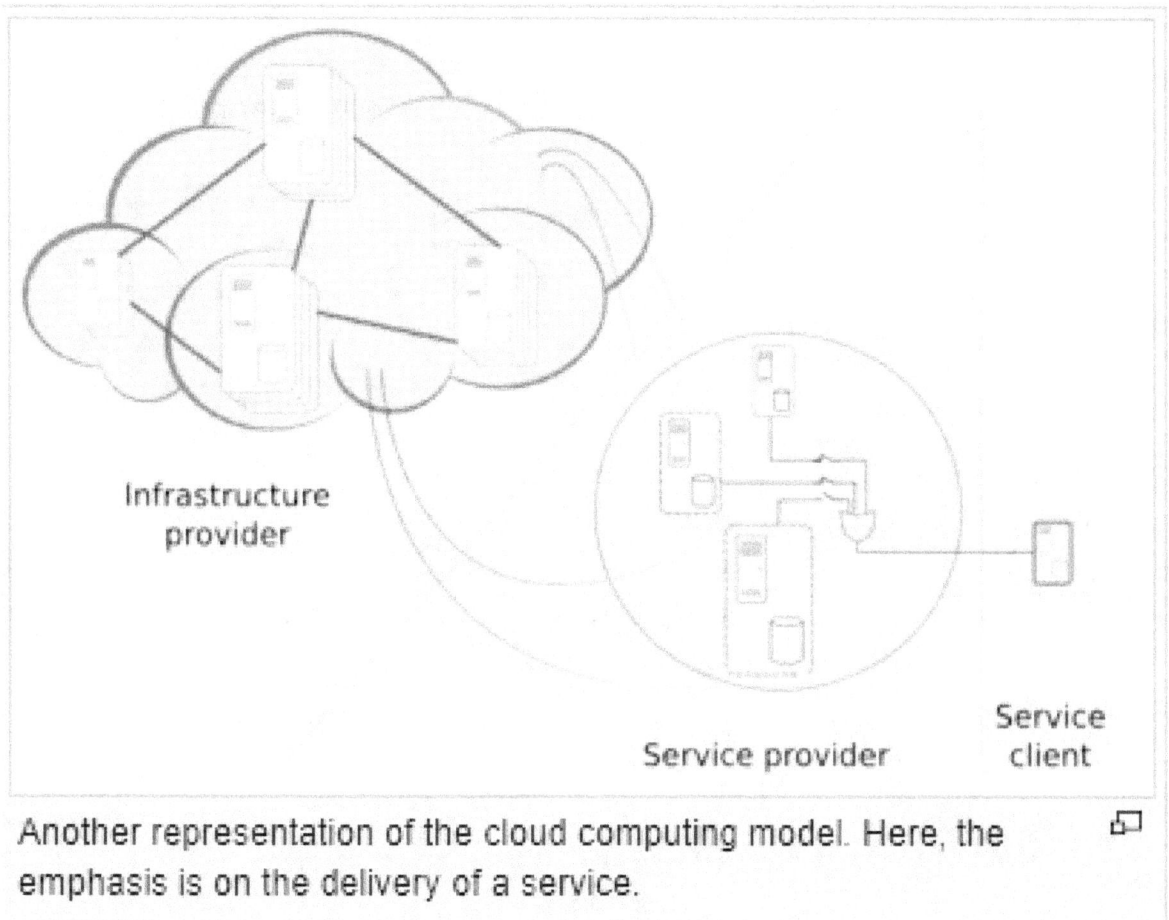

Another representation of the cloud computing model. Here, the emphasis is on the delivery of a service.

http://en.wikipedia.org/wiki/Cloud computing

This illustration of a service provider providing cloud services to many service clients is probably the most common representation for corporate computing migration to cloud computing.

For example, a service provider datacenter with a large computer such as the IBM System i (AS/400) can support many service clients or separate corporate computing clients via high-speed communication lines from each corporation. Each of the service clients processes its corporate computing in a separate Logical Partition

(LPAR), sharing the computing resources of the service provider computer in the remote datacenter.

cloud services

By Vangie Beal

Cloud services means services made available to users on demand via the Internet from a cloud computing provider's servers as opposed to being provided from a company's own on-premises servers. Cloud services are designed to provide easy, scalable access to applications, resources and services, and are fully managed by a cloud services provider.

A cloud service can dynamically scale to meet the needs of its users, and because the service provider supplies the hardware and software necessary for the service, there's no need for a company to provision or deploy its own resources or allocate IT staff to manage the service. Examples of cloud services include online data storage and backup solutions, Web-based e-mail services, hosted office suites and document collaboration services, database processing, managed technical support services and more.

Recommended Reading: Webopedia's Cloud Computing Dictionary Resource and Cloud Computing Security Challenges.

Related Terms

- cloud
- cloud provider
- cloud computing (the cloud)
- cloud computing reseller
- cloud backup service provider
- vertical cloud computing
- cloud computing accounting software
- public cloud
- Red Hat Cloud Computing
- cloud hosting

http://www.webopedia.com/TERM/C/cloud_services.html

copyright webopedia.com Used

cloud management

 11  7

By Vangie Beal

Cloud management means the software and technologies designed for operating and monitoring applications, data and services residing in the cloud. Cloud management tools help ensure cloud computing-based resources are working optimally and properly interacting with users and other services.

Cloud Management Strategies

Cloud management strategies typically involve numerous tasks including performance monitoring (response times, latency, uptime, etc.), security and compliance auditing and management, and initiating and overseeing disaster recovery and contingency plans.

With cloud computing growing more complex and a wide variety of private, hybrid, and public cloud-based systems and infrastructure already in use, a company's collection of cloud management tools needs to be just as flexible and scalable as its cloud computing strategy.

Related Terms

* cloud
* cloud computing (the cloud)
* cloud computing accounting software
* cloud CRM - Customer Relationship Management cloud
* CAMP - Cloud Application Management for Platforms
* storage cloud
* cloud services
* public cloud
* cloud computing reseller
* cloud storage

http://www.webopedia.com/TERM/C/cloud_management.html

copyright webopedia.com

Migration from in-house stored program computer to the Cloud Computing

Corporate computing migration paths over time are illustrated in detail in Appendix A.

The migration paths from manual systems to unit record punched card systems, to in-house computer systems, and now to cloud computing systems and managed services each provided then revolutionary advantages over prior methods. Thus, the early adopters of the new capabilities achieved economic, productivity, and competitive advantages over those who could not or would not change, eventually forcing virtually all to change within perhaps a decade or less to be competitive.

Tens of thousands of large and small companies, including several of the customers I have consulted with have transitioned or are transitioning their in-house corporate computing systems to Cloud Computing or managed services. Managed Services includes many additional services perhaps including collocated datacenters, backup, help desk, backup and recovery and other services.

Thousands of corporate computing in-house systems have already been migrated to the cloud.

Several generalized cloud project implementation scenarios are illustrated below:

A Cloud Migration Checklist

http://www.lawtechnologytoday.org/2015/01/a-cloud-migration-checklist/

The Ultimate Hybrid Cloud Migration Checklist

http://community.netapp.com/t5/Industries/The-Ultimate-Hybrid-Cloud-Migration-Checklist/ba-p/95023

Cloud infrastructure strategy and design - IBM

https://www-935.ibm.com/services/us/its/flash/cloud-strategy_overview.swf

Images for ibm cloud migration chart

https://www.google.com/search?q=ibm+cloud+migration+chart&biw=1464&bih=796&tbm=isch&tbo=u&source=univ&sa=X&ei=YXr0VNf2DNLHsQSFg4L4Bg&ved=0CDoQsAQ&dpr=1

Your Cloud Migration Project Plan

http://blog.integratelecom.com/your-cloud-migration-project-plan/

IBM Cloud Services - United States

http://www-935.ibm.com/services/us/en/it-services/cloud-services/

Successful cloud migration in 5 easy steps

http://thoughtsoncloud.com/2015/01/plan-successful-cloud-migration-5-easy-steps/

DSS Success Story - Pennock Co. - YouTube

https://www.youtube.com/watch?v=ooIRltlJ0uc

4 Mailroom or Intern or Co-op to CEO in Today's Corporation

Ever wonder how and why, in the past, so many CEOs and corporate executives rose from the mailroom and the lowest jobs to the pinnacle of corporate and financial success, while most other people languish in the same dead-end job? The primary reason is that the mailroom was traditionally the focal point of information coming into and leaving the company, and for information flowing among departments within the company, and thus the best source to learn the business for an inquiring person.

The mailroom person delivered the company mail to each department, and between departments, and physically saw the operations of each department and was able to observe and communicate with all levels of staff, even if the conversation was initially "Hi".

This comprehensive exposure to virtually the entire company and key company staff provided a great opportunity for the ambitious mailroom employee to select a desired upward path and the opportunity to communicate that desire to key company staff when appropriate.

Readers of "The One Minute Manager" by Kenneth H. Blanchard and Spencer Johnson are shown how and why a manager can interface with each employee for one minute every day to set and communicate goals and resolve problems for success. My personal experience is that the one-minute personal communication works spectacularly well.

My personal experience is also that the perhaps one-minute observation and communication by the mailroom person delivering the mail with departments in the company provides the opportunity for valuable understanding and advancement from the mailroom. The mailroom job is really a transition job rather than a career-long job as it does not pay well and has little opportunity for advancement within the mailroom.

Contrast the mailroom employee opportunity for advancement and interaction with virtually all company line departments and many of the departmental staff with most other jobs in the company, where a person can be hired in a job and spend the next forty years in essentially the same job.

Jobs in departments such as the boiler room, or stock room, or accounting provide little interaction with many other departments while providing enough compensation stay in the job. .

Today, electronic transmission of information via the Internet and mobile wireless communication has eliminated much of the mailroom documents and mailroom communication with company departments. Important corporate information now resides in computers rather than in paper documents and it is instantly available to authorized users virtually anywhere.

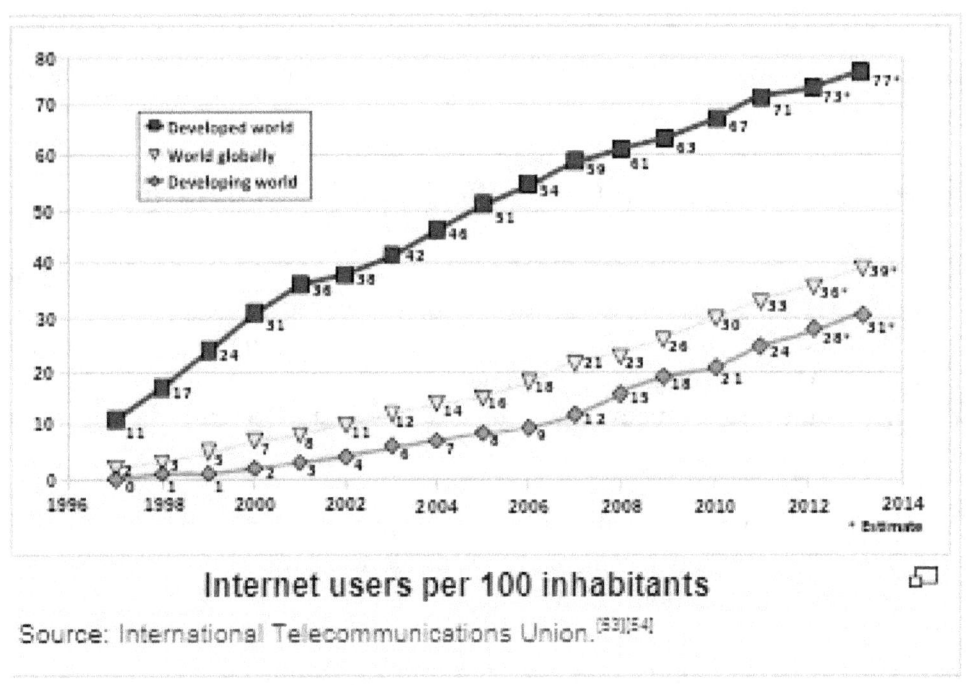

Internet users per 100 inhabitants

Source: International Telecommunications Union.[53][54]

http://en.wikipedia.org/wiki/Internet

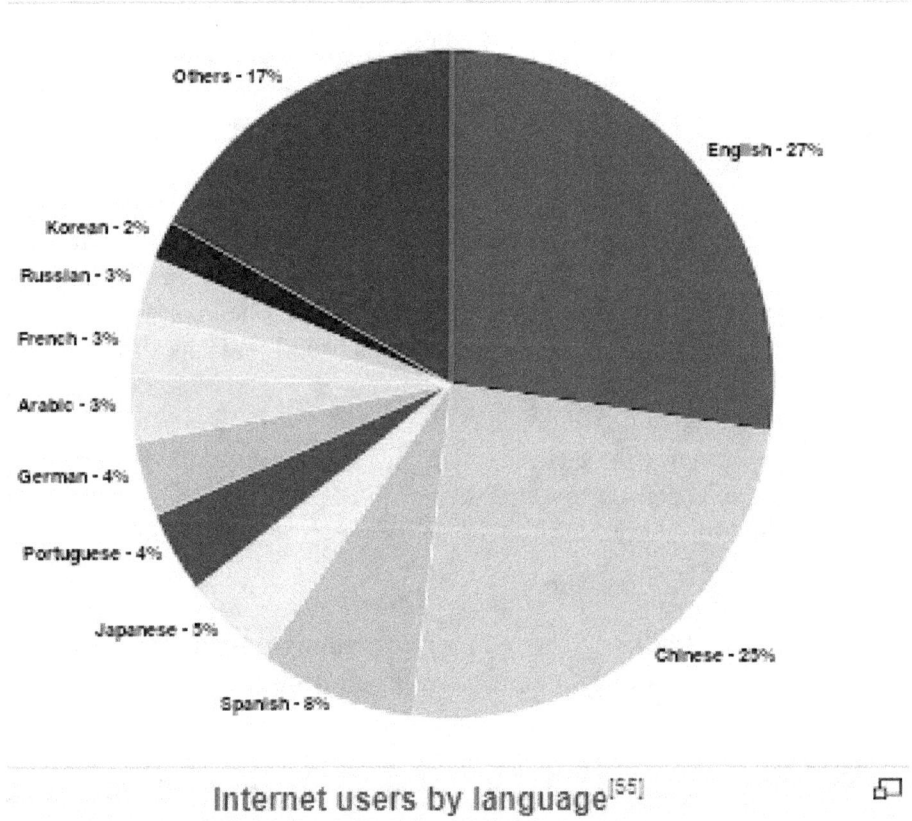

Internet users by language[55]

http://en.wikipedia.org/wiki/Internet

The mailroom person delivering the company mail and interfacing with all departments and levels of management has been replaced by the observant, interested and ambitious business analyst in corporate computing, who can see and potentially understand and analyze virtually all of the corporation's business information without physically moving throughout the company.

Additionally, the corporate computing department is normally not only responsible for the corporate information and security and distribution of that information, but is also responsible to develop, maintain, and often train and implement corporate Standard Operation Procedures (SOP) for most departments. This is because so much of the corporate business processing is now performed by personnel using computers, including real-time plant operations.

Video conferencing and recording software, such as GoToMeeting, Camtasia, and SKYPE provide easy-to-use and high definition video conferencing capability worldwide, and allow recording of the sessions in high definition.

This virtually universal and comprehensive documentation process allows corporate recording of user orientation, education, training, meetings and conferences with attendees worldwide, and posting of the recordings on YouTube and other sites for viewing by authorized viewers anytime.

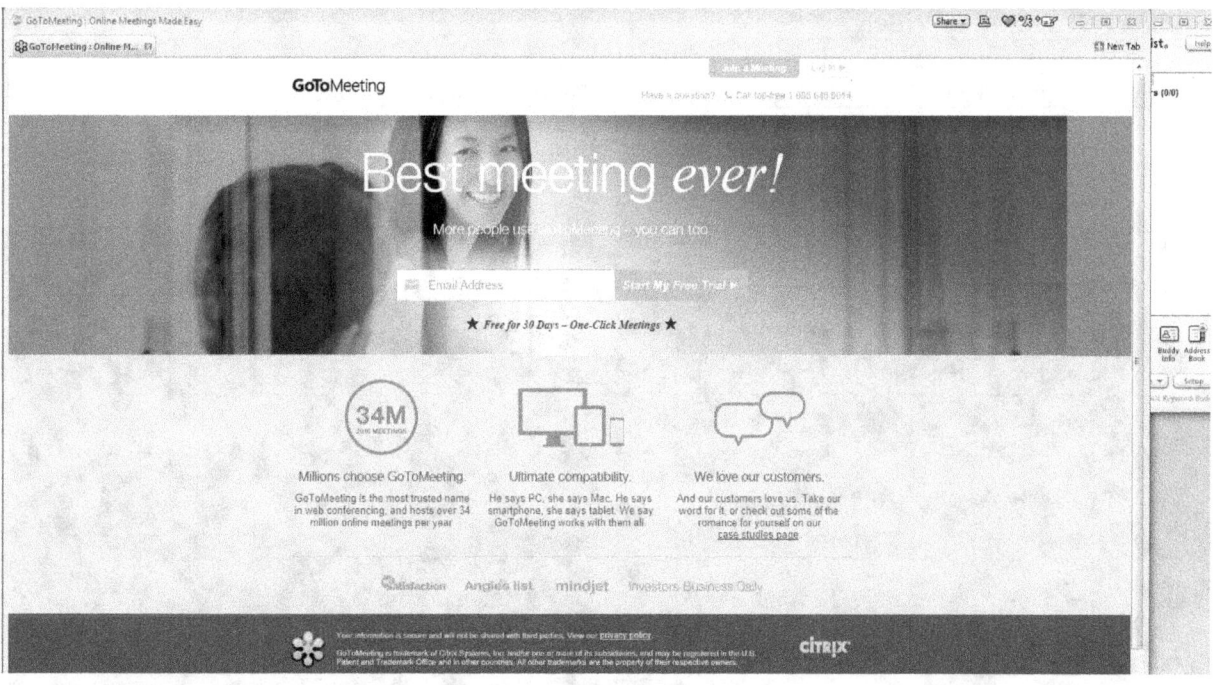

GoToMeeting

https://www4.gotomeeting.com/m/g2msem3.tmpl?Portal=www.gotomeeting.com&c_name=gget-d-c&c_mark=NAPPC&c_kwd=gotomeeting-Exact&c_prod=GTM&c_cmp=sf-70150000000adcs&c_date=CATnumber&c_cell=CPOMy6SsocMCFQQQ7AodIW4AUA&gclid=CPOMy6SsocMCFQQQ7AodIW4AUA&gclsrc=aw.ds

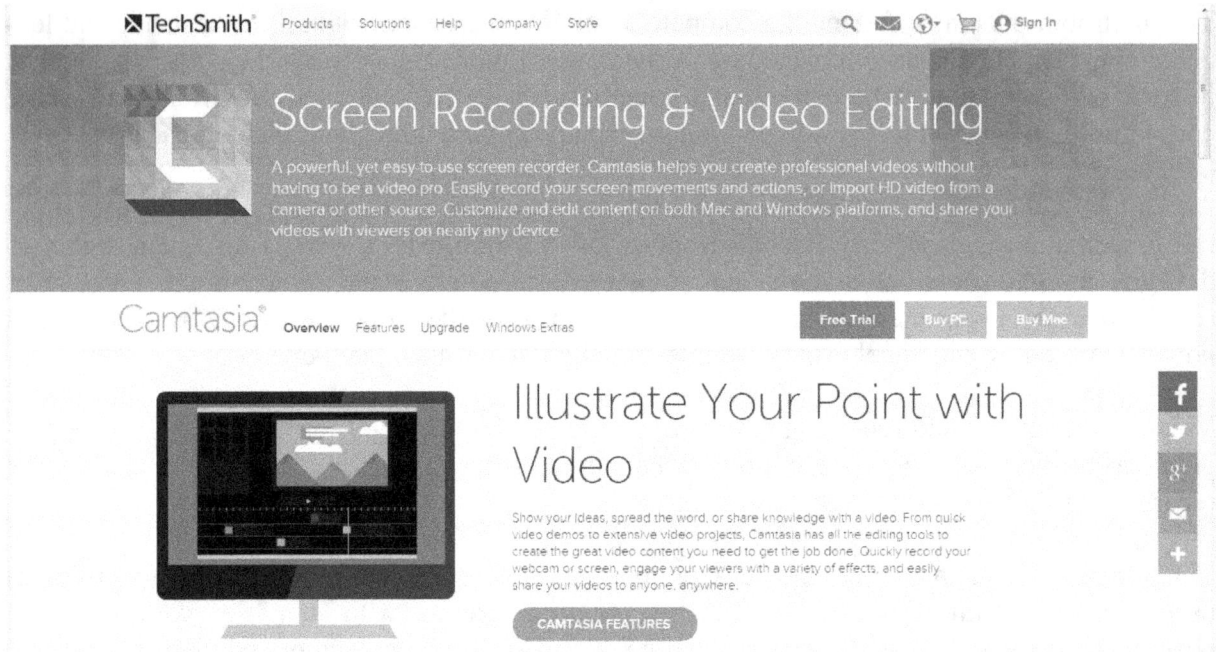

Screen Recording & Video Editing

http://www.techsmith.com/camtasia.html?gclid=CJb93dPej8QCFUojgQodzVEAew

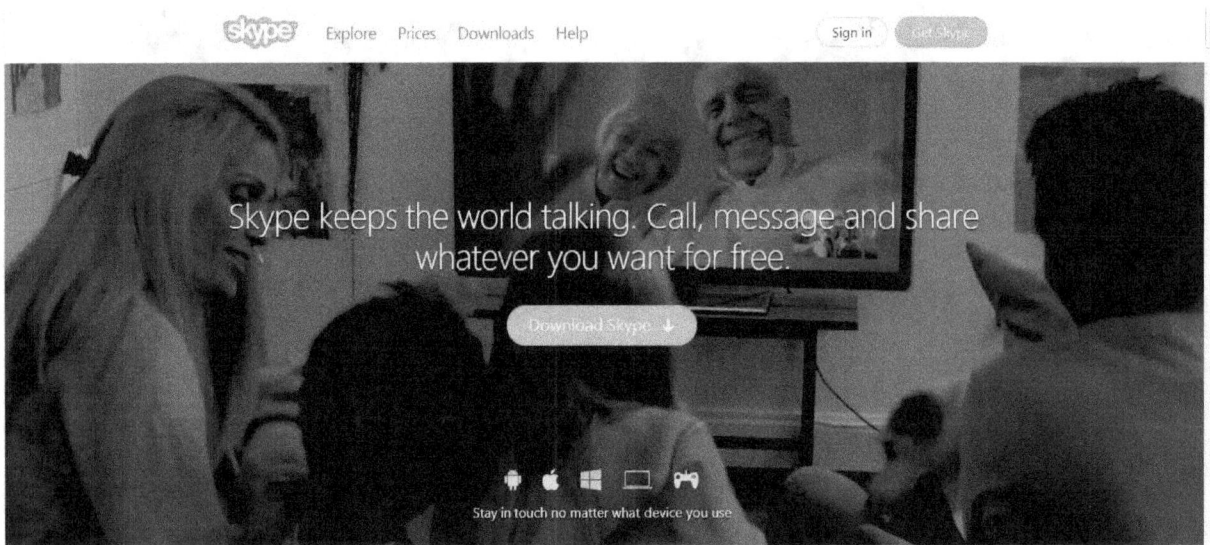

Skype keeps the world talking. Call, message and share whatever you want for free

http://www.skype.com/en/

NOTE – The single most important, valuable, productive, visible to corporate executives, and crucial to your understanding and success thing to do in any business in virtually every company today is to document and record all of the business processes, applications, menus, screens, and exact user interface (UI).

This is illustrated in the steps of an evaluation, or assessment, or study, or a review or an audit performed by the corporate computing department, or best by an independent expert outside consultant familiar with many companies in the same industry.

In my observation and experience, the biggest cause of a myriad of problems and loss of productivity, time, and profit in a company today remains the lack of consistency, speed, and accuracy in following once effective and productive standards and methods and training.

The speed issue is incredibly important, as in my recent experience of telephone customer service from two companies, and I have been involved in telephone customer service applications and issues for decades.

I am utilizing the Amazon Company Createspace to do the book front and back covers and other production functions such as the ISBN number, and I am in awe of the Createspace customer experience and results. I have always preached for rapid response to customer telephone calls, but **Createspace achieves instantaneous response, as perhaps in the same second** the call to Createspace customer service is placed, and that is followed up with expert and friendly service.

As the inventor of the Real-Time Program Audit (RTPA) software, I can really appreciate what the Createspace instantaneous or real-time response means to me the customer and what it accomplishes.

On the other hand, in calls to my bank customer service (a big bank), I virtually always get the dreaded :"We are experiencing very heavy call volumes but your call is valuable to us", and often wait 30 minutes, have lunch, take a nap, while waiting for a call center response.

That is unacceptable, as is any delay of more than several seconds maximum, but that poor customer service continues anyway.

The business analyst, __intern__, or co-op doing the whole company evaluation, assessment, review, or audit will be distressed to witness just such unacceptable response time to customers, most often unknown to executive management except at the company bottom line, and to see the level of general chaos and inconsistency and variation to set standards throughout the company.

Why You Need Interns, and Why You Should Pay Them
http://www.huffingtonpost.com/mike-harden/why-you-need-interns-and-_b_6803050.html

Addressing and correcting that chaos, inconsistency, loss of productivity and inadequate training becomes the next and continuing focus of the business analyst, intern or co-op and often leads to interaction with executive management.

Thus the business analyst, or intern, or co-op in corporate computing can interface with staff at all levels in the corporation as the moderator or instructor or facilitator of corporate information, procedures and best practices, and gain a n important and comprehensive understanding of how the corporation really works. No one else in the corporation is capable of that comprehensive understanding and continual interaction with staff at all levels and in all departments.

Perhaps the very best opportunity for the ambitious corporate business analyst in the corporate computing department is to introduce video conferencing, such as GoToMeeting, to the corporate senior executives as an excellent way for senior management daily communication.

Worldwide video conferencing in high definition with essentially free communications costs is, in my opinion and experience, the best productivity tool available today and for the foreseeable future.

Additionally, the corporate computing department is normally also responsible for helping all departments with traditional business and technical support as in help desk support, and training. Yet again, the corporate computing business analyst is best qualified to work with corporate users in all departments to document and resolve most help desk issues, and to implement procedures to prevent additional user errors. Issues involving programing may require a second level support depending whether the program is maintained in-house, or is an external software package.

Additionally, the corporate computing department is normally also responsible for determining and implementing new applications business requirements or modifying current business application. Yet again, the corporate computing business analyst is best qualified to work with corporate users in all departments to document, confirm, develop and implement modifications to existing corporate business applications.

Additionally, corporate computing is rapidly migrating from in-house programmed and supported applications written specifically for the corporation to externally developed application software, such as SAP or Oracle or IBM.

A primary role of the corporate business analyst is to understand the comprehensive externally developed application software and to interface it to corporate specific needs, perhaps becoming a "super user" in that vendor software. Traditionally, this is developing reports and business analytics via report writers and not through programming traditional programming languages.

Contrast the above corporate business analyst functions and capabilities with the corporate in-house programmer. The corporate in-house programmer normally is focused in writing and maintaining corporate in-house applications in traditional arcane programming languages and sometimes in doing some help desk programming support, and then perhaps in maintaining them for an entire career.

Clearly, in my opinion and experience and for the above reasons and more, the ideal place to be for an ambitious and capable young person in the entire corporation is in corporate computing as a business analyst or intern, not as a programmer.

Said another way, a capable and ambitious corporate business analyst or intern, in six months, can learn and really understand virtually the entire important computer related business applications in a corporation. The best way to do that is simply view the recorded Standard Operating Procedure (SOP) videos of each job in each department, starting at the corporate level, than the application level, than at the screen menu or user job description level, then finally if needed at the underlying computer program level. If these SOP videos are not available, then simply make them, and showcase them as valuable tools for executive management.

So, what might be the ideal job for a capable and ambitious person to start at a corporation? Not in the mailroom anymore, but as an intern in the corporate computing department, with the express job of learning how the entire corporation really works now and how senior management wants it to work, and becoming incredibly valuable by making that happen.

Even a three month summer internship at a corporation would be a valuable and productive experience for both the intern and the company, and no particular knowledge of computing is needed or necessarily desirable.

Looking back at my own career, the Drexel University cooperative six months assignments in industry, including at IBM, were invaluable in gaining such understanding and experience before graduating and selecting IBM as my career.

The real and immediate future for Drexel University and for Drexel Co-op students

In chapter 7 How IBM and SAP can Succeed and Grow: A Revolutionary Strategy, I illustrate my final wonderful Drexel co-op job and how it transformed my life for the better.

I also respectfully promised to not show what would have happened to me, and what did happen to the company that I rejected as a co-op job instead of me fighting for and choosing IBM. And, it happened to some of my Drexel co-op peers

That was in chapter 7, and you really do need to take notice and action to help yourself today. A great many of the "plumb" manufacturing jobs, and blocks and blocks in Philadelphia in 1960s today look like this:

Philadelphia abandoned factories

https://www.flickr.com/search/?q=philadelphia+abandoned+factories&ct=0&mt=all&adv=1

Source: Flickr

Philadelphia PA has changed dramatically since 1960, and today the really plumb Drexel co-op jobs, and indeed the really plumb jobs are not in the traditional industrial engineering manufacturing disciplines taught at Drexel when I was a student.

Today, every company of every size and in every industry has a CEO, or de facto CEO who is responsible for running the company, whatever is its business, and today virtually all companies utilize the corporate computing department, even it is a single PC, to manage and coordinate and communicate with all aspects of the business.

It is in corporate computing and the coordination and communication and services to executive management provided by corporate computing that that is the future for a great many Drexel University co-op students, rather than as 1960s manufacturing industrial engineers, and as other engineers or business students.

And, because of the Internet and other real-time communication capability, such as SKYPE, GoToMeeting and others, Drexel co-op students can largely work worldwide. Think about it, if offshore sourced firms can do local Philadelphia technical jobs, why cannot expertly trained and qualified Drexel students and graduates successfully perform jobs worldwide?

In my more than two generations in corporate computing I have mentored multiple sons of CEOs who were interns in the company corporate computing department and in other line departments, and always with very successful results.

The CEOs placed their sons in corporate computing to learn and understand the entire business, and to coordinate and communicate with other executives, knowing that one day the son would become the CEO and the focus would be the big picture, not in computer computing or in programming.

Drexel co-ops in corporate computing should also utilize the same big picture and coordination and communication opportunities with all executives, and not focus on computer programming.

In chapter 3 Corporate Executive Migration Path to Cloud computing, I illustrate what methods I still use today when I am asked to consult with a CEO or executive staff to help them to evaluate or assess or study and understand the company business, and to recommend what they should do.

I can always understand and document the company business, from top to bottom, within a few weeks, or even days, and there are always significant areas to be greatly improved.

These evaluation and discovery and documentation methods are what an intern in a corporate computing can and should utilize to be the most valuable immediately and in the future.

 The fundamental reason why I make these, true, claims and statements about always finding significant issues and finding valuable solutions is not because of my unique capability or skills, but because humans rather than machines are involved in virtually all of the areas addressed.

Humans are innovative and inventive, and even talkative, but they do not necessarily always do things in the same standard and most productive way, and they make mistakes and quit. Machines also perform in the same exact tireless way, which is why the industrial revolution was so dramatic and productive, and why humans are increasingly being replaced by robots.

Thus the corporate computing intern can and always will be more valuable working with the big picture and the entire company and by focusing on human activity than by programming (see chapter 2), and that is a huge step towards the top.

What to do with the CEO's son or daughter this summer?

I believe the most valuable first corporate intern experience for the son or daughter of a corporate executive is as an intern in the corporate computing department, as illustrated above, and not in a line department. The intern should not waste time becoming a programmer or developer, but actively study and evaluate and audit the entire company operations by observing and recording every business process from top to bottom.

This really is the best way to learn and understand how the entire business works and the issues hampering the company success, and provides information not actually understood by the CEO or other executives. It is the best and most proven method for immediate major improvements that I have observed, partly because the issues discovered by the executive intern can be and are often are fast tracked to the attention of the CEO, sometimes over supper.

What should the Drexel co-op do in the corporate computing department to be the most valuable?

The Drexel co-op should do exactly the same evaluation, study and audit as the executive intern.

The Drexel co-op potentially has the significant advantage of some prior industry co-op experience, and certainly should have the advantage of specific current Drexel courses focused on maximizing the capability to do the study, evaluation or study, and to understand the big picture.

What must Drexel do to best prepare its co-op students to be most valuable now and in their careers?

In my opinion, Drexel University should require its executives and especially its professors to go on a Drexel initiated bus trip, all around Philadelphia starting with Delaware Avenue, and observe the real world of today including the gleaming new office towers in center city. Perhaps Drexel executives could even visit and perhaps consider booming Singapore, as I have suggested.

Then Drexel should require its executives and especially its professors to physically visit the full range of current co-op jobs and to talk with current and previous co-op students and Drexel graduates, and company sponsors about how relevant and complete is the current Drexel education offerings to real world co-op and graduate jobs today, and what new courses would be needed or appropriate.

Then Drexel should do a formal annual comprehensive study and analysis of all of the co-op jobs and co-op corporate sponsors since 1960. This study should be industry by industry, as in manufacturing, accounting, technology, and co-op major by co-op major, as in commerce and engineering, business, electrical engineering, including co-op compensation and co-op location and co-op satisfaction and co-op history of accepting a job with the sponsor on graduation.

These crucial statistics and this crucial information should include assessment of the co-op job and industry as a high value co-op job as at IBM, in compensation and desirability, and a low-value job, as at Lit Brothers, and if the co-op job was considered by the co-op and sponsor as being greatly assisted by the Drexel courses and by Drexel support during the co-op job.

Also if the co-op and sponsor were happy with the co-op experience and would do it again, and what new skills and training Drexel co-ops should bring to the co-op job and how Drexel could best support the co-op and sponsor while the co-op was on the co-op job.

Also (this is just a partial list), if the co-op was satisfied or happy with the sponsor working environment, and if the co-op was well prepared and could have been much better prepared with different courses or subjects prior to the co-op experience, also if there are serious issues or dangers that Drexel should address immediately or otherwise at the co-op job.

Also, what the heck, how the Drexel co-op directly rated the sponsor company, his or her curriculum, courses, compensation, experience, Drexel, and especially his or her professors.

In short, would the Drexel co-op do the co-op or a similar co-op job again, and would the Drexel co-op sponsor company do more Drexel co-op jobs again?

If some of these statistics are new or news to Drexel, they are not new to Drexel co-ops and Drexel co-op sponsors, and they are vitally important to both the co-op and the sponsor, and to Drexel, and they could be easily gathered as a co-op experience summary at the end of each co-op experience, or interactively, by Drexel.

I could assist in the creation and presentation of real-time Big Data analytics, and predictive analytics that should be crucially informative to Drexel, Drexel professors, sponsor companies, co-ops, prospective co-ops and many others, including co-op families.

Of particular interest would be the annual or decade trends, including the trends toward high-value technology co-op jobs, and away from the low-value manufacturing jobs, and the jobs utilizing outdated methods including accounting and auditing.

This formal comprehensive and current graphical analytical study of Drexel actual performance could be a tremendous marketing tool for Drexel University, or not.

There are darn few new Drexel co-op jobs or graduate jobs available in writing compilers for arcane programming languages of the past, or in nanotechnology, or accounting or auditing, as accomplished decades ago, and for a host of courses now offered by Drexel.

Instead, there are an unknown but certainly a huge and growing number co-op and graduate top jobs in current technologies, as illustrated in this book, that are not offered at Drexel. And there is the whole universe of opportunity not apparently known to Drexel.

I suggest, among many courses, On-Demand Forensic Accounting and Analytics, Real-time Predictive Autonomic Computing (using a whole new universe of really big data).

Drexel University will suffer until it can and will face the world of business and technology of today and in the future and adapt, innovate and lead, and provide worldwide new valuable opportunities for its students and graduates.

What must Drexel Co-op students require of Drexel to be the most valuable now and in their careers?

In my opinion, reading and understanding this book would be a great start. I have successfully mentored many people over many decades and I have been mentored by many, including

Drexel's Dr. An Min Chung. It is my obligation to try to mentor Drexel students as best I know how.

Look around you at what are the most needed and the most valuable jobs and vocations, and then think a decade in the future and the trends toward the future, and think of your future.

The crucial productivity tools for humans have evolved from the physical tools of throwing stones, spears, writing with pens, to the mechanical tools of the printing press, train, automobile, to now the electronic tools such as the computer and robotics. This makes the human-computer interaction (HCI) ever more crucial, especially as it is applied to the practical corporate world.

Robots Replacing Human Factory Workers at Faster Pace
http://abcnews.go.com/Business/wireStory/robots-replacing-human-factory-workers-faster-pace-28849861

Human–computer interaction
http://en.wikipedia.org/wiki/Human%E2%80%93computer_interaction

Then set your sights and focus on Singapore, the most expensive city in the world, and the world and not on Delaware Avenue.

World's most expensive cities revealed
http://www.aol.com/article/2015/03/04/worlds-most-expensive-cities-revealed/21149616/?icid=maing-grid7%7Chtmlws-sb-bb%7Cdl20%7Csec1_lnk2%26pLid%3D622532

Then, take the path you think will best get you to your goals and success, and take action towards your own success.

5 The Road to Singapore

In my more than five decades of active involvement in corporate computing, starting with more than twenty one years at IBM, I had traveled alone over most of the world consulting with corporations and executive management in many industries. But, I had never been to a continent that I really wanted to see, exotic Asia. Appendix G Paul Houston Harkins Résumé

Then, one day while I was starting to write this book, I got yet another phone call out-of-the-blue from a recruiter who had read my résumé on dice.com who asked me if I was interested in consulting at a corporation which had lost its CIO and chief developer and programmer and needed help.

The corporation was in the midst of opening a major plant in Singapore, and could not get the corporate computing going, including orientation and training of the new staff, developing Standard Operation Procedures, and proper real-time operation of the multi-million dollar machines in the 24 hour a day and 7 day a week operation.

I initially demurred at the recruiter's persistent offers to consult, but then he mentioned a new plant in Singapore and the probable opportunity to spent several months there, and that previous trips to Singapore by HQ staff had not been successful in getting the corporate computing there operational. Since Singapore is 12 times zones away from the Pennsylvania headquarters of the corporation and there was no one left in headquarters familiar with the in-house developed and supported applications, that meant I would be totally on my own and working directly for the Singapore CEO doing 12 hour shifts at the Singapore plant.

Singapore

http://www.world-finance-conference.com/sites/default/files/beautiful-singapore-cityscape-1600x1066_0.jpg

I finally accepted the Singapore consulting gig, primarily to see Singapore, to work directly for the Singapore CEO, because the job requirements were "Please help us.", and because I would be totally on my own and make all the computing decisions there. This view of Singapore shows the opposite view of the waterfront I had from my suite in the center of Singapore on Somerset Road. I spent three months there last summer, the plant is up and running and Singapore is indeed fabulous. Hint – It takes about a 30 hour door-to-door trip to fly from Newark NJ, to Singapore via Tokyo, so if you fly economy, then sit on at least two pillows and move about often.

That really plumb Singapore corporate consulting experience followed by about two years the very best and most exciting and best compensated corporate consulting experience of my entire working career, and both happened after my seventh birthday because I said yes to properly offered opportunity.

In my more than five decades of active involvement in corporate computing, starting with more than twenty one years at IBM, I had traveled alone over most of the world, except Asia, consulting with corporations and executive management in many industries. But, I had never been an expert forensic accounting investigator in a major fraud case.

Then, one day several years ago while I was starting to enjoy semi-retirement from full time consulting, I got yet another phone call out-of-the-blue directly from an executive involved in the case and who was specifically looking for my unique immediate help.

The computer savvy executive had been tasked with finding an expert in the IBM AS/400 computer, the RPG programming language, and who as expert in auditing computer software, and in searching for an expert he found my web site www.harkinsaudit.com

www.harkinsaudit.com

While the project was confidential, the executive had searched long and hard for a qualified expert and he said the magic words, essentially: "Can you please help?, Can you start immediately?, top money was not an issue, there would be travel and living expenses prepaid, travel is billable, some overnights in New York City, and "Let's start next Monday".

SOURCE: FLICKR

After some consultation with my wife, who is an accountant and who does not think much of my accounting expertise, I finally accepted the New York City consulting gig. The allure for me was once again, primarily to see New York City in a way I never seen it, although I had lived in New York City for over one year, to work directly for the project managers, and to do computer auditing at which I was an expert, and because the job requirements were "Please help us", because I would be almost totally on my own in my investigating, and because it was so incredibly exciting.

Why me, and why not someone else, and why almost guaranteed success after others had failed?

I got that great consulting job in New York City when I lived 100 miles away outside of New York in West Chester PA, in spite of there being thousands of competent computer consultants in and around New York. I got that really plumb job because I apparently had significant unique capabilities and experience that were needed by the executives searching for an expert consultant, I was immediately available and willing, I was visible to them (a reoccurring theme in this book),and I took immediate action and effort to secure the plumb job.

There are several vital things that projected me above those other thousands of available and un-doubtedly capable of my peers, including:

- I was immediately visible worldwide with my resume, experience, unique capabilities and availability, all visible through the Internet
- I was a published author of several books and of current copyrighted articles
- I was the author of an active U.S. Patent important in computer program auditing
- I had a web site (how I was discovered in this case) that related directly to the search needs (AS/400, RPG, Auditing)
- I had posted my current resume to www.dice.com and other such sites such as LinkedIn.
- My extensive IBM experience on the IBM AS/400 was crucial for this opportunity
- My IBM experience and consulting experience made me comfortable with top executives
- My extensive corporate computing consulting experience was important to this opportunity
- I was willing to travel and stay overnight for this opportunity
- I was interested in pushing the envelope of computer auditing
- My wonderful Drexel co-op experiences and my resulting career job at IBM had projected me way above most others in desirability for this job and probable capability to do this job
- I was immediately available and interested and I said so

Most or all of these points could be important or vital for the reader to consider and perhaps to accomplish to increase the potential for significant success in the future.

The net, net is to be accomplished, really expert in something valuable, immediately visible, and to say yes.

Why is this important to you and your success?

The answers to these two questions are detailed next in this chapter— after two illustrations that provide a stark contrast to the the above illustrations of recent opportunjities and events.

In 1960 I was a junior at then Drexel Institute of Technology (now Drexel University), and I spent my third six-month industry co-op stint at the Esso Oil (now (Exxon) credit card processing center in Bala Cynwyd, PA. Esso had an IBM unit record computing center similar to that in the Gulf Oil illustration previously described.

While at Esso, I got the opportunity to see and observe many of the departments, and one day I observed what to me was an epiphany, or at least a very telling moment. Both the Gulf Oil and

Esso operations were very large, and at Esso there was a huge room for accounting, with perhaps forty people at desks doing the clerical work from the unit record accounting machine green bar printed reports, and of course with the electro-mechanical Friden calculators on each desk.

One day we were all called together for an awards ceremony, and the award for the entire accounting department huge room of people was to Frank, for having the cleanest desk.

At that moment I confirmed the realization that I would not go into any job where virtually anyone could do the job, and where I could not excel on my own initiative and with unique and important and demonstrable expertise that I developed.

All of those clerical jobs in huge rooms at Gulf Oil and Esso Oil have long since disappeared, as have those operations, and as have similar jobs everywhere as these commodity jobs were quickly eliminated by computers, and by offshoring.

The movie "The Apartment" in 1960
https://www.youtube.com/watch?v=x356ll3hTxg
Illustrates a similar huge clerical room in New York City, with electro-mechanical Friden calculators and Rollodex card files on most desks, and that each elevator had an operator. Both those manual labor intensive jobs are gone today.

The Apartment (1960)
https://www.youtube.com/watch?v=x356ll3hTxg

As a Drexel Co-op student working at Esso and Sharples Centrifuge Company in Philadelphia, my desk did have a Friden electro-mechanical calculator but did not include a phone or a Rollodex index card file as I was not supposed to make phone calls. The Sharples Centrifuge building in northeast Philadelphia was rubble several years after my six-month co-op job there.

The fourth illustration happens to me several times every week now in my mid-seventies. It illustrates important opportunity, but also an important and I believe a negative shift in how corporate computing jobs are advertised, managed, interviewed and filled from the traditional direct corporation advertised, interviewed, and filled jobs in the past.

Some years ago I received an email from dice.com encouraging me to post my résumé for free on dice.com, so that my résumé would be visible and available to virtually anyone searching for whatever skills that were on my résumé. That free offer by dice.com, and other free offers by other job sites, was probably one of the most fortunate things I have ever done. Appendix G Paul Houston Harkins Résumé

The dice.com and other similar job sites, including www.linkedin.com, index key works from your résumé, such as IBM, AS/400, RPG, consulting, auditing, financial, ERP and essentially every important piece of information on your' and then make it available, similar to the Google search capability to virtually anyone (now mostly recruiters) searching for candidates to fill jobs.

Also my web site www.harkinsaudit.com provides similar worldwide instant visibility to recruiters and anyone by automatically creating key word searches of information on my web site home page. And, all of that worldwide visibility costs perhaps five dollars a month.

Thus, I normally get multiple corporate computing available job inquiries each week, almost always from recruiters who are hired by corporations to find and screen qualified candidate for a corporate computing job, and who are compensated by the corporation for doing so.

All this interest is wonderful and gratifying, except that the recruiter is now responsible to pre-screen and pre-qualify the candidate, including setting what is often a low-ball or commodity rate and conditions for the job.

The corporation does not normally see the candidates' résumé, unless the corporation does the searches, and does not select which candidates may be best qualified for the job, including important industry experience and potential best fit. That is now normally done by the recruiter who does the screening and prodding to get the lowest possible compensation rate among a pool of candidates perceived as a commodity but deemed as qualified by the recruiter.

You probably have already guessed it. The recruiter does not know the corporation applications or know the corporate computing environment, or know the corporate staff. The recruiter is charged with getting the lowest cost probably qualified candidate who says he or she can do the job. The recruiter is also often charged with giving a technical evaluation of the candidate, but the recruiter is not any may never have been a corporate computing staff person, so the technical evaluation is often seriously flawed and irrelevant, which causes the wrong candidates to be offered to the corporation.

Then, there is sometimes the recruiter who thinks he knows more than the expert candidate, because he says so.

Anyone who has been in the U.S. Army and remembers receiving his or her GI (Government Issue) uniform knows the power of the private in the supply room who tells you what your uniform size and boot size are without asking, because he can, and you are just a commodity to him.

So, what do I do with these welcome and interesting emails and occasional phone calls from recruiters?

I reject every one that has a long list of specific skills and requirements and conditions.

I wish I could tell the corporation or recruiter how counter-productive it is to list a page of requirements and duties instead of just selecting candidates with expert résumés and asking "Please interview with us."

Every one that low balls the consulting compensation, I reject.

Every one that requires unpaid overnight travel, I reject.

As a corp-to-corp (corporation to corporation) consultant, every one that does not pay at least half the travel time, I reject.

Every one that requires a recruiter technical interview, I reject.

Every one that offers a job as one of many similar jobs in the corporation, I reject.

Every one that offers a less than respectful and cooperative environment, I reject.

Every one that asks for a guarantee of successful work (an impossibility), I reject.

Old, off-support computer hardware and off-support operating system software, I reject.

(Many more requirements), I reject

I strongly suggest and encourage you to do the same.

Fortunately, if you are an expert—and, even better, a published expert—there will be the occasional "Would you please help us"? and money will not be an object, and you will work directly with the CEO and the executive staff, and you will be successful.

Strive to do most of your consulting that does not require personal contact remotely, using a Virtual Private Network (VPN) secure connection from your home or office to the client. This remote capability saves hours of travel time, transportation costs, living costs and hassle and is much more productive and can speed project completion. A great way to accomplish remote consulting is to charge fully for all travel time, or to charge more for on-site consulting.

6 The Bernie Madoff Case - The Forensic Accounting Investigation

The Bernard L. Madoff Ponzi scheme was the largest financial Ponzi scheme in history, with investors being defrauded out of more than $17 billion in investments. The fraud involved thousands of investors over a period of decades, from the early 1970s until December 2008. The fraud was not uncovered by the Securities and Exchange Commission or other regulators over the decades that it was taking place.

In the Sources section of this book I reference detailed public record documents and voluminous sworn testimony produced during the government trials that show exactly how this fraud was accomplished without Madoff ever having made any actual investments. The Sources section also includes links to many books authored by defrauded investors illustrating how this fraud ruined their lives.

The almost daily reporting by Erik Larson of the recent more than five month trial of five Madoff employees, including two Madoff programmers provides fascinating detail of what the jury was told. Google: Erik Larson Madoff trial reporting

I believe that the type of fraud Madoff perpetrated is continuing largely undetected today, since the government's auditing, detection, and enforcement systems have not been significantly enhanced in order to stop these frauds from happening. I can offer my proven patented solution for preventing this kind of fraud from ever happening again.

Madoff U.S. Marshals Service Auction
https://www.flickr.com/search/?q=Madoff&l=comm&ct=0&mt=all&adv=1

SOURCE: FLICKR

In this book I review information available on the public record, ending with the recent more than five-month trial and the subsequent conviction of the five indicted Madoff employees, including the Madoff programmers. However, unlike previous books and documents made public before the recent trial of those five employees, this book can spotlight public record documents as well as indictment and trial document testimony showing exactly how the Ponzi scheme was actually so easily accomplished and not discovered by the government for decades.

I also give my opinion as to how government auditors, including the Securities and Exchange Commission (SEC) could have and should have implemented available computer auditing technology to uncover this Ponzi scheme, to uncover other ongoing and undiscovered financial frauds, and to deter financial frauds from starting.

Perhaps shockingly, I ask how the government could not uncover the largest fraud in US history, spend six years over $1 billion in investigating the Madoff Ponzi scheme, spend additional unknown amounts of money and resources on the criminal prosecution of Madoff personnel, and still not make needed and available changes to government auditing. And, I give my opinion as to why.

Adv. Pro. No. 08-01789 (BRL) - Bernard L. Madoff ...
https://www.google.com/?gws_rd=ssl#q=I+am+Bruce+Dubinsky&kpevlbx=0

UNITED STATES DISTRICT COURT
SOUTHERN DISTRICT OF NEW YORK

In re: BERNARD L. MADOFF INVESTMENT SECURITIES LLC. Debtor.	Adv. Pro. No. 08-01789 (BRL) SIPA LIQUIDATION (Substantively Consolidated)

IRVING H. PICARD, Trustee for the Liquidation of
Bernard L. Madoff Investment Securities LLC.
 	
     Plaintiff.
 	
v.
 	
SAUL B. KATZ, et al.,
 	
     Defendants.
	Adv. Pro. No. 10-05287 (BRL)
	
	11 Civ. 03605 (JSR) (HBP)

DECLARATION OF
BRUCE G. DUBINSKY, MST, CPA, CFE, CVA, CFF, CFFA

http://www.madofftrustee.com/document/dockets/001036-kwdeclaration11-03605docket107.pdf

In my opinion, the following 279 page declaration document provides the most comprehensive, complete, and detailed information about exactly how the entire Bernard L. Madoff Ponzi scheme was accomplished.
Google: I am Bruce Dubinsky

The following document lists the dockets for the USA v O'Hara Case No 1:10-cr-0228

USA V O'Hara et al New York Southern District Court, Case No. 1:10-cr-00228

The following 98 page indictment document 36 lists the counts in the USA v O'Hara Case No 1:10-cr-0228

Case 1:10-cr-00228-LTS Document 36 Filed 11/17/10 Page 1 of 49
SUPERSEDING INDICTMENT FILED as to Jerome O'Hara (1) count(s) 1ss, 3ss, 4ss,
http://www.pietragallo.com/library/files/show_temp.pl-24.pdf

Case 1:10-cr-00228-LTS   Document 36   Filed 11/17/10   Page 1 of 49

```
UNITED STATES DISTRICT COURT
SOUTHERN DISTRICT OF NEW YORK
- - - - - - - - - - - - - - - - - x

UNITED STATES OF AMERICA          :

          -v-                     :

DANIEL BONVENTRE,                 :
ANNETTE BONGIORNO,
JOANN CRUPI,                      :
     a/k/a "Jodi,"
JEROME O'HARA, and                :
GEORGE PEREZ,
                                  :
          Defendants.
                                  :

- - - - - - - - - - - - - - - - - x
```

INDICTMENT

S2 10 Cr. 228 (LTS)

CNBC Exclusive: CNBC Transcript: Securities and Exchange Commission Chairman Mary Jo White on CNBC's "Closing Bell" Today

http://www.cnbc.com/id/100891221#.

Source CNBC (excerpt)

"WHITE: WE NEED MORE RESOURCES.

BARTIROMO: YOU NEED MORE MONEY.

WHITE: WE NEED MORE MONEY. WE NEED MORE MONEY TO COVER THOSE RE-SPONSIBILITIES. WE'RE IN THE CURRENT BUDGET PROCESS NOW. UNDER THE PRESIDENT'S REQUEST, WE WOULD BE ABLE TO ADD 600-PLUS NEW POSITIONS. THAT WOULD HELP. BUT WE DEFINITELY NEED IT FOR I.T., WE NEED IT FOR EN-

FORCEMENT, WE NEED IT FOR EXAMINATION. IF WE'RE GOING TO DO THE JOB RIGHT, WE'VE GOT TO HAVE THE MONEY.

BARTIROMO: EXACTLY. AND A LOT OF PEOPLE WONDER IF, IN FACT, THE PEOPLE THAT ARE ON THE JOB, OR THAT YOU WILL HIRE, HAVE THE SKILL SET REQUIRED. I REMEMBER BACK IN 2008, SOME OF THE GUYS WHO WE THOUGHT KNEW WHAT THEY WERE DOING – SO WHAT IS A CDS?

WHITE: WELL, ONE OF THE THINGS THAT THE AGENCY HAS DONE PRIOR TO MY ARRIVAL AND CERTAINLY AFTER AS WELL, IS TO ADD MARKET EXPERTISE TO THE STAFF. OBVIOUSLY WE ARE A LAW ENFORCEMENT AGENCY. WE HAVE A LOT OF LAWYERS, A LOT OF ACCOUNTANTS, NEEDLESS TO SAY A LOT OF FINANCIAL STATEMENTS. BUT YOU NEED THAT MARKET EXPERTISE. A LOT HAVE BEEN ADD-ED. A LOT MORE ARE NEEDED".

I believe that the Securities and Exchange Commission (SEC) would be many times more effective and productive and successful and need far fewer employees than it has today by immediately implementing On-Demand Forensic Accounting and Analytics as is illustrated in Appendix C On-Demand Forensic Accounting and Analytics

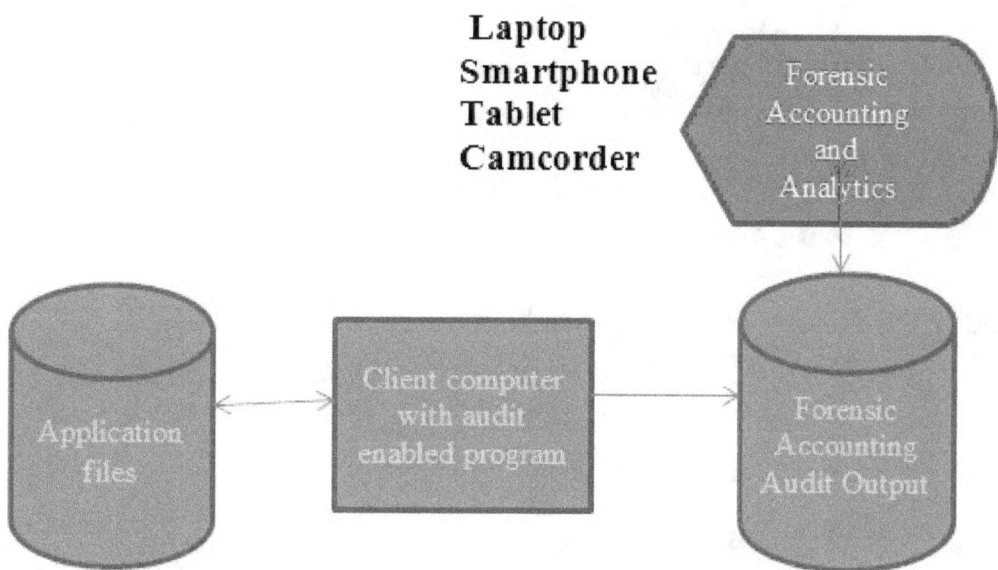

Figure 6: Forensic Accounting and Analytics (can be remote and mobile and real-time).

The Bernard L. Madoff Ponzi scheme was accomplished and went undetected for more than a decade using an IBM AS/400 (IBM System i) business computer, primarily using an IBM programming language RPG (Report Program Generator), as detailed on page 23 of the above declaration.

I have focused on corporate computer program auditing and analytics for many years. I have authored an active U.S. **Patent on a computer program electronic auditing tool, "The Real-Time Program** Audit (RTPA)", which is described in
Appendix H U.S. Patent – Real-Time Program Audit (RTPA) 6,775,827.

Hundreds of thousands of IBM AS/400 (IBM System i, or now IBM i) computers have been installed in companies, primarily for corporate business computing, and there are today still many thousands of IBM AS/400s (IBM i) computers installed in corporations. There are many thousands of programmers still developing and maintaining corporate applications in the RPG programming language, programmers with similar technical skills as the Madoff programmers.

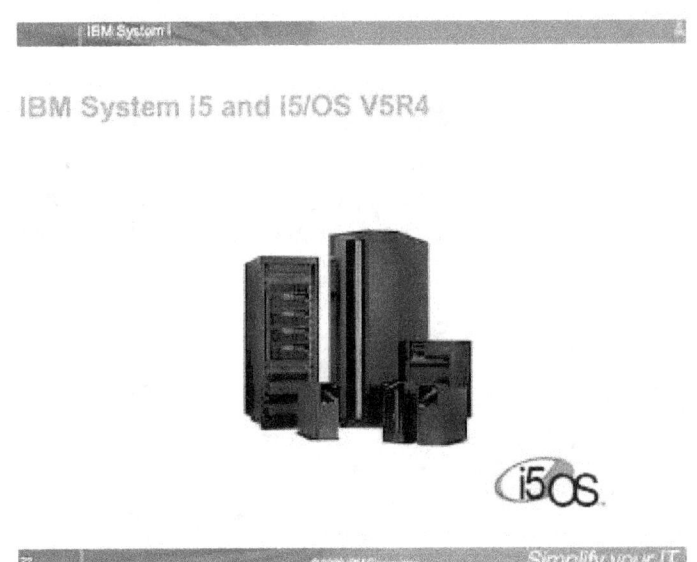

https://www.flickr.com/search/?q=AS%2F400&l=comm&ct=0&mt=all&adv=1

(Source: Flickr)

IBM RPG

http://en.wikipedia.org/wiki/IBM_RPG

The IBM Report Program Generator language (RPG) used by the Madoff programmers to prepare fake statements and other fake documents was originally developed *over half a century* ago to allow programmers to easily create reports using computer source programs rather than by wiring Herman Hollerith unit record control panels.

The RPG programming language, and virtually all other corporate programming languages such as COBOL and the C programming language, do not provide for full electronic program auditing—a process that shows, as if in a video recording, what was processed by the executing program statements and the data processed. This trail is unalterable. Without electronic program auditing, only the final output of the program, such as customer statements, is produced, allowing program computations and data manipulations to go unrecorded and be lost for review and auditing.

This is what happened in the Madoff case: the lack of full electronic auditing allowed the Madoff scheme to go undetected. Full electronic program auditing would have shown in real-time exactly how the Madoff fake statements were computed and the source of the information, rather than just the fake printed customer statements, thereby providing proof of the fraudulent activity.

The following RPG Example illustrates a very simple RPG source program. It is the way corporate programmers writing in the IBM RPG programming language instruct the computer such as the IBM AS/400 computer used by Bernie Madoff to perform a job, such as compute and print customer statements.

Typical RPG application source programs may have hundreds or thousands of RPG source statements, and may link to or call many other programs.

The Madoff SEC auditors would have had to review and hopefully understand this kind of Madoff RPG source programming, the Trustee forensic accounting investigators eventually did.

IBM RPG

From Wikipedia, the free encyclopedia

RPG is a high-level programming language (HLL) for business applications. RPG is an IBM proprietary language and its later versions are only available on IBM i or OS/400 based systems.[1]

It has a long history, having been developed by IBM in 1959 as the **Report Program Generator** - a tool to replicate punched card processing on the IBM 1401[2] then updated to RPG II for the IBM System/3 in the late 1960s, and since evolved into an HLL equivalent to COBOL and PL/I.

It remains a popular programming language on the IBM i operating system, which runs on IBM Power i platform hardware. The current version, **RPG IV** (a.k.a. ILE RPG), provides a modern programming environment.

Example code [edit]

The following program receives a customer number as an input parameter and returns the name and address as output parameters.

```
      * Historically RPG is columnar in nature, though free-formatting
      * is allowed under particular circumstances.
      * The purpose of various lines code are determined by a
      * letter code in column 6.
      * An asterisk (*) in column 7 denotes a comment line

      * "F" (file) specs define files and other i/o devices
     F ARMstF1   IF   E       K    Disk    Rename(ARMST:RARMST)

      * "D" specs are used to define variables
     D pCusNo        S             6p
     D pName         S            30a
     D pAddr1        S            30a
     D pAddr2        S            30a
     D pCity         S            25a
     D pState        S             2a
     D pZip          S            10a
     * "C" (calculation) specs are used for executable statements
     * Parameters are defined using plist and parm opcodes
     C     *entry       plist
     C                  parm                    pCusNo
     C                  parm                    pName
     C                  parm                    pAddr1
     C                  parm                    pAddr2
     C                  parm                    pCity
     C                  parm                    pState
     C                  parm                    pZip

      * The "chain" command is used for random access of a keyed file
     C     pCusNo       chain     ARMstF1

      * If a record is found, move fields from the file into parameters
     C                  if        %found
     C                  eval      pName  = ARNm01
     C                  eval      pAddr1 = ARAd01
     C                  eval      pAddr2 = ARAd02
     C                  eval      pCity  = ARCy01
     C                  eval      pState = ARSt01
     C                  eval      pZip   = ARZp15
     C                  endif

      * RPG makes use of switches.  One switch "LR" Originally stood for "last record"
      * LR flags the program and its dataspace as removable from memory

     C                  eval      *InLR = *On
```

http://en.wikipedia.org/wiki/IBM_RPG

Thus the Madoff programmers could write programs using the arcane RPG programming language, while the SEC auditors and other non-programmer auditors, including lawyers and accountants, could not understand what was actually being performed—they could not follow the audit trail that electronic real-time program auditing would have provided, nor could they see, had they tried, exactly how the fraudulent data had been computed.

Thus the Madoff programmers and staff could create fake documents, as in pages 61 and 62 of **Bruce Dubinsky's testimony at trial in the above documents,** by essentially just entering (keying) whatever information was desired and printing it.

I believe that financial statements and documents are still produced by this virtually unaudited—and certainly not real-time—method today some 25 years after being implemented on the Madoff computer. And the inability to real-time audit and record critical financial information to prevent fraud still exists on virtually every computer system in corporate use and in personal use today.

In 2013 I sent the letter below to the Chairman of the Securities and Exchange Commission. detailing how the SEC could quickly, effectively, and economically stop the type of Madoff fraud and the anguish it caused to so many people. My specific and detailed recommendation to the Securities and Exchange Commission for implementation in months, not years, is detailed in Appendix C On-Demand Forensic Accounting and Analytics

There has been no acknowledgement of the letter or response from the Commission.

July 26, 2013

Paul H. Harkins
Founder and CTO
Harkins & Associates, Inc.
816 Daisy Lane
West Chester, PA 19382

Securities and Exchange Commission Chairman
SEC Headquarters
100 F Street, NE
Washington, DC 20549

(Duplicate to)
Securities Investor Protection Corporation Chairman
805 Fifteenth Street, N.W
Suite 800
Washington, D.C. 20005-2215

Subject: **A critically needed Transformational Opportunity and Requirement for the SEC**

Dear SEC Chairman:

I am writing this letter directly to you, the chairman of the SEC, to inform you that the SEC can and should immediately and economically develop and implement real-time forensic accounting auditing to prevent, detect, investigate and prosecute criminal securities costly fraud cases such as the Bernard L. Madoff case, the Allen Stanford case and many other recent major securities and financial fraud cases. This SEC real-time forensic accounting auditing system provides a security camera like recording of all financial reporting as it is created and an instantaneous forensic accounting analytics of fraud directly to SEC management.

The Bernard L Madoff criminal securities case has cost the SEC dearly in of its reputation, cost the government and SIPC huge costs, now over $700 million dollars for SIPC alone, and enforcement costs, disgusted and infuriated the investing public and identified that the auditing model of the SEC, which is basically just belatedly respond to investor complaints, was ineffective and obsolete for decades and is broken today.

The following are just a few of the many published articles and books relating to the Bernard L. Madoff Ponzi scheme case available on the public record:

Madoff lawyers collect $700 million in fees - May. 6, 2013

money.cnn.com/2013/05/06/news/companies/madoff.../index.html

May 6, 2013 - **lawyers** and other consultants have racked up $701 **million** in fees as they work to recover the $17.5 billion lost to Bernard **Madoff's** Ponzi ...

5.44 billion now distributed to madoff victims - SIPC

www.sipc.org/Media/NewsReleases/Release20130401.aspx

Apr 1, 2013 - **Madoff Trustee's** Third Distribution Sends Approximately $506.2 Million to ... To date, **SIPC** has committed approximately $807 million to **pay** ...

1. **Amazon.com: The Club No One Wanted To Join-Madoff Victims In ...**

   www.amazon.com › ... › True Accounts › True Crime

   The Club **No One Wanted** To Join-**Madoff** Victims In Their Own Words ... of its kind about the **Madoff** Ponzi scheme, in which twenty nine **Madoff** investors **band ...**

1. **An AS/400 was critical to Madoff's Ponzi scheme- The Inquirer**

   www.theinquirer.net/inquirer/.../an-as-400-critical-madoff-ponzi-scheme

   Aug 14, 2009 - The IBM **AS/400** was **used** by him and select other employees to ... Central to the scam was that "no one touched" the computer but **Madoff.**

   AN INTERVIEW WITH IRVING H. PICARD, MADOFF TRUSTEE

   http://www.bakerlaw.com/files/Uploads/Documents/News/Articles/BUSINESS/Picard-FRAUD_7-1-2010.pdf

   2012 Annual Report - SIPC

   www.sipc.org/Portals/0/PDF/2012AnnualReport.pdf

   Apr 30, 2013 - **2012 ANNUAL REPORT.** 3. MESSAGE FROM THE ACTING CHAIR. In **2012, SIPC** continued to make meaningful progress on a number of ...

   The SIPC 2012 Annual report Chairman's letter discusses major fraud cases including: Lehman Brothers Inc., Bernard L. Madoff Investment Securities LLC, MF Global Inc., and the Stanford Group Company, apparently none of which were timely and effectively audited by the SEC before huge investor losses, and huge investigation costs.
   The SIPC 2012 Annual report also illustrates huge spikes in SIPC revenue and expenses in 2007, which are reflected in large costs to the SIPC members for SIPC investor protection. Those costs are ultimately born by the investing public, until the costs of this SIPC insurance and investigation and claims become too great, or until the investing public stops investing.

   The increasing use of computers in securities fraud, together with the demonstrated inability of the SEC to effectively and timely audit the multitude of proprietary and uniquely developed computer systems, as in the Madoff IBM AS/400 system, **require the SEC to develop and implement a sophisticated yet simple and effective securities auditing system to automatically audit and analyze all financial reporting.**

1. **Press Release: SEC Solicits Software Industry's Input for Helping ...**

   www.sec.gov/news/press/2005-141.htm

   Oct 4, 2005 - **SEC Solicits Software Industry's Input** for Helping Manage Interactive Financial Data. FOR IMMEDIATE RELEASE 2005-141. Washington, D.C. ...

   The SEC real-time forensic accounting system would be in a single language (English) and in format and presentation immediately known by a qualified accountant such as a CPA, and easily learned by SEC examiners and authorized government regulators.

   This SEC real-time financial reporting auditing is at the time of and part of the creation of the financial documents and reporting by all publicly traded companies and major private companies, and is

(end **of**

automatically and dynamically analyzed with analytics developed by the SEC and is instantaneously available remotely to authorized government regulators.

My registered U.S. copyrighted paper <u>"On-Demand Forensic Accounting and Analytics"</u> (attached) illustrates exactly **how the SEC could quickly and easily develop and implement Real-Time Forensic Accounting auditing capability in less than one year, and at a cost of less than seven million dollars, which is of less than one percent of the Madoff investigation costs to SIPC of over 700 million dollars and counting.**

This SEC real-time Forensic Accounting auditing capability would automatically and instantaneously and dynamically audit every publicly traded company's financial statements the instant they were produced, without human intervention, and apply the most effective SEC analytical tests for fraud, and instantly alert SEC management of securities fraud.

I propose that the SEC, together with SIPC (which is bearing huge costs), and other government agencies such as the FBI, immediately develop and implement the best real-time forensic accounting analytics, utilizing the federally funded Software Engineering Institute (SEI) at Carnegie Mellon and the Association of Certified Fraud Examiners, using my U.S. patented computer software as illustrated in <u>"On-Demand Forensic Accounting and Analytics"</u>.

<u>**Association of Certified Fraud Examiners - Fraud Training Education ...**</u>

www.acfe.com/

The ACFE is the world's largest anti-**fraud** organization and premier provider of anti-**fraud** training education and certification. ... 5 Introduction to Digital **Forensics** Boston, MA; AUG ... Nominations Now Open For 2014-2015 **Board of Regents ...**

The SEC can and should overpower the fraudsters and enable itself and protect the investing public, before the frauds are even executed and pervasive, and I am most happy to help empower the SEC do so.

Best Regards,

Paul H. Harkins
Founder and CTO
Harkins & Associates, Inc.
816 Daisy Lane
West Chester, PA, 19382
www.harkinsaudit.com
610-431-1755
paulhark@aol.com

Copy – Selected members of the U.S. Senate and the U.S. House of Representatives

Attachment - <u>"On-Demand Forensic Accounting and Analytics"</u>

(End of letter)

<u>Appendix C On-Demand Forensic Accounting and Analytics</u> provides for continuous, real-time, remote and unattended computer auditing, recording and analysis of all financial reporting now subject to SEC auditing.

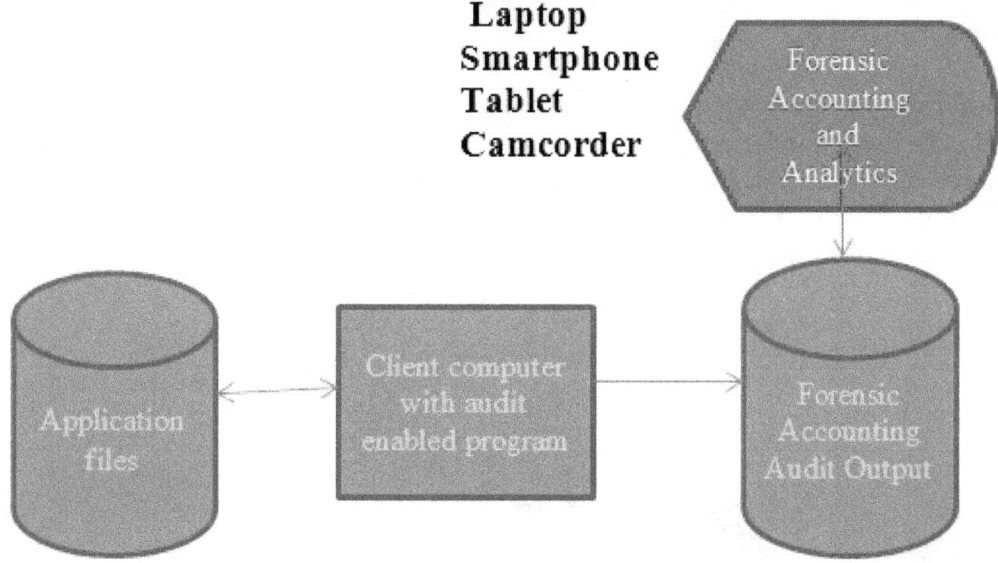

Figure 6: Forensic Accounting and Analytics (can be remote and mobile and real-time).

```
302       torder = 1500;
            1500
303        iorder = 78.543;
            78.543
304    // value of iorder has now been computed
305        xorder = torder + 13.45  +
            1618.19       1500
306    // this is a continuation free form statement preceded with +
307                26.2 + iorder;
                         78.543
308      sorder = torder +  xorder +  iorder + rorder + morder + norder;
      93330.496      1500
                          1618.19      78.543
                                       32109.876
                                            34567.098
                                                 23456.789


(partial Client Stock Account Summary forensic accounting audit output)
```

Figure 4: Client Stock Account Summary forensic accounting audit output.

This continuous, real-time, remote and unattended computer auditing, recording and analysis of all financial reporting audits the actual financial data (numbers) in real-time as they are being computed, analyzes the data and automatically reports possible fradulent computations and processes to SEC headquarters, *without any SEC human auditor activitity.*

Instead of arcane computer language source statements, an SEC auditor, lawyer or accountant can review and focus on the actual financial information (numbers) being created in the financial statements as they are being prepared and before they are distributed to investors, together with auditing analytics messages and information automatically created from the data as it is created.

Why would the SEC not want to implement that real-time, unattended and remote auditing analytical activity and information at the moment the information is created from every company creating financial statements and documents?

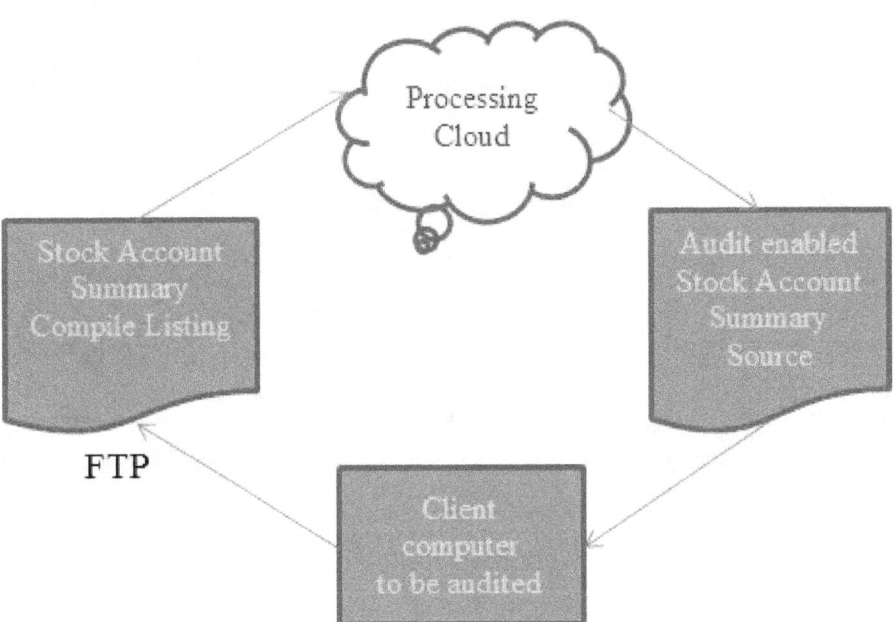

Figure 1: Stock Account Summary program compile listing for forensic accounting.

Perhaps shockingly, I ask the question: How cannot the government uncover the largest fraud in US history, spend six years and probably over one billion dollars in investigating the Madoff Ponzi scheme, spend additional unknown amounts of money and resources on the criminal prosecution of Madoff personnel, hire hundreds of more auditors, and still not make needed and available changes to government auditing?

Also perhaps shockingly, I believe the decades long success of the Madoff Ponzi scheme without ever being discovered by government auditors and the relatively mild punishment of Madoff employees, provide a potentially very attractive low deferred risk and an immediate huge reward and gratification opportunity today for many similar fraudulent schemes.

In my opinion, successful, long undiscovered financial fraud as in the Madoff case and profiled in the TV show American Greed is an available and potentially all too attractive option for a great many like the Madoff employees. They had incredible temptation for decades, and little thought of distant possible consequences. People who think that they would never steal are advised to read The Good Earth by Pearl S. Buck.

A Ponzi Pandemic: 500+ Ponzi Schemes Totaling $50+ Billion in 'Madoff Era'

http://www.forbes.com/sites/jordanmaglich/2014/02/12/a-ponzi-pandemic-500-ponzi-schemes-totaling-50-billion-in-madoff-era/

Today the annual budget of the Securities and Exchange Commission is over one billion dollars, with staff of about four thousand employees, and there are apparently hundreds of current Ponzi Schemes being uncovered and perhaps many, like Madoff, not being uncovered.

Today the Big Four audit firms' annual revenues are well over one hundred billion dollars annually, with staff of over 750,000 employees.

Big Four (audit firms)

From Wikipedia, the free encyclopedia

The **Big Four** are the four largest international professional services networks, offering audit, assurance, tax, consu finance, and legal services. They handle the vast majority of audits for publicly traded companies as well as many p auditing large companies. It is reported that the Big Four audit 99% of the companies in the FTSE 100, and 96% of index of the leading mid-cap listing companies.[1] The Big Four firms are shown below, with their latest publicly avai

Firm ⬦	Revenues ⬦	Employees ⬦	Revenue per employee ⬦	Fiscal year ⬦	Headquarters ⬦	Source ⬦
Deloitte	$34.2 billion	210,000	$162,857	2014	United States	[2]
PwC	$34.0 billion	195,000	$174,359	2014	United Kingdom	[3]
EY	$27.4 billion	190,000	$144,211	2014	United Kingdom	[4]
KPMG	$24.8 billion	162,000	$153,209	2014	Netherlands	[6]

http://en.wikipedia.org/wiki/Big_Four_(audit_firms)

Are the Big Four audit firms using the same or similar methods as is the Securities and Exchange Commission to attempt to detect financial fraud, for the same reasons, and with similar results?

The Big Four audit firms are billing over one-hundred dollars annually to their clients, and there are thousands of smaller auditing firms also.

I believe that all of these auditing firms would catch more frauds and much faster using On-Demand Forensic Accounting and Analytics, and that their clients would be spared huge current losses.

Why, and are the Big Four audit firms' results at uncovering financial fraud any better than the results obtained by the Securities and Exchange Commission?

The Securities and Exchange Commission could today not only catch the Bernard L. Madoff Ponzi scheme immediately, or almost immediately, but also prevent other Ponzi schemes from being attempted and investors from being severely harmed, by implementing the Real-Time Forensic Accounting and Analytics software illustrated in Appendix C.

The Bernard L. Madoff Ponzi scheme investigation and prosecution, which took six years and cost over one billion dollars and involved hundreds of talented and expensive investigators whose services accounted for most of the one billion plus dollars of cost, did not and could not return all of the many billions of dollars to the defrauded investors.

While the investigators were talented, educated, diligent, experienced and experts in their own areas, they were not properly equipped to promptly uncover and prosecute this type of modern electronic computer fraud. They still are not properly equipped today.

This area of real-time forensic accounting and analytics is yet another incredibly huge opportunity for IBM, SAP, or for someone else.

If this chapter's detail of forensic accounting investigation seems difficult to understand, it is described to illustrate to show you how forensic accounting investigation actually works, and just how easy and powerful the real-time results of forensic accounting can be, now:

1. The SEC would be able, easily, to immediately and automatically--- and remotely--- monitor and detect potential fraud and analytics as in the Bernard L. Madoff case Ponzi scheme in real-time as the fraudulent information was being computed.
2. The Big Four audit firms could have the same instantaneous remote fraud detection alert and analytics, with proper authorization
3. Ultimately, the investor could have the same remote monitoring and detection alerts, with proper authorization, as the fraudulent information was being computed.

7 How IBM and SAP Can Succeed and Grow: A Revolutionary Strategy

Today IBM is a diminishing shell of what it was during my twenty-one-plus years at IBM. IBM is relying, with significantly diminishing revenue, on its vast but shrinking store of hundreds of thousands of installed customers with significantly diminishing revenue, while floundering against growing competition. SAP is succeeding and growing and is poised, I believe, to overtake IBM. This revolutionary strategy is crucial to the future success and significant growth of both IBM and to SAP.

I have been directly but fruitlessly communicating to IBM executive management a strategy for succeeding and growing, a strategy I illustrate in this chapter.

In my opinion, which is buttressed by financial performance metrics, IBM has been in relative decline compared with its competitors—and sometimes in actual decline—for the more than three decades since I left IBM in 1984. And, the key reasons for IBM's decline today are essentially a continuation of the reasons why I left IBM in 1984, which I outline in this chapter.

The overarching reason for the decline of IBM since the glory days in the 1960s and 1970s is that since the retirement of CEO Thomas J. Watson in 1971, IBM's IBM executive management and the IBM Board of Directors have been hopelessly out-of-touch with the reality of the changing customer environment and the immense new opportunities for IBM growth and success.

It does not take a genius to comprehend that IBM historically made its revenue and its profits on **renting** its products. An example: the $2,500 a month rent for the IBM 1401 computer in 1961, when IBM System Engineers' monthly pay was perhaps $600 per month. This IBM rental income, or licensing revenue, from its customers not only provided a huge continuing stream of revenue and profits from IBM customers, but it also provided IBM with an incentive to keep the customer happy and productive and growing, and on rent.

The wildly successful IBM Installed User Program (IUP) of the early 1970s, illustrated later in this chapter, provided IBM with the opportunity to strengthen the customer relationship and success by providing sophisticated industry applications already running at key customers' locations to the entire IBM customer base worldwide. The highly profitable customer IUPs generated significant license (rental) revenue for IBM at low cost and generated many new IBM customers worldwide.

However, IBM tossed away the IBM IUP program and the concept of developing and licensing customer end user applications solutions in the 1982 "low-cost producer" initiative, and today has, to my knowledge, virtually no corporate end-user applications licensed products to offer IBM customers or IBM prospects. IBM's successful competitors such as Microsoft, with the Dynamics applications suite, SAP SE, with many customer industry applications suites, and Oracle, with Oracle applications, do now offer comprehensive and powerful licensed applications software that are very widely used and produce significant revenue and new customers.

IBM can yet again succeed now by taking bold and revolutionary action to leapfrog its competition, as it did so dramatically in the 1960s with the development and implementation of the IBM System/360 computer and customers.

In this chapter, I document and illustrate several of what I consider to be some of the most significant achievements that propelled IBM to spectacular success and growth, starting from the time of my full-time employment at IBM in 1962 until today. I also document and illustrate some of what I consider to be the most significant and spectacular failures the have diminished and crippled IBM starting with the time of my full-time employment at IBM in 1962.

I also document how five ex-IBM engineers formed SAP in 1972 to focus on applications software when IBM did not, and how today I believe that SAP is poised to overtake IBM because of that focus on applications software and on constant leading-edge development of improvements, and in developing an application software licensing model.

See **S4/HANA: What does SAP's next generation ERP mean for customers?**

http://www.computerworlduk.com/in-depth/it-business/3596790/s4-hana-what-does-saps-next-generation-erp-mean-for-customers/

Yet, neither IBM nor SAP has recognized or implemented my revolutionary strategy, which would lead to a quantum jump in corporate computing capability, as is illustrated in this book.

These spectacular IBM successes and failures have much less to do with technology, such as the visual display, the PC, the Internet, and Watson, as they do with the decisions of IBM executive management over the last five decades. The profound actual effects of these fundamental, industry-changing executive decisions have been largely shielded from the view of those outside of IBM, but are well known to those inside IBM, to those who have left IBM and continued to work in the computing industry, and to long retired IBMers still enjoying the fruits of their time and efforts while at IBM during its glory days.

These same IBM successes and failures are the direct result of actions taken or not taken by IBM executive management and the IBM Board of Directors over the last five decades, and often illustrate the immense and lasting unintended consequences of these actions. My revolutionary strategy for IBM's success and growth in both the short term and long term is largely based on learning from and building on the remarkable innovations and successes while avoiding the dramatic failures of IBM.

It all seems so obvious and understandable now, but it was apparently not obvious to IBM executive management then, at enormous cost, and apparently is not obvious and understandable to IBM now, at enormous continuing cost.

I offer my perspective as a branch-office ground-level or field IBM employee who spent virtually all of my working hours directly working with and at IBM corporate computing customer locations. I, along with thousands of other field level IBM Systems Engineers (SEs) and marketing representatives (salespeople) were focused on actually implementing the IBM computer hardware and IBM software products sold to the customer.

We often did the actual programming and application development and teaching the customer while at the customer location, often for months, and sometimes years. We were always under some pressure to sell and install more IBM products while at the customer, but we were always most focused on getting the customer to develop and implement additional innovative function to drive the customer business. I personally worked with many customer executives towards success.

Whatever was then and is now the perspective of IBM executive management is still a puzzle to me and to some other retired IBMers and customers in my circle of associates. Whatever is that IBM executive management perspective and vision now, it does not seem to be customer focused and customer centric, perhaps because there is virtually little or no IBM branch office systems engineering and marketing representative customer field force as that was eliminated in 1993 with some 60,000 layoffs.

As always, these opinions and statements are my honest opinions and observations and are mine alone, but I believe are buttressed by historical events now visible to all who look for them and at them.

Perhaps the long decline of IBM and the spectacular creation and successes of at least four upstart technology corporations since the early 1970s in what could have been, and probably should have been IBM successes is really as simple at looking at and analyzing the performance of five technology companies, IBM, Apple, Microsoft, Google and SAP SE, then asking why, and then asking if failing performance can be and is being changed to winning performance.

IBM From Wikipedia, the free encyclopedia

Key people	Ginni Rometty (Chairman, President, and CEO)
Products	See IBM products
Revenue	▼ US$ 92.793 billion (2014)[1]
Operating income	▼ US$ 19.986 billion (2014)[1]
Net income	▼ US$ 12.023 billion (2014)[1]
Total assets	▼ US$ 117.53 billion (2014)[1]
Total equity	▼ US$ 11.868 billion (2014)[1]
Number of employees	431,212 (2014)[2]

http://en.wikipedia.org/wiki/IBM

IBM financial performance trends – all down (red)

Apple Inc. From Wikipedia, the free encyclopedia

Products	Mac · iPod · iPhone · iPad · iPad Mini · Apple TV · OS X · iLife · iWork · iOS · And soon, Apple Watch
Services	Apple Store · Apple Store online · Mac App Store · iOS App Store · iTunes Store · iBooks · iCloud
Revenue	▲ US$ 182.795 billion (2014)[2]
Operating income	▲ US$ 52.503 billion (2014)[2]
Net income	▲ US$ 39.510 billion (2014)[2]
Total assets	▲ US$ 231.839 billion (2014)[2]
Total equity	▼ US$ 111.547 billion (2014)[2]
Number of employees	98,000 (2014)[3]

http://en.wikipedia.org/wiki/Apple_Inc.

Apple financial performance trends – all up (green) except total equity, which is ten times that of IBM

Microsoft From Wikipedia, the free encyclopedia

Products	Windows · Office · Servers · Skype · Visual Studio · Dynamics · Azure · Xbox · Surface · Mobile · more...
Services	MSN · Bing · OneDrive · MSDN · Outlook.com · TechNet
Revenue	▲ US$ 86.83 billion (2014)[1]
Operating income	▲ US$ 27.76 billion (2014)[1]
Net income	▲ US$ 22.07 billion (2014)[1]
Total assets	▲ US$ 172.38 billion (2014)[1]
Total equity	▲ US$ 89.78 billion (2014)[1]
Number of employees	128,076 (June 2014)[2]

http://en.wikipedia.org/wiki/Microsoft

Microsoft financial performance trends – all up (green)

Google From Wikipedia, the free encyclopedia

Products	*See* list of Google products
Revenue	▲ US$ 66 billion (2014)[5]
Operating income	▲ US$ 13.966 billion (2013)[5]
Net income	▲ US$ 16.5 billion (2014)[5]
Total assets	▲ US$ 110.92 billion (2013)[5]
Total equity	▲ US$ 87.309 billion (2013)[5]
Number of employees	53,600 (Q4 2014)[5]

http://en.wikipedia.org/wiki/Google

Google financial performance trends – all up (green)

SAP SE From Wikipedia, the free encyclopedia

Products	See list of SAP products
Revenue	▲ €16.81 billion (2013)[1]
Operating income	▲ €4.46 billion (2013)[1]
Profit	▲ €3.32 billion (2013)[1]
Total assets	▲ €27.09 billion (2013)[1]
Total equity	▲ €16.04 billion (2013)[1]
Number of employees	74,400 (2014)[2]

http://en.wikipedia.org/wiki/SAP_SE

SAP SE financial performance trends in euros – all up (green)

SAP Business Suite S/4 SAP HANA Launch Event

http://events.sap.com/s4hana/en/session/14013

Oracle Corporation From Wikipedia, the free encyclopedia

Products	Oracle Applications, Oracle Database, Oracle Enterprise Manager, Oracle Fusion Middleware, servers, workstations, storage (See Oracle products)
Revue	▲ US$ 38.27 billion (2014)[2]
Operating income	▲ US$ 14.75 billion (2014)[2]
Net income	▲ US$ 10.95 billion (2014)[2]
Total assets	▲ US$ 90.34 billion (2014)[2]
Total equity	▲ US$ 46.87 billion (2014)[2]
Number of	122,458 (2014)[3]

http://en.wikipedia.org/wiki/Oracle_Corporation

Oracle financial performance trends – all up (green)

IBM had almost as many employees (431,000) in 2014 than all of the other five successful technology corporations above combined (476,000 employees), yet IBM's 2014 revenue of about 93 billion dollars was less than one quarter of the revenue (392 billion dollars) of the other five successfully growing technology companies combined.

IBM's other key financial performance metrics of Operating income; Profit, Total assets, and Total equity were all falling. Even Apple's single falling financial metric, total equity of about 110 billion dollars is almost ten times the IBM total equity of almost 12 billion dollars.

Yet, these five very successful technology corporations were founded after I started to work at IBM in 1962, each by just several people with very limited funds, when IBM was the largest and most successful technology corporation in the world with hundreds of thousands of employees and billions of dollars in assets.

Microsoft was founded in 1975 by Bill Gates and Paul Allen, SAP SE was founded in 1972 by five IBM engineers in Germany, Google was founded in 1998 by Larry Page and Sergey Brin, Apple was founded in 1976 by Steve Jobs, Steve Wozniak and Ronald Wayne, and Oracle was founded in 1977 by Larry Ellison, Bob Miner, and Ed Oatesy.

Why is IBM failing in financial performance and not growing when all of the five other technology corporations--- Apple, Microsoft, Google, SAP SE, and Oracle--- are succeeding?

Why does IBM have, by far, the smallest total equity of these technology corporations, when IBM had such a huge start and advantage?

The answer, again in my opinion, is that ***IBM has a failing business model*** which is not focused on the ultimate consumer, or company actual use of corporate computing, and is offering largely antiquated, ancient, and costly products focused on a vast and unproductive programming development and support environment of IBMs own making.

None of the five young upstart and successful technology corporations illustrated above, took IBM's failing path of turning away from the ultimate consumer, and instead focused directly on the ultimate customer, either through hardware, as in the iPhone, or application software for the ultimate end user consumer, or through corporate application software as in SAP SE.

You want proof beyond the stunning financial performance metrics above?

Proof of the major reasons for success of the five successful technology corporations above and the reasons for the failure of IBM above are detailed in what the corporations actually make and sell to customers to produce the revenue and incur costs, and in how they accomplish it.

The **Products** link for each of the six technology corporations illustrated above lists the products these corporations sell to create revenue and make which creates costs.

A detailed review of the Products these corporations sell essentially tells the whole story of success and failure.

Only IBM primarily makes and sells so much middleware and programming development-focused software, as opposed to direct end user applications software. This is somewhat understandable, as the IBM customer base was largely installed decades ago.

Also, IBM purposely got out of the application software business in the early 1980s, as is illustrated below, to become the "Low-cost hardware producer", leaving IBM with little or no applications software to sell to its customers.

All of the other five younger technology companies, the first of which started in 1972, purposely bypassed the programmer development and support market, which may have had one million total largely programming related technical customers (BLS statistics in Chapter 1), an instead focused on providing largely sophisticated applications software directly to the many millions of customer end users, thus bypassing the huge and costly programmer development and support environment supported by IBM.

All of these tiny upstart technology companies: Microsoft, SAP SE, Oracle, Apple and Google, apparently immediately realized what IBM still today apparently does not realize, and that is that the huge and costly, and I believe grossly unproductive corporate programmer development and support environment was and is actually a huge 100 billion dollar annual personnel payroll burden and cost for corporations.

The tiny upstart technology companies simply developed end user application solutions that they could offer and license directly to corporate users and bypass the entire burden of the in-house programmer development and support environment.

The huge annual 100 billion dollar (one million programmer/developer/support/manager personnel times' one hundred thousand dollars payroll and overhead costs) annual cost is a payroll cost that does not go to IBM revenue and is lost to IBM and is lost to the end user corporations, every year.

NOTE – IBM is also losing at least other 100 billion dollar annual revenue business opportunities, as is illustrated later in this chapter.

So, the tiny upstart technology companies focused on developing sophisticated end user software application and end-user products, like the iPhone, that made the corporate end user much more productive, without requiring large and expensive in-house corporate development and support environments.

Along the way, Microsoft, SAP SE, Oracle, and other startup companies including CISCO, looked around for useful ideas and implementations being neglected or discarded by larger companies and universities, like IBM and utilized them to great effect.

And, it turns out that corporate end users and even individual end users were and are willing and even eager to pay significant monthly and annual license fees to enjoy needed and useful and so-phisticated technology end user and corporate user applications.

Illustrations of sophisticated applications software offered include:

Oracle

Products	Oracle Applications, Oracle Database, Oracle Enterprise Manager, Oracle Fusion

Microsoft

Products	Windows · Office · Servers · Skype · Visual Studio · Dynamics · Azure · Xbox · Surface · Mobile · more...
Services	MSN · Bing · OneDrive · MSDN · Outlook.com · TechNet

SAP SE

List of SAP products

From Wikipedia, the free encyclopedia

This presents a partial list of products of the enterprise software company SAP AG

- SAP
    - Customer Relationship Management (CRM)
    - Enterprise Resource Planning (ERP)
    - Product Lifecycle Management (PLM)
    - Supply Chain Management (SCM)
    - Supplier Relationship Management (SRM)

Business Solutions [edit]

- SAP Advanced Planner and Optimizer (APO)
- SAP Analytics
- SAP ABAP
- SAP Apparel and Footwear Solution (AFS)
- SAP Business Information Warehouse (BW)
- SAP Business Intelligence (BI)
- SAP Catalog Content Management ()
- SAP Convergent Charging (CC)
- SAP Enterprise Buyer Professional (EBP)
- SAP Enterprise Learning
- SAP Portal (EP)
- SAP Exchange Infrastructure (XI) (From release 7.0 onwards, SAP XI has
- SAP Extended Warehouse Management (EWM)
- Governance, Risk and Compliance (GRC)
- Enterprise Central Component (ECC)
- SAP HANA (High-performance Analytics Appliance)
- SAP Human Resource Management Systems (HRMS)
- SAP Internet Transaction Server (ITS)
- SAP Incentive and Commission Management (ICM)
- SAP Knowledge Warehouse (KW)
- SAP Manufacturing
- SAP Master Data Management (MDM)
- SAP Rapid Deployment Solutions (RDS)
- SAP Service and Asset Management
- SAP Solutions for mobile business

Of particular interest might be:

SAP Apparel and Footwear Solution (AFS)

Industry Solutions [edit]

- SAP for Retail (ISR)
- SAP for Utilities (ISU)
- SAP for Public Sector (IS PSCD)
- SAP for Oil & Gas (IS Oil & Gas)
- SAP for Telecommunications (IST)
- SAP for Healthcare (ISH)
- SAP for Banking (SAP for banking)
- SAP for Insurance (SAP for Insurance)
- SAP Financial Services Network (FSN)
- SAP Shipping Services Network (SSN)
- Engineering Construction & Operations (EC&O)

IBM

Middleware and applications [edit]

IBM distributes its diverse collection of software products over several brands; mainly:

1. Lotus: collaboration and communication;
2. Rational: software development and maintenance;
3. Tivoli: management, operations, and Cloud;
   Main article: Tivoli Software

4. WebSphere: Internet.
   Main article: IBM WebSphere

- 9PAC Report generator for the IBM 7090 (709 PACkage)
- IBM Administrative Terminal System (ATS) Online Text Entry, Editing, Processing, Storage and Retrieval
- IBM Assistant Series (Filing Assistant, Reporting Assistant, Graphing Assistant, Writing Assistant and Planning Assistant)
- IBM Audio Distribution System
- IBM BS12 (IBM Business System 12)
- IBM CICS (Customer Information Control System)
- CICS Transaction Gateway
- CICS Web interpreter, IBM OD390
- IBM Cloudscape Pure Java Database Server. Now open source Apache Derby
- IBM Cognos 8 Business Intelligence Business Intelligence Suite
- IBM Concurrent Copy, backup software
- IBM DB2 Relational DBMS (DataBase 2)
- IBM DB2 Content Manager
- IBM DB2 Document Manager
- IBM DB2 Records Manager
- IBM Deep Computing Visualization for Linux V1.2
- IBM DISOSS Distributed Office Support System
- IBM Document Composition Facility (DCF), previously known as SCRIPT
- IBM Document Library Facility (DLF)
- IBM FileNet products, P8 Business Process Management and Enterprise Content Management(FileNet bought by IBM)
- IBM Graphical Data Display Manager (GDDM).
- IBM Websphere Host On-Demand (HOD) Host On-Demand Web-based TN3270, TN5250 and VT440 Terminal Emulation.
- IBM HTTP Server

A large percentage of the revenue for Microsoft, SAP SE, and Oracle (direct competitors of IBM) is generated from end user or consumer application licensed software, while IBM has virtually no revenue generated from end user application software licensing. For instance, Microsoft commercial licensing is 47 % of Microsoft revenue and consumer licensing is 23 % of Microsoft revenue. The largest revenue producer for Microsoft is the Office suite of applications.

<u>Microsoft's global revenue in the fiscal years from 2002 to 2014 (in billion U.S. dollars)</u>

http://www.statista.com/statistics/267805/microsofts-global-revenue-since-2002/

Apple, Google, Microsoft: Where does the money come from?

http://www.●●com/article/apple-google-microsoft-where-does-the-money-come-from/

While many additional useful charts and graphs are available on the Internet, many cannot be illustrated here due to licensing requirements. However the reader may easily find this information using Google with searches such as: "Where does Microsoft's revenue come from" and "IBM's global revenue from 2010 to 2014, by business segment".

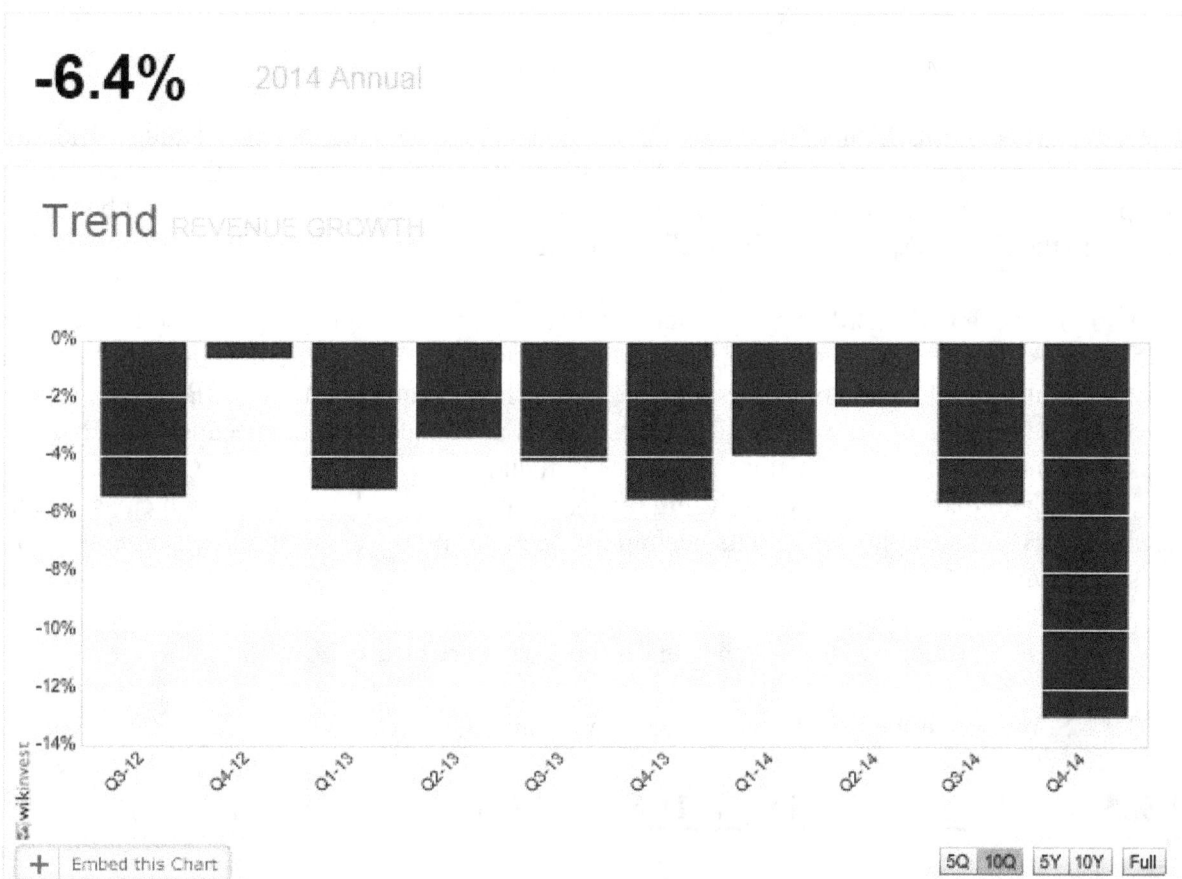

http://www.wikinvest.com/stock/International_Business_Machines_(IBM)/Data/Revenue_Growth

So, it is clear that IBM's financial metrics are falling while its technology competitor's financial metrics are rising, and it is clear, at least to me, that IBM alone does not offer the end user or consumer comprehensive direct user licensed application software and services. Yet, IBM once did offer the end user consumer, including corporations, comprehensive and very profitable application software and support including licensing user application software, and that the IBM business was growing and thriving before these five other startup companies even existed.

What happened, and why, and can and will IBM possibly recover, grow and succeed now?

How and why did IBM get into the failing position today of not having applications software to sell to end users, as do all of its major technology competitors? And is there a revolutionary strategy for short-term and long-term success?

How and why did IBM lose command and control of its destiny and virtually disappear from direct contact with its previously huge, successful, loyal customer base?

I provide what I believe are the detailed reasons and detailed answers, perhaps way too detailed answers for what I believe is the continuing decline of IBM starting in 1982.

There are literally dozens of similar relevant and important questions that could and should be asked and answered. Many books about IBM have been written addressing some of these issues and providing some perspective on the how and why of IBM's decline, and more will be surely written in the future, especially if the decline accelerates.

My two plus decades at IBM as a very successful IBM Systems Engineer (SE), and then my three plus decades after IBM as a corporate computing consultant at IBM customers around the world must be totally foreign and not understandable to the IBM executives running IBM from IBM headquarters in Armonk New York. I say foreign and not understandable because the IBM executives were making strategic decisions totally foreign and not understandable to what made obvious sense to me and many other IBMers during the last five decades, all too often with catastrophic results for IBM, its employees, and its customers. Many of those catastrophic strategic decisions are still playing out today.

My opinions just reflect what I saw then and I see ever more clearly now.

NOTE – Some of these key IBM events are also listed in Chapter 8 My Conclusions.

__IBM Key Events starting in 1961__ (my co-op employment at IBM)

IBM System/360 Computer - 1964 – A revolutionary computing system

In 1961, when I started working at IBM as a Drexel cooperative student on my dream six month cooperative work assignment, Thomas J. Watson Jr, CEO of IBM, who was IBM CEO from 1956 to 1971, made a huge "bet the company" decision to develop the revolutionary IBM System/360 computer system. The wonderfully detailed and explicit 1961 IBM SPREAD project illustrates the real need for IBM back then to reinvent itself and details the powerful opposition of many of the

IBM executives to resist the development of the System/360 and instead attempt to enhance the existing flagging IBM offerings, and their jobs.

In 1961 Watson had the courage, vision, wisdom--- and luckily the power--- to overrule the many IBM executives resisting needed change, and invested 5 billion dollars, twice the IBM annual revenue of 2.5 billion dollars in 1962, for the three year development of the IBM/360 computer.

As a full-time IBM systems engineer employee in 1964 I attended the announcement of the IBM System/360 computer system on April 7, 1964 along with 65,000 other people worldwide. It was an absolute sensation and it was immediately clear that IBM, IBMers, and IBM customers would immensely benefit from this courageous decision to "bet the company".

And, we IBMers and IBM customers did immensely benefit for more than a decade beyond our wildest dreams, as IBM crushed its competitors and we developed important close customer working relationships and we had the opportunity to develop and support sophisticated customer industry applications worldwide.

In 1969 CEO Watson oversaw two other very significant and successful major changes to IBM that again greatly enhanced the company's success financially, enhanced the careers of many IBMers, and most importantly, greatly enhanced IBMs working relations and success with a great many more customers and new customers.

Those two new major changes to IBM were the decision to charge customers for the services of IBM systems engineers (which had be provided at no cost) and to create the General Systems Division, which brought in a huge wave of new customers.

IBM Systems Engineering Services (SES) - 1969 – Fee instead of free IBM Systems Engineers

On June, 23, 1969 IBM announced that IBM Systems Engineers, like me and thousands of other IBMers, would no longer work at no charge to the customer, as we has up until that moment. This announcement was the realization of the flip-flopping economics of inexpensive Systems Engineer (programmer/developer) labor cost and the incredibly high cost of the computer hardware cost.

For instance, in 1961 the *rent* of a tiny IBM 1401 computer was 2,500 dollars a month, while the salary of a typical young hot-shot IBM Systems Engineer was about 600 dollars a month. That meant that IBM could supply two IBM systems engineers FREE, at no charge, to work at the customer location for the IBM customer installing a new IBM computer to write their applications for them, and IBM could still make money.

I was personally a star at IBM Systems Engineering Services, a working and billing machine more than 40 hours a week, and this SES provided some systems engineers with an objective way to impress IBM management with our real value.

IBM Systems Engineering Services later became a preferred way for IBM to develop and document sophisticated customer industry applications in the wildly successful Installed User Program (IUP) program, which was probably implemented as a result of the 1972 Catamore lawsuit against IBM for non-performance in developing custom applications for specific customer.

I personally developed, programmed, documented, marketed and supported five IBM Apparel Business System (ABS) IUPs, starting in 1973 with the Apparel Business System System/3 model 6. These IUPs were licensed to hundreds of customers of IBM, and smoothed the installation of many new customer accounts worldwide for IBM.

IBM Systems Engineering Services (SES) was the predecessor of the current IBM Global Services, which is made up of Global Business Services (GBS) and Global Technology Services (GTS).

A key difference between the IBM Systems Engineering Services of my day, the 1970s, and the Global Services IBM offers today, aside from costs, is that IBM Systems Engineering Services were then performed locally by the possibly long-term resident IBM systems engineer probably familiar with the customer and the customer personnel and applications, while IBM Global Services appears to be mostly outsourced remotely provided services possibly using IBM contractors.

IBM General Systems Division (GSD) - 1969 – A huge wave of new IBM customers for computers

In 1969 IBM under CEO Thomas J. Watson Jr. also announced the creation of a major new division, the General Systems Division (GSD), headquartered not in White Plains New York, but far away in Atlanta Georgia. GSD would market to a whole new set of smaller potential customers, primarily new IBM customers, with different IBM products which were largely developed in Rochester Minnesota rather than in New York State, where the IBM mainframe computers were produced and largely supported.

GSD produced an entirely new and different line of IBM computers which were incredibly easy to program and use and were perfect for the forthcoming sophisticated customer developed Installed User programs.

The net result is that over the next few years GSD sold and installed perhaps twenty times as many new IBM customer accounts as did the older mainframe division, including the still most widely installed IBM corporate computing system today, the IBM AS/400 or IBM i computer.

I bring all this up because the GSD computers, starting with the System/3 and System/34 computers were so easy to program, develop and use that I also left the IBM mainframe division and transferred to the GSD. It was simply too hard to do things with the old mainframe technology, particularly the programming language technology (See my Master's Thesis), and so easy to do it in GSD.
See Fortress Rochester: The Inside Story of the IBM i Series by Dr. Frank G. Soltis.

The brilliant and fearless Dr. Frank G. Soltis and other GSD Rochester key personnel were crucial to the ongoing growth and success of IBM, in spite of significance resistance from IBMers elsewhere.

The Catamore Lawsuit - 1972

548 F. 2d 1065 - International Business Machines Corporation v. Catamore Enterprises Inc
http://openjurist.org/548/f2d/1065/international-business-machines-corporation-v-catamore-enterprises-inc

The Catamore lawsuit against IBM, originally filed in 1972, had a profound influence on IBM and, in my opinion, caused IBM to change the way it supported customers as is detailed in the lawsuit.

The positive key affect for IBM and its employees and customers is that this litigation caused IBM to take action to announce and actively support the wildly successful customer Installed User Program (IUP) initiative in 1973.

IBM Installed User Program (IUP) - 1973 - IBM developing, marketing, licensing and supporting proven successful Industry applications worldwide

The IUP concept was simple and powerful and wonderfully successful. It was to search for an already installed IBM customer with supplicated and comprehensive computer applications already implemented, and to verify, document, package and have IBM market and distribute the customer successful applications, and to have IBM do some support of the applications anywhere worldwide.

The concept was wonderfully simple and elegant. It was to completely bypass the time and effort and risk of developing industry applications for each and every customer, and to implement the most sophisticated and proven applications with virtually no effort for all but the customer sponsoring the IUP. The additional benefits of almost all profit, almost no cost, almost no individual account IBM effort, almost certain success, powerful marketing and customer reference opportunities seemed very attractive when compared to the Catamore Lawsuit.

The customer sponsoring the IUP would get a royalty from IBM each time IBM sold and installed and licensed the IUP, plus the fame and glory of showing off its system potentially worldwide. The IBM license was generally a monthly payment spread over two years, for what was really an essentially turnkey proven successful system, matched to the normally new computer system being installed by IBM.

What was really perhaps most important to the success of the IBM Installed User Program (IUP) was that the local IBM marketing representative (salesperson) who sold the IUP to a customer got a nice additional royalty or commission for selling the IUP, on top of the normal IBM compensation for selling the IBM computer.

Upon reflection, what was really perhaps most important to the success of the IBM Installed User Program (IUP) was getting the local IBM Systems Engineer who probably had actually written the sophisticated customer applications to agree to nominate the customer industry application for the IUP program. That meant that if the IUP nomination was accepted and the IUP was accepted that the SE had to document the IUP (User manuals), prepare the IUP distribution package for IBM distribution worldwide, prepare marketing brochures, host the verification process, present the IUP to prospects, and support the IUP worldwide, all in addition to the normal SE activities, typically doing normal SES billing for more than 40 hours a week.

Why did a very few ambitious IBM SEs bite for that immense additional effort to author and support IUPs? Well, IBM gave the IUP author SE royalty payments when the IUP was installed at IBM customers worldwide and it gave the lowly branch System Engineer a worldwide opportunity and perspective and experience never before possible to grow out of the SE technical job.

And, because there was literally no one else who knew the IUP details but the SE author, IBM encouraged the author SE to travel and demonstrate the IUP anywhere worldwide that an IBM branch or salesman requested. Thus, my multiple trips to Australia and my multiple trips to Europe, and my multiple trips all over the United States for the five IBM Apparel Business System IUPs that I authored, were as the visiting expert and simply wonderful.

Upon final reflection, what ultimately was the very most important to the success of the wildly successful IBM Installed User Program (IUP) was that the sponsoring IBM branch where the IBM SE worked got worldwide duplicate sales credit for sales of the IUP worldwide, if wisely negotiated by the branch and region managers. The message was simple and powerful: "If you want that IUP sale to the new account prospect in Sydney Australia, give our IBM branch and region full duplicate points (sales and sometime install credit), and pay all; expenses and then Paul Harkins will come".

Little did I really know how far the IUP duplicate credit really went until I checked the value of the homes of my managers of that time on Zillow.com, and remembered how many times our regional and branch management went to the IBM Golden Circle, and I many times I went to the IBM Systems Engineering Symposium for outstanding performance.

Our IBM branch and IBM region had both the IBM National Apparel Support Center and the IBM National Hotel and Casino support center, which supported the IUPs in those two industries worldwide. Great credit then and now goes to those outstanding IBM branch and regional managers who thought out of the IBM box and excelled.

Two of the IBM Apparel Business System Installed User Program (IUPS) that I authored are illustrated below, along with a sign from the IBM National Apparel Support Center which was headquartered in my IBM branch office.

INSTALLED
USER
PROGRAM

Program Number   5796-RAC
5796-RAD
5796-RAE
5796-RAJ
5796-RAK

GB30-1457-0

System/34

Apparel Business System

- Apparel Order Entry and Control (5796-RAC)
- Apparel Accounts Receivable (5796-RAD)
- Apparel Order Allocation (5796-RAE)
- Apparel Incentive Payroll (5796-RAJ)
- Apparel Gross-To-Net Payroll (5796-RAK)

Installed at: Goodimade Manufacturing Company, Philadelphia, PA

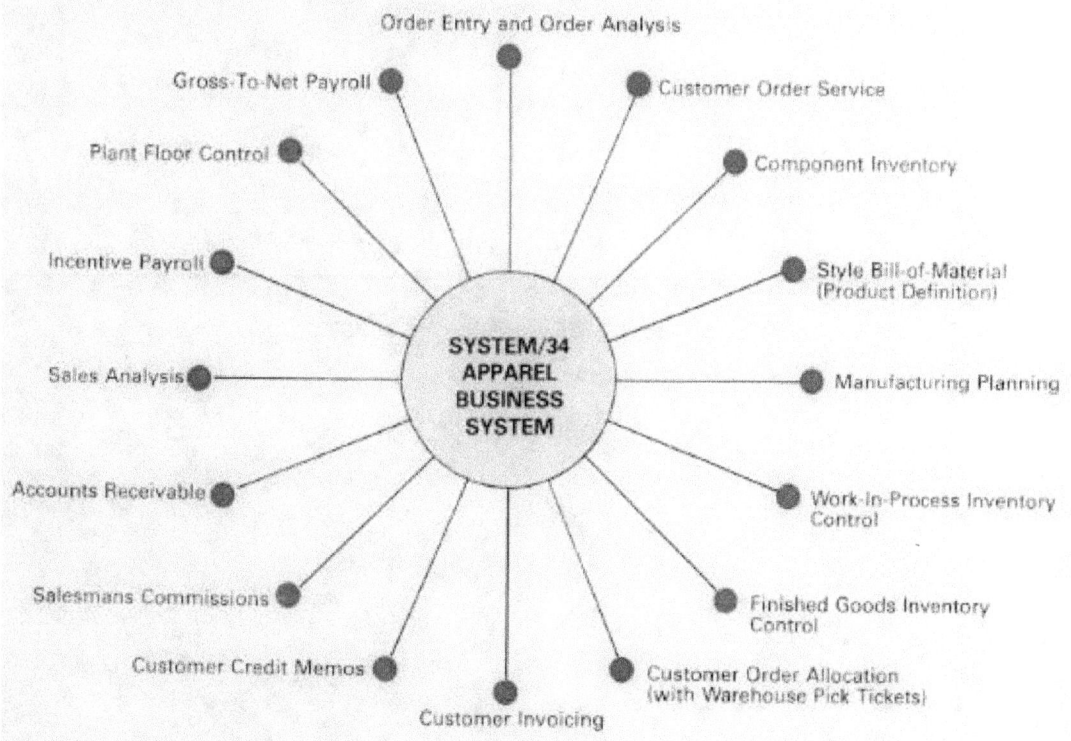

Support Center Overview

Industry Perspective

S/34 Demonstration Package

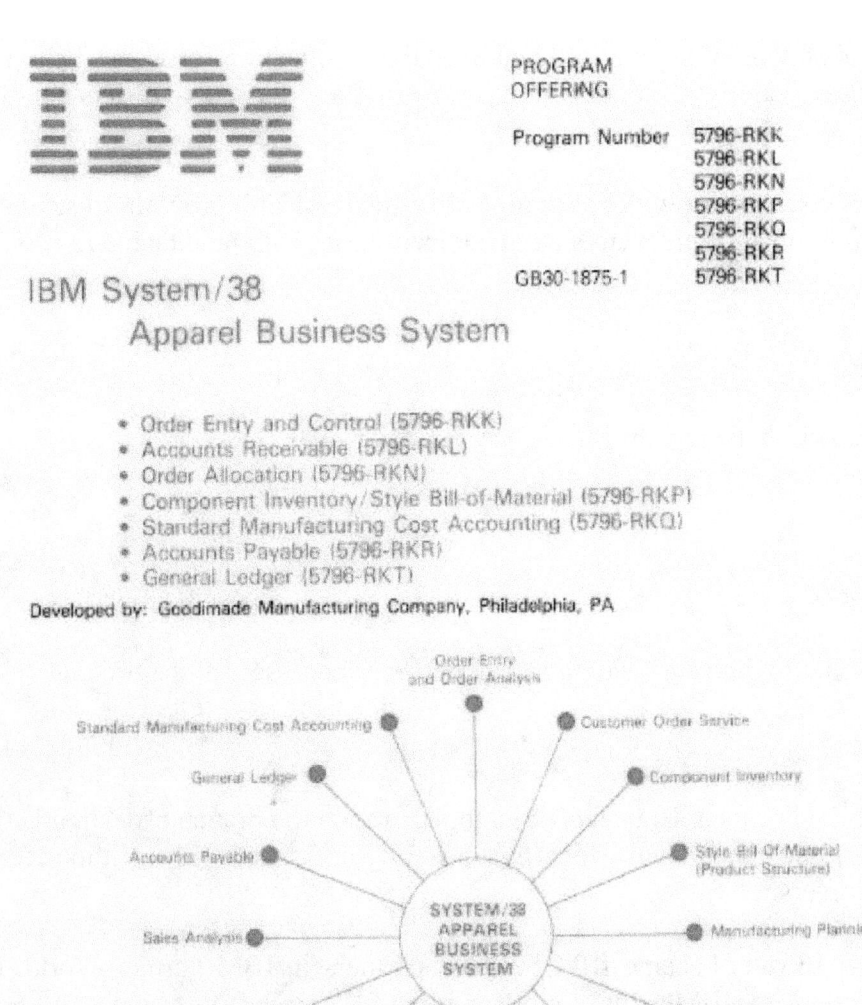

All of that vanished with the IBM executive "Low-cost producer" initiative, along with many IB-Mers, like me, and much needed and available IBM business, and huge opportunity for IBMers and IBM customers.

NOTE – At this moment in time, 1973, the five IBM engineers in Germany working on the Xerox account were about to leave IBM and start SAP SE, with very similar objectives to the IBM IUP program, which is to take advantage of supplicated and available application software. Today the annual revenues of SAP SE exceed 20 billion dollars, and growing and those ex-IBMers could be billionaires.

Today, most current IBMers have no known opportunities like the IBM IUP program to strive for incredible success and recognition and achievement and compensation, with predictable results.

IBM "Low-cost producer" - 1982

A profound change to IBM, and I believe a disastrous one.

Still in effect today

60,000 IBM layoffs - 1993

A profound change to IBM, and I believe a disastrous one, however necessary at the time.

Still in effect today

The elimination of the IBM field or local Branch offices, together with the branch office marketing representatives (salespeople) and the branch office Systems Engineers, left IBM without direct local contact with IBM customers.

Many of the 60,000 laid-off IBMers became IBM business partners in IBM Partner World, but more than two decades later these ex-IBMers have mostly retired.

IBM Business Partners - ongoing

A profound change to IBM made more difficult as ex-IBMer business partners retire, and as IBM changes focus to include: cloud, analytics and mobile.

IBM business partners are developing and offering multiple variations and enhancements of IBM middleware such as IBM i (AS/400) graphical user interface (GUI) software.

IBM long ago virtually stopped of greatly slowed enhancements to the IBM i (AS/400) computer which is still the most widely installed IBM corporate computer, relying on IBM business partners to enhance the IBM middleware.

While initially apparently attractive for IBM to reduce or eliminate its development costs, the prospective customer is often offered many different and non-compatible IBM business partner solutions, and the customer often seems to be selecting none of them.

I believe that IBM can and must replace all of the current middleware now provided by IBM business partners to the still popular IMB I corporate computer with revolutionary software directly developed and supported by IBM as illustrated below, and in the book appendixes.

Current IBM initiatives, business units and focus – 2015

I do not pretend to understand nor do I attempt to provide advice to IBM about the current IBM 2015 focus and newly organized business units, and their probability of success and revenue growth.

However, I do have a revolutionary strategy that I believe could dramatically reverse the decline of IBM and accelerate the success of SAP, and open a new universe of opportunity in corporate computing.

My revolutionary strategy for the success of IBM and SAP

I do have some strong opinions about how valid and complete are several of the focuses and definitions currently presented by IBM, and I have several questions that IBM executives might consider.

Big Data, Analytics, and Cognitive Computing

I realize that the IBM definition of Big Data is not just the amount of data, but includes multiple ways to manage it and process it.

I believe that IBM's definition of Big Data is severely limited to the data recorded under current computing methods, primarily data that is written and recorded by programs external to the program execution, typically as disk or flash memory records, or available with external probes and thus is severely deficient.

I believe that the true definition of Big Data needs to include all of the computer internal execution of statements and data in real-time as in my Real-Time Program Audit (RTPA) active patent (Appendix H).

Only by including all of the really (all of the program statements and data processed) Big Data captured and recorded by the Real-Time Program Audit (RTPA) process can true Autonomic be accomplished, and can true Analytics be performed real-time of critical information now not ever recorded (as in a video camera of the program actual execution.

Big Data that includes only analytical information that has been written externally from the computer program, typically to disk storage as a formatted disk record such as customer invoice detail record, is by definition not real-time and is not big data. The disk invoice detail record was deemed to be important enough to be written to disk external from the executing program, but it is by definition a summary of perhaps hundreds of computer statements and pieces of data processed internally in the executing computer program.

All of those executing computer statements and all of the data processed to produce the disk record written externally to the computer executing program, together with the disk record (and additional information such as the moment of time) is the *really* big data.

Today only data written externally to disk, or captured with a probe, such as in a Honeywell room thermostat, is available for big data analytics as is currently defined and implemented. That greatly limits the amount of crucial information captured, relegates the information to historical, not real-time, information, and limits the value of analytics performed on the historical information.
.

This Real-Time Program Audit (RTPA) recording is fundamental to the next revolutionary success for IBM and to make each and every person fundamentally more capable, or 'smarter"

All I can say about Cognitive Computing is when? and why not have cognitive computing be an integral part of the revolutionary strategy for IBM or SAP success ?

Real-Time Predictive Autonomic Computing

The following references may serve as a useful background for the following illustration of what I mean as a practical implementation of *real-time* predictive autonomic computing that I experienced, and that was only possible when using *really big data* is available for real-time analytics (as implemented with the Real-Time Program Audit (RTPA) software.

Autonomic computing From Wikipedia, the free encyclopedia

http://en.wikipedia.org/wiki/Autonomic_computing

Reverse engineering From Wikipedia, the free encyclopedia

http://en.wikipedia.org/wiki/Reverse_engineering

Towards a Real-Time Reference Architecture for Autonomic Systems

http://ieeexplore.ieee.org/xpl/login.jsp?tp=&arnumber=4228610&url=http%3A%2F%2Fieeexplore.ieee.org%2Fiel5%2F4228597%2F4228598%2F04228610.pdf%3Farnumber%3D4228610

About twelve years ago I was the top corporate computing consultant to a multi-billion dollar annual sales corporation in the branded wholesale apparel business, whose customers included many of the women's and men's apparel major retail chains.

While consulting at another large branded wholesale apparel company, I had received a phone call asking if I could please immediately come to this new company and take over responsibility for enhancing and maintaining the critical warehouse management and shipping computer application.

Even though the new company had several dozen corporate computing staff, no one was apparently able or willing to effectively and accurately support and enhance the packing and shipping computer software provided by a major warehouse management system software vendor.

Thus, needed custom enhancements required by the retail chain customers and ongoing support to the warehousing packing and shipping operations applications software were not made and the customer was suffering from some fifty thousand dollar chargebacks from the retail chains for late and inaccurate shipments from the customers distribution centers. And, the corporate computing staff causing the expensive chargebacks due to incorrect support was at severe risk.

I was not familiar with the vendor supplied warehouse management software and its millions of lines of source code, let alone with the customer's extensive customization of the supplied software that had been made over a period of years. However, I was familiar with warehouse and distribution center processing and with the programming language, RPG, so I took the job, thinking how hard can it be, and how much pressure can there be?

Well, the very first morning I was "in charge of things warehousing", the warehouse computer system stopped, or "blew up", and I found out that I, of course, had no clue of what happened or how to find it or how to fix it, just like the previous staff, even with the pressure of the ringing telephone and visits by executive management.

I reasonably quickly realized that I had to know for sure what was happening inside the huge computer, which serviced up to several hundred "packer" who used radio frequency (RF) wands to pack cartons with expensive dresses to the exact customer order and exact carton weight for shipment on pallets with manifests from the massive distribution centers in several states.

I could not guess what was happening or what had happened and looking at the computer source programs was pointless and a waste of time.

So, I did what for me was the obvious thing to do, and that was to make myself much "smarter" by being able to see and record exactly what the computer was doing all the time with the exact data being processed at every moment in time.

I made the warehouse source programs much "smarter" by enhancing them and enabling them to audit and record to disk or a printer literally everything the program was doing, as is illustrated below: See Appendix C On-Demand Forensic Accounting and Analytics

NOTE – The numbered lines are the RPG ILE computer source statements being executed in real-time. **302   torder = 1500;**

NOTE – The red lines are the data resulting from the above source statement.   1500

302   torder = 1500;

> 1500

Thus I could virtually instantly visualize and understand from a permanent record and whenever I wanted, exactly what the program and data actually did as it executed that exact instance of data and time and in that exact operating environment and I did not need to guess like all the other programmers did, mostly wrongly and with disastrous results.

And, I could use this productivity tool on all of the programs in the huge warehouse management system and quickly understand and support them all, as if it was simple and easy.

```
302      torder = 1500;
            1500
303      iorder = 78.543;
            78.543
304    // value of iorder has now been computed
305        xorder = torder + 13.45 +
            1618.19       1500
306    // this is a continuation free form statement preceded with +
307                 26.2 + iorder;
                        78.543
308      sorder = torder +  xorder +  iorder + rorder + morder + norder;
      93330.496      1500
                        1618.19     78.543
                                32109.876
                                    34567.098
                                        23456.789


(partial Client Stock Account Summary forensic accounting audit output)
```

Figure 4: Client Stock Account Summary forensic accounting audit output.

And, now all the other programmers could do the same, multiplying their productivity and value and confidence, if they only wanted to stop guessing and utilize this programmer productivity tool.

The schematic below illustrates how ***real-time predictive autonomic computing and real-time analytics*** can now be implemented for the very first time as illustrated below, opening a new universe of crucial information not being utilized by IBM or by SAP today, and using this same warehouse packing and shipping example of ***really big data***.

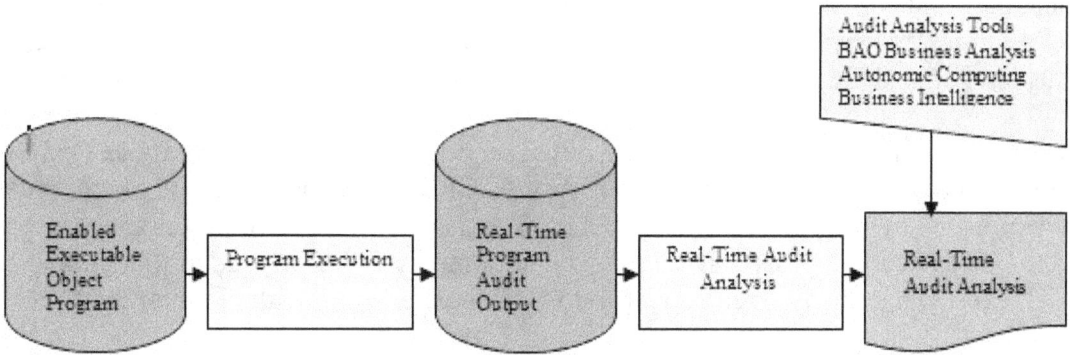

Figure 4. Real-Time Program Audit (RTPA) audit output and analysis.

Some of the major reasons for the many fifty-thousand dollar chargebacks for error or late shipments in the warehouse distribution system were directly caused by things beyond the immediate responsibility of the corporate computing programmers. There were many human packing errors, and for many reasons.

There were always dozens of warehouse packer with Radio Frequency guns with small screens who scanned bar coded expensive garments individually into a carton based on a customer order, or pick slip at a packing station.

A huge problem was that the packers were in several huge warehouses or distribution centers in several states, and the packer turnover rate was very high, training was minimal, and the training personnel were largely at the distribution center at company headquarters, and the packer pay was low. Also the packers encountered many unexpected issues or problems during a shift which caused expected productivity to be missed and unexpected issues such as bad scanners, bad bar codes, missing cartons, dead batteries, and many personal issues such as phone calls from school.

None of this was ever really an area of concern for corporate computing, except for the late and error shipments and the chargebacks.

I had participated is some packer training when implementing enchased new RF scanning and packing features, working with the HQ trainer and packers to implement important packer prompting messages to be displayed on their RF gun screen and important error messages to help the packer, particularly new packers to be correct, and productive, and fast in their packing of cartons.

Being as I had already aced this corporate computing top job, only because of the "smarter" program auditing, I had some time to burn, and I started to look through the audit program output of different packers to see what additional productivity analytics could be achieved. These productivity analytics were real-time and comprehensive over the entire shift for each packer.

And there it was all of the RF scanner gun display prompting and error messages that were sent from the computer to each packer were in the real-time program audit along with the source statements and data and conditions and the moment in time of the prompt and error messages. None of these RF prompts and error messages were written to disk by the original unaudited program, and were thus lost for analytics and big data reporting, and lost for productivity improvements.

I was suddenly and inadvertently the master of packer retraining and productivity as I could see the causes of the many errors and issues that really created the fifty-thousand doll chargebacks accumulate while the training supervisor was taking a personal day off or on the corporate jet. However, I demurred and passed that newfound and important knowledge to the training supervisor in HQ, even as her unanswered emails and voice mails piled up with pleas for help.

I discovered **a whole new universe of real-time computer crucial information** trapped and discarded inside the computer that could and should have been automatically predictively analyzed to increase productivity, reduce errors and cost, and improve performance and profitability.

A whole new universe of real-time computer crucial information

I realize that this book is not about optimizing distribution center operations and about industrial engineering, but I briefly illustrate several of the *dozens of areas* where automatic real-time availability of all computer generated information and predictive analytics would dramatically increase the company profit and the satisfaction of its customers.

The chairman of SAP recently presented a new computing SAP Business Suite and he specifically discussed warehouse processing and the need for same day shipping and pick tickets and productivity and the immense benefits of real-time processing. However, he has not apparently imagined multiplying that new capability by accessing the new universe of real-time computer information, specifically real-time program audit (RTPA) audit output. That means catching and responding to and analyzing every error and issue in real-time, not minutes later if ever.

SAP Business Suite 4 SAP HANA Launch Event
http://events.sap.com/s4hana/en/session/14013

Simple but common daily warehouse problems such as wrong picking, wrong warehouse generated bar item codes, miss-picking, miss-packing, wrong cartons, wrong labels, wrong item weights, bad bar RF scanners, dead RF scanner batteries, wrong carton weights, packer packing errors, weigh scale and carton weight issues, packer personal interruptions, packer training and turnover issues, and many more unexpected issues all delay the required same day shipment from the warehouse and potentially create the chargebacks.

Virtually all or certainly most of those error issues and problems I was able to see and understand by simply looking at the real-time program audit (RTPA) output by packer from the audit information only available inside the computer, and now available instantly to me.

Software vendors such as SAP, IBM, Oracle, Microsoft, and others simply cannot be ultimately t productive and their customers as profitable without using the new universe of real-time computer information as recorded by the real-time program audit (RTPA).

My point is neither IBM nor SAP is capturing, recording and performing really big and crucial analytics or real-time autonomic computing, because they are not using the Real-Time- Program Audit (RTPA) patented capability to open a whole new universe of real-time computer generated information which is now lost. In my opinion, until they do utilize this new universe of crucial real-time audit information their solutions are deficient and are not nearly as valuable as they should be and eventually must be.

Then, perhaps Bernie Madoff could have been remotely and automatically caught by the SEC using predictive analytics as the fake customer statements were being computed as in the illustration below, using vendor supplied application software. Appendix C On-Demand Forensic Accounting and Analytics

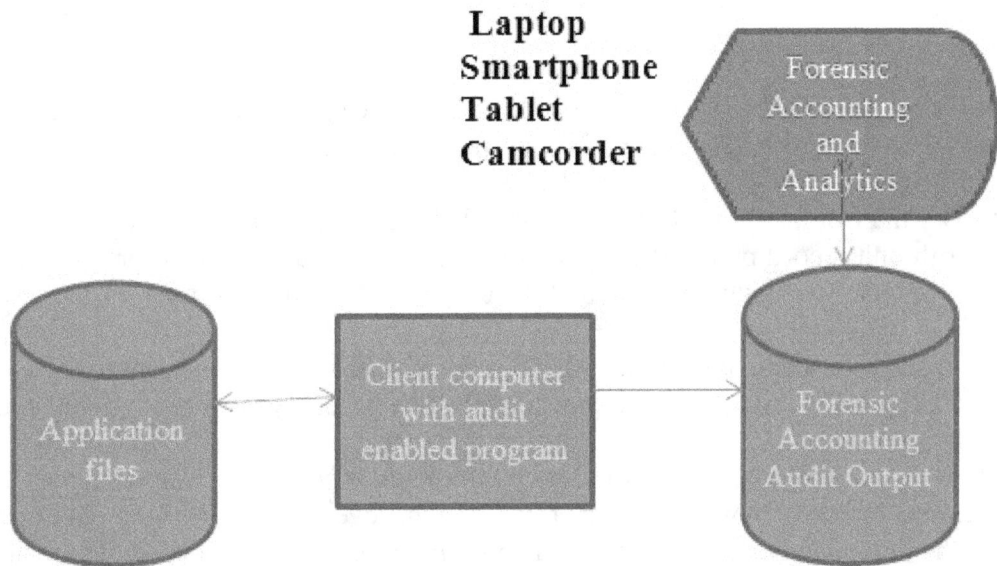

Figure 6: Forensic Accounting and Analytics (can be remote and mobile and real-time).

How will IBM Succeed and Grow?

Some fundamental questions I have included:

Does IBM have a good long-term business model?

How can IBM gain revenue from the 100 billion dollar annual cost now paid to corporate development personnel?

How can we create revolutionary new computing software that will eliminate the need for corporate development personnel?

How can we create and sustain a recurring stream of huge licensed revenue and attract new IBM customers, as all of our competitors are doing?

How quickly and how surely can we right this ship and grow IBM revenue and customers?

In order for IBM to succeed and grow in the future, it must learn from the most significant past successes and failures, why they happened, and understand the profound unintended consequences of some of those decisions.

The IBM SPREAD project in 1961 that developed the IBM System/360 computer was a revolution that kept IBM from failing at the end of the Herman Hollerith Unit Record punched card era to overwhelming its competition in the 1960s.
Bob Evans, the line manager who had the major responsibility for designing this gamble of a corporate lifetime, was only half joking when he said, "We called this project `You bet your company.' "
http://www.cedix.de/Literature/History/FiveMillGamble1.pdf

I was an IBMer on April 7, 1964 and I attended the announcement of the IBM/System/360. The IBM System/360 computer literally changed the corporate computing game for decades.

IBM had to "Bet the Company" in 1961 with the SPREAD project because the sixty-year era of Herman Hollerith unit record punched cards was rapidly ending, and competitors like Honeywell with the H200 computer were winning much of the current IBM 1401 computer business.

Luckily, IBM made a fortunate choice in 1961 to scrap virtually all current computing capability, including IBM's capability with the development of the revolutionary IBM System/360 computer.

Ended is the sixty-year era of the stored program computer as we know it in customer accounts, using ancient, and I believe now deficient programming development software and application software, and the unproductive in-house corporate programmer. This is evidenced in the drastically declining IBM revenues and stock price and the turmoil within IBM and in declining number of IBM customer accounts.

So, once again as in 1961, 1982 and in 1993 IBM must make a "bet the company" decision. The previous "bet the company" decisions profoundly affected my career and life and the careers and lives of hundreds of thousands of families, and thousands of companies for better or worse.

Each of the IBM top executives who made the final "bet the company" decision should have had the very best information and counsel of the very best people, and yet some of these IBM "bet the company" initiatives did not turn out well.

I have been directly interacting and working with and listening to IBM customers for more than five decades unlike anyone in IBM executive management, and I believe that I do know what IBM should do and must do to succeed and grow now and in the future.

What should IBM do now, and what will IBM do?

It is now past time for IBM to initiate another major project to "bet your company" again, before it is too late. The good news is that IBM can succeed as it did in 1964 with a bold and revolutionary strategy, and it can develop and implement that strategy quickly.

Will IBM make a fortunate and successful choice now when it bets the company on the next technology, or will IBM fail to implement critically needed technology at all, or choose the wrong direction entirely?

Several articles and documents available on the Internet provide important background information and perspective of what actually happened over the last half century of my direct involvement in corporate computing, and why.

In the Sources section of this book I reference many articles pertinent to this chapter, with links to the information.

A Revolutionary Strategy for IBM success and Growth

It is clear, at least to me, that IBM could immediately embrace and quickly develop and implement a revolutionary strategy to replace the ancient and primitive sixty year old initial wave of stored program computing and capability with a quantum leap of capability and simplicity.

It is equally clear, at least to me, that if IBM does not revolutionize its offerings and correct its business model that someone will seize this huge opportunity, as did the five young upstart companies starting with Microsoft and SAP SE in the 1970s.

The six decades long reign of the once revolutionary electro-mechanical Herman Hollerith unit record punched card era ended in the early 1960s, replaced with the new revolutionary electronic stored program computer. Each revolutionary invention multiplied the capability and speed of corporate computing possibly by at least ten times and dramatically lowered the cost of corporate computing.

How will SAP Succeed and Grow?

Some fundamental questions I have included:

Does SAP SE IBM have a good long-term business model?

How can SAP use Analytics and Big Data if its customer base is shrinking and new customers' are using other technologies to capture Big Data?

How can SAP gain revenue from the 100 billion dollar annual cost now paid to corporate development personnel?

How can SAP create revolutionary new computing software that will eliminate the need for corporate development personnel?

How can SAP create and sustain a recurring stream of huge licensed revenue and attract new IBM customers, as all of our competitors are doing?

How quickly and how surely can SAP overtake IBM in technology, revenue, profits, customers, and future success?

In order for SAP to multiply success and grow in the future, it must take full advantage of its revolutionary new S/4 HANA Business Suite initiative and multiply that new capability and value beyond what even SAP executives imagine, as is illustrated in this book. Appendix C On-Demand Forensic Accounting and Analytics

SAP Business Suite 4 SAP HANA Launch Event | SAP S ...

http://events.sap.com/s4hana/en/session/14013

A Revolutionary Strategy for SAP success and Growth

It is clear, at least to me, that SAP could immediately embrace and quickly develop and implement a revolutionary strategy to make a quantum leap in corporate computing by multiplying the capability and value of the new and revolutionary S/4 HANA Business Suite.

Not only would the revolutionary SAP new software be virtually real-time and simple, as already announced, it would also record and make available real-time a whole new universe of crucial computer generated information and real-time predictive analytics. That would create a whole new universe of new applications and new customers, all made possible by the Real-Time Program Audit (RTPA) software.

SAP is today following the immensely successful and immensely profitable business model of Microsoft, Intuit, and others by licensing supplicated and full-functions applications to corporations and even ultimately to end-users, including processing cloud .capability and support.

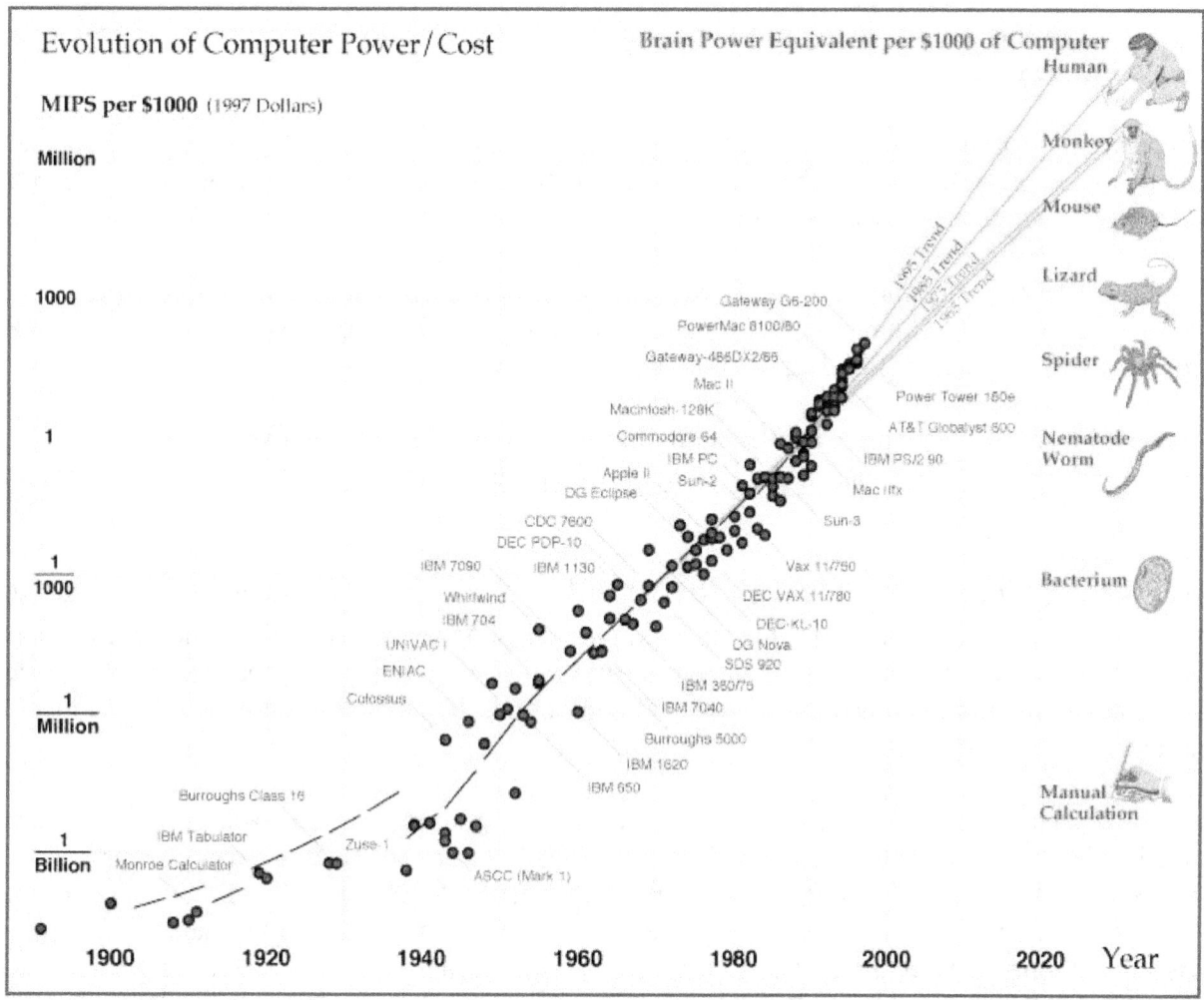

http://www.transhumanist.com/volume1/moravec.htm

Today, corporate computing is literally stuck in limbo as significant corporate computing productivity advancements cannot be made based on hardware technology advancements. Computer hardware is about *one million times* faster now and is infinitely less expensive than in the 1960s, and that speed enhancement can no longer generate the quantum productivity advancements now needed by IBM and its competitors and future competitors to be the most successful and to grow.

So what is the problem of stuck corporate computing productivity now, and is there a revolutionary and available effective solution now?

It should be almost laughingly clear that, as always, the answer to increasing productivity of humans is through productivity tools which multiply human productivity. And, this is all so obvious and understandable that there must be important reasons why implementing known available human productivity tools is being resisted and rejected by IBM and others, such as the SEC.

Paul Houston Harkins

The sociology of resisting change, including topics such as **Resisting Social Change** is critically important towards understanding and implementing needed change. A major reason for resisting needed change is vested interests.

Increasing human productivity is the basis and result and value of virtually all the inventions and patents reviewed earlier, and if this seems so simplistic, it really is this simple and this important, and this applies directly to *your success.*

Most of the earlier inventions, or tools, which greatly multiplied human productivity and reduced effort were to increase human physical productivity, such as the knife, axe, hammer, hoe, rake, broom, wheel, shoe, gloves, shovel, scythe, paper, pen, etc.

The next inventions were more subtle and multiplied a combination of human physical and mental productivity or capability, such as the typewriter, the printing press, and the Herman Hollerith unit record punched card system.

But what productivity tools could actually most directly greatly increase the productivity of the human brain? These include languages, and tools to increase the capability of the human five external senses like hearing aids, microphones, visual recording devices, and probably most importantly eye glasses. Vision or sight being is considered to be the most important human external sense.

Image your business and personal life today without being able to see really well, even with corrected vision as with glasses, contact lenses, or surgically inserted eye lenses, as I now have thanks to Medicare. When my eye surgeon asked me if I wanted "Perfect" both long and short vision, I agreed, especially as it was free to me and took only about ten minutes to permanently and painlessly accomplish perfect and invisibly corrected vision without glasses or contact lenses.

A primary reason why an eye surgeon can perform many eye cataract and lens insertion operations in a day, often one every 15 minutes, with virtually 100 percent success, is that the surgeon has seen and photographed inside the human eye with sophisticated instruments and thus does not have to guess or wonder might he or she will find during the operation.

Apparently over 60 % of the U.S. population needs some sort of vision correction to be able to legally drive a car or even to see from the first row in school.

VISION FACTS AND STATISTICS - MES Vision

https://www.google.com/?gws_rd=ssl#q=percentage+of+population+requiring+correction+vision

The stunning part is that even today no one is born with the understanding that he or she cannot see well enough to effectively compete and flourish in society just because they cannot see well as they need to see for success.

I was born with extremely nearsighted vision, 20/400, and not able to see essentially anything on the blackboard at school from the first row, or the big E at the top of a vision chart when I did finally get my first vision check and the resulting coke bottle eyeglasses at age 11. How I survived 11 years and five grades of school without being able to see much except colors beyond 10 feet is a blur to me today as it was then. I simply did not know that I could not see well.

My sister tells a very similar story of not being able to see from the first row at school and having her face an inch from the paper while writing before having her first vision test and glasses at age 11, and of being called four eyes. She later graduated from the University of Pennsylvania, with honors.

 We both got our nearsightedness from out maternal grandfather Edwin Schubert, who when as an adult he put on his first pair of glasses, looked out the window and said in amazement in Pennsylvania Dutch (German) "Der Voggel" or the bird.

How does this need for good vision affect every corporate CEO, CFO, CIO corporate developer, every corporate computing customer, and you today?

My short but honest answer and opinion is that today virtually all corporate computing, including application development and support is accomplished while working 100 percent blind of what is happening inside the computer, cannot review what happened inside the computer, and cannot utilize the vast and important information created by the computer. There is no real capability to see inside the computer with real-time program auditing, without permanently recording what happens inside the computer where computations are made and where all data is processed, and without the capability perform real-time analytics on the crucial data being generated inside the computer.

IBM can hire 40,000 new potentially hot-shot employees and layoff 50,000 apparently no longer hot-shot employees and it will make little difference, and perhaps have a negative result, as the experience, skills, and relationships of those laid-off employees are lost to IBM. That has already happened several times before over several decades with relatively declining results compared to IBMs competitors.

One hundred percent of all of the current IBM employees and potential new IBM employees are severely crippled in their potential ability to greatly improve their productivity and performance for twenty-first century computer work.

They may now have glasses or contact lenses or surgically inserted eye lens, as I have now. I went through all three wonderful vision corrections methods and amazement at my new vision and capability, starting at age 11 and I finally could see quite well for normal human daily activity. I could even see as well probably as a fairly good hunter or gatherer or farmer, where before I could not have even have used a hoe in the fields.

That is the problem of having 100 percent corrected human vision for hunter gatherer work, but not having the specialized and extraordinary vision needed for extraordinary work with science or with computers in the twenty-first century of virtually infinitely powerful and complex computing.

That is the problem, like me and my sister at age ten and without corrected vision, sitting in the front row of school and not being able to see anything on the blackboard, but not knowing that we were crippled because we did not know it and no one bothered to find out.

We just did the best we could with crippled vision and it had to be enough.

We were both very lucky to have gained reasonable eyesight at about age 10, unlike billions of people today with uncorrected vision or related limitations like Dyslexia.

So, what is the extraordinary vision required being incredibly productive in the twenty-first century for *all* of the 40,000 new hot-shot employees that IBM may now hire, and for the 50,000 IBMers who may be laid-off now to be competitive and productive now and in the future?

It is the extraordinary and spectacular and revolutionary vision of the **eight power refracting telescope invented by Galileo in the early 1600s, which allowed him to see what no one else had ever seen, and to prove the rest of the world's thinking for more than a millennium wrong.**

Imagine Galileo viewing images of the Hubble telescope, or viewing images of an electron microscope, and what these inventions have enabled.

It is the extraordinary vision and capability to see and understand and remember and analyze and immediately act on a whole new world of important information never before captured or seen by anyone.

It is a new world like the fabulous world and sights beneath the surface of the oceans, which is virtually invisible to a person with hunter-gatherer corrected eyesight on a ship or plane looking out over the waves to the horizon, with the waves shielding the incredible world underneath the surface of the ocean.

It is a new world like the fabulous world of atoms and electrons, which are invisible to a person with only our hunter-gatherer corrected eyesight, without the human performance enhancing tools of microscopes.

It is a new world of advanced internal medicine and routine open heart surgery and the Electrocardiogram, and the Echocardiogram which lets the doctor literally see and hear and have a permanent record of the heart working in real-time. I have also directly benefited from those inventions.

Why medical Doctors with perhaps ten years of intense graduate school education and residency would need Echocardiograms to literally see and hear into a beating heart, is because they and you cannot afford to guess with your life, and they want and need to work a rapidly as they successfully can with the knowledge these productivity tools provide.

And then there is the frozen-in-time six decades old world of computer software development, programming and support, where the million plus expensive corporate programmers, developers and support personnel use essentially the same ancient and primitive tools of the early 1960s.

Software programmers, developers and support personnel today have to guess at what might have happened inside the computer, without a permanent record as in a security camera video recording, by staring at the static source program programs and simply imagining what might, could, or perhaps should have happened based on their uncorrected and crippled and limited understanding.

That incredibly ancient and unproductive, error-prone and expensive process of guessing in corporate computing is about to end now, and those who resist that productive and effective change will disappear as did virtually all the people and companies who were displaced by inventions created to increase human productivity through history.

That revolutionary technology is the Real-Time Program Audit (RTPA) patented software illustrated in Appendix H, and the On-Demand Forensic Accounting Universal Program Auditing Language illustrated in Appendix I.

So, how does one of the million-plus corporate computing people who are now subject to being displaced because they are not productive and are very costly succeed in a new and changed environment?

NOTE – The current corporate computing environment is rapidly changing now, and the rate of decline is accelerating.

My answer and opinion is possibly best illustrated in chapter 5 The Road to Singapore and that is to recognize impending change, face it, understand it, utilize it to your unique advantage and success even if you must create change yourself. Simply resisting change is mostly useless and damaging.

I was able to consult successfully in Singapore for ten weeks this past summer, at age 75, and in Europe and all over the United States and Canada working with corporate executive management as well as with corporate computing staff at all levels simply because I could virtually always provide valuable solutions and answers to difficult issues that seemingly no one else could or would.

The reasons for whatever my long-term success, crippled as I was including intellectually compared to many others, are the very same reasons that most others now at risk of being displaced can achieve significant success in similar circumstances by taking focused *action*. .

While this is not intended to be a counseling book, I believe that my personal experiences at Drexel Institute of Technology, now Drexel University relating to corporate computing some fifty-five years ago apply generally to almost everyone today. I believe that every Drexel University cooperative (co-op) education student today, and really every job seeker today, should know and understand these points to ponder for success and many other critical things before taking his or her very first co-op six-month job in industry, or taking his or her first job. The reason is that your very first job may be your job or your industry for a long time, as long as it lasts.

These points to ponder for success, for lack of a better name, may seem basic and obvious, but are not followed by most of my peers, and they were crucial in whatever has been my success.   .

Some of these points are fully illustrated in my book **"How to Become a Highly Paid Corporate Programmer"**

http://www.amazon.com/Become-Highly-Paid-Corporate-Programmer/dp/158347045X/ref=sr_1_1?ie=UTF8&qid=1424554704&sr=8-1&keywords=how+to+become+a+highly+paid+corporate+programmer

Points to Ponder for Your Success

- Do not guess, instead get the correct answer
- Work smarter, not necessarily harder by utilizing productivity tools
- Just give me the answers
- Make it look easy
- Find a way to make it easy with productivity tools
- Simplify
- Be economically valuable, not a commodity
- See the whole picture
- Think and act top down
- Reach out for your own success, now
- Focus on your unique strengths
- Take advantage of opportunity
- Take action towards your future
- Never be satisfied
- Consider the future and your future, now
- Think globally

Perhaps by now not surprising to the reader, I consider university level education and training, as I experienced it at Drexel for my Bachelor of Science and my Masters degrees, to be a full participant in resisting needed change, and in particular in resisting needed corporate computing change.

Once again, as for example; the Securities and Exchange Commission (SEC), IBM and other corporations, and individual in-house corporate computing departments, universities are frozen in time and development and experts in resisting needed change.

My observation and experience is that in universities this is directly because of the vested power of the university professors who essentially have jobs for their career and who can and do resist needed change to make university students, and the university itself succeed.

Once again, there is little or no pain for the professors resisting change and they can present essentially the same material for decades, but there is immense pain for the students who do not have the knowledge, skills or understanding to succeed throughout their working careers. There is also pain for the university itself when it cannot attract enough desirable students, struggles to advance in its academic ranking of universities, and ultimately suffers in its endowment, and rejection by its graduates and alumni.

Harsh perhaps, but I believe true, and I am totally grateful to Drexel for my very practical education, but distressed at Drexel for resisting much needed change and rejecting offers to help make the needed changes for the benefit of Drexel and future students, and for not taking opportunities to greatly increase its endowment.

It seems to me that Drexel University executive management, while friendly and seeming competent is not able to effectively manage the professor led departments in the university and to require needed change. This is actually quite similar to my observation of public and private corporations, where seemingly competent executive management is not able to require and implement needed corporate change, particularly corporate computing change.

Thus, for example corporate computing departments which are typically managed by a Chief Information Officer (CIO) are seemingly immune from effective command and control of corporate executive management and are able to resist needed corporate computing change.

Grab the Brass Ring: My direct advice to all Drexel Co-op students today

The wonderful Drexel University five-year cooperative education program helped me greatly in getting my dream IBM job in 1962, but I had to reach out on my own and desperately grab for the brass ring to achieve it.

The following true short story about my last Drexel co-op experience hopefully illustrates how wonderful is the five year Drexel cooperative education, and how it launched my career in corporate computing at IBM. It also hopefully illustrates the crucial importance for every Drexel co-op student to realize the he or she is ultimately responsible to consider and apply maximum effort from their very first co-op industry experience and *take action* to achieve the most and lasting success.

This advice also applies to virtually anyone and anyone, including high school students searching for a future and the ultimate career they consider to be most successful for their unique abilities and desires.

I got my dream career job in 1962 working for IBM as a Systems Engineering trainee, upon my graduation from my five-year Drexel Institute of Technology cooperative education program. During my five years I had worked four six-month periods in industry at co-op jobs sponsored by employers such as IBM, Esso (Exxon) Oil company, Sharples Centrifuge Company, and Lit Brothers, gaining real world job experience, money to continue my education at Drexel and also gaining a good idea of what I could do well and what I might do upon graduation. These co-op jobs were coordinated by Drexel through Drexel co-op advisors or administrators who matched Drexel co-op students with companies wanting Drexel students to essentially intern with them for a six-month period.

The brand new IBM 650 computer installed at Drexel in about 1960 was the very first computer at Drexel, and it totally changed my career.

An IBM 650 at Texas A&M University. The IBM 533 Card Read Punch unit is on the right.

http://en.wikipedia.org/wiki/IBM_650

Source: Wikipedia
NOTE – The several illustrations of 1960s corporate computing and university computing devices, such as the IBM 650 computer below, seem archaic today, but in 1960 **they were brand new** and incredibly powerful and expensive (million dollar machines) computing technological advancements, as were the Friden electro-mechanical calculators on office desks.

I would illustrate the computing devices of today, but you can reach into your pocket while relaxing on the beach and hold them in your hand while seeing and communicating around the world, or glance at your wrist at a "smart" watch. Possibly you will literally see and interact real-time in a more sophisticated real-time Google glasses, or with a military pilot's advanced vision equipment, or even in a surgically implanted transmitting computer eye lens.
Students taking computer courses and working with the most current computer technology today might want to consider that these devices and courses will seem archaic like the IBM 650 is now, sometime later in their own careers, and that they will have to change and adapt to succeed.

No one really knows what the computing devices will look like in twenty years, the heart of the careers of today's Drexel co-op students, but for sure they will be much more powerful and productive and probably different than today's computing devices, and worlds more powerful and productive than in the 1960s when I started and in the decades when today's professors started their teaching careers.

I had taken the very first computer course offered at Drexel in 1960, a class taught by Dr., An Min Chung in Operations Research (OR). Operations research was useful in oil exploration matrix inversions and a potential for a dream career job at an oil company like Esso, or Gulf, or Sunoco.

The class was our introduction to computers, to computer languages and programming (SOAP programming language), to operations research, and to the massive IBM 650 computer which weighed about 2,500 pounds, and a major technological jump from the K&E slide rules we all had attached to our belts.

SOAP II program
https://www.google.com/?gws_rd=ssl#q=IBM+650+SOAP+II

Drexel professor Dr. An Min Chung was a wonderful teacher in every one of the areas new to the class, and a wonderful mentor and advisor to the entire class.

We were mostly successful in writing SOAP programming language solutions to the Newton-Raphson Square Root approximation formula as our first ever source language computer program.

Newton's method From Wikipedia, the free encyclopedia
http://en.wikipedia.org/wiki/Newton's_method

We were all successful and even somewhat confident in this new world of electronic computing and computer programming only because professor Dr. An Min Chung walked us all through every step in this challenging class, and provided needed help and encouragement when asked to do so.

To me is seemed to be easier than using our analog K&E slide rules to approximate answers to almost everything.

We wrote our source program statements on a SOAP programming coding pad, and then keypunched the perhaps 50 source statements on the coding pad into punched card source (symbolic) programs. We then used the IBM 533 card reader to read the source program into the IBM 650 as a SOAP II source (symbolic) program. We got several attempts trying to get our source program to compile (assemble) successfully with the SOAP II bootstrapped card assembler preceding our programs, as there was no disk storage on the IBM 650 computer to hold programs.

After a successful program compile (assembly), we punched the number for which we were to compute the square root into a card and read the card into the IBM 650 with the IBM 533 card read punch. The IBM 650 calculated our single numerical answer and punched it into a blank card on the 533 card punch. WE could then manually look at the punched card holes to read out result, or use the IBM 407 Accounting machine to print the answer.

The IBM 650 computer utilized a drum for storage rather than core memory, and utilized the IBM 407 Accounting Machine to print results from the IBM 650 output punched cards.

It took perhaps a minute to process our very first computer program, *but it turns out my whole future working career depended on that revolutionary IBM 650 computer and computer programming experience and on that success, and really on the wonderful Dr. An Min Chung*.

Our class had experienced a revolutionary new technology that multiplied our productivity and multiplied the power of the human brain. It opened potential new and exciting and valuable opportunities, giving us a glimpse into the future for us all thanks to Drexel taking the key revolutionary step by approving and installing its very first computer. And, we never had to use our analog K&E slide rules to approximate our answer in this new digital world of electronic computing.

Today, Drexel may think that new revolutionary technology is perhaps nanotechnology, but I believe that far more Drexel students and graduates will benefit from quantum advancements in computing and in real-time analytics and real-time predictive autonomic computing, which are available today but not fully recognized and accepted.

To me this was the most important and exciting class I had taken at Drexel, made even more exciting and important by our wonderful teacher Dr. An Min Chung, who made the complex new topic seem doable and understandable, and clearly important for our future.

But one year later now it was 1961 and I was sitting in the Drexel co-op coordinators office about to take my last and most important six-month co-op job before my graduation from Drexel.

I was quite a good student at Drexel and I thought I deserved a really good final co-op six-month industry assignment before graduation, hopefully in a field I was good at and liked and where my final co-op employer might consider hiring me in a desired field at graduation.

A major problem for me, and apparently for many of my Drexel co-op peers, including my twin brother Peter, was that our prior three co-op six-month assignments were not what we discovered we really liked or were particularly good at, or especially and not where we gradually discovered that we really excelled over others in performance. And, these prior co-op jobs did not pay as much as we wanted or needed.

For me there was too much previous co-op time sitting at a desk in the dreaded big office using an electro-mechanical calculator as illustrated in the movie "The Apartment" or hand posting massive ledger books, or even being a floor coordinator of paper documents.
https://www.youtube.com/watch?v=x356ll3hTxg

I never did like doing a job along with many other people doing the same job, as that type of job invariably turned out to be a "commodity" job that was targeted for elimination, one way or another, with a productivity tool or now by offshoring.

Looking way back now at my Drexel co-op experiences, I realize that it was my own fault that I got the less than wonderful co-op jobs of my early Drexel co-op jobs. There was a major recession in 1958 when I took my first co-op job after my successful freshman year, my father was anxious that my twin brother Peter and I would get co-op jobs to help pay the tuition, and most problematically, Peter and I were good, polite, respectful kids who had never had to actually ask or compete for jobs. Peter and I lived at home and commuted to Drexel, thus missing the social life and much information easily available to resident students.

So in good Drexel co-op coordination job assignment tradition, when the Drexel coordinator sat you in his office and looked at his typewritten piece of paper of available co-op jobs and selected one for you, you took it, and you were glad you had a job interview and possibly a co-op job.

Only later did you wonder "What if I had asked about other potential jobs?", but to us that would have not been respectful.

But now it was June 1961 and I was sitting in the Drexel co-op coordinators office for the final crucial co-op experience.

My Drexel final co-op coordinator was, as I remember, a retired U.S. Army colonel, and he really seemed to like me and my Drexel achievements and academic record, and I really liked him. I did not realize it at the time, but his long and distinguished army career was long before computers and was focused on heavy machines, not in office environments.

It was finally time to apply some real industrial engineering skills and training in the real booming manufacturing environment thriving in Philadelphia PA in 1960, which had a 1960 population of over two million people and was growing.

So, my Drexel co-op coordinator offered me a final cooperative job interview at what he must have thought was a plumb job. It was at a corrugated box manufacturer on **Belgian-block cobblestoned Delaware Avenue** at the docks of the Delaware River, in the oldest and heavy industry part of Philadelphia, far away from center city office buildings, air conditioning, restaurants, and possible interaction with female co-workers. Imagine the movie: **On the Waterfront - Wikipedia, the free encyclopedia**

http://philadelphiaencyclopedia.org/archive/delaware-avenue-columbus-boulevard/

http://en.wikipedia.org/wiki/On_the_Waterfront

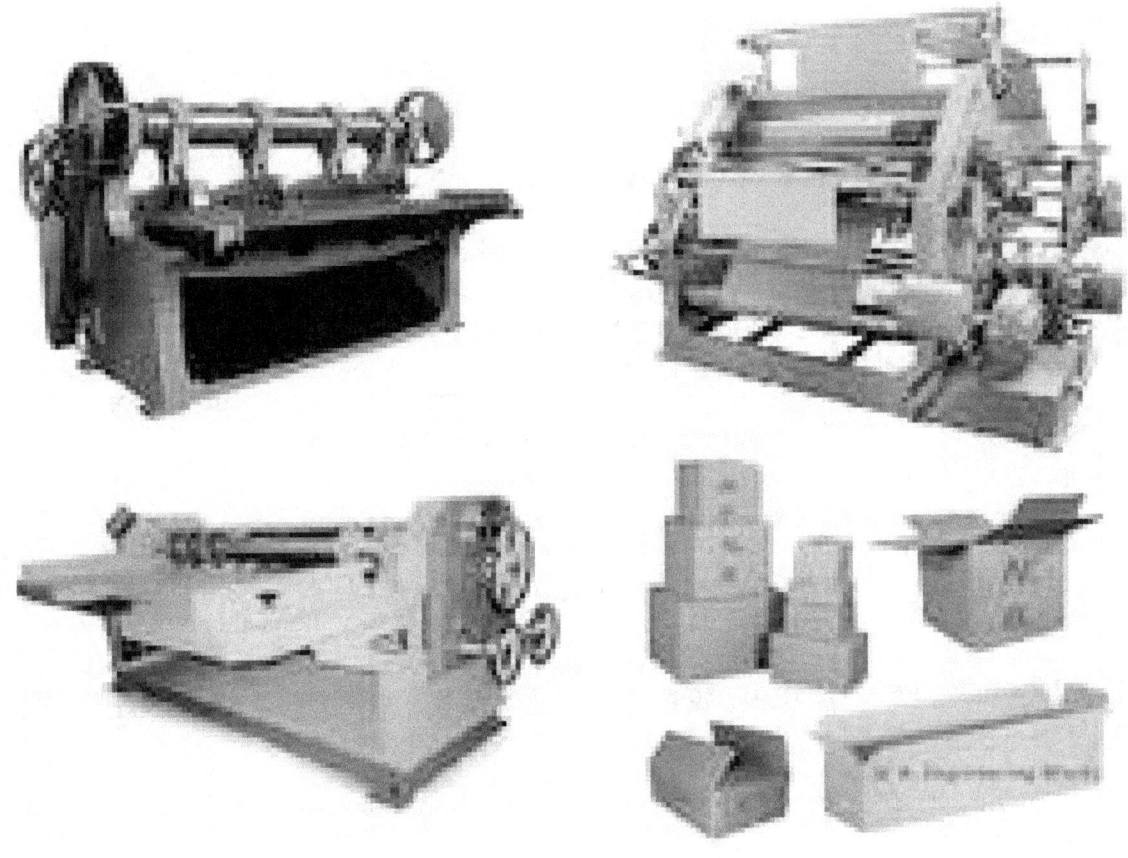

http://3.imimg.com/data3/BG/GF/MY-2938074/corrugated-box-making-machines-250x250.jpg

I was somewhat taken aback at doing my final and most important co-op assignment at a heavy manufacturing company on the other side of town, but being the polite and respectful and grateful person I was brought up to be, I took the long and hot trip to the cobblestoned Delaware Avenue, where the Drexel co-op student working there would give me the scoop on this new and perhaps to him coveted assignment.

Words cannot adequately describe my feelings of despair and shock as my co-op predecessor at the corrugated paper box company showed me what he did, and what I would be soon doing, perhaps for the rest of my working career.

It was boiling hot in the huge room, with thunderous sounds and vibrations and smells and glue coming from the huge box presses, and he was dripping in glue as he reached gingerly into his shirt pocket for a tensile tester to test the tinsel strength and compression strength of a corrugated box right off the thundering press next to us.

Effect of Manufacturer's Joint Fastening Techniques on Compression Strength of Corrugated Fiberboard Boxes
http://digitalcommons.calpoly.edu/cgi/viewcontent.cgi?article=1034&context=it_fachttp://3.imimg.com/data3/BG/GF/MY-2938074/corrugated-box-making-machines-250x250.jpg

And there was no air conditioning or a single female in sight, the pay was middling at best, and Delaware Avenue was over an hour public transportation commute from our family apartment in Drexel Hill PA.

I somehow exited the building after shaking hands with my new Drexel co-op associate for longer than I intended, and I returned to Drexel shell shocked and worried that I had to tell my co-op coordinator and friend that I did not want that co-op job.

Several years later that corrugated box factory on Delaware Avenue was rubble, along with blocks of surrounding factories. I will respectfully not illustrate that sad result.

When I again met with my Drexel co-op coordinator, he was indeed disappointed that I had not taken what he thought was a plumb job, but once again he pulled out his typewritten page of available co-op jobs and prepared to offer me yet another plumb job.

As he mulled over the list of available co-op jobs, I was so distraught that I leaned over his desk and snatched the page from his hand, without even realizing I was doing it.

I quickly scanned the page, saw IBM, and instantly remembered wonderful Dr. An Min Chung and the IBM 650 computer class, and that revolutionary technology of the future.

My final co-op job was at IBM in the heart of Philadelphia PA at 14th and Locust streets, in a beautiful air-conditioned office tower, surrounded by bright eager IBMers including females, wearing a suit and white shirt and a tie, and the pay was great, and our futures bright. I got my dream Drexel co-op, and I was 14 blocks from the docks along Delaware Avenue, really a world away.
.

Directly across 14th street was the spanking new IBM datacenter and education center which featured the IBM 407 Accounting Machine which I had used in the Drexel IBM 650 class, and at which I soon became an expert board wirer. I even got to help the recently retired pitching Paul

Arizin, the MVP of the National Basketball Association start his IBM career as a marketing representative with 407 Accounting Machine board wiring during his training. And, some of the female IBM education instructors talked about weekend bus ski trips to the Pocono Mountains.

IBM offered me my dream full-time systems engineering job when I graduated from Drexel in 1962, the pay was great, and my future was even greater.

Grab the Brass Ring: My direct advice to all Drexel Co-op students today

Each and every Drexel University co-operative student today goes through similar experiences to mine and possibly the roller coaster emotions that I did four times in his or her Drexel co-op years.

Each and every Drexel co-op student today has the opportunity to grab the brass ring rather than politely and respectfully waiting his or her turn and grabbing one of the many iron rings of virtually no value.

Each and every Drexel co-op student today can and should prepare to grab the brass ring by seeking out and taking the revolutionary technology classes of today and of the future, as was the IBM 650 computer class in my day.

Each and every Drexel co-op student today can and should demand that Drexel University search for, embrace, implement and teach the revolutionary technology of today, and perhaps demand those opportunities before matriculating at Drexel.

Several of my good Drexel classmates and friends did take those co-op manufacturing jobs and later full-time jobs at manufacturing companies, and they liked their management jobs and the golf outings on weekends, while the companies lasted.

I believe that the plumb Drexel co-op jobs of the future will be at the plumb and profitable companies who embrace the new and revolutionary technologies illustrated in this book. Technologies that like the invention of using metal shipping containers replacing cargo nets on the docks add immense value and productivity to now costly and unproductive huge industries.

It is the world created inside the computer and now visible and recorded with the Real-Time Program Audit (RTPA).

You can grab the brass ring by preparing yourself and thinking a decade in the future, and taking *action*, or you can wait your turn and get what you get and what is left and wonder what if?

Looff Carousel - Grab The Brass Ring - YouTube

https://www.youtube.com/watch?v=5a06tGdwKGs

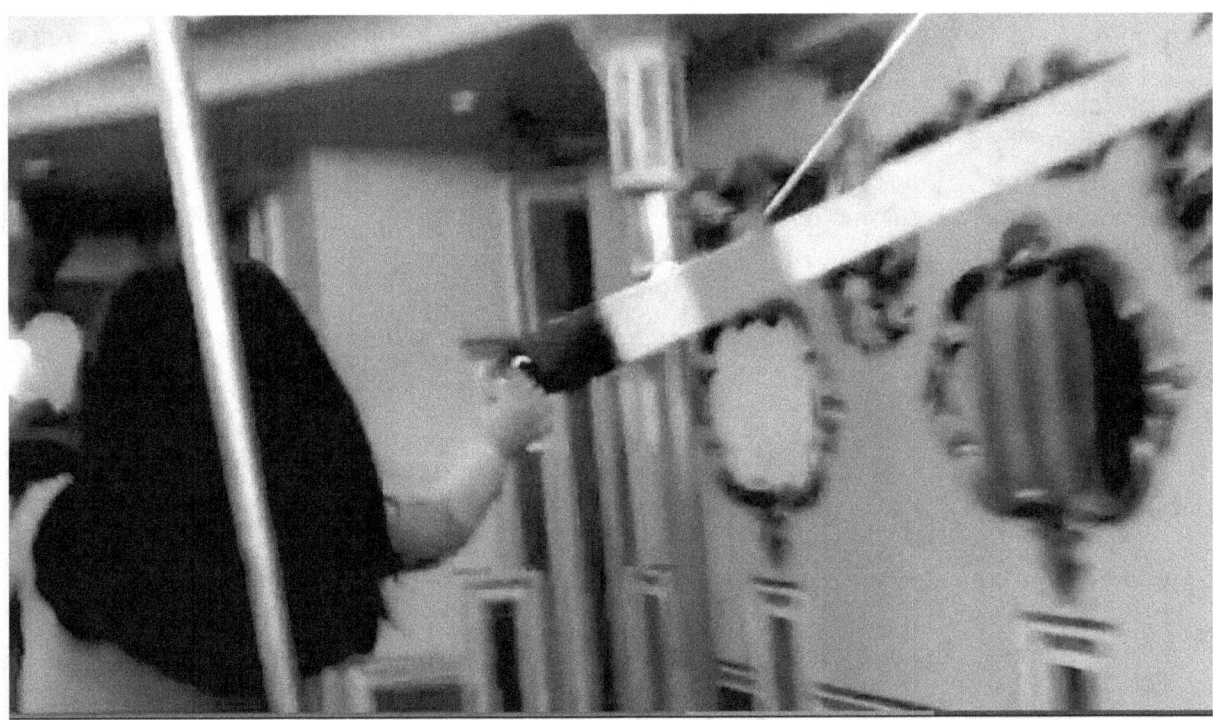

The reward for getting the brass ring on the carousel was a free ride and the admiration of all the other riders who had tried and only gotten iron rings, and it was a reward for taking action to reach out for success along with the fun.

The key to always grabbing the brass ring is not to wait in line and hope to be lucky, but to acquire valuable and needed extraordinary knowledge and skills, to put yourself in a good position to get those very best and selective jobs, and to take action to secure those jobs. Then it is to make those jobs easy and simple for you by utilizing productivity tools, even if you have to invent them.

Philadelphia, Singapore and Shanghai

Today, Philadelphia has a population of about one and one-half million residents, down about half a million residents from in 1960, probably because of the loss of so much manufacturing to off-shore. Today, Philadelphia is not booming, with blocks of rubble where industrial companies once thrived with good industrial jobs.

Today, the future for Drexel co-op students and Drexel graduates is in in acquiring superior new knowledge and a competitive advantage. That demands greatly enhancing their brains and capability with new and revolutionary technology that others resist or do not know exists, and then real-time projecting that knowledge electronically worldwide with a few all-expense-paid trips to exotic Singapore as a bonus.

Today, Singapore has a population of about five and one-half millions residents, up about four million residents from 1960s. That is in spite of strict population control, as there are millions of people in Malaysia and Indonesia who want to move to Singapore.

Singapore is booming with about every kind of business imaginable, including manufacturing and high technology firms. Wealth in Singapore is also staggering with Singapore having all the best luxury stores and some one thousand Lamborghinis', and the sound of them racing late on Saturday nights on Orchard Road is deafening.

There is room and a welcome in Singapore for experts in virtually every technical area who can and will drive growth and success.

Lamborghinis of every colour invade Orchard Road

http://singaporeseen.stomp.com.sg/singaporeseen/this-urban-jungle/lamborghinis-of-every-colour-invade-orchard-road

Today, Shanghai has a population of over twenty-four million residents, more than four times that of Singapore, and that is with population control.

Shanghai Population 2014

http://worldpopulationreview.com/world-cities/shanghai-population/

https://www.flickr.com/search/?q=shanghai&ct=0&mt=all&adv=1

Why is that important to you now and in a decade and in two decades?

It is important because that is where the industry, where the jobs, and where the wealth have gone, and where are the jobs of the future.

And, Philadelphia is not booming today, with mature and aging industries and a lack of current and advanced technological work force. That is an opportunity for Drexel co-op students to change and to multiply their productivity, capability, and their value and to succeed in the worldwide arena.

I spent all of last summer in Singapore doing corporate computing consulting for a U.S company which opened a new, large, expensive, and very modern manufacturing plant is Singapore. I worked twelve hour shifts, seven AM to seven PM plus almost two house commute daily, as did virtually all of the perhaps millions of manufacturing workers in Singapore and nearby Malaysia.

The company local management team often took a quick and inexpensive lunch at one of the more than 400 canteens in the manufacturing districts that provide inexpensive lunches from a variety of essentially Chinese dishes served from woks for the orange jump suited factory labors for about two dollars. You just point at what you want.

The daily lunches were a great opportunity for cultural exchanges, with the Chinese, Malaysia, and other local managers inquiring about life in the USA and for me inquiring about life and customs in Asia.

The net as I understand it is that virtually all the Asian managers would like to go to the USA because of the extreme overcrowding and congestion in Asia, and the life in the USA.

At lunch one day I expressed that Singapore was teeming with people and was very congested compared to my experience, even in Europe. One of the local managers said that she had worked in Shanghai which had almost five times the population of Singapore and was more congested, as was Hong Kong. That is almost incomprehensible to me.

High-Density Living In Hong Kong

http://lsecities.net/media/objects/articles/high-density-living-in-hong-kong/en-gb/

I came to gradually understand why Singapore was so very safe, clean, and vibrant, and all the people I met were courteous and helpful. After several lurid videos of criminal caning punishment, I understood why Singapore is so very safe and clean, why street fights result in arrest and a two thousand dollar fine for all involved, and why smokers rub out their cigarettes with their fingers and put the butts in their pockets rather than tossing them on the street. Not to mention graffiti and chewing gum.

My ultimate net is that the lost USA manufacturing jobs are permanently gone due to the overwhelming economics, growth and work ethic of Asia, and that job seekers in the USA need to focus on intellectual opportunities to make a quantum jump in their productivity and value in new technologies to multiple their brain power and capability with productivity tools and innovations.

My ultimate net to Drexel University executive management and to IBM and to SAP executive management is the same. Revolutionary change is there, just take action to embrace it and benefit from it rather than resist it.

If this book and this chapter on IBM, SAP and necessarily Drexel University seem to group separate topics together and to rehash previous topics, it is because all of the topics are intertwined and interwoven together as one educational and one working career experience in a rapidly changing world.

For instance, had IBM and other computing vendor companies provided more sophisticated and more capable and more productive products, such as Real-Time Program Auditing (RTPA) to companies and to educational institutions, perhaps the companies and educational institutions would have developed more productive and competitive environments, and opened huge new opportunities for all students.

However, had educational institutions taken the lead in technological advancements, or had university students demanded advanced technological advancements and current curriculum to better prepare themselves, and then the USA would be in a far different place and a competitive gainer rather a competitive follower.

And, Drexel University co-op students and Drexel graduate would have many more really plumb jobs and careers awaiting them.

Grab the Brass Ring: My direct advice to IBM executive management today

I have been directly communicating to IBM executive management for several years, as is illustrated in my several letters to the IBM Chairperson in this book, and in my submission of a formal IBM external submission to IBM several years ago of my patented Real-Time Program Audit (RTPA) software. There have been no meetings or direct conversations between me and IBM executive management, and no interest by IBM in my help or advice.

Without being cute or disrespectful or impertinent, I believe that IBM has lost its way and is in severe trouble for the future, and perhaps even its existence, like the BUNCH of its competitors it eliminated in the 1970s.

http://en.wikipedia.org/wiki/BUNCH

There appears that no one can effectively pierce the culture and environment at IBM Headquarters, let alone a loyal and inventive and successful and respectful exIBMer like me.

It may be now too late for IBM to buy SAP SE, as I have been suggesting for years, to get back in the applications software licensing world of Microsoft and SAP SE. And, for SAP that may be a very good thing.

However, I urge the IBM chairperson and the IBM board of directors to view the recent SAP S/4 HANA Business Suite launch presentation, and seriously ponder their future.

S4/HANA: What does SAP's next generation ERP mean for customers?

http://www.computerworlduk.com/in-depth/it-business/3596790/s4-hana-what-does-saps-next-generation-erp-mean-for-customers/

The current SAP chairman co-founded SAP AG in 1972 as an ex-IBMer and is now has a net worth of over eight billion dollars.
http://en.wikipedia.org/wiki/Hasso_Plattner

And, I urge the IBM chairperson and the IBM board of directors to then also briefly review my own Real-Time Program Audit (RTPA) patented software and this book, and seriously ponder their future without it.

All in my humble but expert opinion, the world of IBM today is as I describe it below, as an expert of more than five decades working directly with customers, trying to help IBM and watching its products age and decay.

As for Watson, ask Watson about which employees are making the most errors and need training, and how to implement real-time predictive autonomic computing, when that information is unused and unrecorded, as in lost, outside the executing program. .

Today, this is essentially the same computing processing world provided by corporate computing vendors as in the 1960s at the dawn of the stored program computer, when computers were a million times slower than computers today.

Today's programming languages and compilers are essentially the same ancient and arguably deficient, if not arguably defective, programming languages and compiler designs as in the 1960s, which provide no vision or sight or audit record, as in a security camera recording of the incredibly complex stream of billions of executing program statements and data and the exact moment-in-time of statement execution.

The result is that corporate computing customers are collectively wasting billions of dollars annually on unproductive corporate development staffs, who are blind to what is happening and must guess, and guess, and guess, at what they think could have or might have happened, rather than simply seeing what happened.

The additional huge costs of this unrecorded and unaudited real-time computer processing go far beyond the billions of dollars of payroll costs wasted annually on flat-out guessing and slowed development and slowed problem diagnosis and recovery. The often bloated corporate computing departments, the resistance to implement new applications and functions, and the need to retain "experts" who should understand how the programs work and how to maintain them and how to fix them are only several of many costs involved in this massive waste of corporate assets.

Corporate CEOs, CFOs, and stockholders can and should eliminate this massive waste of corporate assets while achieving high productivity and application capability by requiring that current and available technology be implemented, and they should search for corporate computing vendors or sources that will provide it.

IBM and others can hire tens of thousands of bright and eager new employees, as they have over the last five decades and expect similar results even up to the maximum unaided (uncorrected) capability of their employees.

However now IBM and others must make those bright and eager new employees, and its current employees, and its customers much, much "smarter" and capably and be highly productive and valuable, by providing them all with the productivity tools of today to, for the very first time, actually see and understand and manage what they are doing a million times faster than before.

I have directly communicated key elements of this to IBM executive management, including the following two letters to the IBM CEO and the IBM Board of Directors, without even a meeting.

July 4, 2013

Paul H. Harkins
Founder and CTO
Harkins & Associates, Inc.
816 Daisy Lane
West Chester, PA 19382

(Duplicate to)

Virginia M. Rometty
Chairman, President and CEO   IBM Board of Directors
IBM Corporation   IBM Corporation
1 New Orchard Road   1New Orchard Road
Armonk, New York 10504-1722   Armonk, New York 10504-1722

Subject: A critically needed Transformational Opportunity for IBM

Dear Ms. Rometty:

I am writing this letter directly to you, the CEO of IBM, as a fellow ex IBM Systems Engineer.

My primary objective is to provide you with my expert and independent perspective of more than 50 years in the IBM ecosystem, of the critical issues and critical decisions and potential huge opportunities really facing IBM now and in the future, without the dark cloud of having to project and protect and expand my turf and projects as a current IBMer.

You by now must be keenly aware, and perhaps distraught, of the immense difficulties of trying to wring revenue and profits and new IBM customers from the current aging portfolio of IBM offerings, most importantly the loss of IBM direct added value, and awareness of IBM to IBM customers and prospects. You must also be keenly aware of the declining morale of current IBMers in their ability to compete and succeed.

My forthcoming book *The Future of Corporate Computing* illustrates and details exactly how IBM can quickly succeed and return to greatness in the near future by embracing innovative initiatives of which it is incredibly apparently unaware, and I offer to IBM my consulting expertise and my revolutionary software patent and patent pending and my independent and honest analysis to IBM executive management now.

On July 4, 1976, the 200th anniversary of the United States of America, my fellow IBM Systems Engineer, Garry L. Reinhard, and I (employee number 740009) spent our holiday day and night alone (we had the keys) at the closed IBM Philadelphia Datacenter on the 22nd floor in the IVB building, frantically working as the authors of the announced but unfinished and undelivered IBM Installed User Program (IUP), "The System/370 Apparel Business System."

As we gazed at the spectacular fireworks from the darkened IBM datacenter windows, Garry and I both wondered aloud why we were not at home with our one-month-old baby daughters, or, like the other IBM employees we knew, enjoying the holiday at the Jersey shore.

Our answer was that we wanted to succeed and do extradinary things in our IBM careers, and this was a huge opportunity for us, one that all of the other IBMers we knew had laughingly rejected by tossing the IUP development opportunity blue letters (IUP development was in addition to normal IBM responsibilities and on off-hours time) in the wastebasket, sometimes as paper airplanes.

I had already been recognized in 1972 with an IBM national outstanding achievement award (a brass ship's clock) on the stage of the Fairmont Hotel in San Francisco as a top Systems Engineering Services (SES, the forerunner of Global Services) revenue producer. I was also the author of all other IBM IUP Apparel Business Systems program products, starting with the IBM System/3 Model 6 Apparel Business System IUP in 1973. These IBM Apparel Business System program products were installed in many hundreds of IBM accounts, mostly as net new accounts for IBM, and much of our design and code are still running today. And our IBM branch earned the top ranking throughout IBM largely because of the Apparel and Hotel and Casino IBM products that we developed.

My Apparel Business System IBM systems engineer co-author, Garry Reinhard, later was the primary developer of the IBM Hotel and Casino software in 1978 that has enabled IBM to dominate—even today—the hotel and casino industry. Garry won the prestigious IBM double eagle award (two suitcases full of cash), presented by the IBM GSD president, for his unique and critical development for IBM on the hotel and casino software.

And then someone much higher up in IBM decided that the company should become "the low-cost, high-volume hardware producer and to cut the fat," and that eliminated our opportunity for extradinary success at IBM—as well as the opportunity for IBM to dominate the applications software critical to keeping and expanding its customer base and revenue, including hardware, services, and software revenue. That IBM management decision turned out to be a mega-billion dollar disaster for IBM then and continues to negatively affect IBM today.

Since I left IBM in 1982, I have been continuously active in Information Technology, as a top-level consultant and adviser, author of several IT-related books, the author of U.S. software patent 6,775,827 **The Real-Time Program Audit (RTPA), and U.S. patent pending On-Demand Forensic Accounting Universal Program Auditing Language** U.S. PTO October 2012. My last major IT contract in 2012 was as an expert in a major Forensic Accounting criminal fraud case.

My books, software, patents, and consulting work reflect a unique knowledge and understanding of the IT industry today and are a continuation of our efforts toward extradinary success as IBMers, which were cut short when IBM decided to get out of the software business.

My very first customer interaction in 1961, as an IBM systems engineer while a Drexel Institute of Technology cooperative student for IBM, was to install an IBM unit record 402 Accounting Machine at a new account, Diamond Brothers Clothing in Philadelphia, Pennsylvania. I had taken a one-week customer 402 Accounting Machine wiring (control panel) class, and off I went to be an IBMer at a new customer.
Luckily, I was an ace at wiring the 402 control panel to do a simple invoice printing from punched cards fed at 50 cards per minute on the huge machine, and the customer was thrilled,

even though the 402 accounting machine could not even multiply or divide, just add and subtract, and was introduced by IBM about 1935. I installed many new IBM accounts in my exciting six- month IBM co-op effort.

Thus my IBM career opened in 1962 upon graduation from Drexel, and the understanding and conviction that customer satisfaction, true value added, and innovative application solutions are paramount, and hardware technology ultimately is almost meaningless to the customer.

Today, as in your letter from the Chairman in the IBM 2012 annual report (through page 11), IBM faces another fundamental transformation change away from hardware revenue to services and software, and a rapidly changing customer environment.

IBM must know that much of the software it acquired to drive revenue, such as Lotus, Websphere, Rational, and many others, is aging and outdated; is used by an ever smaller customer base; and is not recognized as added IBM value by end users.

"Big Data" and analytics today do not include any of the real-time computer- generated data provided by my U.S. patent, The Real-Time Program Audit (RTPA), which provides a quantum leap in autonomic computing and forensic accounting real-time capability, leading to huge productivity gains.

IBM must also know that there is a very real limit to the number of customers and prospects who are willing and able to spend extraordinary Global Services fees for results that can or soon will be products available elsewhere at much lower cost and effort.

As an IBMer who has observed the results of the work hundreds of thousands of IBMers over 50 years, it is clear to me that IBM is not on a long-sustainable growth path now.

My expertise and U.S. software patent and patent pending will greatly help IBM participate and succeed in significant new areas including Forensic Accounting, real-time true autonomic computing, true "Big Data" capture and analytics of computer program execution and data processes, and ultimately customer user applications, among many other new growth opportunities for IBM.

I propose a month long consulting contract directly to IBM executive management, with deliverables including executive presentations, interviews as desired, a formal published report, and an honest and independent analysis what IBM should and must do to return to greatness.

Best Regards,

Paul H. Harkins
Founder and CTO
Harkins & Associates, Inc.   www.harkinsaudit.com
816 Daisy Lane   610-431-1755
West Chester, PA, 19382   paulhark@aol.com

October 21, 2013

Paul H. Harkins
Founder and CTO
Harkins & Associates, Inc.
816 Daisy Lane
West Chester, PA 19382

(Duplicate to)

Virginia M. Rometty
Chairman, President and CEO
IBM Corporation
1 New Orchard Road
Armonk, New York 10504-1722

IBM Board of Directors
IBM Corporation
1 New Orchard Road
Armonk, New York 10504-1722

Subject: **Critically needed and Urgent Transformational Opportunities for IBM**

Dear CEO Rometty:

I am writing this letter directly to you, the CEO and Chairperson of IBM, as a follow-up to my enclosed letter to you and to the IBM Board of Directors of July, 4, 2013.

Thank you very much for directly responding to my July 4, 2013 letter by tasking two IBM senior vice presidents to meet with me on September 9, 2013 at 9:30 AM in Armonk to discuss my letter and to explore critically needed transformational opportunities for IBM.

Many thanks also to Stacey L. Lettis, Office of Rodney Adkins, who worked valiantly and very cooperatively to schedule and coordinate this important meeting. Unfortunately, neither senior vice president could or would attend the meeting on September 9, or at any other date known to me.

Thus, this follow-up letter to IBM executive management must serve as my sincere and honest attempt as a loyal and dedicated and very successful IBM ex-employee to rescue IBM from disaster, and to provide IBM with transformational opportunities for immediate success.

IBM today is in crisis and is in danger of slipping much further into the background and possibly into oblivion, as predicted in many current Internet articles and in financial reporting.

Greenberg: Risk Finally Catches Up With IBM - TheStreet

IBM faced very similar significant threats to its superiority and dominance and success in 1961, when I was first working at IBM as an IBM Systems Engineering trainee while a cooperative student at Drexel University.

In 1961 IBM competitors such as Honeywell had produced much faster and cheaper alternative computers modeled after the IBM 1401 computer, such as the Honeywell 200 computer, which were killing IBM sales and discouraging many IBMers who were helpless in competing with the competitor's faster and cheaper and actually much better offerings.

Honeywell 200 - Wikipedia, the free encyclopedia

The courageous actions of then–IBM CEO and Chairman Thomas Watson Jr. and the courageous IBM board of directors, to recognize the serious threats to IBM in 1961 resulted in a top-secret executive task force code named SPREAD whose purpose was to transform IBM into a powerhouse, resulting in the IBM System/360 announcement on April 7, 1964.

I was at that worldwide IBM System/360 announcement meeting in Philadelphia in 1964, and IBM once again ruled the computing world for decades.

Reviewing the fascinating **SPREAD** project documentation reveals the massive differences and infighting in the executive ranks of IBM in 1961—perhaps similar to that of today—and how that was overcome to the benefit of IBM and the world by strong executive leadership and action.

System 360 - IBM

www-03.ibm.com/ibm/history/ibm100/us/en/icons/system360/words/

The team, code-named SPREAD Task Group (Systems Programming, Research, Engineering and Development) were told by Learson to stay at the New ...

High stakes

Indeed, production and sales of the System/360 meant a complete re-engineering of the company's development resources, processes and strategy. In addition to posing a daunting marketing challenge, it would also kill off IBM's golden goose—a disorganized but very profitable line of existing computer products. As with any bold risk worth taking, there were passionate experts on either side of the System/360 debate.

"Bob and I fought bitterly with two separate armies against and for the 8000 series. He was arguing that we ought not to do a new product plan for the upper half of the business, but for the total business. I was arguing that that was a put-off, and it would mean delaying at least two years. The battle ... went to the Corporate Management Committee twice. We won the first time, and they won the second time—and Bob was right. The wonder is that it developed at all."

Ms. Rometty, as CEO and Chairperson of IBM you and your IBM board of directors have the opportunity and I believe the responsibility, to rescue IBM once again and to once again have IBM rule the computing world with your own SPREAD project and action.

Fortunately, this SPREAD project would produce incredibly successful results—in a few months rather than in three years—and cost magnitudes less than the cost of the 1961 SPREAD project. You can transform IBM into an effective and efficient and successful and more profitable leader in computing once again.

This new SPREAD project would open vast new markets for IBM and directly enhance the cognitive capability of IBMers and customer and user personnel many times, thus resulting in much less than one-half of the number of people doing far more and better work than is done now.

Someone in IBM must eventually recognize that many of the IBM software offerings today are based on the ancient and now severely deficient design and architecture of the original IBM System /360 of 1964, which I personally programmed while I was a very successful IBM Systems Engineer, and programmed for decades while I was a top software consultant.

Someone at IBM must also realize that IBM is acquiring the wrong companies and the wrong technologies, as is evidenced in the declining revenues and competitive position of IBM, and the apparent hodgepodge of technologies and products.

Someone at IBM must also realize that utilizing low-cost and inexperienced personnel is not the way for superior products or superior service; in fact, a very few superior people, or even one superior person, such as Dr. Frank Soltis (inventor of the IBM System/38 computer), consistently and spectacularly outperform a multitude of average people.

Someone at IBM must also realize that the huge "store" of the installed IBM customer base, the source of revenue and potential for IBM for half a century, is crumbling–and why.

Someone at IBM must recognize the huge stifling bureaucracy of IBM, and its deadening effect of the success and innovation of IBM, and its immense cost.

Someone at IBM must recognize that IBM offerings and services must directly face and directly benefit the customer, including the public, and that IBM has largely disappeared from the view and the appreciation of the customer and the public.

My IBM Installed User Program (IUP) program products as in the enclosed GSD magazine article were a huge success because IBM customers could directly buy the IBM IUP software product and the GSD IBM computer and be productive immediately because of IBM.

Someone at IBM must recognize that there is a vast and untapped opportunity for real-time, mobile, visual, graphical, and auditable software and hardware as used in accounting, forensic accounting, government regulation, and in autonomic computing, among others directly from IBM.

For instance, the Intuit Corporation (INTU) offers QuickBooks and other very popular accounting software to millions of customers, and now offers a QuickBooks Enterprise Solutions Hosting Service for the Cloud.

Intuit Debuts New Products at Innovation Gallery Walk

My wife is an accountant with multiple customer clients who all use Intuit QuickBooks, and she said they all particularly like the QuickBooks software and especially the drilldown feature.

My patented IBM i (AS/400) Real-Time Program Audit (RTPA) software provides the real-time data recording used for drilldown in corporate computing, forensic accounting, and autonomic computing, but IBM has rejected it, which illustrates another possible or probable major shortcoming of the current IBM External submission process and evaluation.

CEO Rometty, I believe that you have the courage and the opportunity and capability to successfully transform IBM from severe difficulty to incredible success, as did CEO Tomas Watson Jr. and the IBM board of directors in 1964.

I am happy to help IBM as appropriate.

Best Regards,

Paul H. Harkins
Founder and CTO
Harkins & Associates, Inc.
816 Daisy Lane
West Chester, PA, 19382

www.harkinsaudit.com
610-431-1755
paulhark@aol.com

8 My Conclusions (and my Opinion)

My conclusions and my opinion about the Future of Corporate are mine and mine alone, and are as objective and honest and fair as I can be. They are based on fifty-five years of observing and actively participating in corporate computing and watching successes and failures on a personal scale and on a monumental scale, and on interactions with hundreds of companies and thousands of my peers around the world.

My conclusions and my opinion are necessarily heavily influenced my own personal career, especially with having my dream IBM career of more than twenty years come crashing down due to forces beyond my control or even my comprehension. Then I had picked up the pieces that I could control and strive for success essentially on my own capability and ambition in a world after IBM.

My conclusions are very painful for me and bring me no joy, but are what I see is the reality of today and the hope for the future for those who seize immense opportunity as others have before them.

In summary, corporate computing has been dominated by IBM for generations, long before the 1960s when I started my career, and for good reason. IBM was able to invent itself under Thomas Watson, and then reinvent itself in 1961 with the IBM System/360 computer under his son Thomas Watson Jr with revolutionary "bet the company" technology initiatives that transformed corporate computing and created huge success, and importantly kept IBM ahead of its competitors.

IBM was also able to reinvent itself again during my IBM career, again under Thomas Watson Jr., in 1969 with a whole new line of business computers developed by the new upstart GSD division of IBM in Rochester MN. The new computers were very easy to use, immensely productive, and profitable for IBM, multiplied the IBM customer installed base, and enabled the easy and rapid development of customer application software.

These revolutionary transformations of IBM enabled IBM to dominate the corporate computing industry and drive most of its competitors out of business, as the BUNCH and also driving Xerox out of the computer business, thus starting SAP.

But then, the IBM crucial major inventions and reinventions, as above, stopped and have remained stopped until today. Thomas Watson Jr. retired as IBM chairman in 1971 and in my opinion the IBM vision was lost, replaced by executive shuffling and varying executive strategies which are still going on today and which have left IBM in a three decades-plus long relative or even absolute decline without apparent end.

IBM essentially just stopped innovating and apparently tried to play it safe and hold on while it enabled SAP, Microsoft, Oracle, Apple and others to evolve and prosper, often using ideas that IBM discarded.

However, there was no penalty for IBM executive management then or now, with immense compensation, bonuses, stock options, and perks being showered on many, and with no chargebacks except perhaps the declining IBM business and the weight of history.

So, what does this all mean, and how can IBM and others survive, grow and succeed in the future?

I believe that the single most significant trigger event that transformed IBM from the dominant powerhouse to its status today was the 1982 IBM executive decision to become "the low-cost producer" as has been already discussed in this book.

That decision, in my opinion, set the path for IBM from then on until today with its multiple alternate layoff (termination) and hiring of tens-of-thousands of IBMers, with the hope that somehow brand new people not familiar with IBM will be able to save IBM and effectively work with IBM customers.

That decision, in my opinion, effectively ended the ability of IBM to develop, support market crucial customer sophisticated applications software and reap close customer relations and a huge and continuing source of licensed revenue. That has not been lost on SAP or Microsoft, among others.

So what should IBM do now?

I asked that question to a group of some long retired IBMers at our monthly retiree luncheon meeting. All of the retired IBMers were very successful in their long and productive IBM careers and are happy and comfortable in retirement. For the most part, they just shrugged and continued eating their soup, as that is now not their problem or challenge.

I think that IBM must stop the many decades of shuffling executive management directives and shuffling hot topics of the day and press releases, and realize what got IBM so deeply in trouble in 1982, and how IBM might get out of it now and in the future.

IBM must once again reinvent itself, and make a quantum leap forward by multiplying the power, capability and productivity of the human brain and utilizing the whole new universe inside the computer.

IBM should not buy SAP, but instead embrace the brilliance of SAP, and together develop a whole new universe of computing and success.

Sap is brilliant to strive for simplicity, not complexity, as were Steve Jobs and the U.S. Navy with the KISS principle.

My personal experience with IBM is just the opposite, including requiring programmers to guess what is happening inside the computer rather than showing them the information.

IBM seems focused on making the computer execute nanoseconds faster, when the computer is already a million times faster than when I started at IBM, by making the human interface, as in arcane programming and sub-programming, ever more unreadable.

Perhaps the SAP motto: Keep it Simple is a huge reason for their brilliance and for their huge success.
http://www.sramanamitra.com/2014/08/11/saps-new-motto-keep-it-simple/

Or, perhaps it is **SAP's Run Simple Strategy** as in **Run Simple with SAP - Technology Solutions from SAP** is the reason for their brilliance and for their success.
http://discover.sap.com/runsimple?campaigncode=CRM-XH15-POR-PPC-BRND&utm_source=google&utm_medium=PPC&utm_term=run%20simple%20+sap&utm_campaign=NA-NA-AC-Brand-General%20(Paid%20Search-%20Google%20-%20Br)

How Steve Jobs' Love of Simplicity Fueled A Design ...

http://www.smithsonianmag.com/arts-culture/how-steve-jobs-love-of-simplicity-fueled-a-design-revolution-23868877/?no-ist

KISS principle - Wikipedia, the free encyclopedia
http://en.wikipedia.org/wiki/KISS_principle

So what is the result?

IBM finds out that tens of thousands of IBMers hired decades ago cannot perform well enough to be financially viable, after decades of IBM experience, and expects to hire tens of thousands of new people off the street to do a better job.

My view is that virtually all of the qualified people IBM hires over decades are intellectually about the same, and that the way to boost intellectual performance, capability, productivity and value are with productivity tools, such as the Real-Time Program Audit (RTPA) software, and with innovation, and with experience.

I am pro-IBM, not anti-IBM, but this is just the way the world really works in both physical and mental tasks.

Today, corporate computing is literally stuck in limbo as significant corporate computing productivity advancements cannot be made based on hardware technology advancements. Computer hardware is about *one million times* faster now and is infinitely less expensive than in the 1960s, and that speed enhancement can no longer generate the quantum productivity advancements now needed by IBM and its competitors and future competitors to be the most successful and to grow.

Today, this is essentially the same computing processing world provided by corporate computing vendors as in the 1960s at the dawn of the stored program computer, when computers were a million times slower than computers today.

Today's programming languages and compilers are essentially the same ancient and arguably deficient, if not arguably defective, programming languages and compiler designs as in the 1960s, which provide no vision or sight or audit record, as in a security camera recording of the incredibly complex stream of billions of executing program statements and data and the exact moment-in-time of statement execution.

The result is that corporate computing customers are collectively wasting billions of dollars annually on unproductive corporate development staffs, who are blind to what is happening and must guess, and guess, and guess, at what they think could have or might have happened, rather than simply seeing what happened.

The additional huge costs of this unrecorded and unaudited real-time computer processing go far beyond the billions of dollars of payroll costs wasted annually on flat-out guessing and slowed development and slowed problem diagnosis and recovery. The often bloated corporate computing departments, the resistance to implement new applications and functions, and the need to retain "experts" who should understand how the programs work and how to maintain them and how to fix them are only several of many costs involved in this massive waste of corporate assets.

Corporate CEOs, CFOs, and stockholders can and should eliminate this massive waste of corporate assets while achieving high productivity and application capability by requiring that current and available technology be implemented, and they should search for corporate computing vendors or sources that will provide it.

IBM and others can hire tens of thousands of bright and eager new employees, as they have over the last five decades and expect similar results even up to the maximum unaided (uncorrected) capability of their employees.

However now IBM and others must make those bright and eager new employees, and its current employees, and its customers much, much "smarter" and capably and be highly productive and valuable, by providing them all with the productivity tools of today to, for the very first time, actually see and understand and manage what they are doing a million times faster than before.

The world of corporate computing today is far different than the world of electro-mechanical corporate computing in 1960, as illustrated in the movie "The Apartment".
https://www.youtube.com/watch?v=x356ll3hTxg

That seems obvious when now we see how labor intensive corporate business processing was in 1960. But as one, who worked in that environment, it seemed normal and high technology at the time compared to the work environment of the previous generation. Virtually all of those jobs have long since disappeared as employees became ever more expensive and electronic machines became ever less expensive and more powerful.

Today the corporate computing in-house programmers, software developers, and support personnel are once again the people who are no longer productive and cost-efficient as they once might have been necessary and valuable. That is largely because they are using the ancient and outdated tools of the 1960s, resisting change for whatever reasons. They must quickly become significantly more productive and valuable and somehow "smarter" to survive being eliminated and some of them can survive and prosper if they individually take action to leapfrog their peers in productivity and value.

I discovered along the way in my own career road that the real job of the industrial engineer that I trained to be at Drexel, and the job of the computer systems analyst that I became, and the job of the corporate executive that I also became and advised, is to wring out every dollar of value and productivity possible from corporate employees in order to compete and survive and to prosper.

So, I advise corporate computing personnel to understand that their world has changed and they are probably not productive or valuable enough to compete using ancient and outdated technology, and they are probably targeted for elimination.

I advise corporate computing personnel consider and embrace the productivity enhancing and value enhancing technology that I present in this book (**Appendix H U.S. Patent – Real-Time Program Audit (RTPA)**, and to take action immediately to thus leapfrog over those who resist doing so.

I advice corporate executive management, including the CEO and CFO to evaluate their corporate computing environment, including budgets, productivity, security, availability, and competitive advantage with their competitors, and to **require** their corporate computing staffs to utilize proven high-productivity and valuable tools now available. **Corporate Executive Migration Path to Cloud computing**

My personal experiences including some successes and some failures together with my observations of other successes and failures are the only real basis that I have for my advice. If the reader will reflect on his or her own personal successes and failures and reflect on the reasons for success or failure, it may be because of the single factor of being able to compete. It is actually somewhat disconcerting for me to seemingly exhaustively relate my own worldwide computing accomplishments when so many of my intellectually smarter peers worldwide seemed to have floundered or just gotten by. But, I can only relate my experiences and somewhat generalize why I believe the reasons for the disparate results. Specifically, you must find a way to succeed beyond your peers and competition, and take action to succeed on your own,

In short and in my experience, intellectually superior people are most always at the top of their class from kindergarten through university and beyond. And rightly so, as given an approximate level playing field or learning field of academics mostly learned from reading textbooks and interacting in the classroom, intellectually superior people are virtually more successful than average people.

This intellectually superior capability and capacity, and most often equally superior social capability gets intellectually superior people management positions and often executive management positions.

This has always worked out reasonably well, including the ability and capability of intellectually superior corporate computing developers, programmers and support staff to out-perform their more average peers during the 1960s, thus providing some level or results, however unproductive and costly and clumsy.

The problem is that now computers are one million times faster and more powerful and inexpensive than in 1960, and the computing environment is much more complex.

The intellectually superior corporate computing developer or programmer is today simply overwhelmed whit what is being processed inside the computer and having to literally guess (speculate) what is happening or did happen inside the computer with no permanent record of what happened.

Consider the TV quiz show *Jeopardy!* where the IBM Watson computer beat intellectually superior human contestants handily. And consider how these defeated human must have felt, aside from their guaranteed prizes that a machine was "smarter" than they were.
Apparently other *Jeopardy!* format shows of the Watson computer vs human competitors have been publicly run where the human competitors could not even press the clicker to answer without the response time of Watson being delayed. And then there is the consistent Watson computer beating the chess grand masters.

The short of this is that even the "smartest" humans are not as capable or "smart' in seeing, understanding, analyzing and acting on computer information as is the computer itself for information intensive tasks.

That the "smartest" human is crippled or not able to successfully compete with the computer in information intensive tasks is actually only acknowledged in the face-to-face contests such as *Jeopardy!* or a chess match, where the winner is immediate and obvious. This is similar to other physical face-to-face contests such a track and field, where a physically superior (or perhaps sometimes a mentally superior) athlete clearly wins and accepts the prize for victory, and the losers take action to succeed the next time.

This drives athletes to strive for every possible advantage, legal or otherwise, to achieve immediately recognized success and the rewards of success, and to avoid immediately recognized failure. And, this immediate and obvious competition for success drives superior performance.

Conversely and incredibly importantly, in non-face-to-face information intensive environments such as in corporate in-house computing, in Securities and Exchange Commission (SEC) financial fraud auditing, in the Internal Revenue Service (IRS) auditing, in the National Security Agency (NSA) auditing, and in corporations such as IBM and others, there is virtually no competition, certainly no face-to-face immediate competition for success and victory or defeat. And there is rarely a penalty for failure, as there is rarely if ever an acknowledged failure.

There is no race or contest, and there is only the in-place, in-house winner, who is understandably resisting change.

IRS says it's using technology from JFK's time - Feb. 3, 2015
http://money.cnn.com/2015/02/03/pf/taxes/irs-budget-cuts/
(Note the Herman Hollerith plug board)

The winners are always the entrenched and in-place personnel as there is no face-to-face direct competition to determine success or competence, and the victory is continued unproductive employment and continuing nice paychecks and perks. Unfortunately the losers are defrauded investors such as in the Madoff Ponzi scheme, ineffective and expensive and unproductive auditing systems in government costing the U.S. taxpayer, and finally corporations failing to compete.

The Club No One Wanted To Join-Madoff Victims In Their Own Words

http://www.amazon.com/Wanted-Join-Madoff-Victims-Their-Words/dp/0982250932/ref=sr_1_1?ie=UTF8&qid=1422216300&sr=8-1&keywords=No+one+wanted+to+join+the+club

 Thus my invention, The Real-Time Program Audit (RTPA) software to audit, record, and real-time analyze the entire computer generated information and data processed inside the computer. This will make you incredibly "smarter", much more productive, more valuable, and much more competitive, if *you* take action to use it.

The good news is that now IBM, or someone after IBM, has a huge and a viable opportunity to do what IBM has refused to do and resisted from doing over the last four decades.

That is to reinvent itself from the ground up by leapfrogging over all competitors and entering huge and available vast new markets with current available revolutionary technology.

The even better good news is that every single person now has a huge and a viable immediate opportunity to become incredibly "smarter" in corporate computing information intensive capability and to leapfrog those who resist change to incredible success

Even to the exotic Road to Singapore.

It is now time for a yet another set of Stanford or Harvard students, or a few frustrated IBM engineers like the founders of Microsoft, Oracle, SAP SE, Apple, Google, Cisco and others to seize the available opportunity to change the world, become famous, and become multi-billionaires.

These current multi-billionaires picked over the bones of failing or failed companies for discarded or neglected or distained or otherwise available huge opportunity, they found it, and they took action to succeed.

Appendix A Corporate Computing Migration paths over time

Corporate executive migration path to the processing cloud, normally from in-house corporate computers, follows tried and true and successful previous corporate migrations from manual systems and computing as in hand posted ledgers to Herman Hollerith unit record accounting machines starting in 1890, to stored program computers starting in about 1958.

Each of the corporate computing migrations were initially implemented by a few companies to achieve efficiencies and productivity and some competitive or economic advantage over their competitors, Ultimately, virtually all companies and competitors were forced to migrate to the most productive and economic environment to compete and survive, and the personnel who could not or would not make that migration were displaced.

The migration paths then and today are purposely generalized and somewhat simplified as corporate executive management did not then and do not today need to be involved in the minute details involved, except for objectives, schedules, costs and quality issues, as the conversions were routine and cost effective if properly managed. A typical IBM systems engineer would do many, if not dozens of these conversions in that time period.

All of the migration paths involved in corporate computing: from manual systems to Herman Hollerith unit record machines, from Herman Hollerith unit record machines to stored program in-house computers, and from in-house stored program computers to the processing cloud are relatively routine and may take about three or more months depending on the size and complexity of the migration.

Migration of corporate in-house computers to cloud processing typically includes all of the in-house computing capability including IBM type mainframe or midrange computers such as the IBM i (AS/400) and all of the network based systems of the corporation.

Migration from manual systems to Herman Hollerith unit record accounting machines

The conversion plan from manual system processing to the first Herman Hollerith corporate computers was normally a standard conversion plan provided by the computer vendor, such as IBM, that consisted of an implementation plan such as this:

- Finding a large room or space for the massive IBM unit record processing machines, including keypunch machines, machine operators, and supplies including tons of blank cards

- Construction and installation of the space and electrical requirements
- Identification of the current manual processing environment and applications
- How and when to convert the manual applications to the new unit record accounting machines
- Assignment of qualified personnel to perform the conversion (usually including IBM systems engineers to document the paperwork information flow and wire (program) unit record machines for the desired applications
- Installation of the new unit record facility and unit record machines
- Conversion of the data into punched cards and testing
- Implementation of the new unit record applications
- Termination of any no longer needed manual equipment and displaced personnel
- Hopefully but not necessarily documentation of the new system including Standard Operation Procedures (SOP)
- Implement new advanced applications with the new and better technology

I personally converted dozens of companies from manual processing to IBM Herman Hollerith unit record machine processing (a punched card was a unit of record), and from Herman Hollerith unit record processing to stored program computers, and also from manual processing directly to stored program computers, almost always three or four companies concurrently.

One particularly interesting and educational conversion for me from manual computing to Herman Hollerith unit record computing was at the Wheaton Glass Company in Millville New Jersey.

Wheaton Glass installed a large IBM 407 Accounting Machine (top-of-the-line) installation in the company headquarters, and in fact displacing the glass laboratory of the president Frank H. Wheaton, while he was in Europe. Apparently the (unnamed) executive president had a dilemma as to where he could install the critically needed IBM equipment, a dilemma he shared with me, his young IBM systems engineer who was responsible to make the new IBM equipment work before Mr. Wheaton returned home to his lab. The executive vice president needed a really big space and could only choose between president Wheaton's glass lab (something like what I imagined Thomas Edison's glass lab must have looked like a few miles away in Menlo Park), and the Wheaton ballroom where I understood that president Wheaton's daughter was to be soon married.

I got the new IBM installation up and running, including interfacing the Friden Flexowriter billing machines to the new IBM installation with what seemed like miles of eight channel punched paper tape with a new machine for me, the 047 paper tape to punched card converter. This created an 80 column IBM punched card as the unit of record for each billing line from the Flexowriter.

I was not at Wheaton Glass the day president Wheaton returned from Europe, but I did observe and learn much about corporate management at that installation in my first year at IBM.

Wheaton Glass Company could release and reclaim that large and useful space now, if they have not already, by migrating their in-house computing systems to the processing cloud.

The WheatonArts Glass Studio is a state-of-the-art glassblowing facility. The Studio offers eleven glory holes, ranging in size from 9"-21". There are three furnaces on site, with one available for hot casting. We also boast twenty annealing ovens, including a 48"x 24" bell kiln, 2 garages and two pick-up ovens available for rent.

Rentals are scheduled from Tuesday-Sunday between 9am-5:00pm.

• Glory Hole rental includes approximately 10 lbs of glass per hour.
• $2.00 charge for each additional pound per hour, including moil and scrap glass.

http://www.wheatonarts.org/artiststudios/glassstudio/rent

Migration from Herman Hollerith unit record to stored program computer

Tens of thousands of large and small companies, like the previous Gulf Oil processing center illustration transitioned their data processing from Herman Hollerith unit record systems to computers in the 1960s and 1970s, and did so quickly and effectively by following a known successful conversion strategy and plan.

The computer vendor even offered some conversion tools such as the "From Control Panel to Stored Program" manual on the IBM 1401 to the data entry utility programs (later used by Bernie Madoff) to enter raw data into the computer.

That conversion plan from Herman Hollerith unit record processing to computers was normally a standard conversion plan provided by the computer vendor, such as IBM, that consisted of several major parts including:

- Identification of the current unit record environment and applications
- Identification of the relatively small space needed for the stored program computer
- How and when to convert the data and applications to the new computer
- Assignment of qualified personnel to perform the conversion including writing computer programs (usually including IBM often systems engineers)
- Installation of the new computer facility and new computer
- Conversion of the data and applications and testing
- Implementation of the new computer applications
- Termination of the unit record equipment and displaced personnel
- Hopefully but not necessarily documentation of the new system including Standard Operation Procedures (SOP)

Migration from in-house stored program computer to the Cloud Computing

Tens of thousands of large and small companies, including several of the customers I have consulted with have transitioned or are transitioning their in-house corporate computing systems to Cloud Computing or to managed services. Managed Services includes many additional services perhaps including collocated datacenters, backup, help desk, backup and recovery and other services.

That migration or conversion plan from in-house corporate computers to cloud computing or to managed services where computing is performed remotely is probably the easiest of all the prior migrations. This is because instead of changing the corporation in-house processing procedures and personnel, this conversion to remote processing is primarily changing the computer and computer operations from in-house at the corporation to remote locations via communication lines.

The cloud computing vendor, or datacenter normally hosts or provides computing services to many corporations via communication lines and has very comprehensive and tested procedures and staff to do virtually the entire conversion.

Corporations migrating from in-house computers to cloud computing or managed services can expect 24 hour by 7 day availability of corporate computing and current powerful hardware and software and very high speed communication lines, along with a host of additional services at a surprisingly reasonable cost.

Many corporations with in-house computing systems migrate virtually all of their in-house computers, including network computers to managed services or cloud computing, not just the in-house computer processing business applications.

Once corporate computing is off-site, executive management can focus on effectively managing the corporate computing with a very much wider and flexible and economically viable range of options.

Another IBM customer that I installed from along with a host of other manual systems when I was a Drexel Cooperative student at IBM in 1961, Samual S. Pennock, has recently made the complete cycle from manual processing, to unit record processing by me, to an in-house IBM AS/400 computer, and recently to cloud computing. I consider this to be a home run, and Pennock has finally released the in-house space and in-house resources after some fifty years, while achieving 24 hour by 7 day availability as is illustrated below.

DSS Success Story - Pennock Co. - YouTube
www.youtube.com/watch?v=ooIRltlJ0uc ▾
Jan 30, 2014 - Uploaded by Distributed Systems Services, Inc.
Pennock Company shares how DSS has helped simplify their IT infrastructure and managed their data center ...

It is somewhat exhilarating for me to view the success of SS Pennock and viewing the Pennock Co. video and realize that I started that long process more than fifty years ago by designing their IBM 402 Accounting Machine Accounts Payable check.

Appendix B The Power of Traceability

The ability to record and verify exactly what has happened (or is happening) inside the computer at a particular moment has widespread usefulness in matters of consequence in Autonomic Computing.

Paul H. Harkins

Harkins Audit Software, Inc.

www.harkinsaudit.com.

An increasingly critical problem confronting corporate computing and programmer capability is the inability of computer programs to record and analyze the entire execution of the program and data in real time. This lack of traceability prevents true autonomic (self-healing) computing and prevents real-time and permanent analysis of exactly what executing program statements and data are actually processed. Therefore, as computers become millions of times more powerful and program environments become ever more complex and critical, the programmer is still using tools developed at the dawn of computing—tools like step debugging, reconstruction of events, and guessing--to attempt to <u>understand</u> what happened, rather than simply <u>observing</u> exactly what happened and automatically implementing true autonomic computing to self-heal the program.

*In this paper I present a technique--**Electronic Program Auditing**—and a software tool–**The Real-Time Program Audit**—designed to capture and record all of the executing source program statements in virtually any programming language, along with all of the data being processed and the moment-in-time of the statement execution without programmer intervention. This technique and unique tool provide a video-camera-like recording of the exact environment of the entire program execution (or selected conditions of the execution) as the program executes—thus delivering the potential of true autonomic computing and capturing previously unrecorded critical information. This paper presents my technique and tool, some actual and possible applications, and evidence of the value of my approach.*

1 Introduction

Today's computer hardware is incredibly powerful: Indeed, IBM recently announced a supercomputer reaching 1.026 petaflops (1 petaflop is equal to a quadrillion, or one thousand trillion, calculations per second) [1]. However, much of that processing power is wasted, since even the latest software cannot come close to fully harnessing it and fully utilizing the information generated.

Current corporate computer software programming languages were introduced more than a decade ago (Java, in 1995); COBOL, introduced in 1959, has been in use for half a century [2,3]. When all these corporate languages were introduced, computers were millions of times less powerful than they are today, and software applications and environments were significantly more simple than the sophisticated applications and hardware now driving corporate computing—including, for example, the "stream computing" for real-time data analysis that IBM introduced in May 2009 [4].

Full Electronic Program Auditing [5]—which I define as "the complete real-time recording, auditing, and analysis of all executing computer source statements, all data processed, and the moment-in-time of each statement execution to electronic storage (normally disk)"—is the most obvious, comprehensive, and powerful technique for enabling today's software to take full advantage of today's hardware and application requirements and implementation true autonomic computing [6]. Electronic program auditing provides a video-camera-like, real-time permanent record of everything happening in the computer.

This ability to record and verify exactly what has happened (or is happening) inside the computer at a particular moment has widespread usefulness in matters of consequence, as in true Autonomic Computing. Since full recording, auditing, and analysis of all program execution allows for a permanent and unalterable record of the actual program execution, this technique could be used, for example, to expose financial fraud; provide verification—without the possibility of alteration—of actual ballots cast in an election; and provide proof of transactions for Sarbanes-Oxley legislation [7] purposes. The importance of moment-to-moment verification of activity has already been recognized in other contexts: For instance, the city of London [8], hotel casinos [9], and even cruise ships [10] have installed thousands of video cameras to record and analyze virtually all public activity in order to provide a true, unaltered, real-time, and contemporaneous permanent record of significant activity.

Electronic program auditing was initially implemented by using a patented software invention—**the Real-Time Program Audit (RTPA)** [11]—to make existing programming languages capable of recording to disk the execution of all source statements, data processed, and the moment of time as a pre-processor to make the existing source statements smart enough to record their execution in real time, together with all data processed.

Figure 1 shows a partial source program in a free-format programming language that is an example for real-time program auditing. The executable source statements end with a semi-colon, similar to Java and C++ programming languages, and contain programming language commands that are audited based on the command, and program variables that are audited with the data processed by the executing statement. This source program reads a data file named DATAFILE and converts the program variable DATA to hexadecimal (two hexadecimal characters in a program variable **szhex** per input data character) using a function **cvthc**, then the program converts the hexadecimal variable back into the input variable character data with function **cvtch**. This sample source program is a modified source from www.rpgworld.com.

```
0001.00 H BNDDIR('QC2LE')
0002.00 H Dftactgrp(*NO)
0003.00   * Source program from www.rpgworld.com
0004.00 fdatafile  if   e              disk
0005.00
0006.00 D cvthc         PR                        extproc('cvthc')
0007.00 D   ssRtnHexVar                65532A     OPTIONS(*VARSIZE)
0008.00 D   ssSourceVal                32766A     CONST OPTIONS(*VARSIZE)
0009.00 D   nHexLen                      10I 0    VALUE
0010.00
0011.00 D cvtch         PR                        extproc('cvtch')
0012.00 D   ssRtnCharVar               32766A     OPTIONS(*VARSIZE)
0013.00 D   ssInputHex                 65532A     CONST OPTIONS(*VARSIZE)
0014.00 D   nHexLen                      10I 0    VALUE
0015.00
0016.00 D ssHex         S             40A
0017.00 D ssChars       S             20A
0018.00 D Result        S             40A
0019.00
0020.00 /free
0021.00   // Source program example from www.rpgworld.com
0022.00        read datafile;
0023.00        dow not %eof(datafile);
0024.00   // convert character to hex
0025.00           cvthc(ssHex : data : %len(data)*2);
0026.00        eval  result = ssHex;
0027.00        if (ssHex <> *blanks);
0028.00   // convert hex to character
0029.00   cvtch(ssChars : ssHex : %len(%TrimR(ssHex)));
0030.00        eval  result = ssChars;
0031.00        endif;
0032.00        read datafile;
0033.00        enddo;
0034.00        eval  *inlr = *on;
0035.00        return;
0036.00 /end-free
```

Figure 1. Source program for electronic program auditing.

Future programming languages could easily incorporate this real-time RTPA audit recording, auditing, and analysis capability directly into the language itself. And the powerful business intelligence (BI) [12] tools of today could be linked directly into these programming languages in order to provide real-time analysis and autonomic computing.

The processing transactions—relatively small in number in comparison with the exponentially increasing power of the computer—can easily be fully program-audited, stored, and analyzed with electronic program auditing and RTPA without noticeable processing overhead.

The reality of corporate business computing is that the vast majority of computing processes a quite small number of transactions—typically, several thousands of customer orders, invoices, inventory transactions, employee payroll processing, etc., in a typical program execution, rather than millions or billions of transactions. And the number of transactions processed each year in a typical application, such as data on the students in a university, gets only incrementally larger even if the business grows rapidly. Another characteristic of corporate business computing is that the corporate databases such as customer, inventory item, employee and transaction activity are typically changed or updated by normal transaction processing, making rerunning or reconstruction of the exact same processing conditions in exactly the same processing environment (including time) impossible.

State of the Art. There are many program step-through debuggers, interactive program debuggers, and capture-replay techniques and tools [13,14,15] that attempt to display the details of program statement execution. All of these techniques have critical limitations in that they stop the program execution (as in debuggers), allow program and data alteration, or capture only selected parts of the program execution, and require programmer intervention and knowledge of the program. These debuggers can provide, at best, a tiny part of the information needed for program analysis. All of these techniques fail to provide the exact processing conditions as the original processing program, as at least the time has changed and other programs may be altering or have altered the data files. However, there is no known software other than the Real-Time Program Audit (RTPA) that provides full electronic program recording, auditing, and analysis of all executing program statements and all data processed in real time as the program executes, without intervention and without program or data alteration, while providing a permanent record of the original exact environment of the program execution for real-time or future analysis.

Advantages of This Approach. The objective of recording, auditing, and analyzing the entire program statement execution, all data processed, and the moment-in-time in real time (as in video-camera recording) is simple, paradigm-shifting, powerful, and takes advantage of advancing computer capability and greatly reduced cost. This objective has been proven to be easily achievable in multiple programming languages, and it does not require any programmer or operational intervention at the time of program execution.

Real-time recording, auditing, and analysis of the original program execution, with the exact data and conditions at original program execution, provides a permanent record of exactly what happened, thereby eliminating the need for program rerunning, debugging, and guessing what happened. And the wealth of information recorded from the executed source statements, data, and moment-in-time provides information for real-time autonomic computing, business analysis and optimization, and business intelligence that is not possible without full electronic program auditing.

The programmer and operations need not even be aware that electronic program auditing is being performed by the smarter enabled source program, which, like a concealed video camera, provides a permanent and unobtrusive record of events. Electronic program auditing, like that provided by RTPA, audits and records in real time, but does not change or alter the program statements or data, as does most debugging software.

Newly emerging software, such as the IBM System S real-time business analysis [16] would benefit greatly by using Real-time Program Audit output, including data processed, to view not only externally available data now written to disk by other programs, but also the information of the executing source statements and all data processed as the majority of program computation and data is never written to external files. Only electronic program auditing records and audits the actual program statement computations and data content of every statement executed and thus eliminates the opportunity for fraud by manipulating summarized data. For example, the classic fraud of altering summarized voting machine tabulations by adding 25 votes to one candidate's totals and subtracting 25 votes from a competing candidates total vote count is exposed (and thus prevented) only by electronic program auditing which audits the computation and summarization of each and every voter. Additionally, electronic program auditing as in RTPA provides the capability for all logically related sub-programs in an application to be sequenced by the moment-in-time each statement was actually executed, regardless of the architecture or structure of the programs.

2 Real-Time Program Audit Technique

The Real-Time Program Audit (RTPA)[11] software overall technique is to enhance the capability of source programs in virtually all corporate (mainstream) programming languages to record the execution of source program statements (including auditing all source statements executing in real time, all data processed, and the moment-in-time) to an independent audit log or receiver. This independent audit log file is normally a disk file.

Thus, the RTPA auditing provides full electronic program auditing by enabling or enhancing the input source program to audit itself, even if the programming language does not provide recording and auditing capability.

2.1 Overview of the Approach

This technique consists of two phases: audit-enabling or enhancing the original input source program and the resulting executable object program to make it smart enough to completely audit its execution, and then executing the audit-enabled object program in the normal program execution environment to produce the real-time audit file and audit spool file and real-time business analysis. Future programming languages could easily provide this auditing capability as part of the standard programming language capability by providing for the automatic auditing and recording of all of the source statements and data executed similar to current disk file journaling.

2.2   Audit-Enabling the Original Input Source Program

Figure 2 shows the initial implementation of full electric program auditing in the Real-Time Program Audit (RTPA), U.S. Patent 6,775,827 [17], as a pre-processor that inputs source programs of audited programming languages, copies the source program to an enabled source program, and allows the enabled program source statements to be fully audited and recorded in real time during program execution together with all data processed, and outputs an expanded or enabled source program. Executable program object programs are compiled from the enabled source programs and have the capability of auditing themselves during program execution. The audit default is to record and audit all executing program statements and all data processed. However, extensive conditional auditing is also provided to allow focus and auditing on issues of interest.

RTPA provides real-time full recording and auditing capability of executing programs by examining every executable statement or command in the original source program, and adding the capability to log the source statement, the content of statement variables (the data processed by the executing statement), and the moment-in-time to an independent audit file when the statement is actually executed.

The basic process for RTPA auditing is quite similar for most programming languages, and is defined in detail in U.S. Patent 6,775,827.

For the programming language being audited, define all valid language commands, or operation codes, and the auditing to be performed when processing a source statement using that command. For example, in COBOL the IF reserved word (command) would be defined, together with all other commands such as MULTIPLY, together with their RTPA auditing attributes.

1. For instance, the COBOL statement with a MULTIPLY command would be audited in real time in the enabled source program *after* the MULTIPLY command was executed, together with the data of program variables in the MULTIPLY source statement. The COBOL statement with an IF conditional command would be audited in real time in the enabled source program *before* the IF command was executed, together with the data of program variables in the IF source statement, in case the IF condition was not true, so the RTPA audit would show the contents of the IF statement variables that caused the IF condition statements not to be executed.

2. Define an audit recording file for logging all audit output. This file will be included in the audit-enabled source program.

3. Optionally define a printer spool file audit log.

For each original source program to be audit-enabled:

1. Copy the original input source program to an audit-enabled source program. The original input source program is not altered.

2. Compile the original source program and retrieve all detailed program information needed to fully audit the program and program variables.

3. Read the copied source program and audit every executable source statement so that it is recorded in the audit file when the statement is executed, together with the content of statement variables and the moment-in- time of execution.

4. Scan each executable source statement to identify the language command and program variables and special conditions such as complex statement groups such as IF, AND conditional statements.

5. Audit enable each executable source statement including the statement itself, program variables data processed, and the moment-in-time when the statement is executed, together with control information such as the program name.

6. Audit complex statements (commands) such Execute Format (EXFMT) which is a WRITE then READ as a group with the elapsed time between them (user wait time), and audit complex conditional statements like IF, AND as a group.

7. Audit comment statements to provide better program comprehension.

8. Time stamp the moment-in-time of the executing statement to the audit file.

9. Output control and analysis information including the program ID and statements group level to the audit file, so that real-time auditing and analysis may be easily accomplished.

10. Output the file definition for the independent audit file, which will contain the full electronic program audit of the executing program statements, and optionally output the printer spool audit file definition.

11. Optionally selectively audit based on audit criteria or conditions or audit output limits.

12. Compile the audit-enabled source program and create an audit-enabled executable object program.

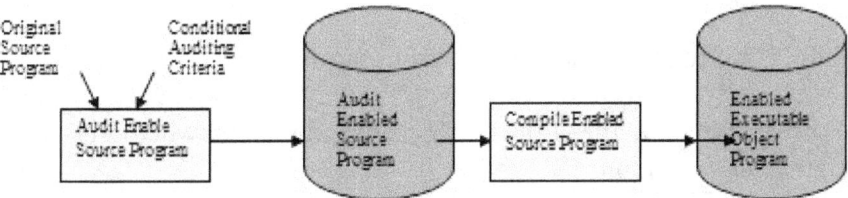

Figure 2. Real-Time Program Audit (RTPA) pre-processor overview.

Figure 3 shows a partial listing of the audit-enabled source program statements with RTPA inserted statement to record and audit every executing source program statement, all data processed, and the moment-in-time the statement was executed. The subroutines or sub-procedures actually accomplishing the output to the RTPA audit file and RTPA audit analysis (spool) file, such as EXSR Z$INIT to initialize the audit file and analysis spool file, vary by the programming language being audited. However, these routines always audit and output the source statements being executed, the data content of program variables in the executing statement, date, and the moment-in-time the statement is executed, together with control information such as the program name.

The complete input example source program, the RTPA audit-enabled source program, and the RTPA audit file and audit analysis output for this CVTTOHEX example program are available on www.harkinsaudit.com in the Users Manual and in RTPA videos.

The audit inserted source statement EXSR Z$INIT; opens the audit file and initializes the inserted audit routines in the audit-enabled source program (and in the executable audit-enabled object program) and outputs audit control information including the program name, job number, and moment-in-time of the program activation. The inserted Z$INIT source statement also outputs optional spool file audit report headings which include the moment of program initiation. The inserted audit source statement EXSR Z$GENS; outputs the source statement to the audit file.

Note: The RTPA source statements inserted into the audit-enabled source program to accomplish full electronic program auditing could easily be inserted by the language compiler (processor) as part of a smarter audit-enabled programming language by the language vendor. A similar technique for accomplishing disk record journaling before-and-after images has long been available as part of the vendor-provided operating system software.

The elapsed time of complex source statements like EXFMT (Execute Format) is computed including the elapsed time it takes for a terminal user to respond to a WRITE then READ statement and the elapsed time it takes for external program calls to other programs or sub-procedures. The exact time a statement is executed and the elapsed time of the statement is invaluable in program traceability, analysis and optimization.

For example, the expanded audit capable source program contains the following source statements to read the DATA file input disk record and to audit the read statement and the data being read. The inserted audit statement are in blue.

```
66              read datafile;
67                      Z$SRC# =  2      ;
68                      EXSR       Z$GENS;
69                      EXCEPT     Z$00002;
70                      IF         NOT %EOF;
71                      EXCEPT     Z$00002D;
72                      ENDIF;
```

The input source statement **read datafile;** reads the next record from the disk file.

The inserted audit statements below output the audit of the read datafile; statement when it is executed with the moment-in-time of the statement execution

```
67                      Z$SRC# =  2      ;
68                      EXSR       Z$GENS;
69                      EXCEPT     Z$00002;
```

The inserted audit statements below output the audit of the actual data if a disk record was read.

```
70                      IF         NOT %EOF;
71                      EXCEPT     Z$00002D;
72                      ENDIF;
```

```
61 C                    EXSR      Z$INIT
62  /free
63   // Source program example from www.rpgworld.com
64                      Z$SRC# =  1     ;
65                      EXSR      Z$GENS;
66         read datafile;
67                      Z$SRC# =  2     ;
68                      EXSR      Z$GENS;
69                      EXCEPT    Z$00002;
70                      IF        NOT %EOF;
71                      EXCEPT    Z$00002D;
72                      ENDIF;
73                      Z$SRC# =  3     ;
74                      EXSR      Z$GENS;
75         dow not %eof(datafile);
76   // convert character to hex
77                      Z$SRC# =  4     ;
78                      EXSR      Z$GENS;
79         cvthc(szHex : data : %len(data)*2);
80                      Z$SRC# =  5     ;
81                      EXSR      Z$GENS;
82                      EXCEPT    Z$00005;
83         eval  result = szHex;
84                      Z$SRC# =  6     ;
85                      EXSR      Z$GENS;
86                      EXCEPT    Z$00006;
87                      Z$SRC# =  7     ;
88                      EXSR      Z$GENS;
89                      EXCEPT    Z$00007;
90         if (szHex <> *blanks);
91   // convert hex to character
92                      Z$SRC# =  8     ;
93                      EXSR      Z$GENS;
94         cvtch(szChars : szHex : %len(%TrimR(szHex)));
95                      Z$SRC# =  9     ;
96                      EXSR      Z$GENS;
97                      EXCEPT    Z$00009;
98         eval  result = szChars;
99                      Z$SRC# =  10    ;
100                     EXSR      Z$GENS;
101                     EXCEPT    Z$00010;
102        endif;
103                     Z$SRC# =  11    ;
104                     EXSR      Z$GENS;
105        read datafile;
106                     Z$SRC# =  12    ;
107                     EXSR      Z$GENS;
108                     EXCEPT    Z$00012;
109                     IF        NOT %EOF;
110                     EXCEPT    Z$00012D;
111                     ENDIF;
112        enddo;
113                     Z$SRC# =  13    ;
114                     EXSR      Z$GENS;
115        eval  *inlr = *on;
116                     Z$SRC# =  14    ;
117                     EXSR      Z$GENS;
118                     EXCEPT    Z$00014;
119                     Z$SRC# =  15    ;
120                     EXSR      Z$GENS;
121        return;
```

Figure 3. Source program with RTPA auditing.

2.3 Execution of the Audit-Enabled Program

Figure 4 shows the processing of the audit-enabled executable Object Program with the output of Real-Time Program Audit output, including data processed and real-time audit analysis, business intelligence tools, and business analytics and optimization (BAO) tools [18]. The Real-Time Program Audit Query analysis tool provides extensive real-time analysis of the audit output file, including the capability to view executing subprograms, source program statements, and program variable contents of different programming languages in a logical application in moment-of-time sequence as the computer actually executes them.

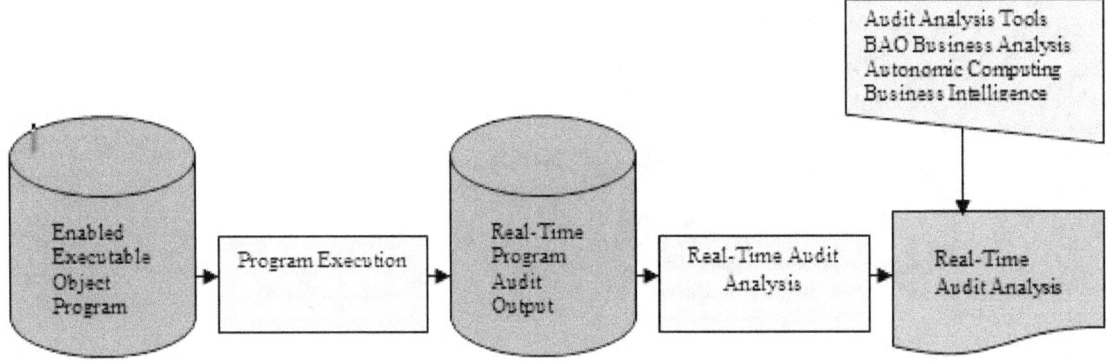

Figure 4. Real-Time Program Audit (RTPA) audit output and analysis.

Figure 5 shows the RTPA real-time audit output file from execution of the audit-enabled program. The audit output file is a *permanent contemporaneous record of the original program execution.*

The electronic program audit of the executed program contains the source program statements as they were actually executed, and shows the compile listing statement numbers as in the original compile listing of the original source program, together with the data executed by the program and the moment-in-time of the statement execution.

The audit output of the read statement below shows the **read** statement and the data read by the read statement with the moment-in-time of the read statement execution The DATA- line is the variable DATA followed by the contents of the variable DATA.

```
   22              read datafile;                                              19.46.37.452
                                                                    File-      00002 Key-
      DATA-1234567890ABCDEFGHIJ
```

The **dow not (eof)** statement (do while not end-of-file) and the source statements 23 and 24 are executed if the read statement read an input record into the variable DATA.

The comment statement at line 24 **// convert character to hex** is audited each time the comment statement is executed. Auditing executing comment statements is very important in programmer comprehension of what actually happened in the executing program.

158

The **cvthc** statement converts the variable DATA into hexadecimal format (two characters per input character) and places the output in the variable szHex.

```
  23           dow not %eof(datafile);
  24      // convert character to hex
  25           cvthc(szHex : data : %len(data)*2);                              B01
                 F1F2F3F4F5F6F7F8F9F0C1C2C3C4C5C6C7C8C9D1
                      1234567890ABCDEFGHIJ
                                1234567890ABCDEFGHIJ
```

```
Program-CVTTOHEX       Convert Character to Hex Data in PF DATAFILE    Obj Lib: Z$AUDITE    Initiated:  6/10/09
          CVTTOHEX     CVTTOHEX
    Job: 334040              User Profile: PHH         Source Type: RPGLE    Y    Source File/Library: QRPGLESRC
    Line#                                                                                          Do# SrcId
     21      // Source program example from www.rpgworld.com
     22           read datafile;
                                                                           File-      00002 Key-
DATA-1234567890ABCDEFGHIJ
     23           dow not %eof(datafile);
     24      // convert character to hex
     25           cvthc(szHex : data : %len(data)*2);                              B01
                    F1F2F3F4F5F6F7F8F9F0C1C2C3C4C5C6C7C8C9D1
                         1234567890ABCDEFGHIJ
                                   1234567890ABCDEFGHIJ
     26           eval   result = szHex;
                    F1F2F3F4F5F6F7F8F9F0C1C2C3C4C5C6C7C8C9D1
                         F1F2F3F4F5F6F7F8F9F0C1C2C3C4C5C6C7C8C9D1
     27           if (szHex <> *blanks);                                           01
                    F1F2F3F4F5F6F7F8F9F0C1C2C3C4C5C6C7C8C9D1
     28      // convert hex to character                                           01
     29           cvtch(szChars : szHex : %len(%TrimR(szHex)));                    B02
                    1234567890ABCDEFGHIJ
                         F1F2F3F4F5F6F7F8F9F0C1C2C3C4C5C6C7C8C9D1
                              F1F2F3F4F5F6F7F8F9F0C1C2C3C4C5C6C7C8C9D1
     30           eval   result = szChars;
                    1234567890ABCDEFGHIJ
                         1234567890ABCDEFGHIJ
     31           endif;                                                           02
     32           read datafile;                                                   02
                                                                           File-DATAFILE  Key-
DATA-KLMNOPQRSTUVWXYZ!@#
     24      // convert character to hex
     25           cvthc(szHex : data : %len(data)*2);                              B01
                    D2D3D4D5D6D7D8D9E2E3E4E5E6E7E8E95A7C7B40
                         KLMNOPQRSTUVWXYZ!@#
                                   KLMNOPQRSTUVWXYZ!@#
     26           eval   result = szHex;
                    D2D3D4D5D6D7D8D9E2E3E4E5E6E7E8E95A7C7B40
                         D2D3D4D5D6D7D8D9E2E3E4E5E6E7E8E95A7C7B40
     27           if (szHex <> *blanks);                                           01
                    D2D3D4D5D6D7D8D9E2E3E4E5E6E7E8E95A7C7B40
     28      // convert hex to character                                           01
(truncated output)
     34           eval   *inlr = *on;                                              01
                    1
     35           return;                                                          E01
```

Figure 5. RTPA audit file output from Audit-Enabled Executable Object Program.

Real-time program audit analysis with the RTPA Query tool, conventional business intelligence (BI) tools, business analysis and optimization (BAO) tools such as the IBM System S, and autonomic computing can access this real-time RTPA audit file and spool file and achieve real-time analysis and true autonomic computing while the program is executing. Audited source statements and source statement data including the contents of program variables provide unprecedented capability to analyze detailed program information never before available for analysis and action.

Figure 6 shows the right side of the audit output containing control information including the conditional do level, source statement number, change date, and time stamp of the moment-in-time of the execution of each statement.

Figure 5 and Figure 6 are actually the left-hand and right-hand sections of the same 198 position audit output, and together illustrate the executing source statement, all data processed by the executing statement, the moment in time of the executing statement , the date and time, and control information including the program do level and the program id. The audit output can ne queried and analyzed immediately in real-time or analyzed later with a variety of existing analytic and business intelligence tools.

```
o Hex Data in PF DATAFILE        Obj Lib: Z$AUDITE    Initiated:   6/10/09 19.46.37.452    PAGE    1    RPGLE    Y

  PHH            Source Type: RPGLE    Y    Source File/Library: QRPGLESRC Z$AUDIT        CVTTOHEX   JOB 297949
                                                 Do#  SrcId ChgDat    Seq#   Time
  www.rpgworld.com                                           080612   2100  19.46.37.452
                                                                            19.46.37.452
                                      File-      00002 Key-

                                                                            19.46.37.452
                                                           080611   2200  19.46.37.452
  %len(data)*2;                                     B01     080612   2300  19.46.37.452
  8F9F0C1C2C3C4C5C6C7C8C9D1
  890ABCDEFGHIJ
      1234567890ABCDEFGHIJ
                                                           080611   2400  19.46.37.452
  F0C1C2C3C4C5C6C7C8C9D1
  5F6F7F8F9F0C1C2C3C4C5C6C7C8C9D1
                                                     01     080611   2500  19.46.37.452
  C1C2C3C4C5C6C7C8C9D1
                                                     01     080612   2600  19.46.37.452
   : %len(%TrimR(szHex)));                           B02     080611   2700  19.46.37.452
  FGHIJ
  3F4F5F6F7F8F9F0C1C2C3C4C5C6C7C8C9D1
            F1F2F3F4F5F6F7F8F9F0C1C2C3C4C5C6C7C8C9D1
                                                           080611   2800  19.46.37.452
  IJ
  0ABCDEFGHIJ
                                                     02     080611   2900  19.46.37.452
                                                     02     080612   3000  19.46.37.452
                                      File-DATAFILE   Key-

                                                           080611   2200  19.46.37.456
  %len(data)*2;                                     B01     080612   2300  19.46.37.456
  9E2E3E4E5E6E7E8E95A7C7B40
  RSTUVWXYZ!@#
      KLMNOPQRSTUVWXYZ!@#
                                                           080611   2400  19.46.37.456
  E3E4E5E6E7E8E95A7C7B40
   (output truncated)
                                                     E02    080611   3100  19.46.37.456
                                                     01     080611   3200  19.46.37.456

                                                     E01    080611   3300  19.46.37.456
```

Figure 6. RTPA audit output right side of report with the moment-in-time of the executing statement.

2.4 Additional Technical Details

This section discusses several of the most relevant technical details of this approach that relate to its implementation into programming languages with varying capabilities to produce audit files (normally disk) and audit spool (printer) files and to allow business analysis and optimization tools (BAO) to be utilized for autonomic computing.

2.4.1 Assumptions

First, this Real-Time Program Audit (RTPA) electronic program audit technique should work for virtually all current corporate programming languages that have the capability to produce an audit file as a disk file output, and optionally a printer spool file output in the programming language. Programming languages without the capability of producing an audit file as a disk file output or a printer spool file, such as the IBM Control Language Program (CLP), can currently be audited with this technique using calls to sub-procedures or subprograms to a language such as COBOL that does provide auditing capability. Future implementation of real-time program auditing in the vendor distributed language would provide this auditing capability in a manner transparent to the programmer for both the executing source statements and for all the data processed with an audit file similar to the current vendor supplied disk journal file for before and after images of disk record updates, additions, and deletes.

Second, the audit enabling statements and techniques currently inserted into the copied, expanded, and enabled source program should not alter the normal execution of the source (enabled object) program. Again, this could be easily incorporated by the vendor of the programming language directly into the language without requiring a separate preprocessor step to audit-enable the source program. Then, audit processing would produce a hugely beneficial and transparent result (similar to video-camera recording) of virtually all corporate computer processing.

Third, the program execution processing time of the audit-enabled statements, including creation of the real-time audit file, incurs very little additional processing time, as is evidenced in the audit output in Figure 5. Real-life execution
of audit-enabled program processing has shown that audit processing requires minimal additional time or overhead for typical corporate application environments for which the original processing time for an application is only a few processing seconds. Additionally, audit recording and logging may be turned on or off based on conditions or the size of the audit file. The emergence of solid-state disk drives (SSDs) [19], which have throughput of some twenty times that of conventional disk drives, ensures that RTPA auditing overhead will be insignificant in the future. That, coupled with the immense and largely unused processing capacity, presents a huge opportunity for pervasive implementation of full electronic program auditing.

3 Possible Applications of This Technique

Eight possible applications of this real-time program audit technique are discussed: Full electronic program auditing of computer program execution; debugging and analysis of computer program execution; business analysis and optimization (BAO) of executing program statements and data; verification of the business initiative "Data as an Asset on the Balance Sheet" [20]; real-time autonomic computing using executing program statements and data; vote-count tabulation verification [21]; and security and authentication verification[22].

3.1 Electronic Program Auditing of Program Execution

This technique, together with the dramatic increase in power and decrease in cost of computing, increases a paradigm shift in how computing is accomplished and analyzed. Full electronic program recording and auditing should become the normal method of corporate computing, making obsolete many of the ancient and inefficient techniques in use today and greatly multiplying the understanding and capability of programmers. This full electronic program audit information would be available as a permanent and unalterable record of the details of exactly how the program executed and exactly how the data were processed.

3.2 Debugging and Analysis of Program Execution

Step-program debuggers and interactive program debuggers were developed literally at the dawn of computing in the 1950s, when programs were small and relatively simple, and only one program at a time was processed by the computer. These debuggers are also slow and labor intensive, requiring programmer intervention by manually stopping the program and they require program knowledge to be used. And, the debuggers can never exactly re-create the original environment, since at least the time and computing environment will have changed by the time the debugging begins. Debuggers also require speculation—guessing about what might have happened or where the problem might be. Real-time electronic program auditing totally eliminates the need for step debuggers and eliminates the need for guessing what happened during program execution.

3.3 Business Analysis and Optimization (BAO) of Executing Program

Much critical business-analysis information processed in executing programs, including exactly how the information is computed statement by statement, is simply not recorded, and therefore is not available for business analysis and business intelligence tools.

For example, end-user screen error messages are typically not recorded, but electronic program auditing records all of the end-user error messages and all the data displayed to the end user and entered by the end user. This error-message recording, auditing, and analysis allows needed end-user training to be customized to the end user and pinpoints how a series of end-user errors can result in error or abnormal processing.

For successful error detection and correction, knowing the content of program variables that are currently not recorded can be crucial. Consider the need for comparison of the estimated carton weight of packed products to the actual packing-line real-time scale carton weight, including the estimated weight of each product. This comparison is critical to successful detection of cartons not matching the estimated carton weight. Real-time recording of all program variable contents at the moment of time of statement execution allows real-time analysis of products in this error carton with products in other error cartons—signaling a potential error in the estimated weight of a particular product, without the need to open the error carton. This allows for the kind of rapid and sure resolution of problems, like errors in estimated weights of a product that may be changed and corrected at any time during the day that would not be possible without this detail information—and it enables the prevention of future packing-weight errors for cartons of the product. Current applications not providing this program-auditing capability simply cannot provide this real-time analysis and correction capability, and result in massive and time consuming error detection and correction procedures and missed shipments.

3.4 Verification of the Initiative "Data as an Asset on the Balance Sheet"

The emerging business initiative that data will become an asset on the balance sheet [20], together with the attention drawn by recent massive corporate financial frauds, requires that summarized data must be verifiable with drilldown not to other summarized data as is normally the output of computer processing, but to the actual program statements and program variable contents used to create the information. Program auditing is the only technique that will accomplish this ultimate drilldown to the original and unalterable audit record created during program execution.

3.5 Real-time true Autonomic Computing Using Executing Program Statements and Data

In order for true autonomic (self-healing) computing [12] to be self-managed or to be self-healing, it is obvious that the executing program must have access to, and utilize, real-time detail information that is often computed in the executing program, such as error messages, and is not available externally outside the program, and never output to disk as part of the application. The RTPA audit file, and spool file do provide all of this internally created program information (all executing source statements, all data processed, and the moment-in-time the statement was executed) and make this information immediately available for a full range of business intelligence tools and business analysis and optimization (BAO) tools, and especially for true autonomic computing. These analysis tools can be utilized by the executing program in real time to provide autonomic computing, as in the case of end-user screen-error message analysis and action, and by the executing program itself in real-time to correct itself. Similar true autonomic computing analysis and correction could be used in automobile "Black box" program real-time analysis of engine, temperature, automatic throttle control, brakes, transmission, seat belt, air bag, electrical, tire pressure, and other systems with self-correcting function to stop the car in extreme emergencies such as "run away" cars. Other major software catastrophes such as the "Blackberry" internet routine software update that caused outages of hours and days, could be either prevented with better testing and analysis as in RTPA, or mitigated, instantly found or corrected with true autonomic computing using RTPA audit output.

3.6 Vote-Count Tabulation Verification

Real-time program auditing can be utilized in vote-count tabulation verification [21] to ensure that all votes counted by a computer program, such as mark sensed voting sheets or electronic voting, are verified with a *permanent and unalterable* audit record of *actual votes* as each vote is accumulated. This auditing technique could be very easily implemented, and, if mandated, would eliminate actual and much attempted electronic-voting machine and online voting fraud at every level of voting.

3.7 Internet Security and Authentication Verification

The emergence of the Internet and remote processing technologies such as Cloud Computing [22], has greatly increased the susceptibility of computer programs to hacking, unauthorized use, and the resulting damage by this hacking of computers at every level of business and government, as the computing is external to the corporate location.

Electronic program auditing and analysis provides unalterable and potentially permanent and accessible proof of exactly what was processed at the program executing statement level; what data were processed at the executing statement level; the moment-in-time of the executing statement level; and the user ID or program name and object information responsible for the processing activity. This, the ultimate drilldown for security and authentication, provides real-time audit information for autonomic computing security and authentication, analysis, and corrective action during the execution of the program and later for detailed review and analysis.

3.8 Ultra-Fast Trading, time is a huge competitive advantage

Ultra-fast stock trading [23] and ultra-fast computers with sophisticated quantitative analysis software give computers closest to the source of stock trades (as in the same building) a time advantage in receiving stock trade information faster than those computers farther away who must use communication lines to access the stock trades. This allows ultra fast trading of information not yet available to the public. Real-time program auditing of the actual programs forming the stock trade , before it is sent to a communication line outside of the computer, would allow true autonomic computing of the trade as it is being computed and before it is available to ultra fast trading techniques.

4 The Tool: RTPA

This implementation of full electronic program auditing is the Real-Time Program Audit (RTPA) software tool [11], which is written in the RPG programming language and is implemented for several programming languages, including RPG, COBOL, and the IBM Control Program Language (CLP). The original source program is not altered in any way, and the copy of the source program is audit-enabled without programmer intervention, so that full auditing is output to an audit file when the audit-enabled program is executed.

During execution of the audit-enabled executable object program, the program is intended to execute the original source statements exactly as in the original source program. The inserted RTPA source statements are executed inline with the executing original source program statements, merely and only to record the executing source program statement, the content of program variables in the executing original source statement, and the moment-in-time of execution of the original source program statement. The executable object program of some programming languages such as RPG, COBOL, and CLP have a program template that includes the source program statement and program variable definitions to allow for step through or interactive debugging and program variable analysis. Implementation of full electronic program auditing by software vendors in the operating system compilers would utilize this available information for audit recording, rather than the auditing preprocessor having to save this information in the audit-enabled executable object program. Thus, software vendor-supplied full electronic program auditing capable compiles would provide the capability to output the executing source statement to the audit file when the source statement was executed and the moment–in-time of execution as part of the operating system.

5 Empirical Evaluation

The feasibility and value of full electronic program auditing in the corporate programming environment was first tested by manually inserting the RTPA additional source statements to a copy of a large production original source program. When the resulting expanded source program was compiled to an expanded object program and executed in a normal corporate processing environment, the resulting real-time audit file and audit spool file was extremely useful in the real-time analysis of the program. This manually inserted program auditing was performed on several important source programs and greatly simplified the development and maintenance and support of these programs.

No step-debugging or program rerunning was required to solve programming issues, since the audit file and audit spool file had already produced the information needed for analysis.

Once the concept and value of full electronic program auditing was proved, the manual auditing process was generalized and automated as in today's RTPA software implementations, and the automated auditing implementation was generalized for other programming languages.

It has been proven that—through its simplification of programming and analysis and its provision of real-time program data, internal to the program, that had never before been available—full electronic program auditing (as in the RTPA implementations), represents a paradigm shift in programming and computing.

Though the need for structured programming is widely acknowledged and useful to programmers viewing the static program source structure, full electronic program auditing diminishes this need, since all the executing statements from many routines or sub-procedures in a logical application written in several programming languages can be sequenced in the moment-of-time the statement was executed, regardless of program organization. The emergence and astonishing capability of online search engines to almost instantly gather together the widely dispersed information to satisfy a search request is an example of how a logical request for related data created at different times does not rely on the data being stored next to or near each other.

Electronic Program auditing is essential and needed in virtually all corporate processing environments and in virtually all corporate applications, including all financial applications. Virtually all of these corporate applications are processed in a multiprocessing environment, where multiple independent jobs are running simultaneously in the computer, and where each program is running in a single processing thread [24]

My book "How to Become a Highly Paid Corporate Programmer" [25] illustrates the capability and usefulness of electronic program auditing, the usefulness of breaking programs into logical phases for development and production analysis, and prototyping the programs during development.

Indeed, thousands of original source programs have been audit-enabled using the Real-Time Program Audit (RTPA) software, and then audited using the resulting expanded audit-enabled executable object program in normal processing environments. Typically, an original source program of several thousand source statements is copied, audit-enabled into an audit-enabled source program as in Figure 2 and then compiled into an audit-enabled executable object program as in Figure 4, in less than 5 elapsed seconds on a small corporate computer.

6 Related Work

I know of no other implementation of full electronic program auditing software, as in the Real-Time Program Audit (RTPA) software—at least in the corporate programming environment.

The many debuggers and capture-and-replay tools such as SCARPE[15] provide useful tools for program review and analysis, but they sometimes allow program and data modification, and they do not provide a full and complete real-time and permanent audit record of the entire program execution of all executing source statements and all data processed as output of the executed programs.

Large hardware and software vendors, such as IBM, Hewlett-Packard, and Oracle, need a new killer application that implements the immense benefits of full electronic program auditing, and utilizes the largely unused capacity of current technology to fully implement the emerging initiatives of autonomic computing, data as an asset on the balance sheet, and real-time business analysis and optimization (BAO) technology.

7 Conclusion

I have described a technique for implementing full electronic program auditing and autonomic computing with the Real-Time Program Audit (RTPA) software. Of the many new applications made possible with electronic program auditing, eight have been suggested. Finally, I have presented the initial implementations of full electronic program auditing in several corporate programming languages, and I have demonstrated how easy, effective, and valuable it is to implement electronic program auditing in a corporate programming language.

One significant conclusion is that the entire world of corporate computing can be made dramatically more productive, auditable, capable, and simple by harnessing the power of the computer to fully electronic program-audit, record, and analyze the execution of all computer programs. Academic computing would also greatly benefit from electronic program auditing, particularly in teaching and learning computer languages and by being capable to fully record and observe the actual statement computations being performed in programs that are often executed only once and that do not have otherwise verifiable results.

Productivity tools that are now conventional—such as the Microsoft Word Spelling and Grammar tool and the security and virus tools that run in the background of Word document processing—are key examples of the significant benefits provided by smarter processing with productivity tools. Full electronic program auditing, as in the Real-time Program Audit (RTPA), provides smarter processing that is revolutionary and more comprehensive—indeed, it will work industry-wide and provide a critical new level of real-time information from the executing program itself.

Mandated standards and regulations in many industries have evolved over the years to provide needed safety and security for all who use cars, such as the automobile industry requirements for airbags and collision protection standards, and health care strict safety standards. These mandated standards have allowed much greater safe use of automobiles worldwide, while greatly reducing risks and accidents. It is now time and feasible that corporate computing and corporate and government develop and implement effective and powerful real-time safety, security and auditing .standards and capability for all corporate computing through tools such as full electronic program auditing.

Key next steps are to improve and expand the capability and use of full electronic program auditing into other corporate programming languages, and particularly to expand the use of real-time audit information in autonomic computing and in business analysis and optimization (BAO) tools.

References
[1] IBM's Roadrunner breaks petaflop barrier, tops supercomputer list June 2008
http://news.cnet.com/8301-10784_3-9971006-7.html
[2] The Java Programming Language http://www.engin.umd.umich.edu/CIS/course.des/cis400/java/java.html
[3] The COBOL Programming Language http://www.engin.umd.umich.edu/CIS/course.des/cis400/cobol/cobol.html
[4] IBM touts 'stream computing' for real-time data analysis
http://www.computerworld.com/action/article.do?command=viewArticleBasic&articleId=9133081
[5] Electronic Program Auditing http://www-949.ibm.com/software/rational/cafe/docs/DOC-3263
[6] Autonomic Computing http://www.research.ibm.com/autonomic/overview/solution.html
[7] The Sarbanes-Oxley Corporate Governance Compliance Guide. http://www.soxtoolkit.com/sox-govern.htm
[8] CCTV in London. http://www.urbaneye.net/results/ue_wp6.pdf
[9] Public and private applications of video surveillance and biometric technologies
http://www.library.ca.gov/crb/02/06/02-006.pdf
[10] Cruise Line: FBI finished preliminary investigation http://blogs.phillyburbs.com/news/bct/tag/norwegian-cruise-lines/
[11] The Real-Time Program Audit (RTPA) software http://www.harkinsaudit.com
[12] Business intelligence http://www.businessweek.com/technology/content/mar2009/tc2009032_101762.htm
[13] Computer Program Debugging http://ponce.sdsu.edu/legacy_tales_so_far_so_good.html
[14] Debugging an interactive application with full prompt
http://publib.boulder.ibm.com/infocenter/iadthelp/v7r5/index.jsp?topic=/com.ibm.etools.iseries.debug.doc/topics/tbisintp.html
15] SCARPE: A technique and tool for selective capture and replay of program executions.
http://www.cc.gatech.edu/~orso/papers/joshi.orso.presentation.pdf
[16] IBM launches new real-time data analysis software
http://www.reuters.com/article/technologyNews/idUSTRE54C0PO20090513?feedType=RSS&feedName=technologyNews
[17] United States Patent 6,775,827 Harkins August 10, 2004 Real-Time Program Audit software
http://patft.uspto.gov/netacgi/nph-Parser?Sect1=PTO1&Sect2=HITOFF&d=PALL&p=1&u=%2Fnetahtml%2FPTO%2Fsrchnum.htm&r=1&f=G&l=50&s1=6,775,827.PN.&OS=PN/6,775,827&RS=PN/6,775,827
[18] IBM Business Analytics and Optimization
http://www-935.ibm.com/services/us/gbs/bus/html/bcs_centeroptimization.html
[19] **IBM makes the case for power systems SSDS. http://www.itjungle.com/tfh/tfh060109-story01.html**
[20] I**BM Council Predicts Data Will Become an Asset on the Balance Sheet http://biz.yahoo.com/iw/080707/0413582.html**
[21] Florida Election Stolen
http://www.americanfreepress.net/html/florida_election_stolen.html
[22] Top five cloud computing security issues
http://www.computerweekly.com/Articles/2009/04/24/235782/top-five-cloud-computing-security-issues.htm
[23] Ultra-fast trading software much sought http://www.upi.com/Business_News/2009/08/24/Ultra-fast
[24] Single Threaded Programs http://wiki.answers.com/Q/Single_threaded_Process_and_Multi-threaded_Process
[25] How to Become a Highly Paid Corporate Programmer McPress 2004
http://www.amazon.com/Become-Highly-Paid-Corporate-Programmer/dp/158347045X/ref=sr_1_1?ie=UTF8&s=books&qid=1259713704&sr=8-1

Appendix C On-Demand Forensic Accounting and Analytics

On-Demand Forensic Accounting and Analytics

Paul H. Harkins

Harkins & Associates, Inc.
www.harkinsaudit.com

Abstract

Forensic accounting, or financial forensics, currently lacks the ability to proactively record, access, examine, and analyze in real time all of the financial activity used in financial transactions and financial reporting.

The "black box' of opaque and inaccessible computing financial detail information has allowed and enabled numerous recent huge "Ponzi schemes," including the Bernard Madoff and Allen Stanford cases, which cost investors billions of dollars while humiliating the responsible government regulators and causing the investing public to lose confidence in stock-market investing.

This paper describes a revolutionary and transformational patented forensic accounting and analytic capability that captures and records all executing program source statements and data, and puts a time stamp inside corporate computer programs as they produce financial reports. This makes ultimate drill-down to the source of financial information available—on-demand, instantly, and remotely—to authorized government regulators, auditors, and investors.

1. Introduction

Forensic accounting, or financial forensics [1], currently lacks the ability to proactively record, access, examine, and analyze in real time all of the financial activity used in financial transactions and financial reporting.

The "black box' of opaque and inaccessible computing financial detail information has allowed and enabled numerous recent huge "Ponzi schemes," including the Bernard Madoff and Allen Stanford [2] cases, which cost investors billions of dollars while humiliating the responsible government regulators [3] and causing the investing public to lose confidence in stock market investing [4].

This paper describes a revolutionary and transformational patented forensic accounting and analytic computer software capability [5] that captures and records all executing program source statements and data, and puts a time stamp inside corporate computer programs as they produce financial reports. This makes ultimate drill-down to the source of financial information available—on-demand, instantly, and remotely— to authorized government regulators, auditors and investors.

The huge potential of forensic accounting was addressed by Dr. James Gordon Brown when he was Britain's Chancellor of the Exchequer: "What the use of fingerprints was to the 19th century and DNA analysis was to the 20th, forensic accounting will be to the 21st century [6]. The above-described patented on-demand Forensic Accounting computer software, "Real-Time Program Audit", or RTPA, enables the pervasive worldwide implementation of Dr. Brown's vision and dramatically empowers forensic accountants. In short, RTPA creates a read-only permanent audit record of exactly what is happening in the computer program, in real-time, including executing source statements, data (the contents of variables) and a timestamp.

On-Demand Forensic Accounting and Analytics provides a video camera–like computer program recording and auditing capability of RTPA [6, 7, 8] software **on-demand via the Internet** to virtually any authorized computer worldwide. This on-demand computer forensic accounting capability enables and empowers government regulators, for the first time, to remotely forensically investigate the recorded actual computer program source statements and data produced in financial reporting.

2. On-Demand Forensic Accounting and Analytics Scenario

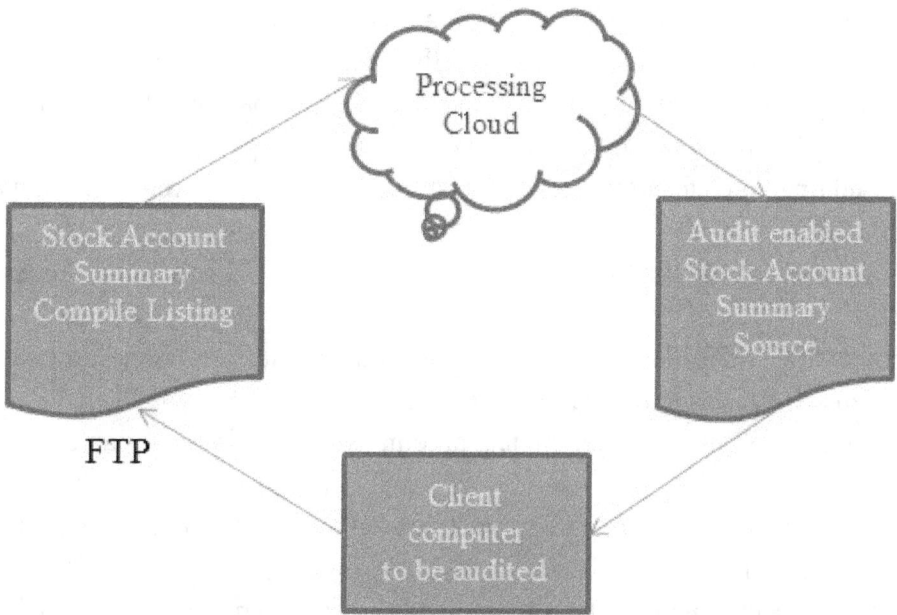

Figure 1: Stock Account Summary program compile listing for forensic accounting.

The government regulator or authorized forensic accountant requires financial reporting (for example, **Stock Account Summary Statements**) of a client to be audited, including source program statement execution and data and timestamp showing exactly how all program information is created (1)

- The client being audited transmits the financial source program listing to the secure government- authorized server or the Cloud for audit enablement via the Internet (2)

- The secure government server enhances the financial source program to enable source statement execution and data recording (3)

- The enabled, smarter and auditable source program source is transmitted back to the client via the Internet, and is compiled with the standard language compiler into a forensic accounting audit environment (4)

- The government regulator supervises processing of the audit enabled financial program at the client site in a secure separate auditing environment, and queries and analyzes the audit output files (5)

Scenario Notes:

(1) The ultimate drill-down to the original program statement execution and data as it is actually created include all levels of summarization and eliminates the often used altering and corruption of summarized information at all levels of reporting.

(2) The Internet or cloud normally uses secure FTP or File-Transfer-Protocol, and is nominally free.

(3) The central secure government server or authorized Cloud server and FTP transmission is required only to enhance or make auditable the client source program, and is NOT required if the language vendor provides this enhanced auditing capability at the client SITE, or if the client has the enhanced auditing capability in-house [7].

(4) The elapsed time to enable a typical client source program for forensic accountant auditing and analytics is less than 10 seconds.

(5) Forensic accounting auditing is performed in a separate and secure environment at the client site.

(6) No client data or client files are needed to audit-enable the client program remotely at the Government secure server or by the processing Cloud.

(7) The audit-enabling process is completely automated and without human operator involvement.

(8) The client production program and productions operating environment is unchanged, as a separate auditing environment is established.

(9) The Forensic Accountant or Government regulator can examine, inspect, analyze, document, and record the audit output in real-time and remotely, including using mobile

devices.

```
302      torder = 1500;
303       iorder = 78.543;
304     // value of iorder has now been computed
305        xorder = torder + 13.45  +
306     // this is a continuation free form statement preceded with +
307             26.2 + iorder;
308      sorder = torder +  xorder +  iorder + rorder + morder + norder;


K e y   F i e l d   I n f o r m a t i o n
   4  CUSTMAST
      CUSTREC1 is the RPG name of the external format CUSTREC.
                    CUCUST              PACK    7,0 SIGNED
                    CUSTOR              PACK    7,0 SIGNED
   2  ORDERDE
      ODETREC
                    ODORD#              PACK    7,0 SIGNED
                    ODLINE              PACK    5,0 SIGNED
 Global Field References:
    IORDER          S(8,3)
    TORDER          S(7,0)
    XORDER          S(9,2)

(partial source program compile listing FTPed to Cloud for audit enablement)
```

Figure 2: Client Stock Account Summary program compile listing for forensic accounting.

```
0323.00      torder = 1500;
0324.00                   Z$SRC# =  16   ;
0325.00                   EXSR     Z$GENS;
0326.00                   EXCEPT   Z$00016;
0327.00       iorder = 78.543;
0328.00                   Z$SRC# =  17   ;
0329.00                   EXSR     Z$GENS;
0330.00                   EXCEPT   Z$00017;
0331.00     // value of iorder has now been computed
0332.00                   Z$SRC# =  18   ;
0333.00                   EXSR     Z$GENS;
0334.00        xorder = torder + 13.45  +
0335.00     // this is a continuation free form statement preceded with +
0336.00             26.2 + iorder;
0337.00                   EXSR     Z$GETI;
0338.00                   EXCEPT   ZF00001;
0339.00      sorder = torder +  xorder +  iorder + rorder + morder + norder;
0340.00                   Z$SRC# =  19   ;
0341.00                   EXSR     Z$GENS;
0342.00                   EXCEPT   Z$00019;

(partial source program FTPed from Cloud audit enabled for forensic accounting)
```

Figure 3: Client Stock Account Summary source program audit enabled

2.3 Method

The FTPed Client Stock Account Statements Summary program compile listing (Figure 2) is received and processed by the processing Cloud server and the program source statements, and variable (data) information is stripped from the compile listing and is used as the input program source, files, and variables.

The inserted audit statements (Figure 3) in the audit enabled source program allow the enabled program to record all of the executing source statements, data (variables) and the timestamp as the compiled object program is later executed at the client site.

The audit enabled source program is FTPed back to the client, compiled into an executable object program, and run by the forensic accountant in a separate secure environment with normal client data and procedures to produce the ultimate recorded drill-down to all program statements actually executed and the data processed by each and every executed source program statement (Figure 4).

Note: If the client already has the source program audit enabling software installed at the client site, then no FTPing or processing Cloud is needed. For instance, this might be the case if government regulators installed that auditing capability during an audit of the client, or if the client already utilized the audit enabling software to enhance productivity.

Note: The program language providers of client financial applications, including IBM, Microsoft, SAP, Oracle, Hewlett Packard, and open source languages could easily provide this program audit enabling capability in their standard compilers.

```
302        torder = 1500;
              1500
303         iorder = 78.543;
              78.543
304     // value of iorder has now been computed
305         xorder = torder + 13.45  +
              1618.19      1500
306     // this is a continuation free form statement preceded with +
307               26.2 + iorder;
                      78.543
308        sorder = torder +  xorder +  iorder + rorder + morder + norder;
      93330.496      1500
                        1618.19     78.543
                                      32109.876
                                         34567.098
                                            23456.789


(partial Client Stock Account Summary forensic accounting audit output)
```

Figure 4: Client Stock Account Summary forensic accounting audit output.

The right side of the audit output shows the source sequence number, change date and the timestamp of the moment-in-time when the statement was executed (Figure 5). These program statements were executed, recorded, and audited in the elapsed time of one millisecond, and in a tiny fraction of a CPU second.

```
  00209 020623   23800                         16.50.19.042 2012-09-19
                                               16.50.19.042 2012-09-19
  00210 020623   23900                         16.50.19.043 2012-09-19
                                               16.50.19.043 2012-09-19
  00211 061201   24000                         16.50.19.043 2012-09-19
  00212 020623   24100                         16.50.19.043 2012-09-19
                                               16.50.19.043 2012-09-19
  00213 061201   24200                         16.50.19.043 2012-09-19
  00214 020623   24300                         16.50.19.043 2012-09-19
                                               16.50.19.043 2012-09-19
  00215 070214   24400                         16.50.19.043 2012-09-19
                                               16.50.19.043 2012-09-19
                                               16.50.19.043 2012-09-19
                                               16.50.19.043 2012-09-19
                                               16.50.19.043 2012-09-19
                                               16.50.19.043 2012-09-19
  (partial Client Stock Account Summary forensic accounting audit timestamp
```

Figure 5: Client Stock Account Summary forensic accounting audit output timestamp.

2.4   Forensic Accounting and Analytics of the Audited Program Output

The forensic accountant now has the capability to remotely actually see from a mobile device and understand exactly is happening at the client's computer inside the audit enabled program at the ultimate lowest level of information, which is the executing program code and data, and can utilize the full set of analytics tools including SQL to select and extract any desired information from the read-only audit output Relational Data Base (Figure 6).

The 64GB flash memory in mobile devices such as smartphones, tablets, laptops, and video camcorders enables the forensic accountant to **remotely access, inspect, analyze, and record** literally everything of interest processing inside the client's computer program, in real time.

The forensic Accountant or Government regulator has the capability to Query the audit output for literally any variable data produced by the audit-enabled program. For instance, the auditor could query for 1618.19 and examine exactly where and how the variable xorder was computed. (figure 4).

```
305            xorder = torder + 13.45  +
               1618.19     1500
306      // this is a continuation free form statement preceded with +
307               26.2 + iorder;
                  78.543
```

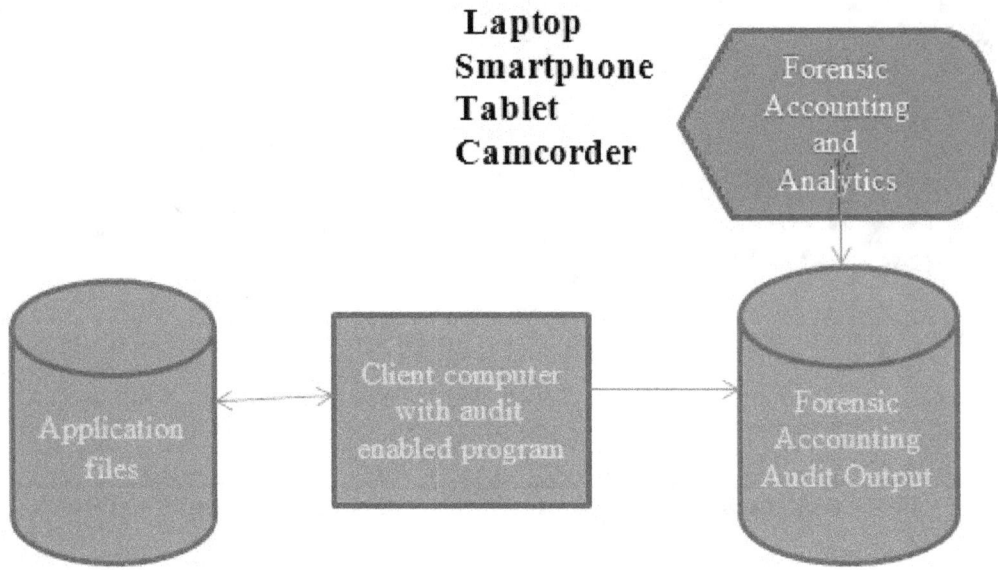

Figure 6: Forensic Accounting and Analytics (can be remote and mobile and real-time).

2.5   Additional Technical Details

The technical details of exactly how computer programs are enabled to audit and record the executing source program statements and all data (variables) processed is fully described on the patented Real-Time Program Audit (RTPA) software web site www.harkinsaudit.com and related documentation, including videos [7].

Detailed information and techniques about exactly how virtually any corporate programming language may be audit-enabled with video camera-like recording of the executing source statements and data are available in the "The Power of Traceability" paper [8].

Detailed information about the emerging and transformative field of Forensic Accounting, and particularly Computer Forensics, is widely available on the Internet, including the book *Computer Forensics: An Essential Guide for Accountants, Lawyers, and Managers* [9]

Computer program source statement and data audit-enabling provides, for the very first time, the capability for true **Autonomic Computing** [10], as all of the source program executing statements and all of the data (variables) are real-time recorded and available for autonomic computing, NOT just the program output written external to the program (normally to disk), or available by program probes. **Thus, a vast new world of critical self-healing capability is now available real-time at the most atomic level of all of the executing program statements and data.**

3. Related Work

The virtually unlimited computing power and data storage of the typical corporate computer is routinely multiplied every several years [10], and smartphones can have 64GB of flash memory [11], making computing power, computing speed, and data storage considerations and cost of little real concern, or no real concern, in implementing source program audit-enablement for forensic accounting.

A potential consideration relating to the speed and capability of creating and indexing forensic analysis audit databases is addressed in the paper "On-Demand View Materialization and Indexing for Network Forensic Analysis" [12]. This paper essentially concludes that commercially available relational database management systems (RDBMSs) and effective indexing techniques can provide sufficient real-time auditing capability and performance.

4 Possible Applications of This Transformational On-Demand Forensic Accounting Technique

The positive and immense benefits of real-time computer source program and data audit-enablement and recording include all corporate (client) computer program related functions, activities, and related personnel, from the programmer, analyst, IT manager, operations, to the compliance officer, auditor, and CFO.

Productivity gains, cost reductions, increased confidence, and large capability gains of each of these jobs, and in other jobs through the enterprise, even down to a packer in a warehouse, are actually enormous.

The immediate economics of audit-enabling forensic accounting, and general accounting, and auditing, may be illustrated in the huge current costs of belatedly discovering criminal fraud and in recovering and prosecuting that **preventable** fraud, sometimes hundreds of millions of dollars in a single case [13], rather than utilizing available forensic accounting tools and techniques pro-actively to look for fraud and to prevent or quickly discover those frauds.

The huge multi-billion dollar revenue generated annually by the **general accounting industry**, together with their relatively similar skills and capability in forensic accounting, would make a transformational capability commanded by one of them a powerful competitive and marketable revenue capability [14] (Figure 7).

Additionally, a huge new opportunity to educate and train and support forensic accounts, public accountants, government regulators and corporate personnel in new proactive techniques of fraud detection and dispute resolution would be available to early adopters of this technology.

Big Four (audit firms)

From Wikipedia, the free encyclopedia

The **Big Four** are the four largest international professional services networks in accountancy and professional services, which handle the vast majority of audits for publicly traded companies as well as many private companies, creating an oligopoly in auditing large companies. The Big Four firms are shown below, with their latest publicly available data:

Firm	Revenues	Employees	Fiscal Year	Headquarters	Source
Deloitte	$31.1bn	193,000	2012	United States	[1]
PwC	$29.2bn	169,000	2011	United Kingdom	[2]
Ernst & Young	$22.9bn	152,000	2011	United Kingdom	[3]
KPMG	$22.7bn	145,000	2011	Netherlands	[4]

Figure 7: Big Four Audit Firms annual revenues

Similarity, the huge **Investment Advisory industry** is very competitive and most firms have relatively similar skills and capability in forensic accounting, which would make a transformational capability, commanded by one of them a powerful competitive and marketable revenue capability.

Similarity, the huge **public and private college and university industry** is also very competitive and most schools have relatively similar skills and capability in forensic accounting, which would make a transformational capability, commanded by one of them a powerful competitive and marketable revenue capability.

Probably the most important possible use of computer audit audit-enabled forensic accounting is in the **U.S. Government and regulatory agencies**. Agencies such as the U.S. Securities & Exchange Commission (SEC) [15], the IRS, the FBI, the Securities Investment Protection Corporation (SIPC) [16], have tens of thousands of highly trained and highly–paid employees who would be able to do their jobs significantly more effectively with this computer program audit-enabling technique.

5 Conclusion

Forensic accounting is in its infancy, but it has already utilized some of the techniques illustrated in this paper to uncover and prosecute major criminal fraudulent activity, and has proven its immense potential and value to society.

Using the computer itself to provide a security camera–like recorded auditing capability at the most atomic level of the executing source program statement and data provides the basis for a revolutionary and transformational change in how auditing and information technology and forensic accounting are performed.

The importance of Dr. Gordon Brown's quote "What the use of fingerprints was to the 19th century and DNA analysis was to the 20th, forensic accounting will be to the 21st century" is being proven true and on a scale unimaginable until now.

References

[1] ACFE Definition of Forensic Accounting http://jemoore.typepad.com/blog/2008/12/acfe-definition-of-forensic-accounting.html

[2] Bernard Madoff's and Allen Stanford's Ponzi Schemes http://money.howstuffworks.com/ponzi-scheme5.htm

[3] Washington Post Reports That SEC Disciplines Eight Employees For Role Failures in Madoff Investigation http://www.fedseclaw.com/2011/11/articles/sec-news/washington-post-reports-that-sec-disciplines-eight-employees-for-role-failures-in-madoff-investigations/#axzz26liZuOunf

[4] Stock Market Loses Face http://online.wsj.com/article/SB10001424052702304065704577429111951625728.html

[5] Patent US6775827 Real-time program audit software www.google.com/patents/US6775827

[6] Forensic Accounting http://www.figl.co.nz/index.php?page=services-1

[7] The Real-Time Program Audit software http://www.harkinsaudit.com/

[8] The Power of Traceability http://www.harkinsaudit.com/docs/the_power_of_traceability_article_2009_final.pdf

[9] Computer Forensics: An Essential Guide for Accountants, Lawyers, and Managers http://www.wiley.com/WileyCDA/WileyTitle/productCd-0471789321.html

[10] IBM's Roadrunner breaks petaflop barrier, tops supercomputer list June 2008 http://news.cnet.com/8301-10784_3-9971006-7.html

[11] Apple iPhone 4S 64GB Smartphone http://www.amazon.com/Apple-iPhone-4S-64GB-Smartphone/dp/B005Z7CLLY

[12] Geambasu i et. al.On-Demand View Materialization and Indexing for Network Forensic Analysis http://db.cs.washington.edu/nids/netdb07nids.pdf

[13] **Madoff Case Is Paying Off for Trustee ($850 an Hour** http://dealbook.nytimes.com/2012/05/28/madoff-case-is-paying-off-for-trustee-850-an-hour/

[14] Big Four (audit firms) http://en.wikipedia.org/wiki/Big_Four_(audit_firms)

[15] U.S. Securities and Exchange Commission (SEC) http://en.wikipedia.org/wiki/U.S._Securities_and_Exchange_Commission

[16] U.S. Securities Investor Protection Corporation http://en.wikipedia.org/wiki/Securities_Investor_Protection_Corporation

Appendix D On-Demand Forensic Accounting Universal Program Auditing Language

The On-demand Forensic Accounting Universal Program Auditing Language (UPAL) provides a universally implemented and understood contemporaneous auditing capability to all accountants, auditors, government regulators and ultimately to the investing public for all financial reporting.

On-Demand Forensic Accounting

Universal Program Auditing Language

Paul H. Harkins

Harkins & Associates, Inc.
www.harkinsaudit.com

Abstract

Forensic accounting, or financial forensics, currently lacks the ability to proactively record, access, examine, and analyze in real time all of the financial activity used in financial transactions and financial reporting.

The "black box' of opaque and inaccessible computing financial detail information has allowed and enabled numerous recent huge "Ponzi schemes," including the Bernard Madoff and Allen Stanford cases, which cost investors billions of dollars while humiliating the responsible government regulators and causing the investing public to lose confidence in stock-market investing.

This paper describes a revolutionary and transformational patented forensic accounting and analytic capability that captures and records critical never before recorded information, including all executing program source statements and data, and puts a time stamp inside corporate computer programs as they produce financial reports. This makes ultimate drill-down to the source of financial information available—on-demand, instantly, and remotely— to authorized government regulators, auditors and investors.

Additionally, the Universal Program Auditing Language described in this paper provides the ability to see the financial document created by the program and the actual program source statements and data creating the information, including ultimate drill-down to the computation of the data in real-time, which is instantly available via mobile device to the Forensic Accountant, CPA, auditor, CFO, government regulator, Judge, or other authorized requestor.

A Rosetta Stone like transformational capability translates the arcane gobbledygook language of multiple programming languages used to produce financial reports, including Customer Stock Summary Statements, Balance Sheet and Income Statement documents, into the language (such as English, French, or German) desired by the requesting Forensic Accountant or other reques-tor, virtually instantly into useful information in a format desired by the requestor, and protected from fraud.

1. Introduction

Forensic accounting, or financial forensics [1], currently lacks the ability to proactively record, access, examine, and analyze in real time all of the financial activity used in financial transactions and financial reporting.

The "black box' of opaque and inaccessible computing financial detail information has allowed and enabled numerous recent huge "Ponzi schemes," including the Bernard Madoff and Allen Stanford [2, 3] cases, which cost investors billions of dollars while humiliating the responsible government regulators [4,5] and causing the investing public to lose confidence in stock market investing [6].

This paper describes a revolutionary and transformational patented forensic accounting and analytic computer software capability [7] that captures and records all executing program source statements and data, and puts a time stamp inside corporate computer programs as they produce financial reports. This makes ultimate drill-down to the source of financial information available—on-demand, instantly, and remotely— to authorized government regulators, auditors and investors.

Additionally, the Universal Program Auditing Language described in this paper provides the ability to see the financial document created by the program and the actual program source statements and data creating the information, including ultimate drill-down to the computation of the data in real-time, which is instantly available via mobile device to the Forensic Accountant, CPA, auditor, CFO, government regulator, Judge, or other authorized requestor.

A Rosetta Stone [8] like transformational capability translates the arcane gobbledygook [9] language of multiple programming languages used to produce financial reports, including Customer Stock Summary Statements, Balance Sheet and Income Statement documents, into the language (such as English, French, or German) desired by the requesting Forensic Accountant or other requestor, virtually instantly into useful information in a format desired by the requestor, and protected from fraud.

The huge potential of forensic accounting was addressed by Dr. James Gordon Brown when he was Britain's Chancellor of the Exchequer: "What the use of fingerprints was to the 19th century and DNA analysis was to the 20th, forensic accounting will be to the 21st century [10].

The fundamental key to unlocking and fully utilizing the huge potential of fingerprints, DNA, and now forensic accounting is to make them all essentially universally available on demand and in a standard easily and immediately understandable format to ultimate consumers worldwide.

The above-described patented on-demand Forensic Accounting computer software, "Real-Time Program Audit", or RTPA, enables the pervasive worldwide implementation of Dr. Brown's vision and dramatically empowers forensic accountants. In short, RTPA creates a read-only permanent audit record of exactly what is happening in the computer program, in real-time, including executing source statements, data (the contents of variables) and a timestamp.

On-Demand Forensic Accounting and Analytics provides a video camera–like computer program recording and auditing capability of RTPA [11, 12] software **on-demand via the Internet** to virtually any authorized computer worldwide. This on-demand computer forensic accounting capability enables and empowers government regulators, for the first time, to remotely forensically investigate the recorded actual computer program source statements and data produced in financial reporting, *in timestamp sequence as the computer executed them,* no matter how the multiple programs producing the financial statements were structured or the computer language used in individual program modules.

2. Critical Need for a new Corporate Computing and Reporting Environment

Students of history who have read Harold Evan's landmark book "They Made America" [13] can recognize and understand both the importance of many key inventions to society, such as the steam boat, and the electric light bulb among scores of others, and also the entrenched resistance and inertia and difficulties against their acceptance and general usage.

Today, the computing industry and specifically the corporate computing software industry as a whole are operating with technology largely designed and developed at the dawn of corporate computing in the late 1950s when computer hardware was extremely slow and primitive and extremely expensive, and when people were extremely inexpensive. IBM used to "give away free" it's System Engineers (programmers), including me [14], to work at customer locations until 1968 to customers who were implementing new IBM systems.

Since the early 1960s, computer hardware has gotten literally thousands of times more powerful and become inexpensive [15, 16], and computer programmers have become more than ten times [17] more expensive than in the early 1960s while largely still writing programs and applications in the arcane gobbledygook and opaque and deficient programming languages developed decades or scores of years ago. [18]

The paradigm change of Cloud computing [19], which essentially provides on-demand remote computing in a virtualized environment without end-user knowledge of the underlying computer hardware or software technology, provides the foundation and capability for a totally new corporate computing and reporting environment.

Medical advances over the past fifty years including the EKG, CAT scan, MRI, mammogram, ultrasound, Echocardiogram [20] (not to mention the previously discovered X-Ray and Stethoscope) have enabled doctors to literally see inside a patient and record what is happening and to save arguably millions of lives, while significant advances in important capability, such as recording and auditing computer program processing and the ability to reproduce the computer processing output with drill-down to the ultimate source of the data processed, in software computing languages are minimal and insufficient, at best.

Conversely the programming languages used today in the computing industry have essentially have the same primitive design as in the 1960s when optimizing the performance of a single available and expensive computer processor (CPU) was key and computers took minutes or hours to process typical applications rather than perhaps a few seconds now needed to execute the same application, and there are multiple processors (CPUs) available for processing at a minimal cost.

Software languages and compilers have never gotten significantly beyond the 1950s and 1960s focus of transcribing a needed action into gobbledygook code to attempt to efficiently utilize a then scarce and expensive computer, by a then inexpensive programmer, while causing an opaque and unrecorded and not audited record of what the computer is doing or actually did inside the program. Thus, virtually none of the super-smart exquisitely trained and superbly qualified forensic accounts, CPAs, attorneys, CFOs, accounting firm auditors, government regulators and certainly not investors have a real clue as to what is happening inside the computer as it produces critical financial documents and reports, because they cannot see or understand what the computer actually did to record its entire execution statement-by-statement including variable data and a processing timestamp, and thus what is really is the ultimate source of the data in the financial documents [3, 4, 5, 6]. This lack of transparency or visibility or knowledge of exactly what is happening in real-time inside the computer and in recording it as in a video camera, allows and enables the types of "Ponzi schemes"[2] and other fraud caused by the "Black Box" of computers by shielding these frauds from real-time and mobile access in an understandable way by government regulators, auditors, and investors, and enables a host of fraud generated by computers in financial reporting and other reporting to remain undetected and not prosecuted at cost billions of dollars annually. [3, 4, 5, 6, 16, 21]

While there are hundreds or actually thousands of spoken languages worldwide, all aircraft Air Traffic Control [22] of airplanes worldwide is required to be spoken in the English language, due to the critical real-time need to understand and react and communicate to situations in a single language. Similarly, virtually anyone (including some 10 year olds) can drive any make or model car from any manufacturer by just stepping on the accelerator and steering and braking in an intuitive manner, worldwide, because of strict regulated standards to make the hundreds of millions or autos easily usable by the hundreds of millions of end-users without an expensive technician driving the sophisticated auto for them.

Additionally, the aircraft industry (FAA), auto industry (DOT), drug industry (FDA), securities industry (SEC and SIPC), among many other industries directly relating to the consumer, have strict safety and consumer protection standards and regulations [23]. However, the Information Technology (computing) industry has never had and today has essentially NO effective consumer standards or effective government regulation, and this lack of consumer (including investor) protection and transparency has directly enabled the opaque and gobbledygook computing systems of today and enabled the multiple massive frauds against the investor and the public.

The auto industry in particular has embraced and responded to the needs for the end-user driver to successfully operate and maintain an ever more sophisticated vehicle and technology by literally just stepping on the accelerator in any auto worldwide, and further has even made the auto virtually scheduled maintenance free for scores of thousands of miles and mandated critical safety equipment such as air bags and catalytic converters even over the protests of some manufacturers. And beyond that, the auto industry regulators have mandated an industry standard of vehicle diagnostics [24], which enables the end-user consumer (driver) to see in real-time inside the vehicle with a PC and a diagnostic tool. This real-time and available auto auditing technology allows literally any auto shop or interested driver to actually see and understand what is really happening or is wrong and directly avoids potential massive fraud previously rampant in the auto industry, while simplifying the maintenance of an increasingly complex and sophisticated and expensive auto.

Nothing like the auto industry mandated diagnostic capability, or safety capability is available to the financial industry investor or to the general public or to the government regulators, or CPAs, or attorneys or forensic accounts or corporations utilizing information technology. They are all literally in the dark with the opaque and gobbledygook software used in Information Technology, and in truth they are all at best guessing at what might be behind that stonewall of Information Technology ancient and deficient technology used as the source of financial information. [2, 3, 4, 5, 6]

Why cannot all forensic accountants, CPAs, auditors, government regulators, CFOs, investors worldwide see in real-time and understand what is happening inside the computer executing program and **recreate the financial documents with ultimate drill-down to the creation of the data updated in an Excel spreadsheet and in a single understandable language su**ch as English (or optionally French or German) on-demand from a remote mobile device such as a computer tablet or smart-phone?

The incredible answer is forensic accountants and others could essentially accomplish the above paradigm change today with huge productivity gains and major fraud reduction and huge cost savings with available technology such as On-Demand Forensic Accounting and Analytics [7, 10, 11, 12].

2.1 Reasons preventing the needed new Corporate Computing and Reporting Environment

Perhaps the primary reason preventing the corporate computing and reporting environment from moving from the antiquated and deficient and un-productive and expensive computing languages and techniques (old technology) used in the past and today is the fact that the primary revenue source of the existing information technology providers is now the hugely profitable software and services businesses rather than the ever diminishing and now less profitable hardware business. [25, 26]

The huge profits generated by having a corporation needing to utilize the services and software of an effectively monopolistic information technology vendor to implement applications or to decode a gobbledygook program problem or application problem at perhaps eight times the average programmer compensation [17] or forty times the federal minimum wage [27] is a powerful incentive to perpetuate the status quo and resist innovation which would eliminate that need. The technical staff of these services providers is not necessarily as well trained or capable as I was when I performed such services for IBM in the 1970s [14]. The huge and profitable services revenue is also a powerful incentive to develop additional software which will require similar services to implement and support it, and to resist simplification and standards which will enable end-users to quickly and effectively utilize these products independent of the vendor.

Perhaps the second biggest reason preventing the corporate computing and reporting environment from moving from the antiquated and deficient and un-productive and expensive computing languages and techniques used in the past and today is existence of often bloated corporate information technology programming and management staffs, who have essentially career high-paying jobs trying to decode the gobbledygook programs and applications used by their companies. The executive senior management of those companies is effectively held hostage by the same unknown and incomprehensive gobbledygook knowledge locked up within the information technology staff and the feared risks of replacing it.

Perhaps the third biggest reason preventing the corporate computing and reporting environment from moving from the antiquated and deficient and un-productive and expensive computing languages and techniques used in the past and today is the inertia and resistance to innovation of educational institutions, like my Drexel University [14]. Apparently the tenured and secure appointments of these PhDs. in teaching essentially the same technology they learned as students overrides the need and opportunity for true innovation and providing their students and alumni with a significant competitive advantage in the changing world of business.

Other significant reasons preventing the corporate computing and reporting environment from moving from the antiquated and deficient and un-productive and expensive computing languages and techniques used in the past and today include the inexplicable lack of mandated government standards and regulations requiring transparency and simplicity of the information technology industry.
And, the apparent total lack of ability by super-smart and capable and apparently dedicated government regulators such as the SEC [23] and the Congress to understand how to solve their huge problems quickly and effectively with fraud and implement those solutions. [3, 4, 5, 6, 11]
And, the forensic accountants, CPAs, auditors, attorneys, government regulators, CFOs, investors worldwide who are in fact are literally in the dark when confronted with this opaque information technology, and who are apparently unwilling to admit it and get transparent and real-time simplified and verifiable information in English remotely on their mobile devices.

3. On-Demand Forensic Accounting and Analytics Scenario

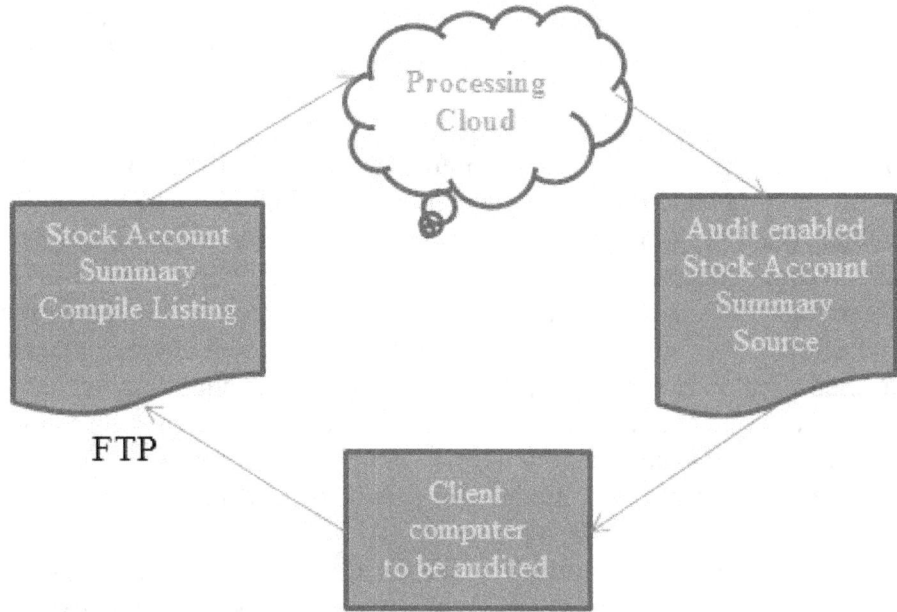

Figure 1: Stock Account Summary program compile listing for forensic accounting.

The government regulator or authorized forensic accountant requires financial reporting (for example, **Stock Account Summary Statements**) (Figure 1) for a corporate client to be audited, including source program statement execution and data and timestamp showing exactly how all program information is created (1)

- The client being audited transmits the financial source program listing to the secure government- authorized server or the Cloud for audit enablement via the Internet (2)

- The secure government server enhances the financial source program to enable source statement execution and data recording (3)

- The enabled, smarter and auditable source program source is transmitted back to the client via the Internet, and is compiled with the standard language compiler into a forensic accounting audit environment (4)

- The government regulator supervises processing of the audit enabled financial program at the client site in a secure separate auditing environment, and queries and analyzes the audit output files (5)

Scenario Notes:

(10)   The ultimate drill-down to the original program statement execution and data as it is actually created include reconstruction of the financial document and Excel spreadsheet detail of all levels of summarization and eliminates the often used altering and corruption of summarized information at all levels of reporting.

(11)   The Internet or cloud normally uses secure FTP or File-Transfer-Protocol, and is nominally free.

(12)   The central secure government server or authorized Cloud server and FTP transmission is required only to enhance or make auditable the client source program, and is NOT required if the language vendor provides this enhanced auditing capability at the client SITE, or if the client has the enhanced auditing capability in-house [10].

(13)   The elapsed time to enable a typical client source program for forensic accountant auditing and analytics is less than 10 seconds.

(14)   Forensic accounting auditing is performed in a separate and secure environment at the client site.

(15)   No client data or client files are needed to audit-enable the client program remotely at the Government secure server or by the processing Cloud.

(16)   The audit-enabling process is completely automated and without human operator involvement.

(17)   The client production program and productions operating environment is unchanged, as a separate auditing environment is established.

3.1 Method

The FTPed Client Stock Account Statements Summary program compile listing is received and processed by the Processing Cloud server and the program source statements, and variable (data) information is stripped from the compile listing and is used as the input program source, files, and variables.

The inserted audit statements (Figure 2) in the audit enabled source program allow the enabled program to record all of the executing source statements, data (variables) and the timestamp as the compiled object program is later executed at the client site.

The audit enabled source program is FTPed back to the client, compiled into an executable object program, and run by the forensic accountant in a separate secure environment with normal client data and procedures to produce the ultimate recorded drill-down to all program statements actually executed and the data processed by each and every executed source program statement (Figure 3).

Note: If the client already has the source program audit enabling software installed at the client site, then no FTPing or processing Cloud is needed. For instance, this might be the case if government regulators installed that auditing capability during an audit of the client, or if the client already utilized the audit enabling software to enhance productivity.

Note: The program language providers of client financial applications, including IBM, Microsoft, SAP, Oracle, Hewlett Packard, and open source languages could easily provide this program audit enabling capability in their standard compilers.

```
302      torder = 1500;
           1500
303        iorder = 78.543;
           78.543
304   // value of iorder has now been computed
305        xorder = torder + 13.45  +
           1618.19      1500
306   // this is a continuation free form statement preceded with +
307               26.2 + iorder;
                  78.543
308      sorder = torder +  xorder +  iorder + rorder + morder + norder;
      93330.496      1500
                        1618.19     78.543
                                    32109.876
                                      34567.098
                                        23456.789


(partial Client Stock Account Summary forensic accounting audit output)
```

Figure 2: Client Stock Account Summary forensic accounting audit output.

ly

The right side of the audit output shows the source sequence number, change date and the timestamp of the moment-in-time when the statement was executed (Figure 3). These program statements were executed, recorded, and audited in the elapsed time of one millisecond, and in a tiny fraction of a CPU second.

```
00209 020623   23800                              16.50.19.042 2012-09-19
                                                  16.50.19.042 2012-09-19
00210 020623   23900                              16.50.19.043 2012-09-19
                                                  16.50.19.043 2012-09-19
00211 061201   24000                              16.50.19.043 2012-09-19
00212 020623   24100                              16.50.19.043 2012-09-19
                                                  16.50.19.043 2012-09-19
00213 061201   24200                              16.50.19.043 2012-09-19
00214 020623   24300                              16.50.19.043 2012-09-19
                                                  16.50.19.043 2012-09-19
00215 070214   24400                              16.50.19.043 2012-09-19
                                                  16.50.19.043 2012-09-19
                                                  16.50.19.043 2012-09-19
                                                  16.50.19.043 2012-09-19
                                                  16.50.19.043 2012-09-19
                                                  16.50.19.043 2012-09-19

(partial Client Stock Account Summary forensic accounting audit timestamp
```

Figure 3: Client Stock Account Summary forensic accounting audit output timestamp.

3.2 Forensic Accounting and Analytics of the Audited Program Output

The forensic accountant, with this On-Demand Forensics and Analytics capability, has the capability to remotely actually see from a mobile device the reconstructed financial document, for example Stock Account Summary or Balance Sheet or Income Statement, including Excel spreadsheet detail data of exactly how the data was created and processed, and understand exactly is happening at the client's computer inside the audit enabled program at the ultimate lowest level of information, which is the executing program code and data, and can utilize the full set of analytics tools including SQL to select and extract any desired information from the read-only audit output Relational Data Base (Figure 4).

The 64GB flash memory in mobile devices such as smartphones, tablets, laptops, and video camcorders enables the forensic accountant to **remotely access, inspect, analyze, and record** literally everything of interest processing inside the client's computer program, in real time.

The forensic Accountant or Government regulator has the capability to Query the audit output for literally any variable data produced by the audit-enabled program. For instance, the auditor could query for 1618.19 and examine exactly where and how the variable xorder was computed. (Figure 4). The data contents of program variables, such as **xorder**, can be updated to an Excel spreadsheet (for example variable **xorder** value 1618.19 and variable **torder** value 1500) so the ultimate drill-down and the total value of variables may be verified independently outside of the executing program.

```
305           xorder = torder + 13.45  +
              1618.19      1500
306      // this is a continuation free form statement preceded with +
307              26.2 + iorder;
                 78.543
```

This real-time audit output of the executing program source statements and data (Figure 2) provides the input for the Universal Program Auditing Language remote mobile display in English to the forensic accountant and others.

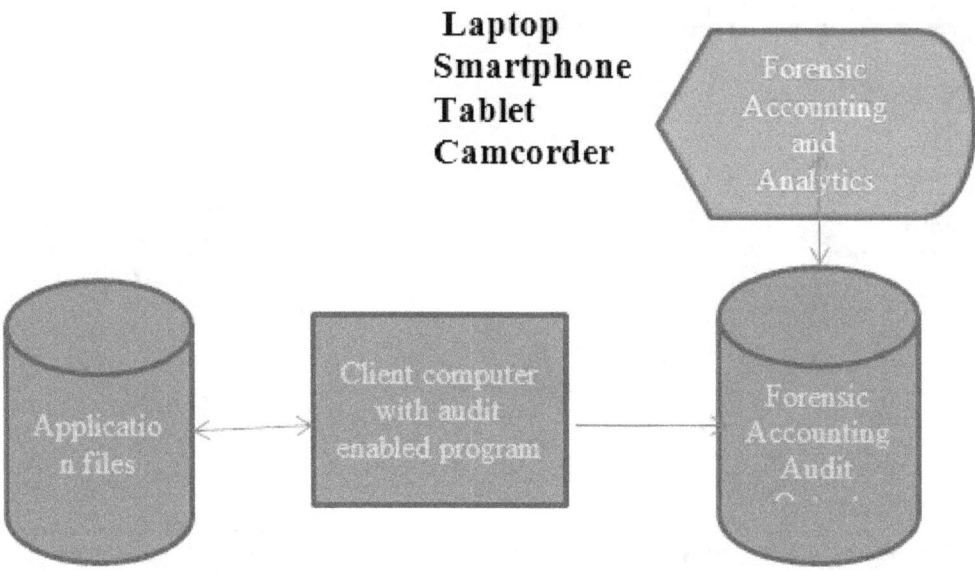

Figure 4: Forensic Accounting and Analytics (can be remote and mobile and real-time).

Also, source program comments statements (statement 306) can be translated into another language of the auditor's choice as in the Google language translator [28].

Ultimately, the entire gobbledygook source program language audit output could be translated in real-time and in English and available remotely on a mobile device in an easily understandable format by a forensic accountant, auditor, CPA, attorney, government regulator, Judge, CFO, investor and the programmer developing the financial document program, starting with a reconstruction and display of the financial document created by the executing program and Excel spreadsheets with the detail computation of the variables (data) used in the program.

Additionally, the **Universal Program Auditing Language** output described above could include fraud detection and flagging capability such as when the detail variable (data) does not correctly match to the total document value for the variable (for example xorder or torder in Figure 4), which indicates manipulation of the data or errors such as "plugged totals" in the program, purposeful or not.

3.3 Additional Technical Details

The technical details of exactly how computer programs are enabled to audit and record the executing source program statements and all data (variables) processed is fully described on the patented Real-Time Program Audit (RTPA) software web site www.harkinsaudit.com and related documentation, including videos.

Detailed information and techniques about exactly how virtually any corporate programming language may be audit-enabled with video camera-like recording of the executing source statements and data are available in the "paper "On-Demand Forensic Accounting and Analytics" [11] and in the "The Power of Traceability" paper. [12]

Detailed information about the emerging and transformative field of Forensic Accounting, and particularly Computer Forensics, is widely available on the Internet, including the book *Computer Forensics: An Essential Guide for Accountants, Lawyers, and Managers* [29]

Computer program source statement and data audit-enabling provides, for the very first time, the capability for true **Autonomic Computing** [30], as all of the source program executing statements and all of the data (variables) are real-time recorded and available for autonomic computing, NOT just the program output written external to the program (normally to disk), or available by program probes. **Thus, a vast new world of critical self-healing capability is now available real-time at the most atomic level of all of the executing program statements and data.**

4. The Universal Program Auditing Language

The forensic accountant, with this On-Demand Forensics and Analytics capability using the Universal Program Auditing Language (Figure 5), has the capability to remotely actually see in real-time via mobile devices [31, 32, 33] the final financial documents produced and *all* of the information and procedures actually used to create the document.

The initial display is the actual financial document or documents (for example; Stock Summary Report, Balance Sheet, Income statement) with data. Ultimate drill-down and spread sheet detail of variables, including the executing program source statements and timestamp and processing user information if desired, is available in the language of the requestor by clicking on the desired information as in a normal drill-down in a financial document or analytical report.

Business analytics software may be utilized, and never before possible **true** autonomic processing may be accomplished using computational program data never before written external to the program, such as error messages sent to warehouse packers that are not now recorded external to the program. The real-time auditing and recording of the executing program statements and data is a **quantum leap** in computing and analytics.

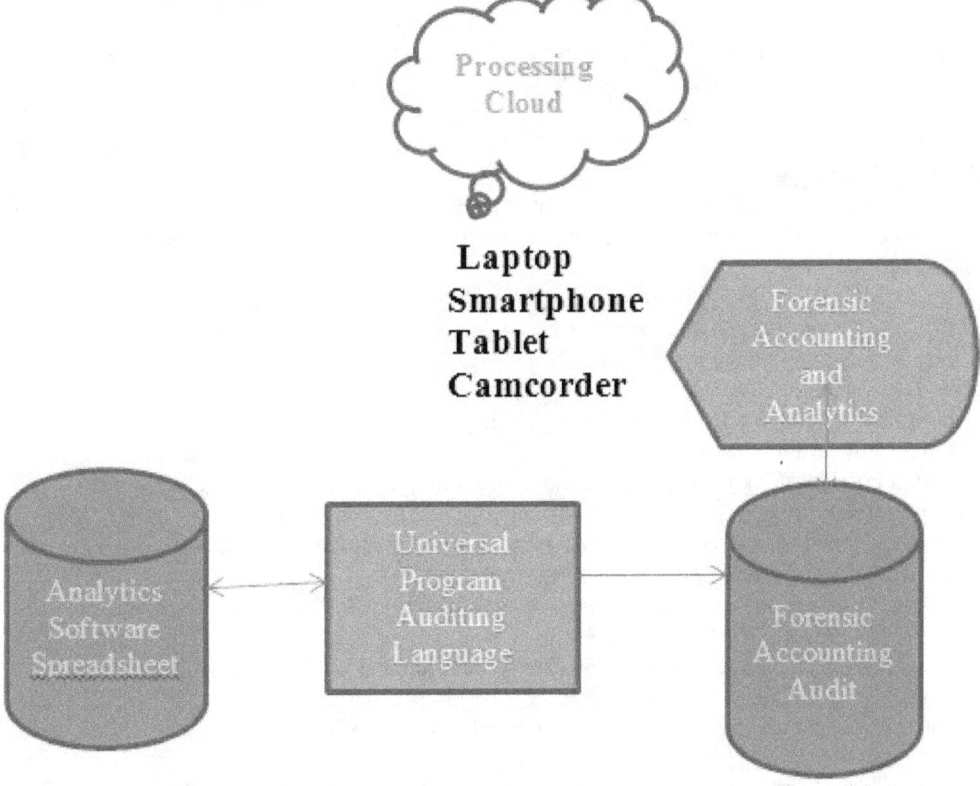

Figure 5: The Universal Program Auditing Language

5. Conclusion

The importance of Dr. Gordon Brown's quote "What the use of fingerprints was to the 19th century and DNA analysis was to the 20th, forensic accounting will be to the 21st century" [10] is being proven true today in the detection, prosecution and prevention of multiple huge financial frauds.

Unfortunately, the gobbledygook antiquated and deficient information technology systems in place, together with the almost total lack of effective government financial document processing and auditing standards and enforcement makes this forensic accounting process cumbersome, slow, and incredibly expensive [34].

The huge productivity gains achievable in many industries, the huge achievable cost reductions, the quantum leap in analytics capability, and the restoration of confidence in the securities industry achievable with the Universal Program Auditing Language will require its recognition and adoption worldwide

The U.S. Securities Exchange Commission (SEC) [35] and the U.S. Securities Investor Protection Corporation (SIPC) [36] and the U.S. Congress should ***mandate*** the implementation of the Universal Program Auditing Language, and additional modern and effective methods, in all financial and securities reporting. This will enable its staffs and the auditing community led by forensic accountants to exercise effective proactive government regulation and fraud detection and prevention and restore consumer confidence in the opaque and fraud riddled financial industry [37, 38].

References

[1] ACFE Definition of Forensic Accounting http://jemoore.typepad.com/blog/2008/12/acfe-definition-of-forensic-accounting.html

[2] Bernard Madoff's and Allen Stanford's Ponzi Schemes http://money.howstuffworks.com/ponzi-scheme5.htm

[3] SEC Enforcement Actions Against Ponzi Schemes http://www.sec.gov/spotlight/enf-actions-ponzi.shtml

[4] Washington Post Reports That SEC Disciplines Eight Employees For Role Failures in Madoff Investigation http://www.fedseclaw.com/2011/11/articles/sec-news/washington-post-reports-that-sec-disciplines-eight-employees-for-role-failures-in-madoff-investigations/#axzz26liZuOunf

[5] The Whistleblower From the Madoff Scandal Tells How to Reform the SEC http://truth-out.org/news/item/2116:the-whistleblower-from-the-madoff-scandal-tells-how-to-reform-the-sec

[6] Stock Market Loses Face http://online.wsj.com/article/SB10001424052702304065704577429111951625728.html

[7] Patent US6775827 Real-time program audit software www.google.com/patents/US6775827

[8] Rosetta Stone http://simple.wikipedia.org/wiki/Rosetta_Stone

]9] Gobbledygook http://en.wikipedia.org/wiki/Gobbledygook

[10] Forensic Accounting http://www.figl.co.nz/index.php?page=services-1

[11] On-Demand Forensic Accounting and Analytics http://www.harkinsaudit.com/docs/On_Demand_Forensic_Accounting_and_Analytics_copyright.pdf

[12] The Power of Traceability http://www.harkinsaudit.com/docs/the_power_of_traceability_article_2009_final.pdf

[13] They Made America by Harold Evans [http://www.pbs.org/wgbh/theymadeamerica/

[14] Paul H. Harkins Résumé http://www.google.com/#hl=en&sclient=psy-ab&q=paul+H.+Harkins+resume&oq=paul+H.+Harkins+resume&gs_l=hp.3...8788.1021562.1.1022368.22.18.0.4.4.0.203.2561.0j17j1.18.0.les%3B..0.0...1c.1.KJKSmcG-cY8&pbx=1&bav=on.2,or.r_gc.r_pw.r_qf.&fp=4bf76621ca799f85&bpcl=35243188&biw=1464&bih=796/

[15] Moore's law http://en.wikipedia.org/wiki/Moore's_law

[16] IBM's Roadrunner breaks petaflop barrier, tops supercomputer list June 2008 http://news.cnet.com/8301-10784_3-9971006-7.html

[17] Computer Programmers http://www.bls.gov/ooh/computer-and-information-technology/computer-programmers.htm

[18] C (programming language) http://en.wikipedia.org/wiki/C_(programming_language)

[19] Cloud computing http://en.wikipedia.org/wiki/Cloud_computing

[20] **Echocardiogram** http://en.wikipedia.org/wiki/C_(programming_language)

[21] Big Four (audit firms) http://en.wikipedia.org/wiki/Big_Four_(audit_firms)

]22] Air Traffic Control http://en.wikipedia.org/wiki/Air_traffic_control

[23] USA > Government > **Regulatory Bodies**
http://www.findouter.com/NorthAmerica/USA/Government/Regulatory-Bodies

[24] Unleash the Diagnostics Power Built into your Vehicle http://www.autoenginuity.com/products.html

[25] A letter from the President and CEO http://www.ibm.com/annualreport/2011/letter-from-the-ceo-and-president.html

[26] CNBC Video: Jobs, Elections and Hewlett-Packard   http://carlyfiorina.com/2012/10/cnbc-video-jobs-elections-hewlett-packard/

[27]   Wage and Hour Division (WHD) **Minimum Wage**   http://www.dol.gov/whd/minimumwage.htm

[28] **Google Translate**

http://www.google.com/#hl=en&sugexp=les%3Bpchsnhc&gs_nf=3&cp=18&gs_id=1y&xhr=t&q=google+language+translator&pf=p&sclient=psy-ab&oq=google+language+tr&gs_l=&pbx=1&bav=on.2,or.r_gc.r_pw.r_qf.&fp=9dac06e9a9126a6e&bpcl=35277026&biw=1464&bih=796

[29] Computer Forensics: An Essential Guide for Accountants, Lawyers, and Managers
http://www.wiley.com/WileyCDA/WileyTitle/productCd-0471789321.html

[30] Autonomic computing http://en.wikipedia.org/wiki/Autonomic_computing

[31] Tech Tablet makes pilots paperless   http://www.cnn.com/video/#/video/tech/2012/10/20/caifa-tablet

[32] Profound UI http://www.profoundlogic.com/prodproui.rpgsp

[33 Mobile Apps for Business http://www.longrangemobile.com/

 [34] Madoff **Case Is Paying Off for** Trustee (\$850 **an** Hour
http://dealbook.nytimes.com/2012/05/28/madoff-case-is-paying-off-for-trustee-850-an-hour/

[35] U.S. Securities and Exchange Commission (SEC)
http://en.wikipedia.org/wiki/U.S._Securities_and_Exchange_Commission

[36] U.S. Securities Investor Protection Corporation
http://en.wikipedia.org/wiki/Securities_Investor_Protection_Corporation

[37]   **Financial services tops internal fraud charts** http://news.silobreaker.com/financial-services-tops-internal-fraud-charts-5_2266054962612011182

[38] Why I Left Goldman Sachs
http://video.cnbc.com/gallery/?video=3000123608&play=1#eyJ2aWQiOiIzMDAwMTI0NjY2IiwiZW5jVmlkIjoiOFBKMjdyUUdiNkUrNjJDYTA-rUmpOUT09IiwidlRhYiI6InRyYW5zY3JpcHQiLCJ2UGFnZSI6IiIsImdOYXYiOlsiwqBMYXRlc3QgVmlkZW8iXSwiZ1NlY3QiOiJBTEwiLCJnUGFnZSI6IjEiLCJzeW0iOiIiLCJzZWFyY2giOiIifQ==

Appendix E www.harkinsaudit.com

The www.harkinsaudit.com web site from Harkins & Associates, Inc. brings together important information about forensic accounting and analytics, including powerful computer tools, educational tools, productivity tools, copyrighted papers on information technology (IT), including videos.

Additionally, implementation of the Real-Time Program Audit (RTPA) U.S. patent is illustrated in detail, including a comprehensive RTPA User's Manual.

The www.harkinsaudit.com home page

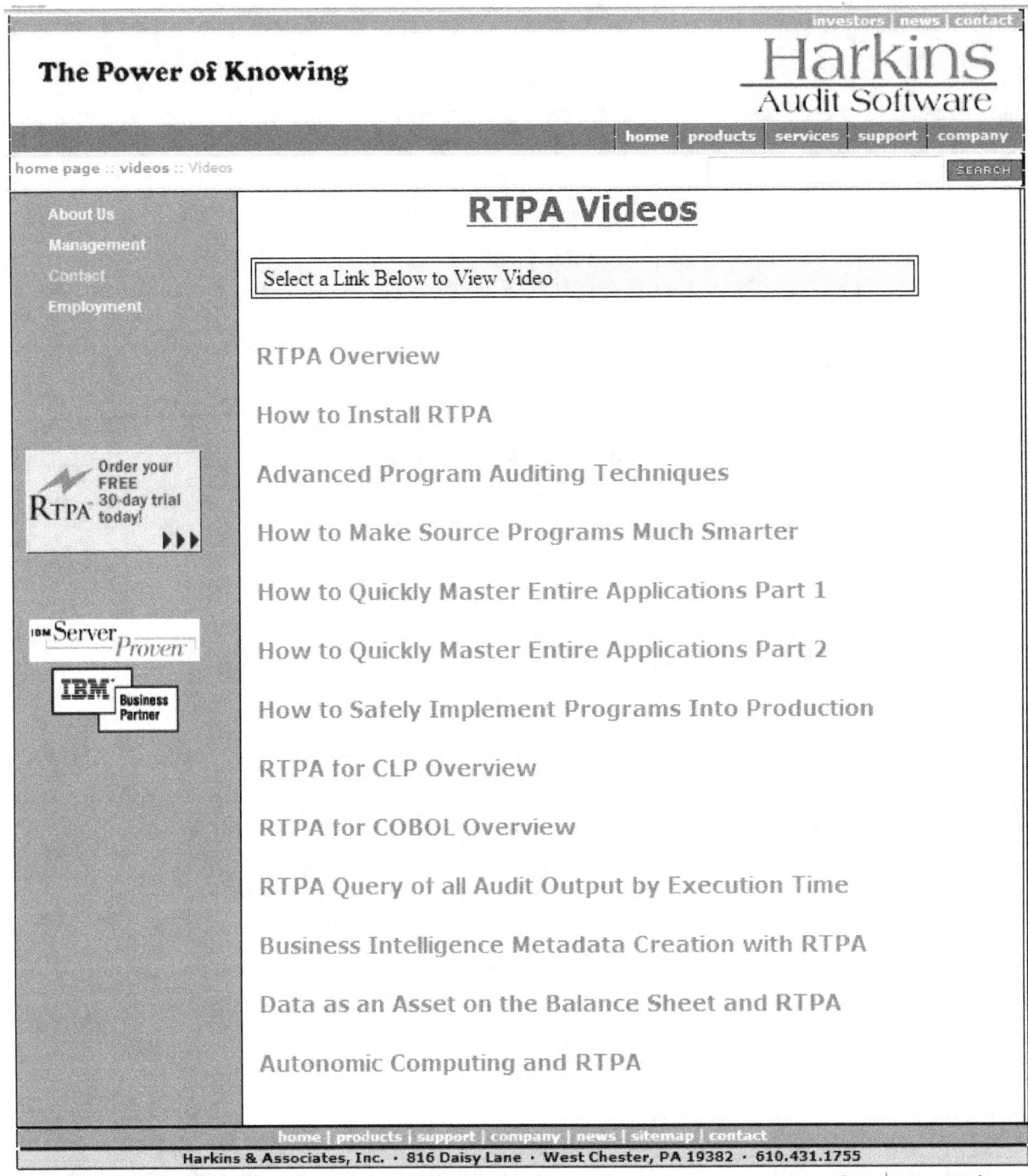

Real-Time Program Audit (RTPA) videos illustrating real-time computer program auditing and video camera like recording

REAL-TIME PROGRAM AUDIT™

RTPA for RPG

RTPA for CL

RTPA for COBOL

RTPA Query

United States Patent No. 6,775,827

Australian Patent – Patent No. 778165

User Manual
V5R1

Real-Time Program Audit (RTPA) User's Manual

Appendix F www.futureofcorporatecomputing.com

The www.futureofcorporatecomputing.com web site from Harkins & Associates, Inc. brings together important additional information relating to this book, including additional resources.

Appendix G Paul Houston Harkins Résumé

Paul Houston Harkins
816 Daisy Lane
West Chester, PA 19382-5709
Tel: 610 431-1755 Cell 610-804-1527 Fax: 610 436-1249
E-mail: paulhark@aol.com
www.harkinsaudit.com

1990 to   Harkins & Associates, Inc. – Founder and CTO
present   Invented and programmed the Real-Time Program Audit (RTPA) software utility, an IBM i
        (AS/400) RPG400 (RPGIII) and RPG ILE (RPGIV and RPG Free) programming
        productivity tool. Also developed RTPA for CLP, RTPA for COBOL, and RTPA
        Query. RTPA for RPG supports RPGII, RPGIII, RPGIV, RPG Free format, RPG
        ILE, and Embedded SQL RPG.

2001 to   Harkins Audit Software Inc. – President and Chief Technology Officer
2011

IBM i (AS/400) Consultant to National Label Company including ten weeks onsite in Singapore implementing a new Asia plant (April 2014 – present)

IBM i (AS/400) Expert Forensic Accounting Information Technology investigator and programming consultant (August 2011 – 12/31/2012)

IBM i (AS/400) programmer consultant at Appcon Consultants Inc. (Appcon)
        www.appcon4.com)
        in Ridley Park, PA., doing RPGIV application development, implementation, and support
        of major ERP systems for Appcon clients including G III, The Apparel Group in Dallas,
        Texas (2009 to present)

IBM i (AS/400) analyst and programmer consultant at the Jay Group in Lancaster, PA
        a fulfillment company with large customers including Heineken, Hershey, CertainTeed,
        Reebok, developing a Web FTP order logging process to highlight processing and errors
        for Web reporting of client orders for fulfillment. (2008)

IBM i (AS/400) programmer consultant at Application consultants (APPCON) in Ridley
        Park PA, consulting with their customers including Warnaco, Inc. Milford CT on
        ERP programming (2007)

Siebel PC Software implementation on 400 Salesperson's PCs Dentsply, Inc. (2006) Supported implementation of the Siebel PC software package York, PA Dallas, TX

IBM i (AS/400) Programmer consultant at GSI Commerce in King of Prussia, PA. (2006)
RPG ILE, CLP, Sub-Files, DDS, Aldon Change Management, JDA ERP package

IBM i (AS/400) Programmer consultant at Dentsply in York, PA. (2005- 2006) FDA environment
Advanced RPG ILE, RPG Embedded SQL and Interactive SQL, BPCS, Aldon Change Management, Electronic Support Center

IBM i (AS/400) Programmer at Jones Apparel Group (Jones New York), Bristol PA (2002-2004)
Staff RPGIII and RPGIV programmer responsible for developing and maintaining PkMS (Pick Ticket Management System RF wanding warehouse system from Manhattan Associates), JNY CRM applications supporting the Apparel Computing Systems (ACS) software package. Also trained and supported JNY programmers in the use of the Real-Time Program Audit (RTPA) for RPG, a programmer Productivity tool.

Consultant to several New York City Apparel companies (1999-2001)
Interfaced Retail Pro (a PC Retail package) to the JD Edwards World General Ledger on the AS/400. Also Interfaced ACS wholesale software to the JD Edwards General Ledger.

Consultant to Jones New York, Bristol, PA (1998 - 2001). Responsible for heavy PkMS enhancements to Radio Frequency applications (the lead PkMS programmer). and many advanced PkMS projects in RPG. Completed 42 significant projects.

Consultant to Fishman & Tobin, Inc., Philadelphia, PA (1999 - 2000).
PkMS programming, implementation and IT consulting to top management.

Consultant (including programming) to Computer Generated Solutions, Inc., New York (1996 -1998) Project Manager for multiple customer installations.
- Clients included Champion (1996), Leslie Fay (1997), Phillips-Van Heusen (1998)
- Applications: All ACS apparel applications, including corporate systems, order processing, manufacturing, distribution, warehouse management, EDI, and financial.
- Custom programming of hundreds of customer-specified reports.
- Custom programming of conversion to AS/400 from other hardware (MVS)

Consultant to Alfred Angelo, Inc., Horsham PA (reporting to the owner, Vincent Piccione) (1990-1995)
- Managed, designed, and implemented AS/400 RPG application development including:
- Corporate systems, order processing, customer service, manufacturing, distribution, and all financials.
- Developed shaded component (piece goods) inventory system
- Developed online Returns (RA) system
- Developed online Telephone Order Entry system
- Developed online Capacity Requirements Planning (CRP) system
- Developed online Material Requirements Planning (MRP) system
- Implemented the Lawson Associates, Inc., financial suite software applications.
- Implemented Focus Forecasting and Distribution Requirements Planning (DRP)

- ISD strategic Planning

1984 to
1990
Apparel Business Systems, Inc., Philadelphia, PA - Principal

- Responsible for software research, development, and implementation at clients
- Responsible for international accounts
- Project management and support of large accounts

1962 to
1984
IBM Corporation, Philadelphia, PA - Senior Systems Engineer

- Sole author of the original IBM Apparel Business System software product 1973
- Co-author of all other IBM Apparel Business System software products 1974 - 1982
- Senior technical person in the IBM National Apparel Support Center
- IBM National Award – Outstanding Achievement, San Francisco, July 6, 1972
- IBM Systems Research Institute 1970 in New York
- Author of twelve IBM publications
- Supported hundreds of IBM customers worldwide
- Member of the IBM IUP Hotel Product team
- IBM product development consultant – IBM store systems, product requirements
- International - Dusseldorf Germany, London and Bristol England, Sydney and Melbourne Australia, La Hulpe Belgium, Vancouver, Montreal, Toronto Canada, Singapore

Inventions and Patents

U.S. Patent No. 6,775,827 Real-Time Program Audit (RTPA) August 10, 2004
Australian Patent No. 778165

Real-Time Program Audit (RTPA) software for the IBM i (AS/400) computer. Languages: RPG, COBOL, CLP copyrighted 2002, 2007

Disk storage Volume Calculator software (VOLCAL) 1970

Software and resources Project Management and Control software 1972

Education and professional development
1962 Bachelor of Science – Commerce and Engineering (Industrial Engineer) – Drexel University
Outstanding ROTC Freshman award and trophy Drexel University
1969 Master of Business Administration (MBA) - Drexel University
Masters Thesis – An Illustrative Comparison of five of the Most Common Computer Programming languages: Assembler, COBOL, Fortran, PL/I, RPG

1970 IBM Systems Research Institute - New York City

2004 Delaware Valley Computer Users Group (DVCUG) Board of directors

2005 RPGWorld RPG computer conference – Las Vegas
2005 IBM COMMON conference – Orlando

2006   DVCUG annual Seminar on XML in RPG and WDSc, RSE

APICS member for many years

Military Service
1962 -1968 United States Army Reserve – Active duty Fort Knox Kentucky

Paul Houston Harkins

Bibliography

"How to Become a Highly Paid Corporate Programmer" McPress March 2004

"The Power of Traceability" 2009 Registered U.S. copyright

Abstract

An increasingly critical problem confronting corporate computing and programmer capability is the inability of computer programs to record and analyze the entire execution of the program and data in real time. This lack of traceability prevents true autonomic (self-healing) computing and prevents real-time and permanent analysis of exactly what executing program statements and data are actually processed. Therefore, as computers become millions of times more powerful and program environments become ever more complex and critical, the programmer is still using tools developed at the dawn of computing—tools like step debugging, reconstruction of events, and guessing--to attempt to <u>understand</u> what happened, rather than simply <u>observing</u> exactly what happened.

In this paper I present a technique--Electronic Program Auditing—and a software tool–The Real-Time Program Audit—designed to capture and record all of the executing source program statements in virtually any programming language, along with all of the data being processed and the moment-in-time of the statement execution without programmer intervention. This technique and unique tool provide a video-camera-like recording of the exact environment of the entire program execution (or selected conditions of the execution) as the program executes—thus delivering the potential of true autonomic computing and capturing previously unrecorded critical information. This paper presents my technique and tool, some actual and possible applications, and evidence of the value of my approach.

"On-Demand Forensic Accounting and Analytics" 2012 Registered U.S. Copyright
Abstract

Forensic accounting or financial forensics, currently lacks the ability to proactively record, access, examine and analyze in real-time all of the financial activity used in financial transactions and financial reporting.
This "black box' of opaque and inaccessible computing financial detail information has allowed and enabled numerous recent huge "Ponzi schemes' including the Bernard Madoff and Charles Stanford cases which cost investors billions of dollars while humiliating the responsible government regulators] and causing the investing public to lose confidence in stock market investing.
This paper describes a patented forensic accounting and analytic capability that captures and records all executing program source statements, data and a time stamp inside corporate computer programs as they produce financial reports and makes ultimate drill-down of the source of financial information on-demand and instantly remotely available to authorized government regulators, auditors and investors.

"On-Demand Forensic Accounting Universal Program Auditing Language" 2012 Registered U.S. Copyright
Abstract
Forensic accounting, or financial forensics, currently lacks the ability to proactively record, access, examine, and analyze in real time all of the financial activity used in financial transactions and financial reporting.

The "black box' of opaque and inaccessible computing financial detail information has allowed and enabled numerous recent huge "Ponzi schemes," including the Bernard Madoff and Allen Stanford cases, which cost investors billions of dollars while humiliating the responsible government regulators and causing the investing public to lose confidence in stock-market investing.

This paper describes a revolutionary and transformational patented forensic accounting and analytic capability that captures and records critical never before recorded information, including all executing program source statements and data, and puts a time stamp inside corporate computer programs as they produce financial reports. . This makes ultimate drill-down to the source of financial information available—on-demand, instantly, and remotely— to authorized government regulators, auditors and investors.
Additionally, the Universal Program Auditing Language described in this paper provides the actual program source statements and data creating the information, including ultimate drill-down to the computation of the data in real-time, which is instantly available via mobile device to the Forensic Accountant, CPA, government regulator, Judge, or other authorized requestor.
A Rosetta Stone like transformational capability translates the arcane goobly-gook language of multiple programming languages used to produce financial reports, including Customer Stock Summary Statements, Balance Sheet and Income Statement documents, into the language (such as English, French, or German) desired by the requesting Forensic Accountant or other requestor, virtually instantly in a format desired by the requestor, and protected from fraud.

"On-Demand Forensic Accounting and Analytics" subtitle "How to Detect and Prevent Financial Fraud" Kindle eBook 2013

"The Future of Corporate Computing" Kindle eBook and paperback book 2015

" Human-Computer Interaction in Corporate Computing" forthcoming Kindle eBook 2015

Author of four articles relating to programming for several major IT magazines

www.mcpressonline.com

Author of twelve IBM program product publications

Appendix H Real-Time Program Audit (RTPA) U.S. Patent

United States Patent	6,775,827
Harkins	August 10, 2004

Real-time program audit software

Abstract

An automated computer-implemented method for generating an audit record of a computer program while the computer program is executing. The computer program has a source program comprising a plurality of source statements written in a predetermined source language. The method includes the steps of: selecting one or more audit options, each audit option being defined by one or more field names; examining each one of the source statements for the presence of one or more of the field names; creating an audit statement in the source language of the computer program corresponding to each one of the source statements in which one or more of the field names is present; and inserting each created audit statement into the source program proximate to the corresponding source statement to form an expanded source program.

Inventors: **Harkins; Paul H.** (West Chester, PA)
Assignee: **Harkins Audit Software, Inc.** (West Chester, PA)
Family ID: 32824981
Appl. No.: 09/611,210
Filed: **July 6, 2000**

Related U.S. Patent Documents

Application Number	Filing Date	Patent Number	Issue Date<TD< TD>
398310	Sep 20, 1999		<TD< TD>

Current U.S. Class:	**717/130**; 714/E11.209; 714/E11.212; 717/128
Current CPC Class:	G06F 11/3624 (20130101)
Current International Class:	G06F 11/36 (20060101); G06F 009/44 ()
Field of Search:	;717/127,130,128,145

References Cited [Referenced By]

U.S. Patent Documents

5559884	September 1996	Davidson et al.
5574898	November 1996	Leblang et al.
5613118	March 1997	Heisch et al.
5754763	May 1998	Bereiter
5771385	June 1998	Harper
5794252	August 1998	Bailey et al.
5813009	September 1998	Johnson et al.
5832271	November 1998	Devanbu
5903730	May 1999	Asai et al.
5950003	September 1999	Kaneshiro et al.
6011920	January 2000	Edwards et al.
6071316	June 2000	Goossen et al.
6202199	March 2001	Wygodny et al.

Foreign Patent Documents

WO 93/01550	Jan 1993	WO

Primary Examiner: Ingberg; Todd
Assistant Examiner: Kiss; Eric B.
Attorney, Agent or Firm: Akin Gump Strauss Hauer & Feld, LLP

Parent Case Text

CROSS REFERENCE TO RELATED APPLICATIONS

This is a continuation-in-part of application Ser. No. 09/398,310 filed on Sep. 20, 1999 now abandoned, the disclosure of which is hereby incorporated by reference.

Claims

I claim:

1. An automated computer-implemented method for generating an audit record of a computer program while the computer program is executing, said computer program having an original source program comprising a plurality of source statements written in a predetermined source language, the method comprising the steps of: selecting an audit profile, the audit profile being defined by at least one field name; examining each one of the source statements for the presence of the at least one field name; creating an audit statement in the source language of the computer program corresponding to each one of the source statements in which the at least one field name is present; inserting each created audit statement into the original source program proximate to the corresponding source statement to form an expanded source program, said audit statement being inserted prior to the corresponding source statement when the corresponding source statement is a branching statement; and compiling or interpreting said expanded source program to form an expanded computer executable program, wherein said audit statement causes said computer executable program to output the audit record, in real time, during the time that said computer executable program is executing, said audit record comprising the at least one field name and a value of the field associated with the at least one field name corresponding to each one of the source statements in which the at least one field name is present.

2. The method according to claim 1, wherein said audit profile provides for including in the audit record, the name of the at least one field and the value of the field associated with the at least one field name contained in each audited source statement.

3. The method according to claim 1, wherein a unique audit code is assigned to each source statement that is audited.

4. The method according to claim 1, wherein the at least one audit profile provides for inserting at least one documentation statement into the source program to form the expanded source program.

5. The method according to claim 4, wherein the at least one documentation statement provides for including in the audit record, at least one file description, at least one file key field name and at least one called program description.

6. The method according to claim 1, wherein the at least one audit profile provides for including in the audit record a date and a time of execution of each source statement.

7. The method according to claim 1, wherein the at least one selected audit profile may be changed while the computer program is executing.

8. The method according to claim 1, wherein the audit record is output to at least one of a storage

media and a print file.

9. The method according to claim 1, wherein the at least one audit record comprises at least one of a program name, a user name, a date and a time of execution, an audit code prefix, the source statement corresponding to the audit statement and field values.

10. The method according to claim 1, wherein the at least one audit profile provides for customizing the audit record by a file name, a record format, an operation code, a field name and a program label.

11. An article of manufacture for generating an audit record of a computer program while the computer program is executing, said computer program having an original source program comprising a plurality of source statements written in a predetermined source language, the article of manufacture comprising a computer-readable medium holding computer executable instructions for performing a method comprising the steps of: selecting an audit profile, the audit profile being defined by at least one field name; examining each one of the source statements for the presence of the at least one field name; creating an audit statement in the source language of the computer program corresponding to each one of the source statements in which the at least one field name is present; inserting each created audit statement into the original source program, proximate to the corresponding source statement, to form an expanded source program, said audit statement being inserted prior to the corresponding source statement when the corresponding source statement is a branching statement; and compiling or interpreting said expanded source program to form an expanded computer executable program, wherein said audit statement causes said computer executable program to output the audit record, in real time, during the time that said computer executable program is executing, said audit record comprising the at least one field name and a value of the field associated with the at least one field name corresponding to each one of the source statements in which the at least one field name is present.

12. The article of manufacture of claim 11, wherein said audit profile provides for including in the audit record, the name of the at least one field and the value of the field associated with the at least one field name contained in each audited source statement.

13. The article of manufacture according to claim 11, wherein a unique audit code is assigned to each source statement that is audited.

14. The article of manufacture according to claim 11, further including code for inserting at least one documentation statement into the source program to form the expanded source program.

15. The article of manufacture according to claim 14, wherein the at least one documentation statement provides for including in the audit record, at least one file description, at least one file key field name and at least one called program description.

16. The article of manufacture according to claim 11, wherein the at least one audit profile provides for including in the audit record a date and a time of execution of each source statement.

17. The article of manufacture according to claim 11, wherein the at least one selected audit pro-

file may be changed while the computer program is executing.

18. The article of manufacture according to claim 11, wherein the output of the audit record is to a storage media or to a print file.

19. The article of manufacture according to claim 11, wherein the at least one audit record comprises a least one of a program name, a user name, a date and a time of execution, an audit code prefix, the source statement corresponding to the audit statement and field values.

20. The article of manufacture according to claim 11, wherein the at least one audit profile provides for customizing the audit record by a file name, a record format, an operation code, a field name and a program label.

21. An automated computer-implemented apparatus for generating an audit record of a computer program while the computer program is executing, said computer program having an original source program comprising a plurality of source statements written in a predetermined source language and executing in the form of a computer executable program, the apparatus comprising: means for receiving an input for selecting an audit profile for auditing the computer program, the audit profile being defined by at least one field name; means for examining each source statement for the presence of the at least one field name; means for creating at least one audit statement in the source language of the computer program corresponding to each one of the source statements in which the at least one field name is present in the selected at least one audit profile; means for inserting each created at least one audit statement into the original source program proximate to the corresponding source statement to form an expanded source program, said audit statement being inserted prior to the corresponding source statement when the corresponding source statement is a branching statement; and means for compiling or interpreting said expanded source program to form an expanded computer executable program, wherein said audit statement causes said computer executable program to output the audit record, in real time, during the time that said computer executable program is executing, said audit record comprising the at least one field name and a value of the field associated with the at least one field name corresponding to each one of the source statements in which the at least one field name is present.

22. The apparatus according to claim 21, further comprising means for including in the audit record, the name of the at least one field and the value of every field associated with the at least one field name contained in each audited source statement.

23. The apparatus according to claim 21, further comprising means for assigning a unique audit code to each source statement that is audited.

24. The apparatus according to claim 21, further comprising means for inserting at least one documentation statement into the source program to form the expanded source program.

25. The apparatus according to claim 24, further comprising means for including in the audit record, at least one file description, at least one file key field name and at least one called program description.

26. The apparatus according to claim 21, further comprising means for including in the audit record a date and a time of execution of each source statement.

27. The apparatus according to claim 21, further comprising means for changing the selected audit profile while the computer program is executing.

28. The apparatus according to claim 21, further comprising means for outputting the audit record to at least one of a storage media or a print file.

29. The apparatus according to claim 21, wherein the at least one audit record comprises a least one of a program name, a user name, a date and a time of execution, an audit code prefix, the source statement corresponding to the audit statement and field values.

30. The apparatus according to claim 21, wherein the at least one audit profile provides for customizing the audit record by a file name, a record format, an operation code, a field name and a program label.

31. A method for a user to interact with a first computer program so as to generate an audit record of a second computer program, the first computer program including an audit profile for the second computer program, the method comprising the steps of: receiving a name of the second computer program, said second computer program comprising an original source program having a plurality of source statements; and receiving a selection of a compile audit profile, wherein said compile audit profile is defined by at least one field name, said at least one audit statement being added to the source program of the second computer program proximate to a source statement of the second computer program containing the field name, said audit statement being added prior to the source statement when the source statement is a branching statement, said audit profile including a profile of substantially every operation code and file description format of the second computer program, wherein said selection of the compile audit profile causes the first computer program to create at least one audit statement in the second computer program, said at least one audit statement being in the form of a source language of the second computer program, the at least one audit statement being added to the source program of the second computer program to form an expanded source program and thereby generate the audit record of the second computer program during the time that the second computer program is executing, the audit record comprising at least one field name and a value of the field associated with the at least one field name corresponding to each one of the plurality of source statements in which the at least one field name is present.

Description

A portion of the disclosure of this patent document contains material which is subject to copyright protection. The copyright owner has no objection to the facsimile reproduction by anyone of the patent document or the patent disclosure, as it appears in the Patent and Trademark Office patent files or records, but otherwise reserves all copyrights whatsoever.

MICROFICHE APPENDIX

Reference is made to the Microfiche Appendix which forms a part of this document and is incorporated herein by reference. The Microfiche Appendix comprises 188 frames located on 2 microfiche.

BACKGROUND OF THE INVENTION

1. Field of the Invention

The present invention relates generally to a method and system for auditing and analyzing the execution of computer programs in real-time, and particularly to a method and system for generating source program auditing statements for debugging an application program.

2. Description of the Related Art

Typically, computer source programs are written in a source programming language by computer programmers. Alternatively, source programs can be generated by a Fourth Generation Language (4GL) or a computer-aided software engineering (CASE) tool. Programs created using a Fourth Generation Language or a CASE tool are automatically translated into source statements of a conventional programming language as an intermediate step to compilation and execution. Conventional programming languages include Common Business-Oriented Language (COBOL), formula translation (FORTRAN), Pascal, and Report Program Generator (RPG), amongst others. These conventional programming languages are source programs that are compiled into executable modules or objects so that they may be executed. Alternative programming languages, such as Java or Basic, allow source programs to be directly executed by an interpreter, bypassing the compilation step.

The programmer using a conventional or alternative programming language, or the application designer using a 4GL or a CASE tool, uses available programming tools such as objects, functions, diagrams, routines, and/or operation codes to translate a perceived or defined need into a programmed solution. The output program must be tested to determine if the program works as designed. The program is executed against data to verify the efficacy and accuracy of the program as executed. Herein both the programmer and the application designer are generally referred to as the programmer.

In the art of computer programming, the quickest and easiest part of programming is writing or generating the source program, while the most difficult and time-consuming part is making the program work correctly. The computer program needs to work correctly both initially and years later. Errors in programming result from a variety of sources. Sometimes the programming specifications are not complete or correct, resulting in errors and rewrites. Also, the programmer's understanding or logic may not be correct. Frequently, the data processed by the program is not as anticipated. In addition, unanticipated error conditions increase the probability of program error or failure. Such conditions include human error resulting from operation and training inadequacies, hardware failures, and network problems resulting from the complex interaction of events at any moment of time in a company with hundreds or thousands of computer users.

When a program does not work properly or fails completely, it is essential to provide tools for quick, comprehensive analysis of the program's execution. In addition, tools that speed identification and resolution of any problems are needed. Tools that allow the source program to be quickly and easily understood and corrected are also desirable. These tools are helpful during initial testing by the programmer to increase programmer productivity, and to increase the quality and reliability of the program. These tools are crucially needed when the program fails or must be changed by a programmer who is totally unfamiliar with the source program while it is in production, often at a time of great stress, of economic loss to the company, and in a high-risk environment. The real-time program audit software of the present invention addresses these needs for virtually any source programming language, and is also applicable in 4GL and CASE programming environments.

Programs purporting to audit the execution of themselves or other programs are found in the prior art. These prior art programs lack the real-time nature of the current invention or are not as comprehensive in their auditing capabilities. The related art is represented by the following patents of interest.

U.S. Pat. No. 5,559,884, issued on Sep. 24, 1996 to Robert L. Davidson et al., discloses a method and system for generating and auditing a signature for executable modules. Davidson et al. do not suggest real-time program audit software according to the claimed invention.

U.S. Pat. No. 5,574,898, issued on Nov. 12, 1996 to David B. Leblang et al., discloses a data processing system and method which feature an object selector including an auditor for recording, as an audit record, which versions of objects are accessed by a processor during a data processing process. Each derived object is associated with an audit record. A system build process starts the auditor prior to executing commands which produce derived objects, and stops the auditor when those commands are completed. The process records any arbitrary sequence of commands. The invention of Leblang et al. is a CASE system and cannot be utilized with other programming languages or source programs, regardless of how they are generated. Also, the invention of Leblang et al. audits which version of a file is being utilized; it is a CASE version control system. The program also generates a configuration record which provides a complete record of software builds which includes a listing of all source file versions used, versions of build tools, and all build options specified. Configuration records can then be compared by showing the differences between two builds of the same program. Other commands label the builds with version labels on object versions listed in the record. The invention of Leblang et al. is designed to monitor the version of a software program, and the objects used within that software program, during the design of the program. It is a tool to be used by computer programmers who are utilizing CASE tools to write a software program and, therefore, is not as useful as the present invention in that it is limited to CASE tool program design. Also, the invention of Leblang et al. is not useful for monitoring the execution of a program in a remote time after the creation of the program. The invention of Leblang et al. is distinctly different from the present invention in that it was not designed to monitor the execution of a program utilizing any type of programming language; the current invention is designed to monitor any type of machine code as it executes. Leblang et al. do not suggest real-time program audit software according to the claimed invention.

U.S. Pat. No. 5,754,763, issued on May 19, 1998 to Thomas W. Bereiter, shows a software auditing program which is designed to monitor the number of users who simultaneously invoke one or more application programs which occur in response to system management tasks. The auditing program therein counts the number of simultaneous invocations in order to determine whether an authorized number of copies of each program within the managed region has been exceeded. The protocol requires a dedicated license server. The sole purpose of the invention of Bereiter is to use a license server to identify violations of the licenses of an organization. The program therein does not audit any other activity nor does it aid in the actual execution of a program. It does not aid in the monitoring of program errors and trouble shooting during the execution of a program or system, as does the current invention. Bereiter does not suggest real-time program audit software according to the claimed invention.

U.S. Pat. No. 5,794,252, issued on Aug. 11, 1998 to Bruce W. Bailey et al., discloses a database management system which utilizes a remote duplicate database facility to monitor changes made to a database on a local system and to maintain a copy of that database on a remote system. The invention of Bailey et al. verifies data files making sure that the data or other file, relied upon by the user, is the most up-to-date file available. The system verifies that the files are protected from interruptions, errors, or failures in the computer operations. Bailey et al. protect database files and other files from being lost by creating a remote backup of those files as they are made and stored. Bailey et al. also make a record of the backups in order to verify that the most recent files are in use and are concurrent with the backup records. The invention of Bailey et al. is distinctly different from the current invention. Bailey et al. protect or audit data files, while the current invention audits program executions. These are very distinct activities. Bailey et al. do not suggest real-time program audit software according to the claimed invention.

U.S. Pat. No. 5,813,009, issued on Sep. 22, 1998 to Johnson et al., describes a computer based records management system which filters information to assure that record data units offered to the system for storage are complete and not redundant. These record data may originate from a variety of sources, such as electronic data, data scanned from paper, data digitally formed from audio, video, or otherwise formed as digital data information media. The goal of Johnson et al. is to provide a record keeping medium which eliminates the need for paper or microform record keeping. The system therein audits itself to assure that only the most up-to-date and accurate records are maintained. Johnson et al. provide for record data unit tracking and audit trails in the event of any requirement for regulatory or legal compliance with discovery or other record unit requests. Johnson et al. also permit reconstruction of the record units of an enterprise in the event of a catastrophic event. Johnson et al. audit storage files but not program execution and is, therefore, distinctly different from the present invention. Johnson et al. do not suggest real-time program audit software according to the claimed invention.

International Patent document WO 93/01550, published on Jan. 21, 1993, discloses a method and system for recording the use of a licensed product, and for controlling its use. International '550 does not suggest real-time program audit software according to the claimed invention.

None of the above inventions and patents, taken either singularly or in combination, is seen to describe the instant invention as claimed. Thus, a real-time program audit solving the aforementioned problems is desired.

SUMMARY OF THE INVENTION

The current invention, a real-time program audit software program, is a software program, a method, and a system for generating source program audit statements which examine and verify program statements and data as the program executes. The audits generated by the real-time program audit provide real-time analysis of the execution of the program. The real-time program audit software may be used with any programming language that uses source program statements, whether the source statements are compiled into an executable object or are interpreted during program execution. Conventional source programs are selected for auditing based on an audit profile. The audit profile is customized for specific compile and initial execution options. The source program is expanded with the selected audit statements. The source program is compiled with a conventional language compiler. Program execution audits are based on the initial execution audit profile, customized execution audits, or dynamic audits specified during program execution. Program audit output is to a disk or print file, and is available for immediate online display or printing, or for expanded auditing analysis. Expanded auditing analysis provides for extensive analysis of the real-time program audit output data from all audited programs based on the desired analysis, which includes program, user, date and time ranges, audit code prefixes, audited file, field, label, and any execution audited data value.

The real-time program audit software is a new approach to auditing the execution processing of programs of virtually any source programming language. The real-time program audit is basically a pre-compiler program that is specific for the type of programming language utilized. In other words, a different version of the real-time program audit software is required for each programming language compiler or interpreter utilized.

Accordingly, it is a principal object of the invention to audit the execution of every program statement selected for auditing in real-time. The audit includes all field names used in the audited source statements and their data values at program execution. Date and time are included in the audit. Real-time online review and analysis of the auditing is an integral part of the real-time audit program software. Real-time printing of the auditing for off-line review and analysis is also provided.

It is another object of the invention to expand the input conventional source program with the audit statements, using an easily understood method of source program expansion that does not materially alter or change the processing, flow or conventional output of the program as it executes. The invention, alternatively, permits the existing conventional source program to optionally remain unchanged by creating a separate expanded source program in another library.

It is a further object of the invention to utilize the expanded source program and the audit statements as the basis for analysis of the program execution audit output. The invention provides for more rapid understanding and correction of errors, problems, or programming logic than is possible with the conventional source program. The source program is expanded with standard comprehensive program documentation. Examples of the documentation provided are file names, file keys, and call program names. This expansion results in source program's being significantly faster to write and test by the original programmer. Also, the program is much easier to read and understand by programmers unfamiliar with it, and therefore programmers can more easily modify the program.

Still another object of the invention is to provide default audit compile profiles which provide for typical auditing environments such as first program test audits, completed program test audits, pilot production audits, and production environment audits. The default audit profiles simplify the process of selecting auditing options to be included in the expanded source program. The invention allows a selected audit profile to be modified for the selected program and used when the conventional source program is expanded with audit statements.

Another object of the invention is to allow virtually any executable source program statement to be audited. The invention also allows virtually any file in the source program to be audited, together with desired file operation codes, and the data for all key fields used in the audited file operations. The invention provides ten levels of auditing which may be dynamically changed during program execution. Any executable operation code may be audited together with all fields referenced in each audited statement. Also, the invention provides standard audit operation code audit prefix codes beginning with the characters Z$, and with a suffix code unique to the operation code.

A further object of the invention is to allow virtually any field or label used in the source program to be audited when either referenced or modified, together with the data value of each audited field. Also, the invention provides select and omit functions which qualify the auditing of operation codes by field name(s).

Another object is to provide program default initial execution profiles, which are provided for typical initial execution environments, such as first program test, completed program test, pilot production, and production environment. The default initial execution profiles simplify the process of auditing the execution of programs by providing frequently selected audit execution options. The invention allows a selected execution profile to be modified for the selected program and used during the execution of the program.

It is a further object of the invention to provide for dynamic modification of program auditing during program execution by changing execution auditing options, or turning auditing on or off completely. Audits must have been previously selected for potential audit and included in the expanded source program.

An additional object is to optionally output audit data to a disk, and to provide for the retention of the audit data for both test and production environments. The invention also provides an audit database in date and time sequences from all audited programs. This provides for analysis of audited statements across all audited programs by date and time sequence. The analysis may include program, user, date and time range, audit code prefix, file, field, label, and/or any execution audited data value. The invention provides formatted audit reporting of historical audit information for use by internal and external auditors at a level of detail and auditability not possible previously.

Another object of this invention is to reduce the cost of developing and maintaining source programs by significantly reducing the skills and training needed by programmers, and to reduce much of the risk involved in implementing and maintaining programs. The invention also reduces the number of programmers required to develop and maintain programs.

Additionally, it is an object of the invention to provide the real-time detailed audit information needed for advanced event detection and event action software functions. This object may be advantageous in a large variety of computer operation settings and is particularly useful with multiple programmers and users that are utilizing the same programming language on the same compiler on a remote computer.

It is an object of the invention to provide improved elements and arrangements thereof in real-time program audit software for the purposes described which is inexpensive, dependable and fully effective in accomplishing its intended purposes.

These and other objects of the present invention will become readily apparent upon further review of the following specification and drawings.

BRIEF DESCRIPTION OF THE DRAWINGS

FIG. 1A is a block diagram of the source program compile and initial execution audit functions (program Z$PGM01).

FIG. 1B is a block diagram of the expansion of the conventional source program with audit statements (program Z$PGM02), and the conventional programming language compile of the expanded source program.

FIG. 2 is a block diagram of the program execution audit options (program Z$PGM03), including the modification of the initial execution audit options, and the conventional execution of the compiled program object with audit outputs.

FIG. 3 is a block diagram of the create or change options and run audit analysis options (program Z$PGM04), including the creation or change of audit analysis reporting options, and the processing of the audit analysis report.

FIG. 4 is a block diagram of the create or change options and run formatted audit analysis reporting options (program Z$PGM05), and the processing of the formatted audit analysis report.

FIG. 5 is a block diagram of the modify source program compile and initial execution audit options (program Z$PGM06), including the capability to undo all or selected audit source statements.

FIG. 6A is a flowchart of the pseudo-code for the create or change compile and initial execution audit options program (Z$PGM01).

FIG. 6B is a flowchart of the pseudo-code for the create or change compile and initial execution audit options program (Z$PGM01).

FIG. 6C is a flowchart of the pseudo-code for the create or change compile and initial execution audit options program (Z$PGM01).

FIG. 6D is a flowchart of the pseudo-code for the create or change compile and initial execution audit options program (Z$PGM01).

FIG. 7A is a flowchart of the pseudo-code for the create or change compile and initial execution audit options program (Z$PGM01).

FIG. 7B is a flowchart of the pseudo-code for the create or change compile and initial execution audit options program (Z$PGM01).

FIG. 7C is a flowchart of the pseudo-code for the create or change compile and initial execution audit options program (Z$PGM01).

FIG. 8 is a flowchart of the pseudo-code for the create or change compile and initial execution audit options program (Z$PGM01).

FIG. 9A is a portion of the flowchart of the pseudo-code for the expand source program with audit statements program (Z$PGM02).

FIG. 9B is a portion of the flowchart of the pseudo-code for the expand source program with audit statements program (Z$PGM02).

FIG. 9C is a portion of the flowchart of the pseudo-code for the expand source program with audit statements program (Z$PGM02).

FIG. 10A is a portion of the flowchart of the pseudo-code for the expand source program with audit statements program (Z$PGM02).

FIG. 10B is a portion of the flowchart of the pseudo-code for the expand source program with audit statements program (Z$PGM02).

FIG. 10C is a portion of the flowchart of the pseudo-code for the expand source program with audit statements program (Z$PGM02).

FIG. 11 is a portion of the flowchart of the pseudo-code for the expand source program with audit statements program (Z$PGM02).

FIG. 12A is a portion of the flowchart of the pseudo-code for the modify the initial execution audit options program (Z$PGM03).

FIG. 12B is a portion of the flowchart of the pseudo-code for the modify the initial execution audit options program (Z$PGM03).

FIG. 13A is a portion of the flowchart of the pseudo-code for the create or change options and run the audit analysis reporting program (Z$PGM04).

FIG. 13B is a portion of the flowchart of the pseudo-code for the create or change options and run the audit analysis reporting program (Z$PGM04).

FIG. 13C is a portion of the flowchart of the pseudo-code for the create or change options and run the audit analysis reporting program (Z$PGM04).

FIG. 14A is a portion of the flowchart of the pseudo-code for the create or change options and run the formatted audit analysis reporting program (Z$PGM05).

FIG. 14B is a portion of the flowchart of the pseudo-code for the create or change options and run the formatted audit analysis reporting program (Z$PGM05).

FIG. 14C is a portion of the flowchart of the pseudo-code for the create or change options and run the formatted audit analysis reporting program (Z$PGM05).

FIG. 15A is a portion of the flowchart of the pseudo-code for the modify source program compile and initial execution audit options program (Z$PGM06).

FIG. 15B is a portion of the flowchart of the pseudo-code for the modify source program compile and initial execution audit options program (Z$PGM06).

FIG. 15C is a portion of the flowchart of the pseudo-code for the modify source program compile and initial execution audit options program (Z$PGM06).

Similar reference characters denote corresponding features consistently throughout the attached drawings.

DETAILED DESCRIPTION OF THE PREFERRED EMBODIMENTS

The present invention is a real-time program audit software that is a method and system for generating source program audit statements which provide analyses of program statements and data as the source program executes. These audit statements provide for real-time analysis of the execution of the program. The real-time program audit software is applicable to virtually any programming language that uses source program statements, whether the source statements are compiled into an executable object or are interpreted during program execution. Conventional source programs are selected for auditing based on an audit profile; the audit profile is customized for specific compile and initial execution options; the source program is expanded with the selected audit statements; and the source program is compiled with a conventional language compiler. Program execution audits are based on the initial execution audit profile, customized execution audits, or dynamic audits specified during program execution. Program audit output is to a disk or print file, and is available for immediate online display or printing, or for expanded auditing analysis. Expanded auditing analysis provides for extensive analysis of the real-time program audit output data from all audited programs based on the desired analysis, which includes: program, user, date and time ranges, audit code prefix, audited file, field, label, and any execution audited data value.

For purposes of the present application, it will be understood that the following definitions apply.

"Conventional programming language" is defined to be any artificial language that can be used to define a sequence of instructions that can ultimately be processed and executed by a computer; a translation process, from the source code expressed using the programming language to the machine code that the computer needs to work with, must be automated by means of a compiler. As used herein, the term "programming language" refers to any series of source codes regardless of whether the program statements are compiled or interpreted.

"Source code" is human-readable program statements written in a high-level or assembly language that are not directly readable by a computer.

A "source program" is the source code version of a program.

"Object code" is the code, generated by a compiler or an assembler, that was translated from the source code of a program. Object code generally refers to machine code that can be directly executed by the system's central processing unit (CPU), but it can also refer to assembly language source code or a variation of machine code.

An "interpreter" is a program that translates and then executes each statement in a program written in an interpreted language.

A "compiler" is any program that transforms one set of symbols into another by following a set of syntactic and semantic rules. Also, a compiler is a program that translates all the source code of a program written in a high-level language into object code prior to execution of the program. As used herein, "compiler" refers to both interpreter and compiler.

"Real-time" refers to a time frame wherein the computer responds to situations as they occur. The analyses which occur in the present invention occur at the rate at which the audited program is executed. Real-time operations are those in which the machine's activities match the human perception of time or those in which computer operations proceed at the same rate as a physical or external process.

"Operation (OP) code" is the portion of a machine language or assembly language instruction that specifies the type of instruction and the structure of the data on which it operates.

The term "validating" refers to accepting a pre-chosen variable or changing that variable to a preferred variable. Variables include program language, conventional source program, and audit profile.

In a preferred embodiment, the present invention provides a method and system for generating computer source code audit statements from input source programs of virtually any commercial programming language. The generated audit source statements are inserted into a copy of the input source program (the conventional source program) , become an integral part of the copied source program (the expanded source program), and are available for optional auditing at any time during program development, program testing, implementation, or in a production environment, without intervention by the programmer, or anyone else. The generated source code audit statements then may be utilized during the execution of the compiled program object, or execution of an interpreted source program, to provide a real-time audit of the detailed processing of the program against the data processed by the program. The resulting real-time audit output may be viewed online as the program execution takes place, or may be viewed later both online or in printed audit analysis reports. Audits may be specified at up to ten levels, providing for no auditing, auditing of only key program functions, to very comprehensive auditing of virtually every executable instruction as it is executed, with all the data processed by the instruction. The level of auditing may be changed dynamically as the program is executing by using dynamic audits.

In addition, this invention provides for the insertion of source program documentation statements into the input conventional source program. This provides comprehensive and useful program documentation not normally found in conventional source programs written by most commercial programmers, and not available in most commercial software products. The resulting expanded source program becomes much easier to read and comprehend, particularly for programmers unfamiliar with the program, and the resulting source program logic is much easier to understand by viewing the audit output of the actual processing being performed against the data being processed. The real-time program audit software provides a separate licensed implementation for each source programming language implementation supported. Thus, each programming language vendor compiler that supports specific language functions and operation codes (OP codes) could have a licensed implementation of the real-time program audit software which would support that specific language implementation. Each programming language requires a separate version of the real-time program audit software.

FIG. 1A shows a block diagram of the initial input and output files needed for the real-time program audit software. FIG. 1A shows the source program compile and initial execution audit functions used. The program module create or change compile and initial execution audit options for program 100 handles the initial input/output files for the real-time program audit software. The create or change compile and initial execution audit options program 100 (Z$PGM01) allows the programmer to quickly and easily audit and document the conventional source program 27 or select additional audits for a previously expanded source program. This program is a setup program for the expand input with audits program, the pre-compiler 200 (Z$PGM02) (FIG. 1B), and provides all the information and options needed to expand the source program with audit statements.

The select compile and initial execution audit options 20 for program 100 represents the screen input. Here the programmer decides which files and additional information is to be audited by the real-time program audit software.

The operation code audit profile and master information file 21 contains an audit profile of virtually every operation code and file description format used by programmers in writing source programs in the vendor programming language implementation. The operation code audit profile and master information file 21 determines exactly how the operation code is to be audited, if selected for auditing, including all variable names and status codes used in the instruction. The profile also determines whether the audit is to be inserted before the source statement (as in branches), or after the source statement (as in file I/O). The operation code audit profile and master information file 21 contains the standard audit prefix code for the operation code, such as Z$R for READ and Z$W for WRITE.

The compile and initial execution audit profiles 23 master file contains a default compile audit profile, and a default initial execution audit profile for typical programming environments such as: initial compile, where comprehensive documentation would be appropriate; initial test, where audits of all file input and output would be appropriate; pilot implementation, where comprehensive auditing would be appropriate; and for production implementation, where selected auditing such as key event auditing may be appropriate. Production implementation auditing is critical for enhanced error correction and for auditing by internal and external auditors.

The data file names, attributes, keys, fields length, and types 25 master file contains all the necessary information about each file used in the source program to insert the audit and documentation statements into the expanded source program. This information is automatically generated by analyzing the compile listing output of the conventional input source program.

The conventional source program library 27 is the existing source program library in the programming language at the licensed customer site. Previously expanded conventional source program library files are included as a conventional source program library 27 because they are handled in the same manner as if unexpanded. Programs to be expanded with audit and documentation statements should compile successfully before program expansion, including already expanded conventional programs. Conventional data files 29 are the existing data files used in the conventional source programs at the licensed customer site.

An appropriate audit profile is selected for the selected program name, together with an initial execution profile. The default audit profile, documentation options, and initial execution options may be utilized, or the profile options may be extensively modified for each program file, operation code, field and label used in the conventional source program. In addition, the ability to bypass auditing of labeled subroutines or procedures that are specified by the programmer or for the entire installation is provided. This provides the ability to bypass the auditing for very repetitive routines such as date validation and field names defined as constants, which can greatly reduce the amount of audit output, allowing focus on key program processing routines. The selected compile audit options file 22 (Z$AUDITC), and the program file and field information file 24 (Z$AUDITM) are output, and used in the next program, the expand input with audits program, the pre-compiler 200, to expand the source program with audit statements. The initial execution audit options file 26 (Z$AUDITO) is also output, and is used during program execution to create audit output. The selected compile audit options file 22 provides output which can also be used as shown in FIG. 2. This is denoted by the circled capital A. The initial execution audit options file 26 also provides output which can be used, as denoted by the circled capital B. Advanced and online review of output audits is also provided, by optionally displaying the source program variable names on a line above the actual audit data being executed. This optional review is available only if the expanded source program is online during review of the audit output file, which is normally the case. The ability to select and sequence virtually any file record (data) field when auditing file record processing is provided, as well as the ability to select and sequence virtually any (data) field when auditing any label in the program. The ability to audit any changed (data) field in a specified labeled subroutine or procedure is provided, in addition to the ability to audit any specified (data) field, including auditing only when the field is changed.

The submit program to insert audit statements 28 (FIG. 1B) represents screen input. Here the programmer decides whether to submit the conventional program to the expanded with audit statements by real-time program audit software. The block diagram shown on FIG. 1A continues to FIG. 1B, as shown.

The expand input with audits program, the pre-compiler 200 (Z$PGM02), provides a one-pass expansion of the input conventional source program 27, utilizing the selected compile audit options file 22, and program file and field information file 24 from the previous program. This expand input with audits program 200 is the major module in this invention, and it may be considered to be a pre-compiler to the conventional programming language compiler 37. The expanded source program audit messages 31 are read into the pre-compiler 200. Each conventional source statement read is examined for insertion of audit and/or documentation statements, using the selected options. Every data field for audited statements is audited, and a unique audit code is assigned to each audited statement, by suffixing the standard assigned audit prefix code with a sequential number starting with 001. Therefore, the first audited READ statement would have an audit code of Z$R001. The pre-compiler 200 is output to a separate expanded source program with selected audit statements library 33, leaving the input conventional source program unchanged. Each of the audit statements are assigned a unique fifteen digit number to provide for a second level file of very detailed audit information for every audited source statement executed. This optional detailed auditing provides for auditing all of the one hundred RPG indicators, and the command keys, and other key information at every audited statement executed in the expanded source program for RPG language implementations. Standard audit printer and disk file definitions are copied into the program, together with routines to initiate and change auditing during program execution. The pre-compiler 200 also includes an express expand source option which utilizes default audit options normally utilized by the programmer. This express expand option allows a programmer to key only the program name and then to press a command key to expand the input source program with real-time program audits. This express option is in addition to the option to fully customize the audits by file, record format, operation code, field, and program label.

The expanded source program with selected audit statements library 33 and the conventional (existing) program language compiler files 35 are read into the conventional programming language source program compiler 37. The conventional programming language source program compiler 37 compiles the expanded source program, producing an expanded executable program object with selected audits 32 having the compiled audit statements. The conventional programming language source program compiler 37 also produces a program source compile listing with audit statements document 39. The source program compile listing may be utilized as the basis for creating real-time programming audit work files. The compile listing completely defines the program files, fields, labels, and operation codes including copybooks utilized in the source program. The expanded source program with selected audit statements library 33 and the expanded executable program object with selected audits 32 are also referred to in other block diagrams denoted by the circled capital letters. The expanded source program with selected audit statements library 33 is utilized in FIG. 5 as denoted by the circled capital C, and the expanded executable program object with selected audits 32 is utilized in FIG. 2 as denoted by the circled capital D. It is possible to include several commonly utilized levels of compilers in the same language implementation. For example, for IBM AS/400 RPG, both the RPGIII (RPG/400) and RPGIV (ILE RPG) can be provided in the same implementation. For IBM AS/400 COBOL, both COBOL/400 and COBOL ILE can be provided in the same implementation.

FIG. 2 shows a block diagram of the program which is responsible for the execution of audit options. The modify initial execution audit options program 300 (Z$PGM03) allows the programmer to quickly and easily modify the selected initial execution options for compiled audit statements, even during program execution. The selected compile audit options file 22 is utilized by the modify initial execution audit options program 300. The modify initial execution audit options for program 41 represents screen input. Here the programmer decides whether to change the selections previously made pertaining to audit options for the program and to write these selections to the modify initial execution audit options program 300. The modify initial execution audit options program 300 is the program that allows the dynamic modification of the auditing options and audit output as the program is in program execution, by modifying the initial execution audit options for program file 26 into the current execution audit options file 43. The initial/current execution audit options program is (Z$AUDITO) utilized to create the initial execution audit options for program file 26 and the current execution audit options file 43.

The current execution audit options file 43 and the expanded executable program object with selected audits file 32 are used in conventional program execution by the executable program object with selected audits 47. Data files used in the program conventional processing 45 are also write to, and are written to, by the executable program object with selected audits 47. The output from the executable program object with selected audits 47 includes an audit execution analysis report 49 and an audit execution output file 42. The audit execution output file 42 is also used in FIG. 3 as denoted by the circled E.

FIG. 3 is a block diagram depicting the create or change options and run audit analysis reporting program 400, and includes the creation, change and processing of audit analysis reporting options. The create or change options and run audit analysis reporting program 400 (Z$PGM04) allows the programmer or any authorized user to analyze the audit execution output file 42 (Z$AUDITF) information, if this file was output during program execution. The display or print execution audit analysis 51 screen display allows the user to decide which menus to choose. The requester may select from a menu of audit analysis functions and create printed or displayed audit output or create formatted disk audit output 59 (Z$AUDITE) for further analysis. The create or change options and run audit analysis reporting program 400 (Z$PGM04) also produces an audit analysis reporting document 57 (Z$AUDITP). Alternatively, a display of audit analysis 55 may be produced. An audit analysis reporting options file 53 (Z$AUDITA) provides the ability to save and retrieve reporting options by a name assigned to the audit analysis request. Typical audit output would be for a specific job execution of the program, or by user, terminal, date, or time range. The printed and disk audit outputs may be viewed and scanned using standard system utility programs and available utility programs in real-time as the program executes, or later for error resolution or analysis.

FIG. 4 shows a block diagram of the create or change options and run formatted audit analysis reporting program 500 and the processing of the formatted audit analysis report 65. The display or print formatted audit analysis 61 screen display permits the user to select options for the create or change options and run formatted audit analysis reporting-program 500 (Z$PGM05). The create or change options and run formatted audit analysis reporting program 500 (Z$PGM05) allows the programmer or any authorized user to analyze the extracted audit execution file 59 (Z$AUDITE), if the extracted audit execution file 59 (Z$AUDITE) was output by the previous program. A formatted audit analysis reporting options file 63 (Z$AUDITS) provides the ability to save and retrieve formatted reporting options by a name assigned to the formatted audit analysis request. The requestor may select from a menu of formatted audit analysis functions, presented by the display of formatted audit analysis 67, and create a printed audit output. The formatted audit analysis reporting 65 allows the user to print audit analysis. Typical audit output would be for a specific application to selected transaction types over a range of dates and times. This focused audit output is most useful for internal and external auditors in verifying the detailed computations, processing, and transactions behind more summary output. These detail transactions may be transient computations that otherwise would never have been written to disk and saved without the audits, and not available on any disk journal.

The modify compile and initial execution audit options program 600 (Z$PGM06) allows the programmer to undo or partially undo the previous expansion of source programs with audit statements, and therefore remove the expanded source program with selected audit statements file 33. The input/output to the modify compile and initial execution audit options program 600 is shown in the block diagram FIG. 5. The expanded source program is read from the expanded source program library and contains the expanded source program with selected audit statements file 33. All audit and documentation statements are summarized and displayed to the programmer on screen by the modify compile and initial execution audit options for program 71 screen display. The programmer may then undo all or some of the auditing or documentation selections. The initial execution options for the program are similarly read, summarized, and displayed to allow the undoing of these selections. The source program may then be expanded with additional audit, documentation, and initial execution options with the expand input with audits program 200 using input/output that is very similar to that shown FIG. 1A, and the same files are frequently used, as shown by both FIG. 1A and FIG. 5. The block diagram shown in FIG. 5 flows to FIG. 1B in the exact same manner as does FIG. 1A. The operation code audit profile and master information file 21 is utilized several times and is the same file throughout even though its position in the block diagrams are not identical. The source program may alternatively be left as a conventional program.

The pseudo-code for the create or change compile and initial execution audit options program 100 (Z$PGM01) is shown in the flowchart depicted in FIGS. 6A, 6B, 6C, 6D, 7A, 7B, 7C, and 8. The flowchart flows linearly from figure to figure as indicated. In particular, FIG. 6A shows the initial selection on the screen display corresponding to the select compile and initial execution audit options for program 20 shown in the block diagram FIG. 1A. The initial display 101 shows the initial screen images. The initial display 101 prompts the user to enter the name of the conventional source program 27 and select the default compile audit profile from the compile and initial execution audit profiles 23 master file. The initial steps involve validating the selection of the program 102 to be audited from a display of conventional source programs 27 listed preferably in a library format, validating a selected program language 103 to determine that the program language is acceptable for auditing by the audit pre-compiler, and validating the entered audit profile 104 or allowing selection of the audit profile.

FIG. 6B includes the steps of retrieving and saving operation codes 105, 106, 107. Retrieving and saving the default audit profile operation codes and the default initial execution audit options 105 are executed at this time. This step 105 includes retrieving and saving the default audit profile operation codes which are to be audited and the default initial execution audit options for the selected audit profile. The next step 106 involves retrieving and matching the operation codes to be audited. The selected program source operation code is retrieved and matched to the default audit profile operation code used. The selected operation codes are to be audited unless deselected subsequently during execution of the real-time program audit software. Next is the step 107 of saving the programs unselected operation codes. This step 107 involves saving the program operation codes which are actually used in the program but are not selected for auditing in the default audit profile. These saved program operation codes may be selected for additional auditing later during the execution of the real-time program audit software.

As shown in FIG. 6C, these steps 108, 109, 110 involve the matching of program operation codes used by the conventional source program 27 but not in the default audit profile with the master list of all operation codes valid for auditing. Also saved are any program operation codes used by the program but that are not valid for auditing, for later optional display 108. Also shown is the step 109 of retrieving or creating the data file names, attributes, keys, fields, lengths, types 25 master file for each file used. The next step 110 creates a cross reference which involves creating a separate file and field label files on a disk with one keyed record per file. This step 110 creates the program file and field information file 24; it creates a keyed record per field including program defined constants and internally described file fields.

As shown in FIG. 6D, the next step 111 deletes all unreferenced fields that are not actually utilized in the conventional program from the program file and field information file 24. This step 111 deletes all unreferenced fields which are not used from the disk cross reference file. The next step 112 displays a menu of the functions specified in the selected audit profile and allows the selection of the menu items for auditing profile overrides. These menu options are grouped by files, operation codes, and fields. The next step 113 allows a command key to be pressed to accept the audit profile options as displayed. This creates the selected compile audit options file 22 and the initial execution audit options file 26. An option is provided for submitting the source program directly to the basic audit pre-compiler program for insertion of the auditing statements utilizing the submit program function.

As shown in FIG. 7A, alternatively to submitting the source program to the basic audit pre-compiler program, a step 114 is provided which enables the user to display the menu options in order to override the default audit options for the program. The menu override options include: Files, Operation codes, Fields and Labels, and initial execution options. If the override option

File is chosen 115, the display will show a summary of the file and audit status utilized. Step 116 enables a user to select or deselect files for auditing, to modify auditing levels, and to permit a command key to display a second line with each operation code used by the file and its auditing status.

FIG. 7B shows selections 117,118,119 pertaining to auditing the operation codes. Step 117 enables the programmer to select (or unselect) to audit each operation code used in each file, and to determine the auditing level. It is important to emphasize that all key fields used in the audited file's operation codes will be audited automatically. The programmer may also select additional non-key fields for automatic auditing. If the programmer chooses to use operation code overrides, step 118 displays each operation code. The display will include the auditing status of the operation code and the level of auditing selected. It will show the assigned audit code prefix and apparent duplicate field names. Step 119 enables the programmer to select (or unselect) each operation code used for auditing, the auditing level, and to change previously assigned audit prefix codes. Fields used in non-file audited operation codes will be audited automatically. Audit prefix codes will be suffixed in the pre-compiler 200 program to uniquely identify an audit point.

FIG. 7C shows additional audit options 120,121,122,123,124. When utilizing the Field or Label overrides, as shown in step 120, a display of each Field and Label used in the program is shown as a single line on a Field summary screen, and a display of the auditing status and which of the ten levels of auditing of each Field and Label used in the program is also shown. Step 121 enables the programmer to select (or unselect) each Field or Label used for auditing, to modify the audit levels, and to allow auditing when a field is used or is modified. When the programmer chooses to select the Initial Execution overrides, step 122 displays the default initial execution profile options. The execution options may be modified and the auditing level may be changed from level 0 to level 9. Note that level 0 has no initial program execution auditing. Step 123 requires the programmer to validate all default profile and override entries. Error messages are displayed as required, wherein the programmer accepts and revalidates input until all input is correct. Step 124 provides a command key which may be utilized to exit the program and to submit the source program for expansion of the auditing statements.

FIG. 8 shows the output for the create or change compile and initial execution audit options program 100. Upon pressing a command key to submit the source program for expansion, step 125 formats and creates the output files required for the program to be utilized in expanding the conventional source code with audit statements. As shown in step 126, the output files which are produced include selected basic audit compile options for source program expansion to the selected compile audit options file 22, program file information, key fields information and field cross reference for source program expansion to the program file and field information file 24, and basic audit initial execution options for the object (executable) program to the initial execution audit options for program file 26. Step 127 prints a summary of the audit options, the program's initial execution options, informational messages, warning messages, error messages, counts of the input conventional source statements, files, fields, and labels used. Step 128 displays a message that the source program has been submitted for expansion of the auditing statements. The last step 129 returns to the calling program.

The steps required to create or change compile and initial execution audit options are complete.

The create or change compile and initial execution audit options program 100 has been executed fully.

The flowchart for the pseudo-code for the expand input with audits program, the pre-compiler 200 program (Z$PGM02), is shown in FIGS. 9A, 9B, 9C, 10A, 10B, 10C, and 11. The first four steps 201,202,203,204 in the pre-compiler 200 program are depicted in FIG. 9A. In the first step 201, the pre-compiler 200 program reads and stores the selected audit compile options which were created by the create or change compile and initial execution audit options program 100. Additional information for the expansion of the conventional source program is stored in the operation code audit profile and master information files 21. In the next step 202, the pre-compiler 200 program reads and stores the program file information, the key fields information, and the field cross reference information that were created by the create or change compile and initial execution audit options program 100. In step 203, the pre-compiler 200 program reads the conventional (existing) source statements for the program from the conventional source program 27 library, and in a single pass of the conventional source program statements, expands the source by inserting the basic audit source statements and expanded documentation statements. In step 204 the pre-compiler 200 determines if expanded documentation is selected. For each file used, comment lines are created with the full file name and a list of the file field names used in the file key. Auditing may be limited to only expanded source program documentation.

FIG. 9B shows the auditing to disk selections 205, 206 for the pre-compiler 200 program. If the programmer has selected the option 205 to audit operation codes or data fields to disk, then the programmer must insert the File description source statements for the audit execution output file 42 into the source program statements. Audit execution output file 42 source statements are copied from the audit master information. Related files, records, fields, and standard processing routines for this function are also copied. All audit disk output will be written to the audit execution output file 42 disk. Alternatively, the programmer may select option 206, to effect the basic auditing of operation codes or data fields to disk. In this case, the programmer must insert the file description source statements for the audit execution output file 42 into the source program statements. The program copies the current execution audit options file 43 source statements from the audit master information. Also, the program copies related file, record, field and standard processing routines for this function. The current execution audit options file 43 is the audit execution options disk files which controls which of the audit options are active during program execution.

As shown in FIG. 9C, if the programmer has selected option 205 to audit operation codes or data fields to disk, and then selects option 207, the programmer inserts the file description source statements for the audit execution analysis printer file into the source program statements. The program copies the audit execution analysis report 49 file source statements from the audit master information and copies related files, records, field information, and processing routines for this function. This print record output is formatted in a manner similar to the previous disk record output. The audit execution analysis report 49 printer file provides real-time analysis of audit output during program execution from a printer spool file. This output is for that specific program execution, for only that specific user, and for only that job. In step 208, the auditing and/or documentation options selected in the previous program, the create or change compile and initial execution audit options program 100, for each executable source statement read are determined.

This determination involves consideration of the statement operation code, the statement variable names, and the conditions, such as indicators or switches. The auditing and/or documentation source statements are inserted using the audit operation code profile for the source statements being processed. The resulting audits may be output to disk via the audit analysis reporting options 53 file and/or to a printer via the audit analysis reporting 57 program based on selections in the create or change compile and initial execution audit options program 100.

The flowchart of the pseudo-code for the expand input with audits program, the pre-compiler, is continued in FIG. 10A. As shown in step 209, a unique audit name for the audited source statement is generated for each source statement to be expanded with audit statements. In assigning a unique audit name, the assigned three character audit prefix code for the operation code from the create or change compile and initial execution audit options program 100 is utilized. The audit prefix code is suffixed with a three digit sequential number each time the operation code is used in the source program. This method results in a unique identifier for every source statement audited during the execution of the program and the audited variable names identify the data being processed. As shown in step 210, changes to the conventional (existing) source statements can occur only if a branch is made to a statement label, and auditing is selected to audit the branch to that label, which results in an audit statement that is inserted at the label statement. These changes are normally made only to the copies of the expanded source program.

The flowchart of the pseudo-code for the expanded input with audits program, the pre-compiler 200 program, is continued in FIG. 10B. In step 211, the audit operation code profile for the source statement being processed inserts documentation comment statements for each source statement expanded. In step 212, the entire expanded source program results are output to an expanded source program library. A new source program is created in an expanded source program library with the same program name. The entire input conventional source program is written to the expanded source program library including the inserted audit and documentation statements. The input conventional source library remains unchanged. In step 213, the inserted audit and documentation source statements and the input of conventional program source statements are counted by program source statements and comment statements. Also, audit and documentation expansion statement errors, if any, are counted by error types.

The flowchart of the pseudo-code for the expand input with audits program, the pre-compiler 200 program, is continued in FIG. 10C. In step 214, the expanded source program audit messages 31 printer file is utilized to print an expanded source program audit messages report. Needed audit expansion or documentation messages may then be printed. The counts of input program source statements and comment statements, and the counts of the inserted audit and documentation program source and comment statements are printed at the end of the basic audit source program expansion. The elapsed time of the execution of the audit source program expansion program is also printed.

In step 215, if the expand source program with audits is successful, then the expanded source program is allowed to be submitted to the conventional -programming language source program compiler 37. An executable program object with the basic audit functions in an expanded program object library is created by successful expanded source program compilation. The output conventional object library remains unchanged, which allows program execution to be performed by the object program either before or after basic audit source program expansion. Successful completion of the expand source program with audits means that no significant errors are detected, and inserted basic audit source statements should compile successfully in the conventional language compile of the expanded source program.

The flowchart of the pseudo-code for the expand input with audits program, the pre-compiler 200 program, is continued in FIG. 11. In step 216, in the event that the expanded source program with audits is unsuccessful, then an error severity code is returned. The error severity code for the job is similar to the error severity code returned by conventional language compilers. In step 217, once the pre-compiler 200 program is finished, the program is exited and returned to the calling program.

The flowchart of the pseudo-code for the modify the initial execution audit options program 300 (Z$PGM03) is depicted in FIGS. 12A and 12B. The modify initial execution audit options program 300 is the program that allows the dynamic modification of the auditing options. The first step 301 is to input the name of the conventional source program 27 by entering the name when prompted by the initial display screen, the modify initial execution audit options for program 41. It is important to note that the program execution options for a program may be changed while the program object is executing when confirmed later during the execution of modify initial execution audit options program 300. Step 302 requires the programmer to validate that the modify initial execution audit options program 300 has selected the audit compile options in the selected compile audit options file 22. Only those audit options which have been used to expand the source program may be selected or modified for and during object program execution. Step 303 retrieves any initial or current initial execution options for the program from the initial execution options for program file 26 (Z$AUDITO), together with the compile audit options for the program from the selected compile audit options file 22 (Z$AUDITC). Step 304 displays the initial or current program execution audit options and all of the compile audit options are displayed. Step 305 allows all the compile options to be turned on or off as execution options, and allows for the ten auditing levels to be changed.

Step 306 causes the current execution audit options for the program to be updated to the current execution audit options file 43 (Z$AUDITO). The changed execution audit options will take effect immediately if the program is being executed. Step 307 enables a command key to be used to confirm that the audit execution options are complete and may be used for current auditing. It is indicated that the execution audit options have been changed for the program in the current execution audit options file 43 (Z$AUDITO), so that if the program is currently executing, and no auditing is taking place, the program is to start auditing with the current execution options. In step 308, a command key is used to end the modify initial execution audit options program 300. In step 309, the calling program is returned to once the modify initial execution audit options program 300 ends.

FIGS. 13A, 13B, and 13C are a flowchart of the pseudo-code for the create or change options and run audit analysis reporting program 400 (Z$PGM04). In step 401 the initial screen is displayed. This display or print execution audit analysis 51 screen display provides for the selection of the desired audit analysis function. Audit analysis reporting is provided for using a selection capability from a menu of functions. Output provided, by the selection includes printing of audit execution output file information and creation of extracted audit execution output file information for formatted reporting. The printed and disk input and output may be viewed and scanned online using standard system utility programs and available utility programs. An option 402 is provided which allows for the entry of an audit analysis report name or the selection of a name from a display of existing audit analysis report names. The audit report name provides the ability to save previously entered audit report parameters for use again in the same, or a similar, audit analysis report. In step 403, when a new audit analysis report name is entered, a menu for audit analysis reporting selection options which allows the selection of the form of output is provided. The selection of the desired audit execution output file information is also provided. Selection parameters include all keyed fields of the audit output file including Job, Program, User, Terminal, Date, and Time.

As shown in step 404, when an existing audit analysis report name is entered, the create or change options and run audit analysis reporting program 400 retrieves the existing options for the audit analysis report name from the analysis reporting options file 53. The same menu of audit analysis reporting selection options is provided and indicates which options were previously selected. The same selection options that were available when creating a new audit analysis name are allowed. Step 405 provides a command key which allows exiting the program without updates. All selections are validated and, when there are no errors, a command key to save the audit analysis selected options to the analysis reporting options file 53 is provided by the entered audit analysis report name. Step 406 provides a command key is provided to allow the audit analysis report to be run.

As shown in step 407, if the audit analysis report is to be run, the selected audit analysis report options are processed against the audit execution output file 42 (Z$AUDITF) to produce the desired printer file (Z$AUDITP), and/or the formatted disk file (Z$AUDITE) output. Step 408 provides a command key to end the program, and step 409 returns to the calling program.

FIGS. 14A, 14B, and 14C are a flowchart of the pseudo-code for the create or change options and run formatted audit analysis reporting program 500 (Z$PGM05). In step 501, the initial screen is displayed providing for the selection of the desired formatted audit analysis functions. The formatted audit analysis reporting using a selection capability from a menu of selection and formatting functions is provided. It is important to note that printed and disk input and output may be viewed and scanned online using standard system utility programs and available utility programs. In step 502, the entry of a formatted audit analysis report name or the selection of a name from a display of existing formatted audit analysis report names is allowed. The formatted audit report name provides the ability to save previously entered formatted audit report parameters for use again in the same or similar formatted audit analysis report. In step 503, if a new formatted audit analysis report name is entered, a menu of formatted audit analysis reporting selection options is provided which allows for the selection of the form of output and for the selection for the desired extracted audit execution file information. The selection parameters include all keyed fields of the extracted audit execution formatted file including Job, Program, User, Terminal, Date, Time, and other parameters selected when the file was formatted.

In step 504, if an existing formatted audit analysis report name is entered, the existing options for the formatted audit analysis report name are retrieved from the formatted audit analysis reporting options file 63. The same menu of formatted audit analysis reporting selection options are provided and the options which were previously selected are indicated. The same selection options that were available when creating a new formatted audit analysis name are allowed. In step 505 a command key is provided to allow exiting the program without updates, all selections are validated, and when there are no errors, another command key is provided to save the formatted audit analysis selected options to the formatted audit analysis reporting options file 63 (Z$AUDITS) by the entered formatted audit analysis report name. Step 506 provides a command key to allow the formatted audit analysis report to be run.

In step 507, if the formatted audit analysis report is to be run, then the selected formatted audit analysis report options are processed against the extracted audit execution formatted file (Z$AUDITE) to produce the desired display or printer file (Z$AUDITR) of the formatted audit analysis reporting 65. Step 508 provides a command key is provided to end the program and step 509 returns to the calling program.

FIGS. 15A, 15B, and 15C are a flowchart of the pseudo-code for the modify compile and initial execution audit options program 600. In step 601, the initial screen is displayed and the program allows a name to be entered. This program is utilized to input previously expanded source programs and to allow the removal of all or selected audit source statements. This allows the complete undoing of the expanded source audit statements back to the original conventional input source program, or the partial undoing of the expanded source audit statements. The program may then be expanded with additional audit statements. In step 602, the expanded source program is retrieved from the expanded source program library into a work file, the source program is scanned for all audit statements, and the audit functions are summarized in the same display as used in the create or change compile and initial execution audit options program. In step 603, the audit functions in the expanded source program are displayed, and any or all of the audit functions are allowed to be removed from the work file of the input expanded source program.

In step 604, the initial (current) execution options are retrieved and displayed for the expanded source program from the initial execution audit options file 26 (Z$AUDITO). Any or all of the initial execution audit options are allowed to be removed (undone). Step 605 provides a command key to allow exiting the program without updates, all selections are validated, and when there are no errors, a command key is provided to save the source program from the work file back into the expanded source program library. Any changes to the initial execution is updated to the initial execution audit options for program file 26. Step 606 produces a variety of printouts. A summary of the auditing options removed and the audit options remaining in the expanded source program are printed. Informational, warning, and error messages are printed as required, including counts of the input and output source statements.

Step 607 provides a command key to call the create or change compile and initial execution audit options program to allow additional audit functions to be selected. Step 608 provides a command key to end the program, and step 609 returns to the calling program.

The microfiche appendix shows four IBM AS/400 RPG source programs of the software according to a preferred embodiment. The microfiche appendix includes programs Z$PGM01D, Z$PGM01R, Z$PGM02R, and Z$PGM04R written in IBM AS/400 RPG III. Program

Z$PGM01D generates a user-friendly display screen for a user. Program Z$PGM01R allows a programmer to quickly and easily audit and document a conventional source program, or select additional audits for a previously expanded source program. This program is a setup program for the expand input and audits program Z$PGM02R. Program Z$PGM02R is the expand input and audits program which is the primary program which expands the input conventional source program with the audit statements based on the options selected. Program Z$PGM04R creates cross reference information needed for the expand input with audits program.

It is to be understood that the present invention is not limited to the embodiments described above, but encompasses any and all embodiments within the scope of the following claims.

* * * * *

US006775827B1

(12) **United States Patent**

Harkins

(10) **Patent No.:** **US 6,775,827 B1**

(45) **Date of Patent:** **Aug. 10, 2004**

(54) **REAL-TIME PROGRAM AUDIT SOFTWARE**

(75) Inventor: **Paul H. Harkins**, West Chester, PA (US)

(73) Assignee: **Harkins Audit Software, Inc.**, West Chester, PA (US)

(*) Notice: Subject to any disclaimer, the term of this patent is extended or adjusted under 35 U.S.C. 154(b) by 377 days.

(21) Appl. No.: **09/611,210**

(22) Filed: **Jul. 6, 2000**

Related U.S. Application Data

(63) Continuation-in-part of application No. 09/398,310, filed on Sep. 20, 1999, now abandoned.

(51) Int. Cl.⁷ G06F 9/44
(52) U.S. Cl. 717/130; 717/128
(58) Field of Search 717/127, 130, 717/128, 145

(56) **References Cited**

5,950,003 A	*	9/1999	Kaneshiro et al.	.... 717/130
6,011,920 A		1/2000	Edwards et al.	
6,071,316 A		6/2000	Goossen et al.	
6,202,199 B1	*	3/2001	Wygodny et al.	.... 717/125

FOREIGN PATENT DOCUMENTS

WO	WO 93/01550	1/1993

* cited by examiner

Primary Examiner—Todd Ingberg
Assistant Examiner—Eric B. Kiss
(74) *Attorney, Agent, or Firm*—Akin Gump Strauss Hauer & Feld, LLP

(57) **ABSTRACT**

An automated computer-implemented method for generating an audit record of a computer program while the computer program is executing. The computer program has a source program comprising a plurality of source statements written in a predetermined source language. The method includes the steps of: selecting one or more audit options, each audit option being defined by one or more field names; examining each one of the source statements for the presence of one or more of the field names; creating an audit statement in the source language of the computer program

U.S. PATENT DOCUMENTS

5,559,884 A		9/1996	Davidson et al. 380/4
5,574,898 A		11/1996	Leblang et al. 395/601
5,613,118 A	*	3/1997	Heisch et al. 717/158
5,754,763 A		5/1998	Bereiter 395/187.01
5,771,385 A		6/1998	Harper
5,794,252 A		8/1998	Bailey et al. 707/202
5,813,009 A		9/1998	Johnson et al. 707/100
5,832,271 A	*	11/1998	Devanbu 717/131
5,903,730 A	*	5/1999	Asai et al. 709/224

corresponding to each one of the source statements in which one or more of the field names is present; and inserting each created audit statement into the source program proximate to the corresponding source statement to form an expanded source program.

31 Claims, 32 Drawing Sheets

Microfiche Appendix Included
(2 Microfiche, 188 Pages)

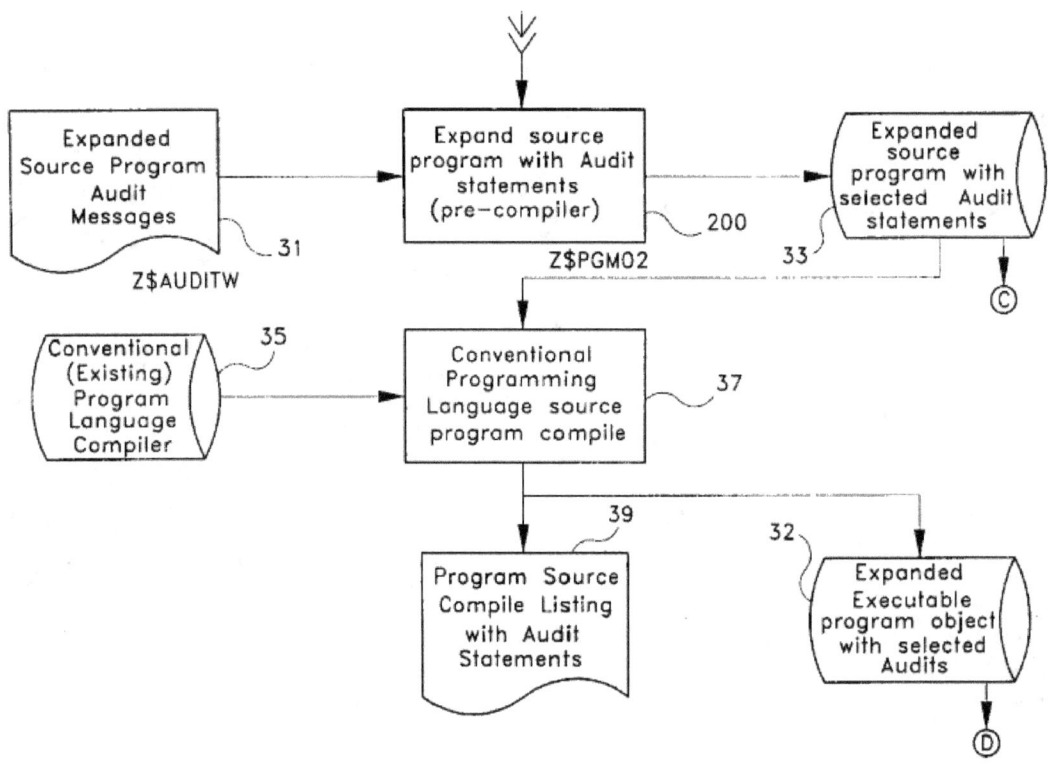

U.S. Patent   Aug. 10, 2004   Sheet 1 of 32   US 6,775,827 B1

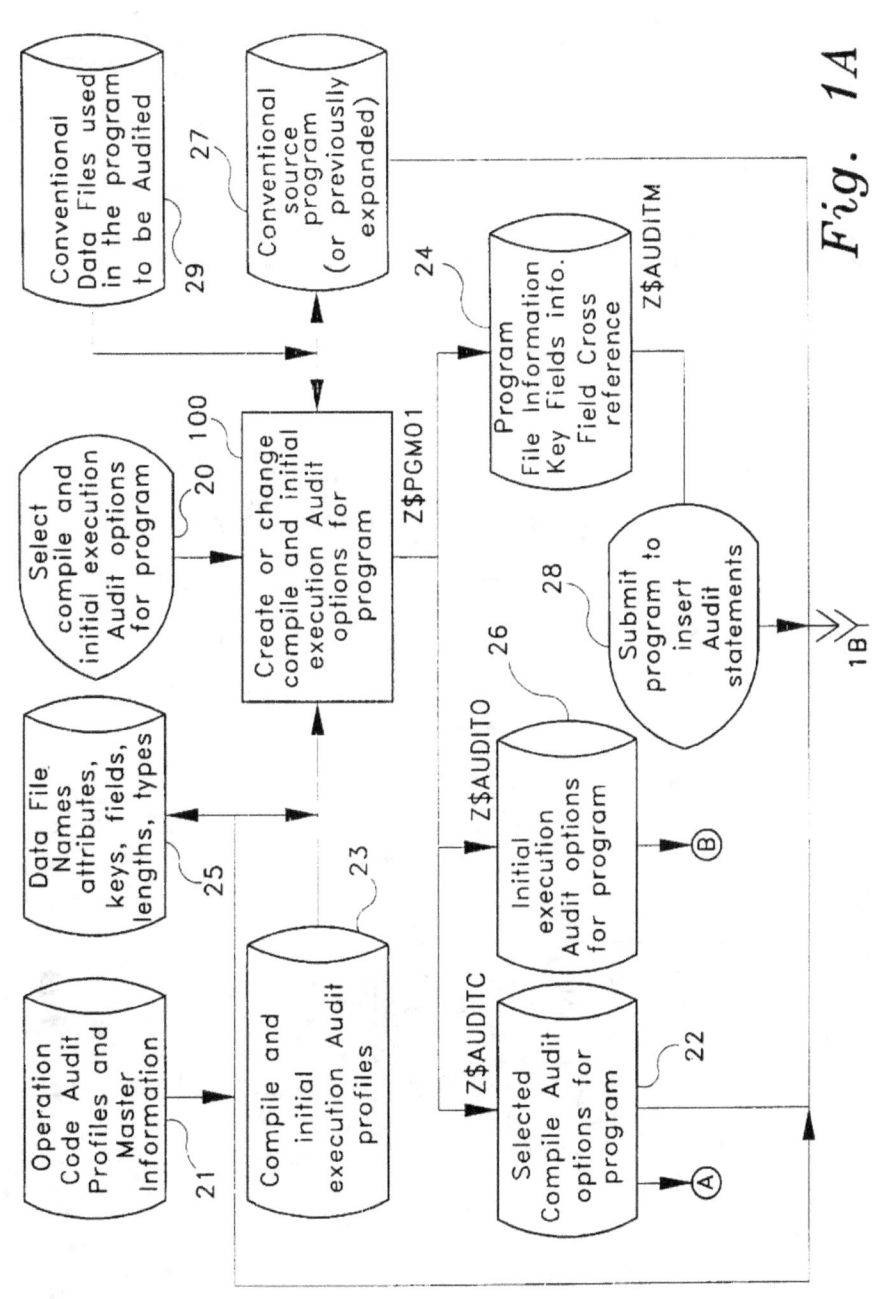

Fig. 1A

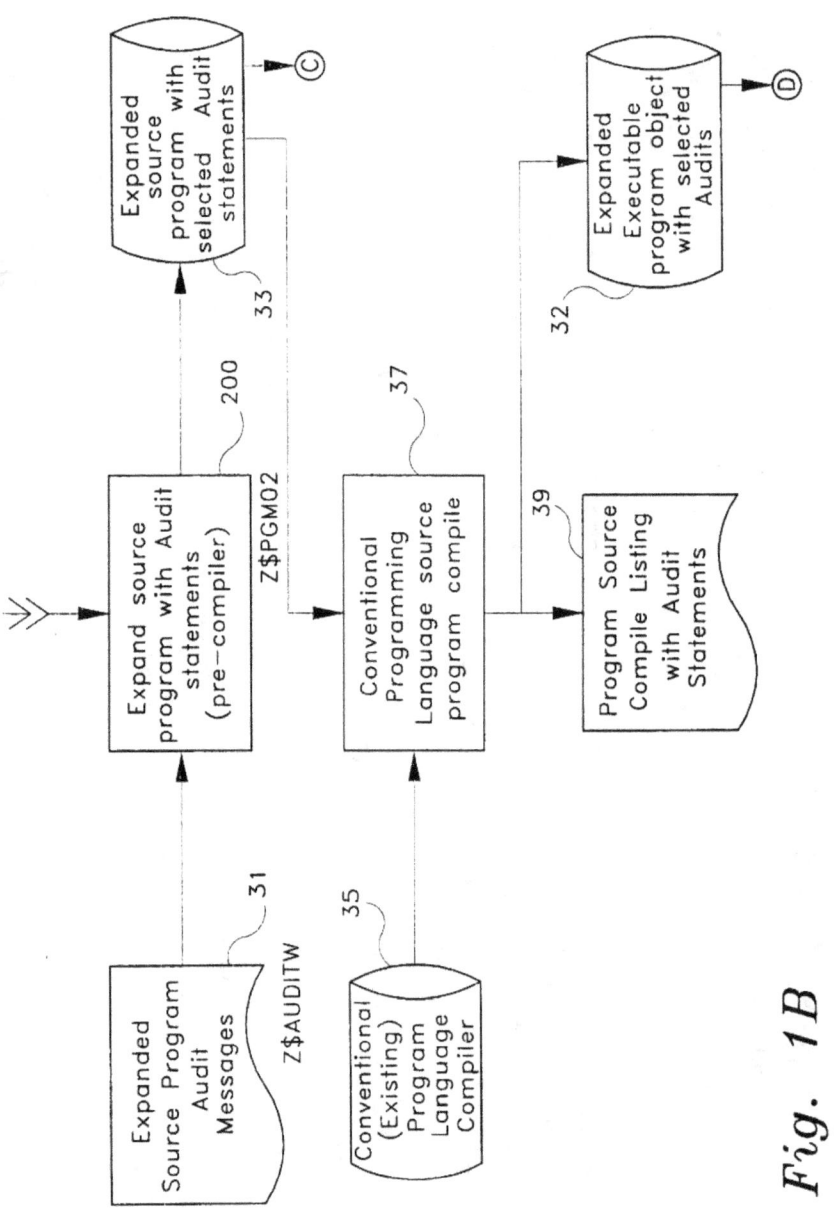

Fig. 1B

U.S. Patent   Aug. 10, 2004   Sheet 3 of 32   US 6,775,827 B1

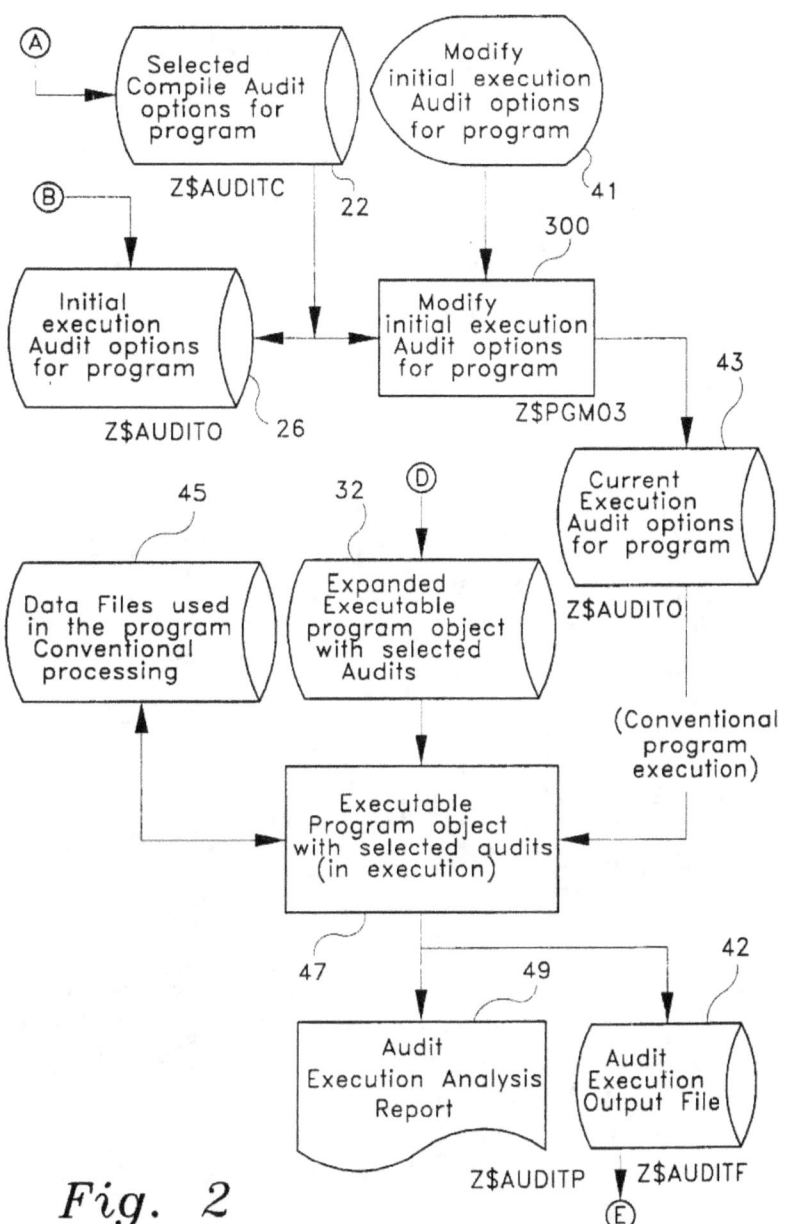

Fig. 2

233

Fig. 3

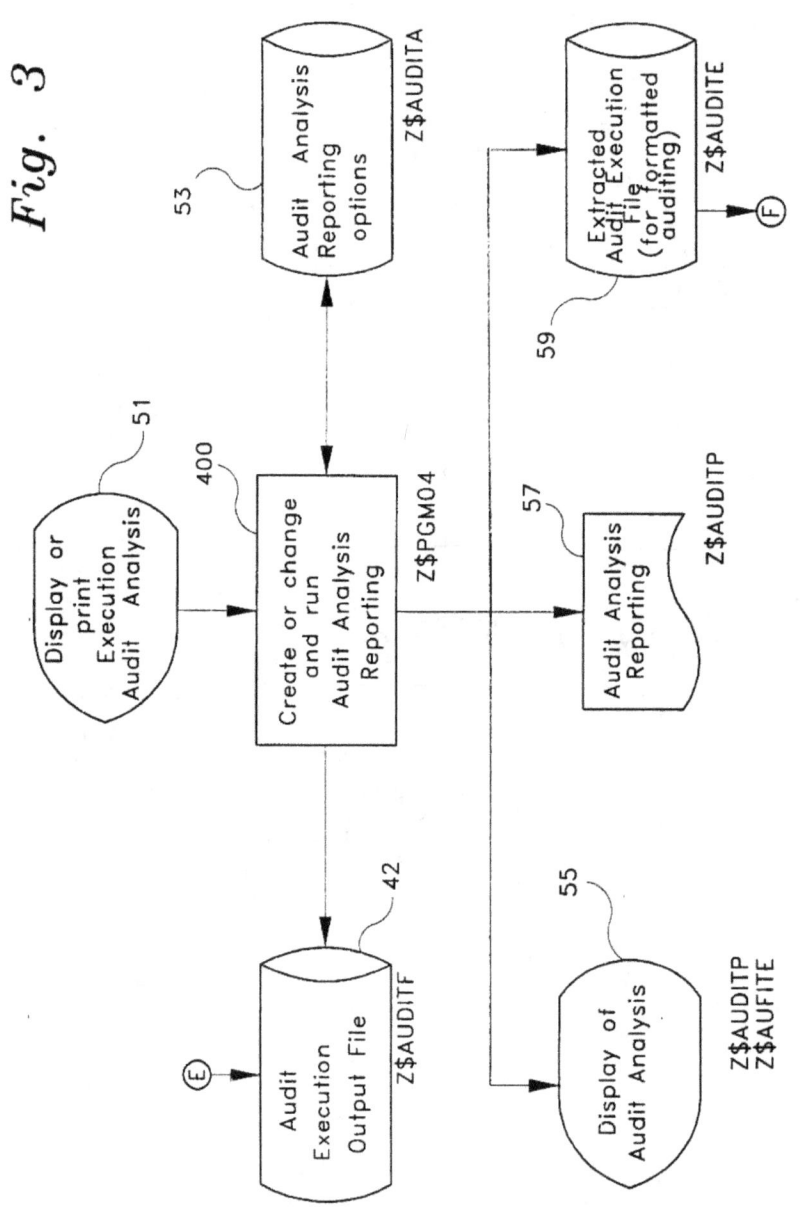

The Future of Corporate Computing

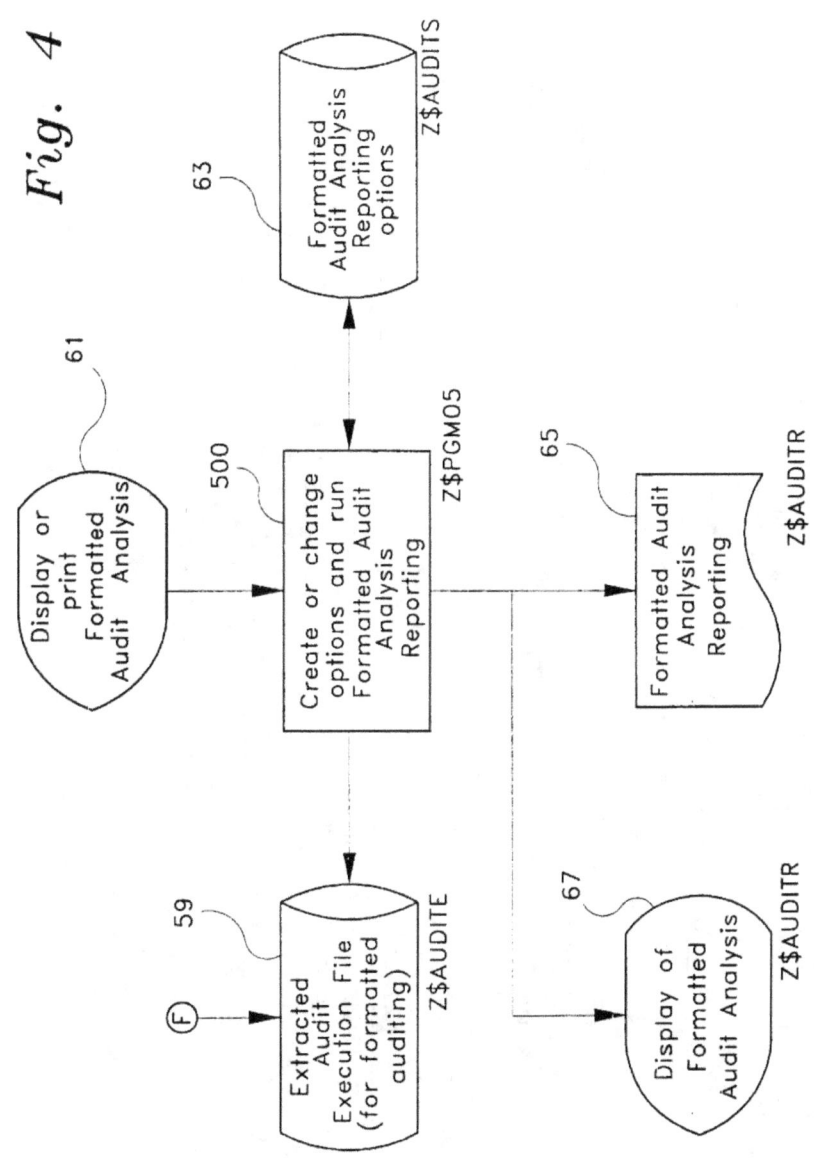

Fig. 4

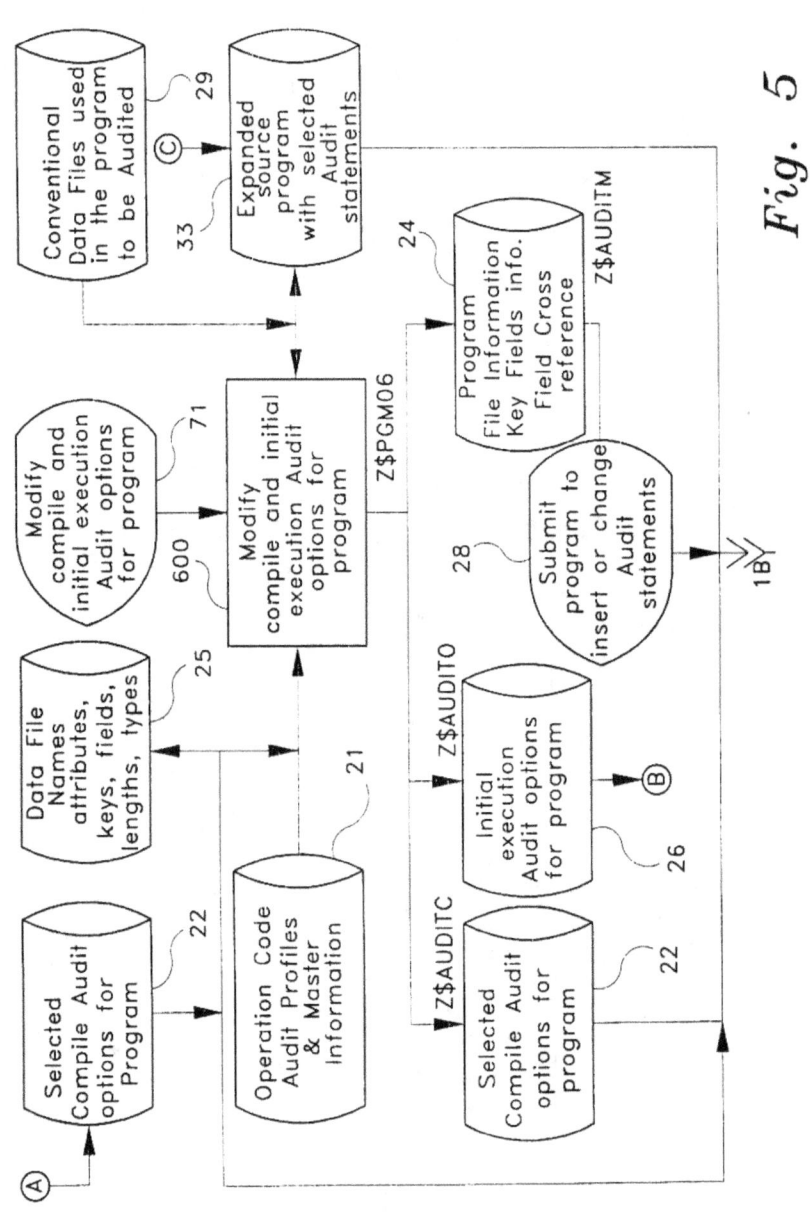

Fig. 5

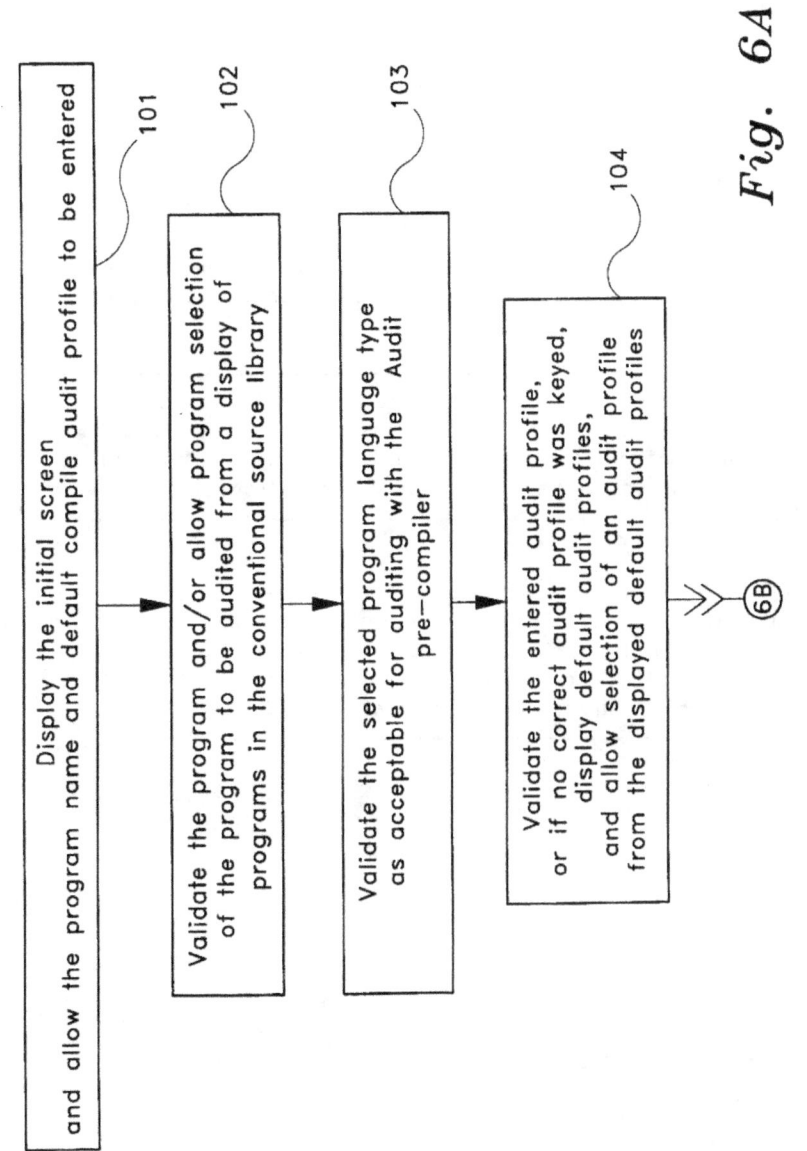

Fig. 6A

Display the initial screen and allow the program name and default compile audit profile to be entered

101

Validate the program and/or allow program selection of the program to be audited from a display of programs in the conventional source library

102

Validate the selected program language type as acceptable for auditing with the Audit pre-compiler

103

Validate the entered audit profile, or if no correct audit profile was keyed, display default audit profiles, and allow selection of an audit profile from the displayed default audit profiles

104

6B

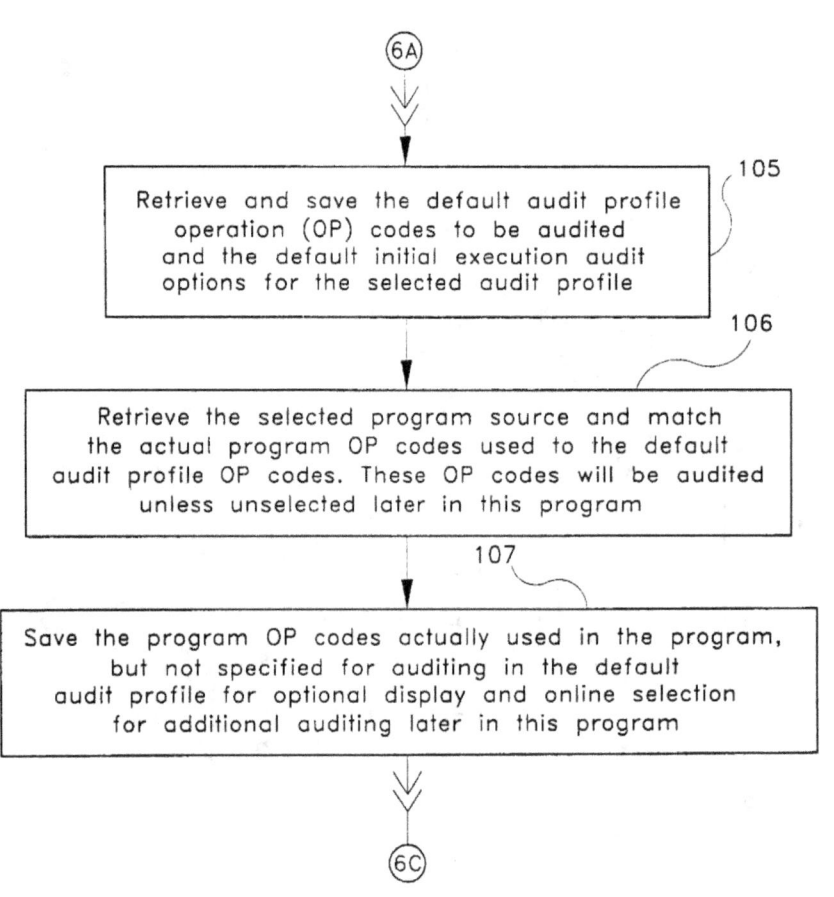

Fig. 6B

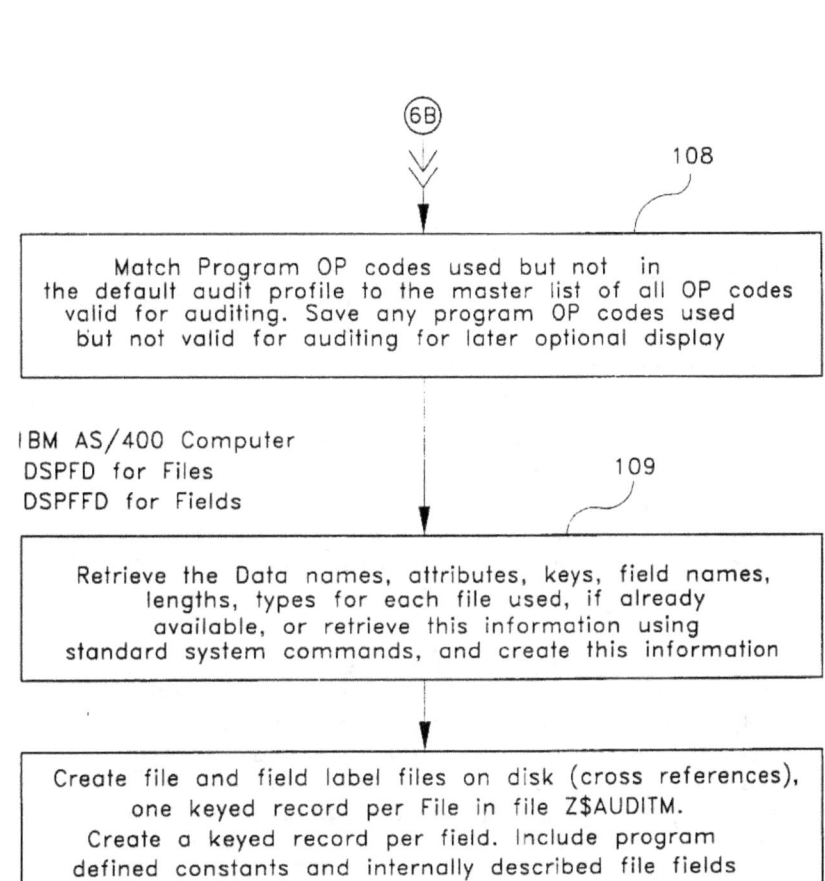

Fig. 6C

6C

111

Delete all unreferenced fields that are not actually utilized in this program from the disk cross reference file of fields utilized in this program

112

Display a menu of the auditing functions specified in in the selected audit profile. Allow selection of the menu items for auditing profile overrides.
Menu options are grouped by: Files, Op codes, Fields

113

Allow a command key to be pressed to accept the audit profile options as displayed. This creates the selected compile options file, and the selected initial execution options file. Optionally submit the source program to the Basic Audit pre-compiler program for insertion of the auditing statements.

7A

Fig. 6D

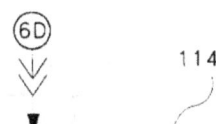

U.S. Patent Aug. 10, 2004 Sheet 11 of 32 US 6,775,827 B1

6D
114
Allow the displayed menu options to be selected to override the default audit options for the program. Menu override options include: Files, Operation codes, Fields and Labels, initial execution options
115
If File overrides: Display each file used in the program as a single line on a file summary screen. Show its auditing status based on the selected profile, and which of the ten levels of auditing was selected for the file. All key fields used in audited files will be automatically audited. Allow additional (non-key) fields for the file to be selected for automatic auditing
116
Allow files to be selected or unselected for auditing, and auditing levels to be modified. Allow a command key to display a second line with each Op code used by the file and its auditing status.
7B

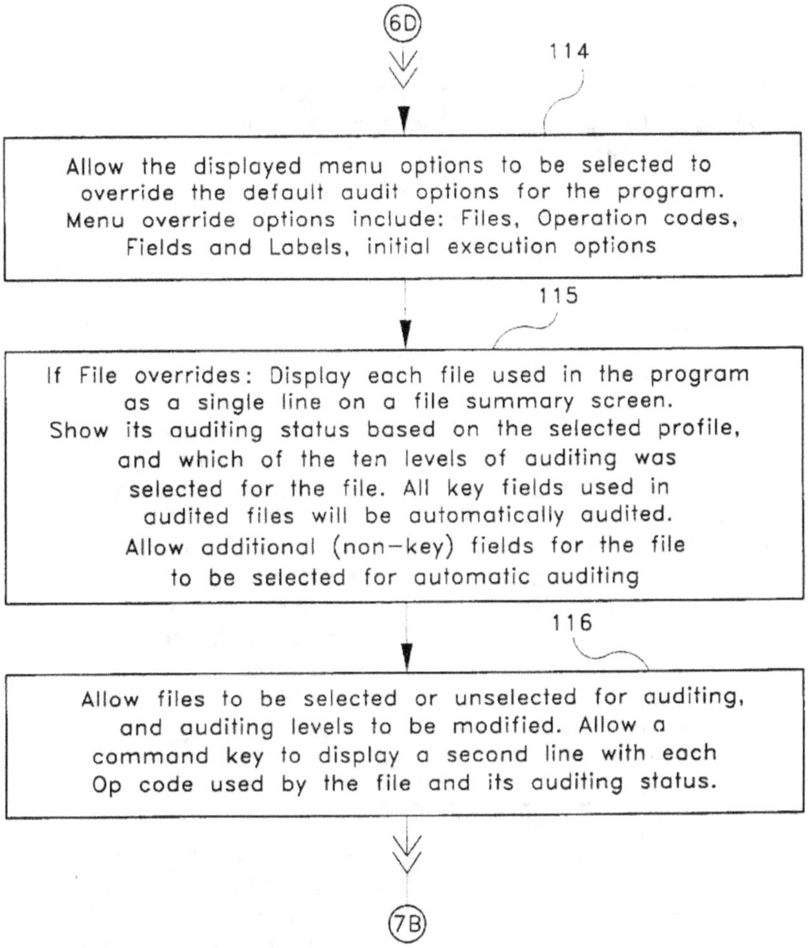

Fig. 7A

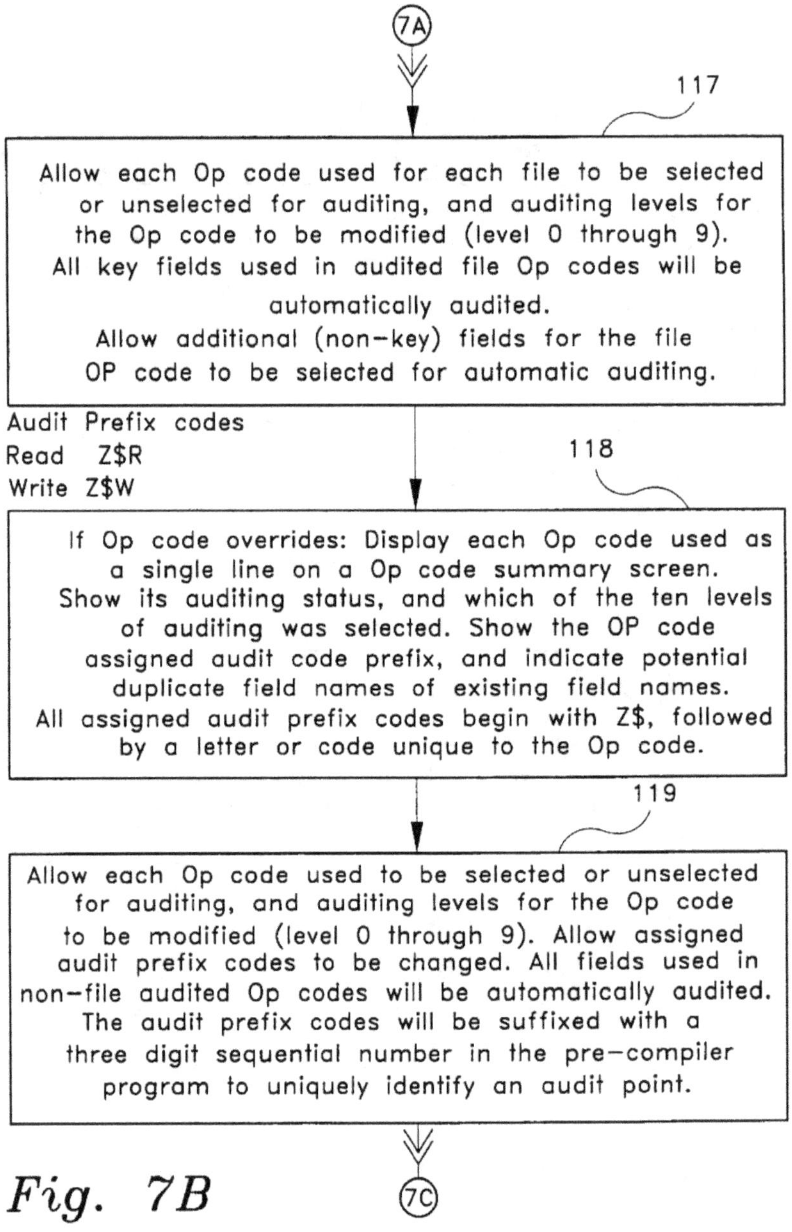

117

Allow each Op code used for each file to be selected
or unselected for auditing, and auditing levels for
the Op code to be modified (level 0 through 9).
All key fields used in audited file Op codes will be
automatically audited.
Allow additional (non-key) fields for the file
OP code to be selected for automatic auditing.

Audit Prefix codes
Read   Z$R
Write Z$W

118

If Op code overrides: Display each Op code used as
a single line on a Op code summary screen.
Show its auditing status, and which of the ten levels
of auditing was selected. Show the OP code
assigned audit code prefix, and indicate potential
duplicate field names of existing field names.
All assigned audit prefix codes begin with Z$, followed
by a letter or code unique to the Op code.

119

Allow each Op code used to be selected or unselected
for auditing, and auditing levels for the Op code
to be modified (level 0 through 9). Allow assigned
audit prefix codes to be changed. All fields used in
non-file audited Op codes will be automatically audited.
The audit prefix codes will be suffixed with a
three digit sequential number in the pre-compiler
program to uniquely identify an audit point.

Fig. 7B

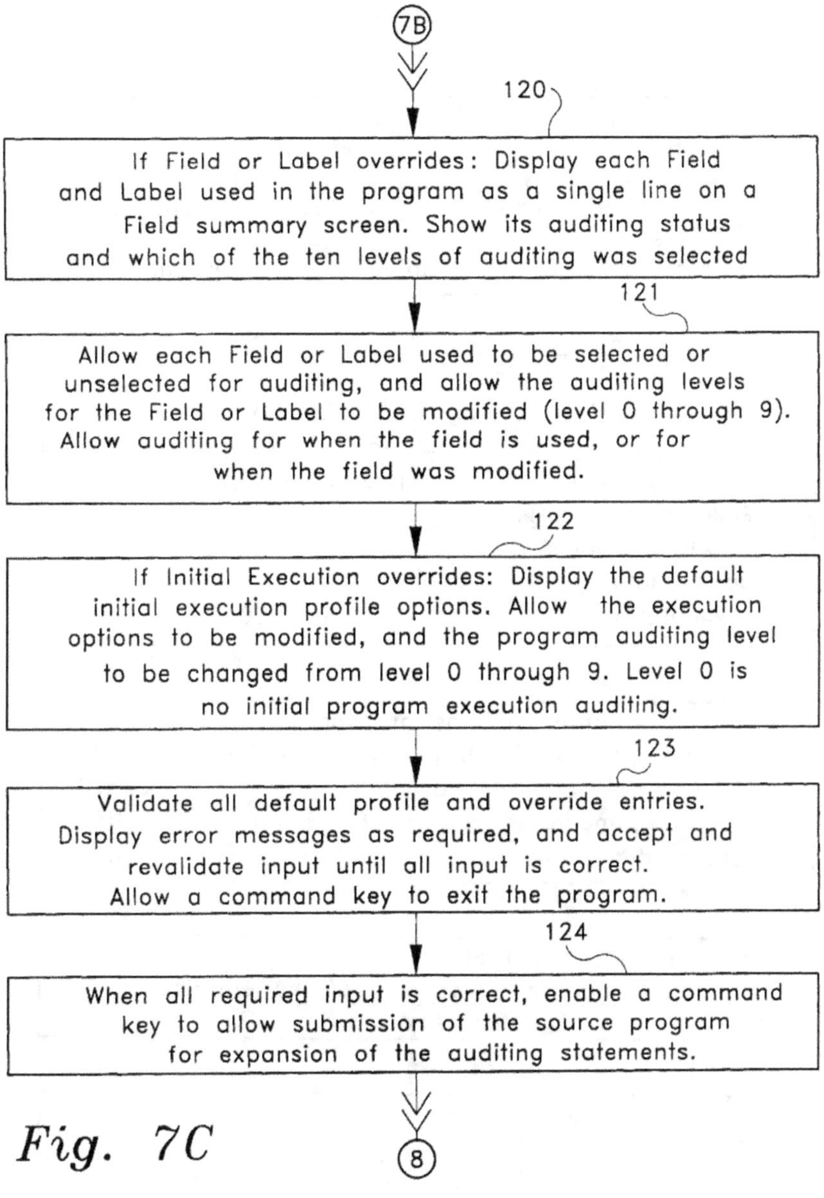

(7B)

120

If Field or Label overrides: Display each Field and Label used in the program as a single line on a Field summary screen. Show its auditing status and which of the ten levels of auditing was selected

121

Allow each Field or Label used to be selected or unselected for auditing, and allow the auditing levels for the Field or Label to be modified (level 0 through 9). Allow auditing for when the field is used, or for when the field was modified.

122

If Initial Execution overrides: Display the default initial execution profile options. Allow the execution options to be modified, and the program auditing level to be changed from level 0 through 9. Level 0 is no initial program execution auditing.

123

Validate all default profile and override entries. Display error messages as required, and accept and revalidate input until all input is correct. Allow a command key to exit the program.

124

When all required input is correct, enable a command key to allow submission of the source program for expansion of the auditing statements.

Fig. 7C

(8)

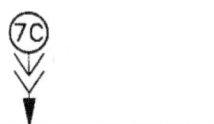

U.S. Patent Aug. 10, 2004 Sheet 14 of 32 US 6,775,827 B1

7C
125
If a command key is pressed to submit the source program for expansion: Format and create the output files needed for the program to be utilized in expanding the conventional source code with audit statements, and for the program initial executions options.
126
Output files include:
1. Selected Basic Audit compile options for source program expansion to file Z$AUDITC.
2. Program file information, Key fields info. Field cross reference for source program expansion to file Z$AUDITM.
3. Basic Audit Initial execution options for the object (executable) program, to file Z$AUDITO
127
Print a summary of the auditing options selected, and the program initial execution options selected. Print informational, warning, and error message as required, including counts of the input conventional source statements, files, fields, and labels used.
128
Display a message that the source program has been submitted for expansion of the auditing statements.
129
Return to the calling program

Fig. 8

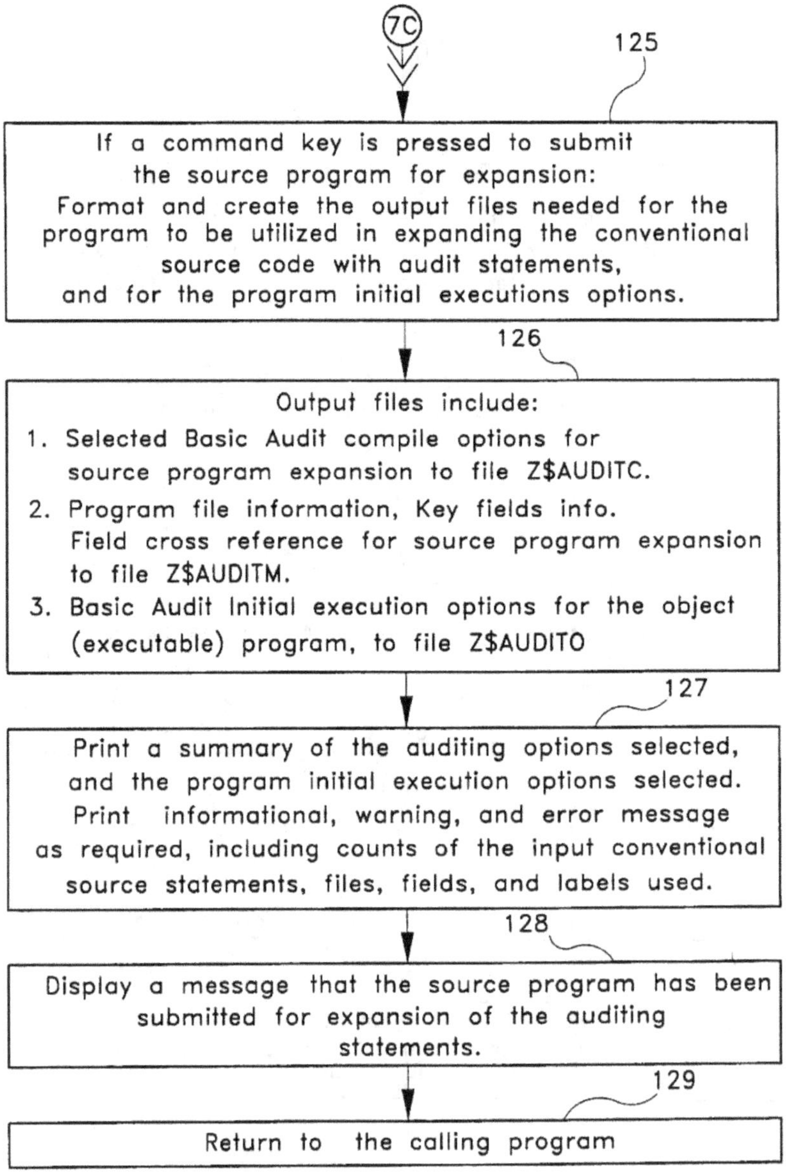

U.S. Patent Aug. 10, 2004 Sheet 15 of 32 US 6,775,827 B1

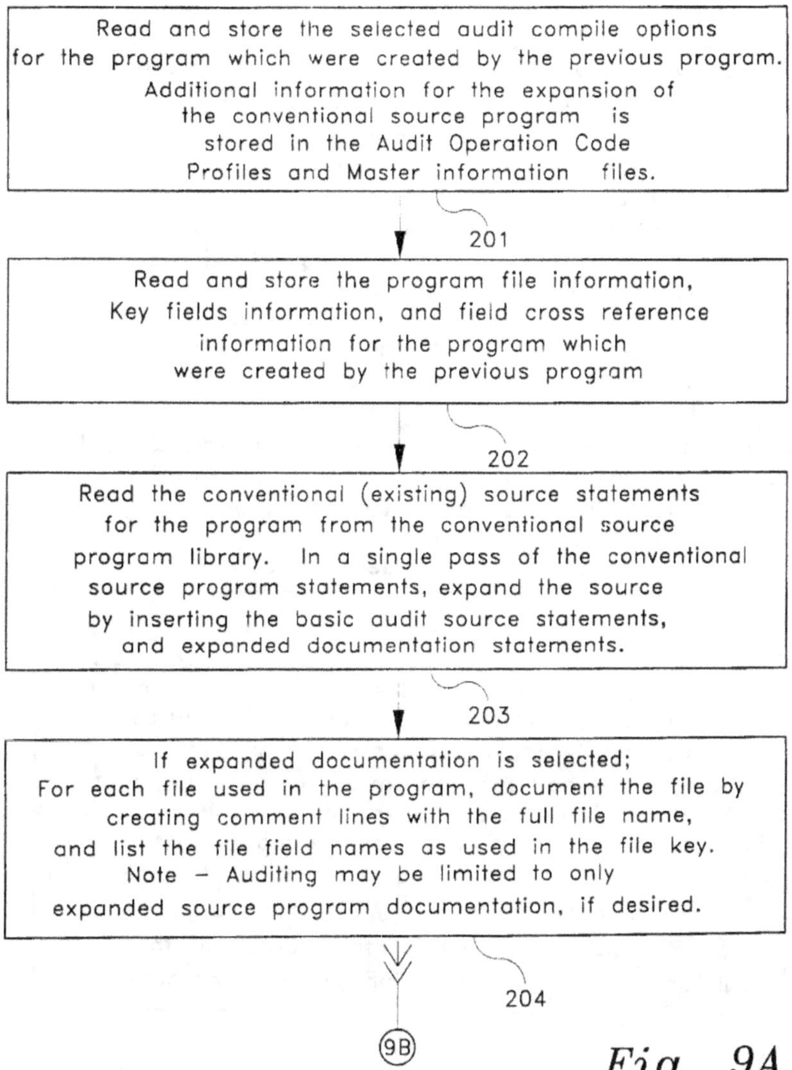
Read and store the selected audit compile options for the program which were created by the previous program. Additional information for the expansion of the conventional source program is stored in the Audit Operation Code Profiles and Master information files.
201
Read and store the program file information, Key fields information, and field cross reference information for the program which were created by the previous program
202
Read the conventional (existing) source statements for the program from the conventional source program library. In a single pass of the conventional source program statements, expand the source by inserting the basic audit source statements, and expanded documentation statements.
203
If expanded documentation is selected; For each file used in the program, document the file by creating comment lines with the full file name, and list the file field names as used in the file key. Note – Auditing may be limited to only expanded source program documentation, if desired.
204
9B

Fig. 9A

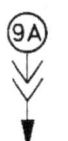

U.S. Patent Aug. 10, 2004 Sheet 16 of 32 US 6,775,827 B1

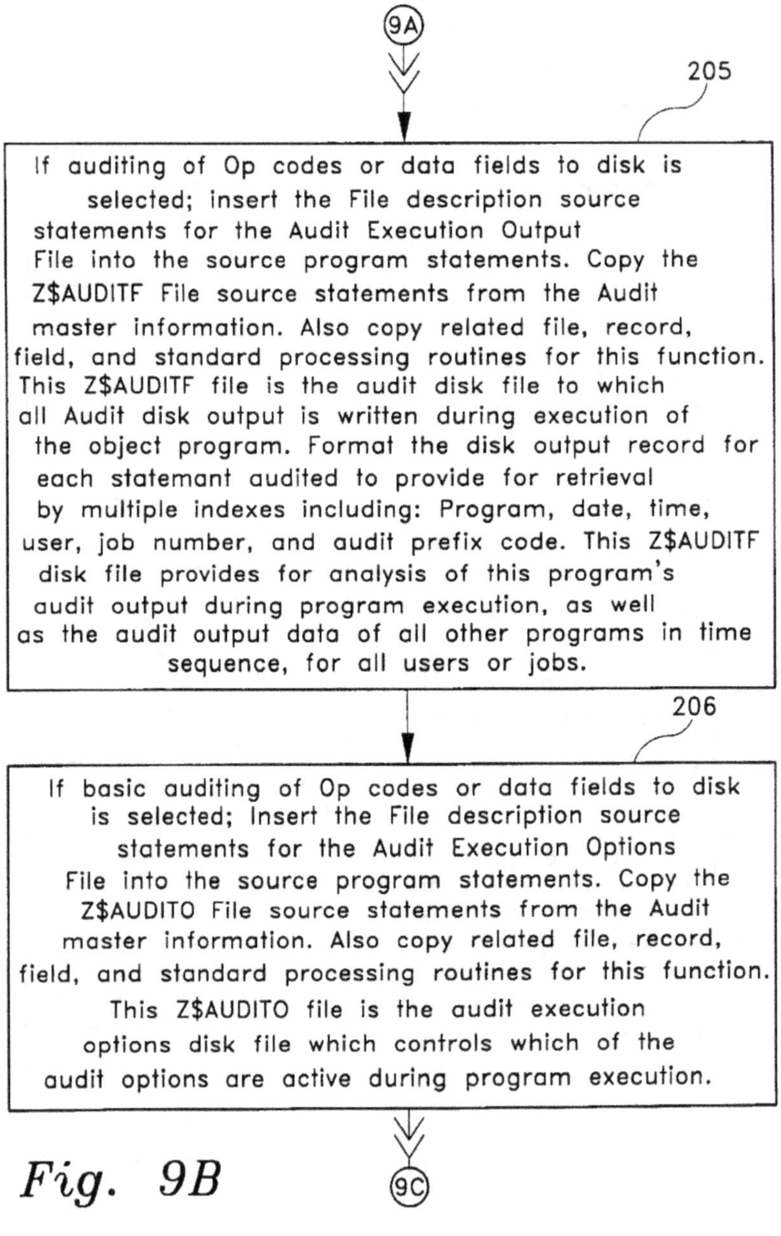
9A
205
If auditing of Op codes or data fields to disk is selected; insert the File description source statements for the Audit Execution Output File into the source program statements. Copy the Z$AUDITF File source statements from the Audit master information. Also copy related file, record, field, and standard processing routines for this function. This Z$AUDITF file is the audit disk file to which all Audit disk output is written during execution of the object program. Format the disk output record for each statemant audited to provide for retrieval by multiple indexes including: Program, date, time, user, job number, and audit prefix code. This Z$AUDITF disk file provides for analysis of this program's audit output during program execution, as well as the audit output data of all other programs in time sequence, for all users or jobs.
206
If basic auditing of Op codes or data fields to disk is selected; Insert the File description source statements for the Audit Execution Options File into the source program statements. Copy the Z$AUDITO File source statements from the Audit master information. Also copy related file, record, field, and standard processing routines for this function. This Z$AUDITO file is the audit execution options disk file which controls which of the audit options are active during program execution.
9C

Fig. 9B

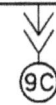

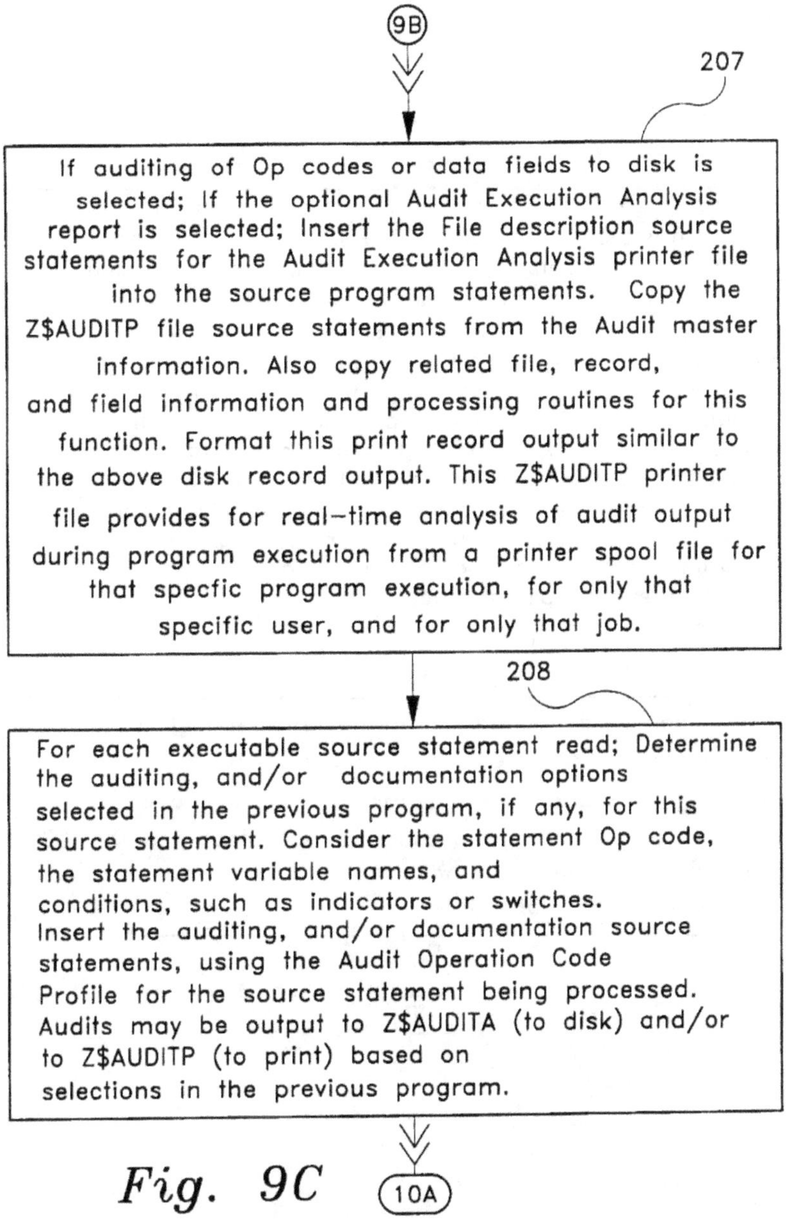

207

If auditing of Op codes or data fields to disk is
selected; If the optional Audit Execution Analysis
report is selected; Insert the File description source
statements for the Audit Execution Analysis printer file
into the source program statements.   Copy the
Z$AUDITP file source statements from the Audit master
information. Also copy related file, record,
and field information and processing routines for this
function. Format this print record output similar to
the above disk record output. This Z$AUDITP printer
file provides for real-time analysis of audit output
during program execution from a printer spool file for
that specfic program execution, for only that
specific user, and for only that job.

208

For each executable source statement read; Determine
the auditing, and/or documentation options
selected in the previous program, if any, for this
source statement. Consider the statement Op code,
the statement variable names, and
conditions, such as indicators or switches.
Insert the auditing, and/or documentation source
statements, using the Audit Operation Code
Profile for the source statement being processed.
Audits may be output to Z$AUDITA (to disk) and/or
to Z$AUDITP (to print) based on
selections in the previous program.

Fig.   9C

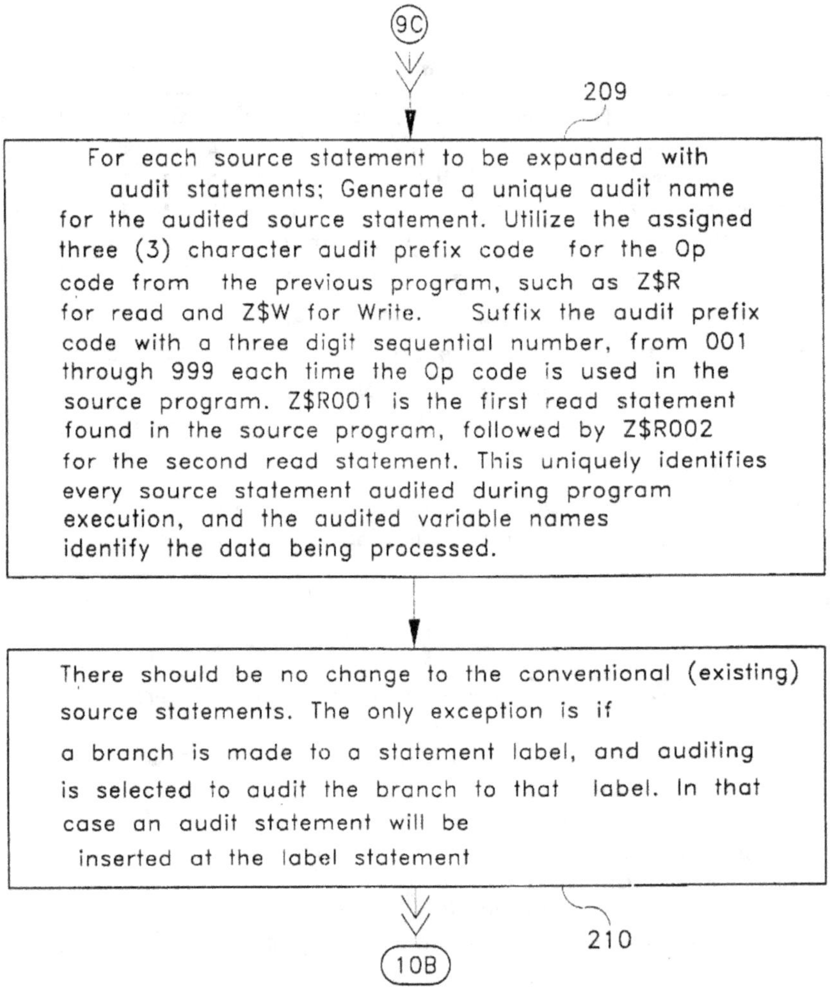

209

For each source statement to be expanded with
audit statements; Generate a unique audit name
for the audited source statement. Utilize the assigned
three (3) character audit prefix code for the Op
code from   the previous program, such as Z$R
for read and Z$W for Write.   Suffix the audit prefix
code with a three digit sequential number, from 001
through 999 each time the Op code is used in the
source program. Z$R001 is the first read statement
found in the source program, followed by Z$R002
for the second read statement. This uniquely identifies
every source statement audited during program
execution, and the audited variable names
identify the data being processed.

There should be no change to the conventional (existing)
source statements. The only exception is if

a branch is made to a statement label, and auditing
is selected to audit the branch to that label. In that
case an audit statement will be

 inserted at the label statement

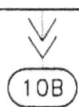

210

Fig. 10A

248

U.S. Patent   Aug. 10, 2004   Sheet 19 of 32   US 6,775,827 B1

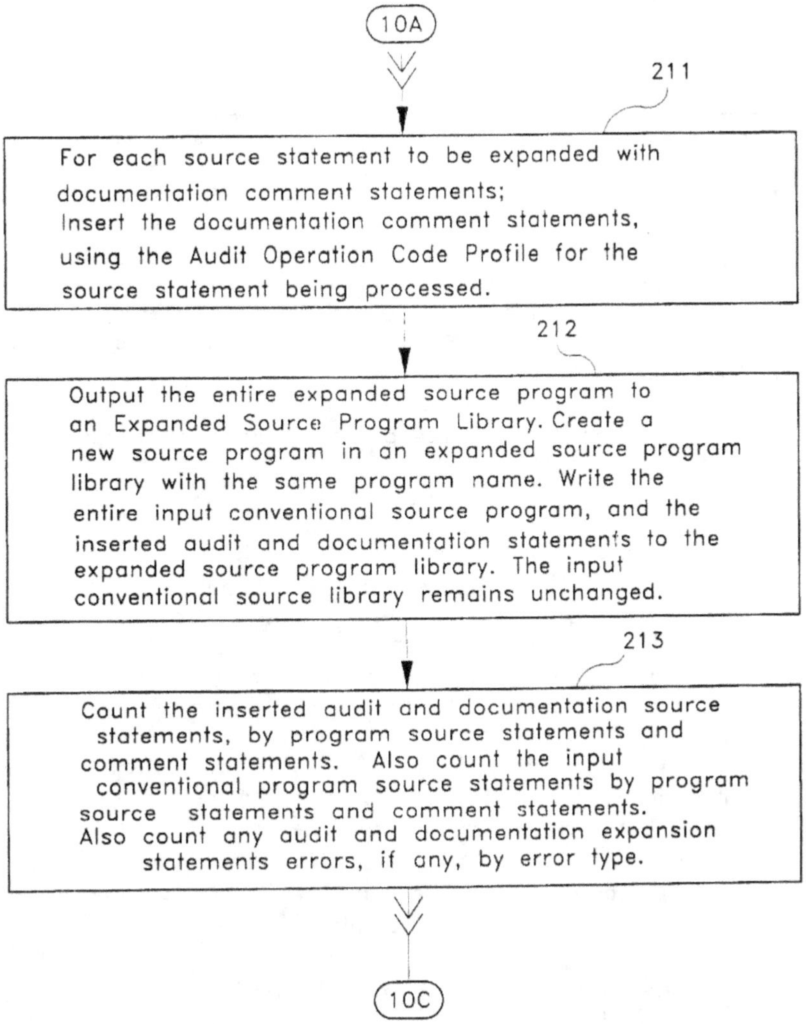
10A
211
For each source statement to be expanded with documentation comment statements;
Insert the documentation comment statements, using the Audit Operation Code Profile for the source statement being processed.
212
Output the entire expanded source program to an Expanded Source Program Library. Create a new source program in an expanded source program library with the same program name. Write the entire input conventional source program, and the inserted audit and documentation statements to the expanded source program library. The input conventional source library remains unchanged.
213
Count the inserted audit and documentation source statements, by program source statements and comment statements. Also count the input conventional program source statements by program source statements and comment statements.
Also count any audit and documentation expansion statements errors, if any, by error type.
10C

Fig. 10B

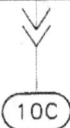

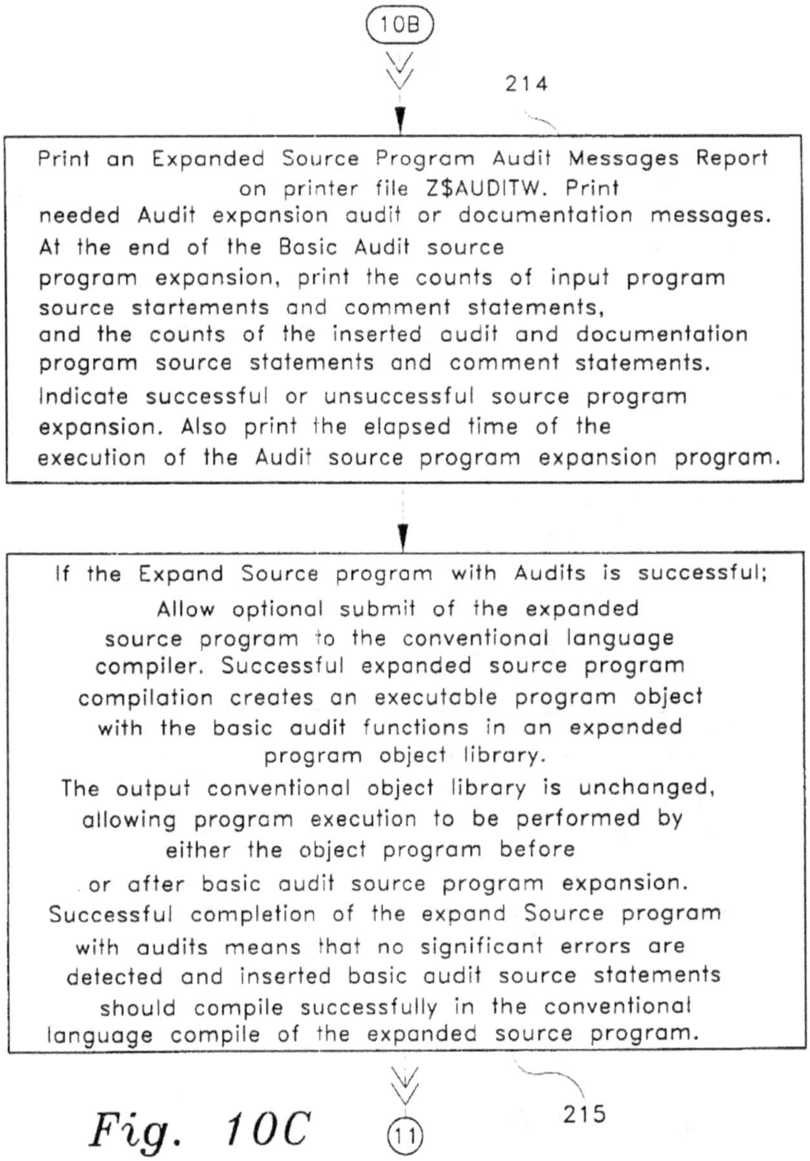

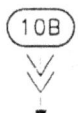

214

Print an Expanded Source Program Audit Messages Report
on printer file Z$AUDITW. Print
needed Audit expansion audit or documentation messages.
At the end of the Basic Audit source
program expansion, print the counts of input program
source startements and comment statements,
and the counts of the inserted audit and documentation
program source statements and comment statements.
Indicate successful or unsuccessful source program
expansion. Also print the elapsed time of the
execution of the Audit source program expansion program.

If the Expand Source program with Audits is successful;
Allow optional submit of the expanded
source program to the conventional language
compiler. Successful expanded source program
compilation creates an executable program object
with the basic audit functions in an expanded
program object library.
The output conventional object library is unchanged,
allowing program execution to be performed by
either the object program before
or after basic audit source program expansion.
Successful completion of the expand Source program
with audits means that no significant errors are
detected and inserted basic audit source statements
should compile successfully in the conventional
language compile of the expanded source program.

215

Fig. 10C   (11)

250

U.S. Patent   Aug. 10, 2004   Sheet 21 of 32   US 6,775,827 B1

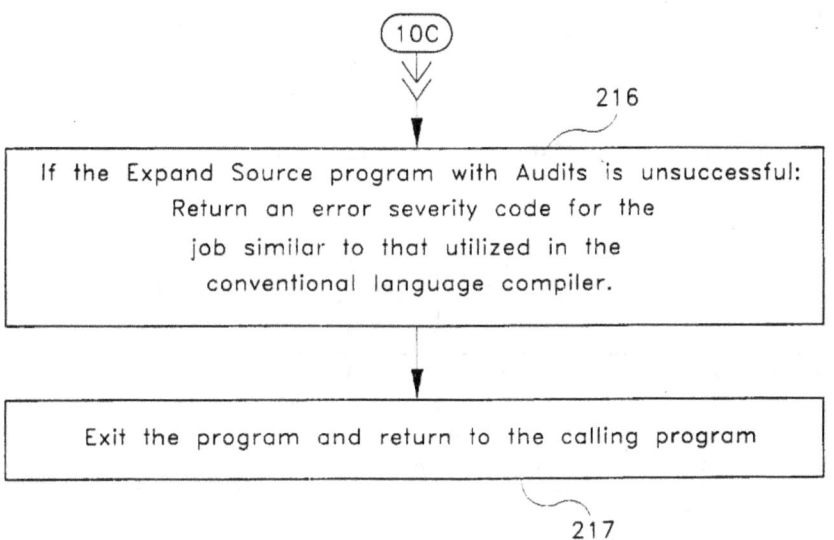

Fig. 11

251

```
┌──────────────────────────────────────────────────┐
│              Display the initial screen            │
│      and allow the program name to be entered      │
│    Note — program execution options for a program  │
│    may be changed while the progrm object is       │
│      executing                                     │
│          when confirmed later in this program.     │
└──────────────────────────────────────────────────┘
                        │ 301
                        ▼
┌──────────────────────────────────────────────────┐
│   Validate that the program has selected audit     │
│   compile                                          │
│   options in file Z$AUDITC. Only audit options that│
│   have been used to expand the source program may  │
│   be selected or modified for and during object    │
│                program execution.                  │
└──────────────────────────────────────────────────┘
                        │ 302
                        ▼
┌──────────────────────────────────────────────────┐
│  Retrieve any initial or current  initial execution│
│  options                                           │
│  for the program from file Z$AUDITO, together      │
│  with the compile audit options                    │
│  for the program from file Z$AUDITC.               │
└──────────────────────────────────────────────────┘
                        │ 303
                        ▼
┌──────────────────────────────────────────────────┐
│ Display the initial or current program execution   │
│ audit options,                                     │
│ together with all the compile audit options for the│
│ program.                                           │
└──────────────────────────────────────────────────┘
                        │ 304
                        ▼
┌──────────────────────────────────────────────────┐
│ Allow all the compile audit options for the program│
│   to be turned on or off as execution options, and │
│   for                                              │
│      the ten auditing levels to be changed.        │
└──────────────────────────────────────────────────┘
                        ▼ 305
                     (12B)
```

Fig. 12A

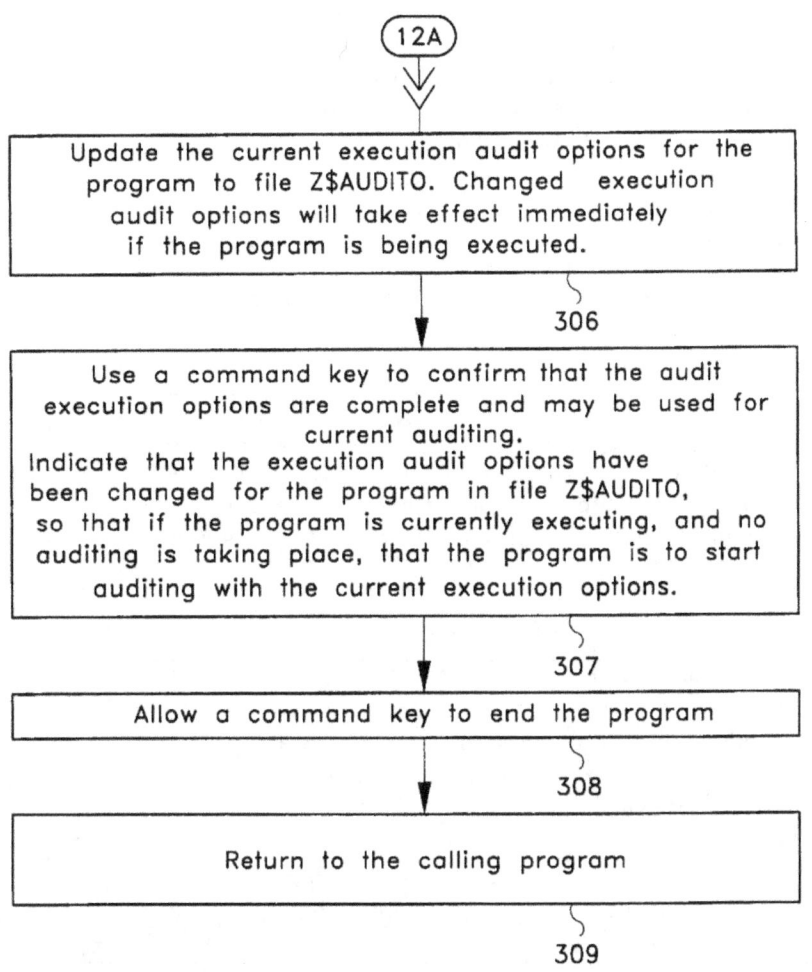

Fig. 12B

U.S. Patent Aug. 10, 2004 Sheet 24 of 32 US 6,775,827 B1

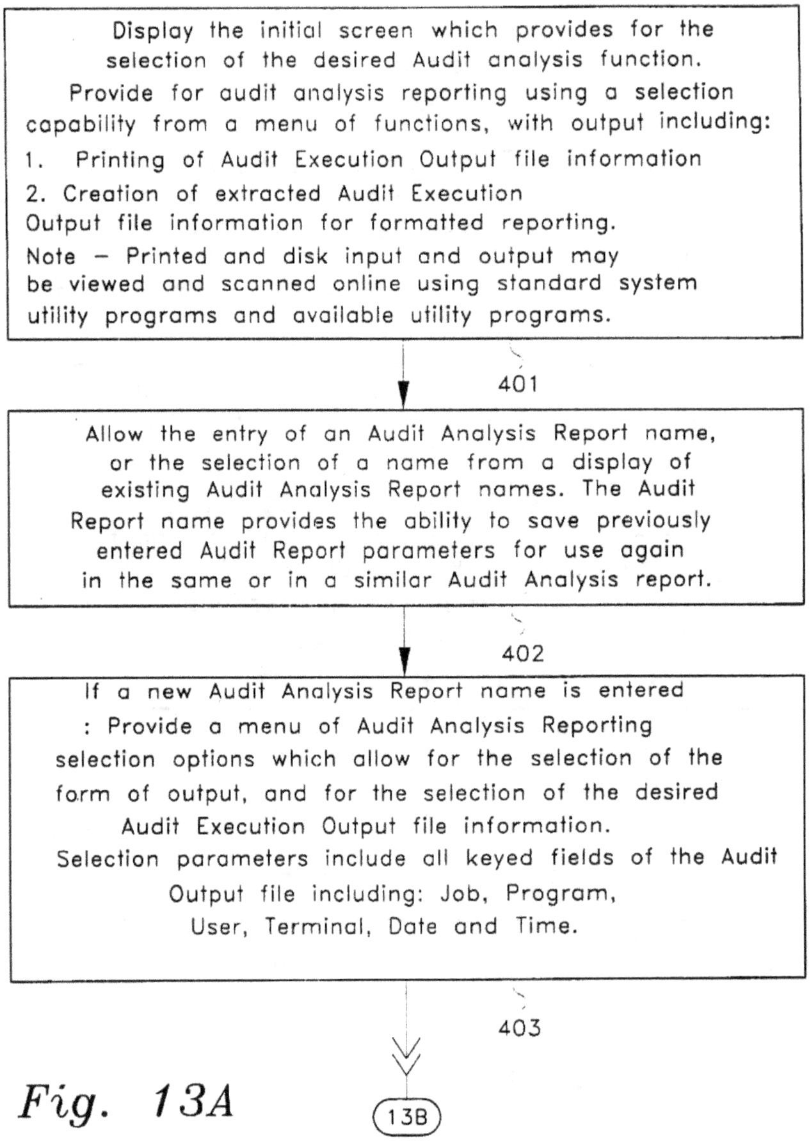
Display the initial screen which provides for the selection of the desired Audit analysis function.
Provide for audit analysis reporting using a selection capability from a menu of functions, with output including:
1. Printing of Audit Execution Output file information
2. Creation of extracted Audit Execution Output file information for formatted reporting.
Note – Printed and disk input and output may be viewed and scanned online using standard system utility programs and available utility programs.
401
Allow the entry of an Audit Analysis Report name, or the selection of a name from a display of existing Audit Analysis Report names. The Audit Report name provides the ability to save previously entered Audit Report parameters for use again in the same or in a similar Audit Analysis report.
402
If a new Audit Analysis Report name is entered : Provide a menu of Audit Analysis Reporting selection options which allow for the selection of the form of output, and for the selection of the desired Audit Execution Output file information.
Selection parameters include all keyed fields of the Audit Output file including: Job, Program, User, Terminal, Date and Time.
403
13B

Fig. 13A

U.S. Patent Aug. 10, 2004 Sheet 25 of 32 US 6,775,827 B1

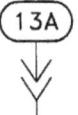

13A
If an existing Audit Analysis Report name is entered: Retrieve the existing options for the Audit Analysis Report name from the Audit Analysis Reporting options file Z$AUDITA. Provide the same menu of Audit Analysis Reporting selection options, and indicate which options were previously selected. Allow the same selection options as available when creating a new Audit Analysis name.
404
Provide a command key to allow exiting the program without updates. Validate all selections, and when there are no errors, provide a command key to save the Audit Analysis selected options to the Audit Analysis Reporting options file Z$AUDITA by the entered Audit Analysis Report name.
405
Provide a command key to allow the Audit Analysis Report to be run.
406
13C

Fig. 13B

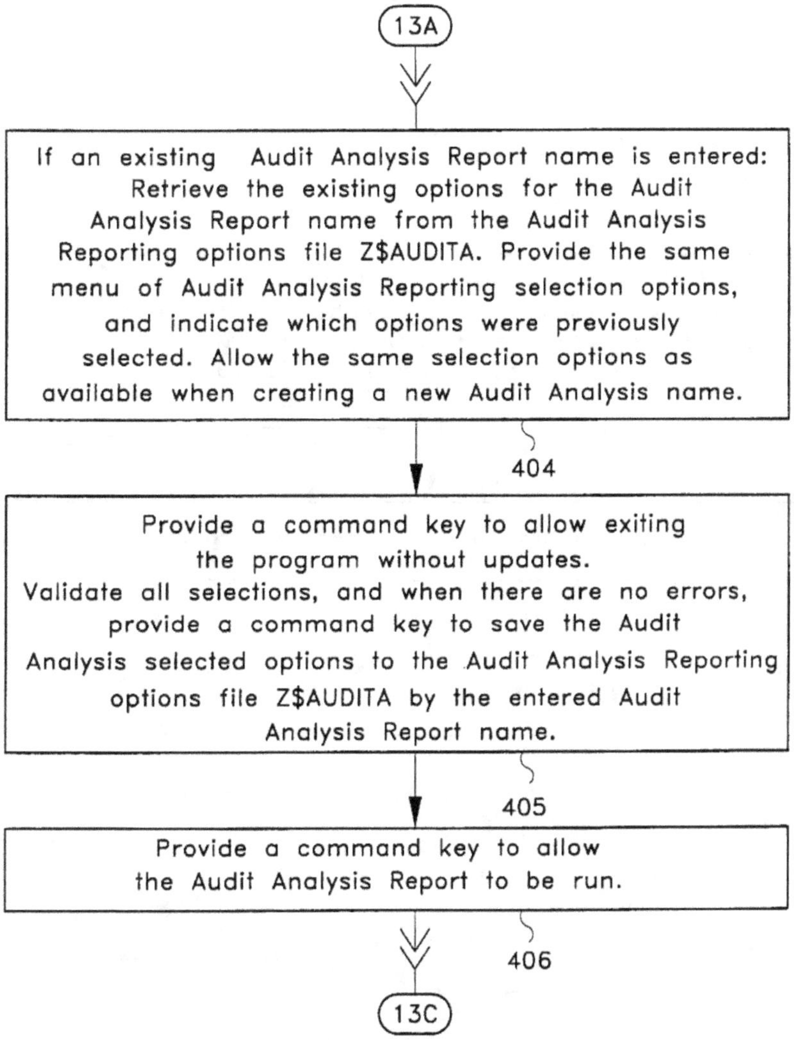

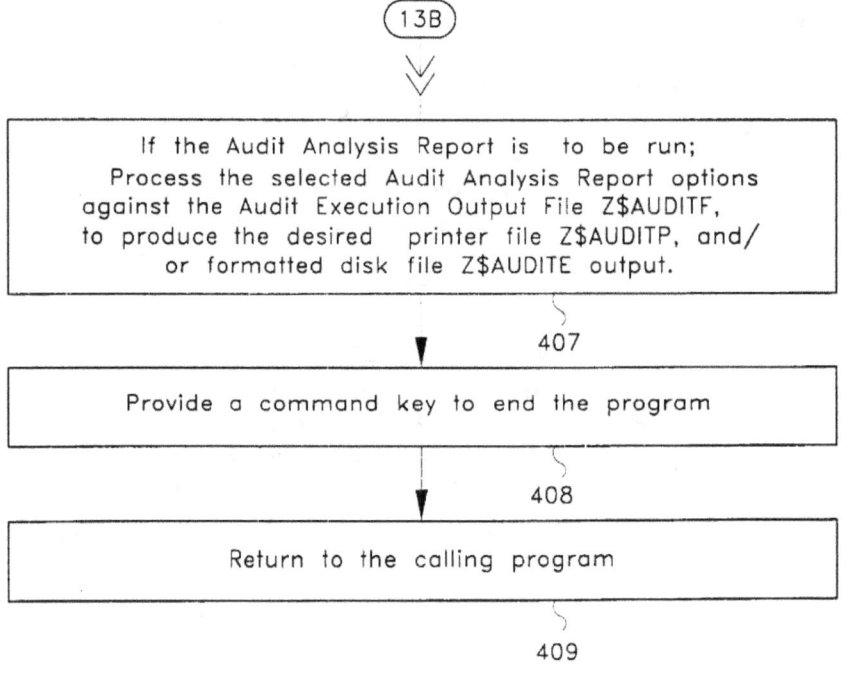

(13B)

If the Audit Analysis Report is to be run;
Process the selected Audit Analysis Report options
against the Audit Execution Output File Z$AUDITF,
to produce the desired printer file Z$AUDITP, and/
or formatted disk file Z$AUDITE output.

407

Provide a command key to end the program

408

Return to the calling program

409

Fig. 13C

U.S. Patent Aug. 10, 2004 Sheet 27 of 32 US 6,775,827 B1

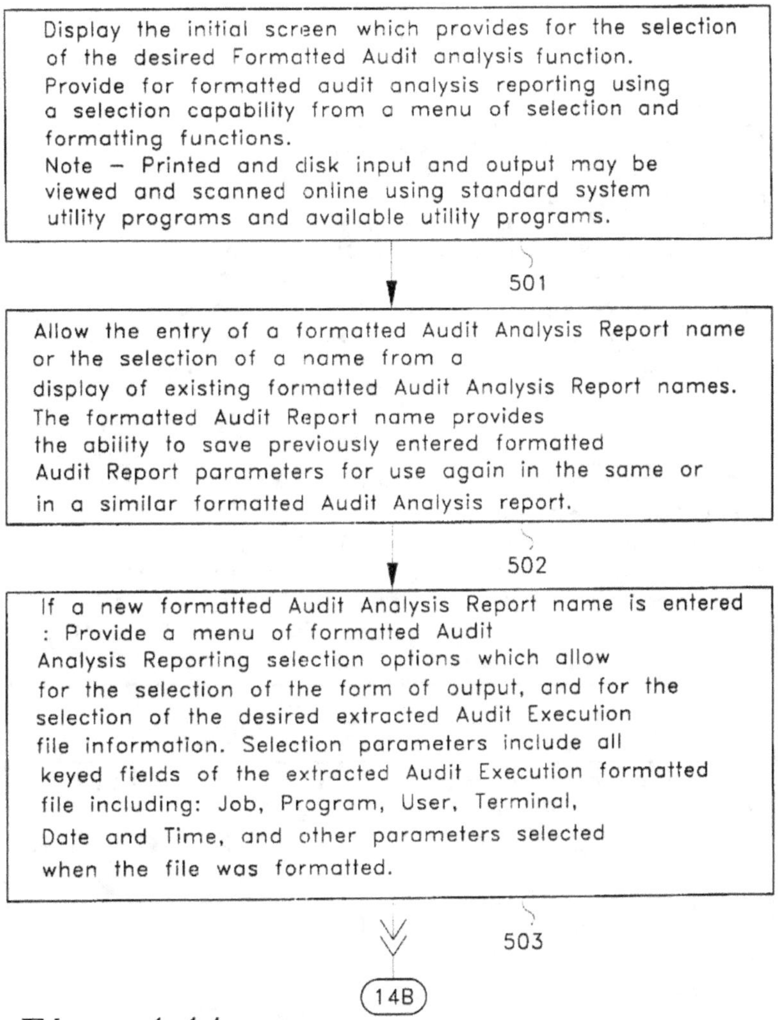
Display the initial screen which provides for the selection of the desired Formatted Audit analysis function. Provide for formatted audit analysis reporting using a selection capability from a menu of selection and formatting functions. Note – Printed and disk input and output may be viewed and scanned online using standard system utility programs and available utility programs.
501
Allow the entry of a formatted Audit Analysis Report name or the selection of a name from a display of existing formatted Audit Analysis Report names. The formatted Audit Report name provides the ability to save previously entered formatted Audit Report parameters for use again in the same or in a similar formatted Audit Analysis report.
502
If a new formatted Audit Analysis Report name is entered : Provide a menu of formatted Audit Analysis Reporting selection options which allow for the selection of the form of output, and for the selection of the desired extracted Audit Execution file information. Selection parameters include all keyed fields of the extracted Audit Execution formatted file including: Job, Program, User, Terminal, Date and Time, and other parameters selected when the file was formatted.
503
14B

Fig. 14A

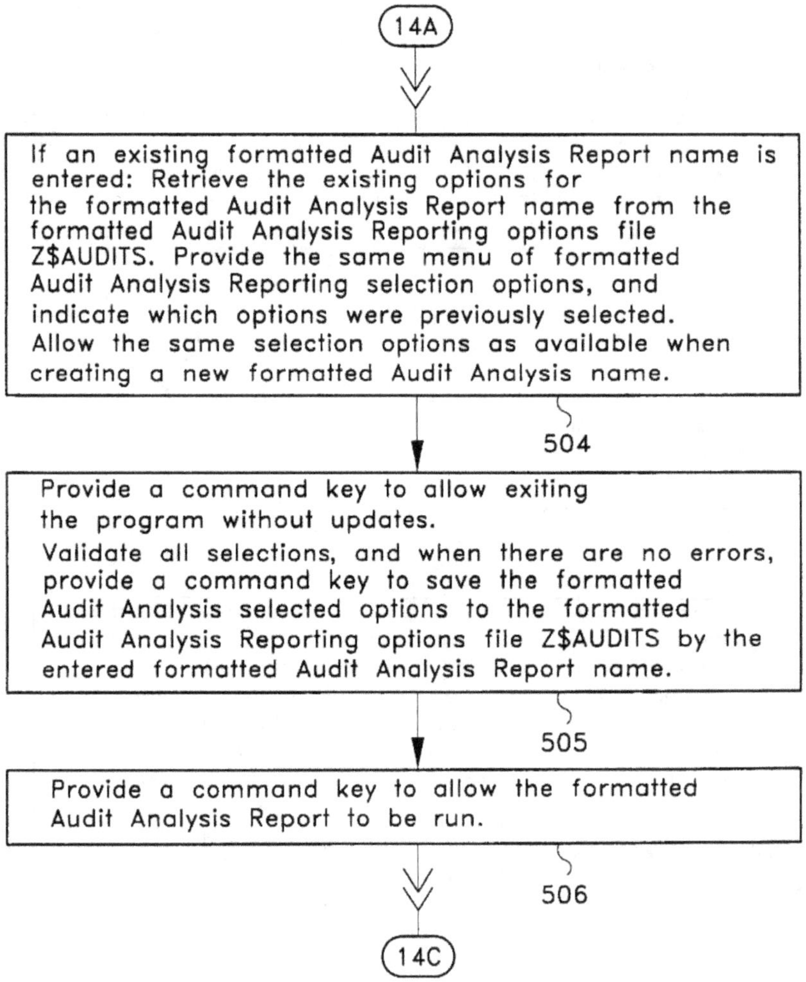

14A

If an existing formatted Audit Analysis Report name is
entered: Retrieve the existing options for
the formatted Audit Analysis Report name from the
formatted Audit Analysis Reporting options file
Z$AUDITS. Provide the same menu of formatted
Audit Analysis Reporting selection options, and
indicate which options were previously selected.
Allow the same selection options as available when
creating a new formatted Audit Analysis name.

504

Provide a command key to allow exiting
the program without updates.

Validate all selections, and when there are no errors,
provide a command key to save the formatted
Audit Analysis selected options to the formatted
Audit Analysis Reporting options file Z$AUDITS by the
entered formatted Audit Analysis Report name.

505

Provide a command key to allow the formatted
Audit Analysis Report to be run.

506

14C

Fig. 14B

258

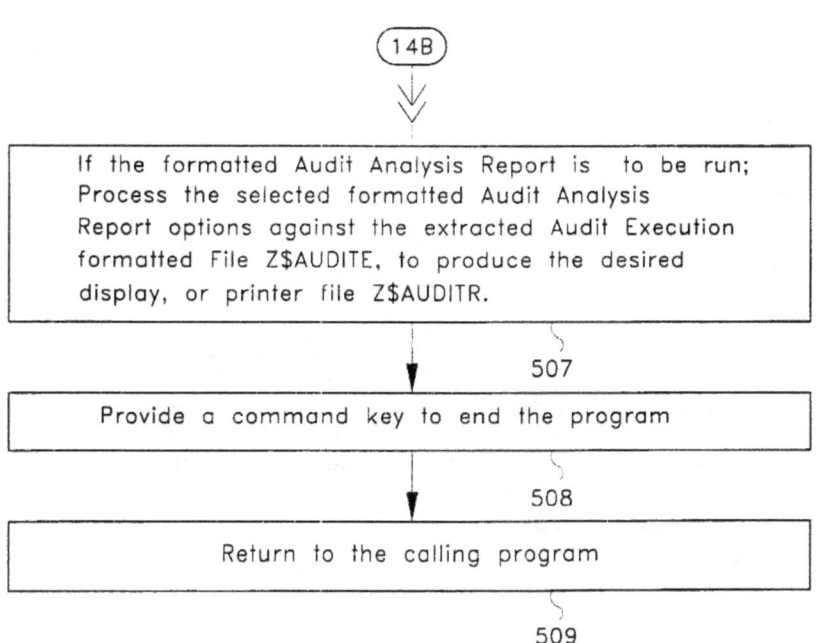

Fig. 14C

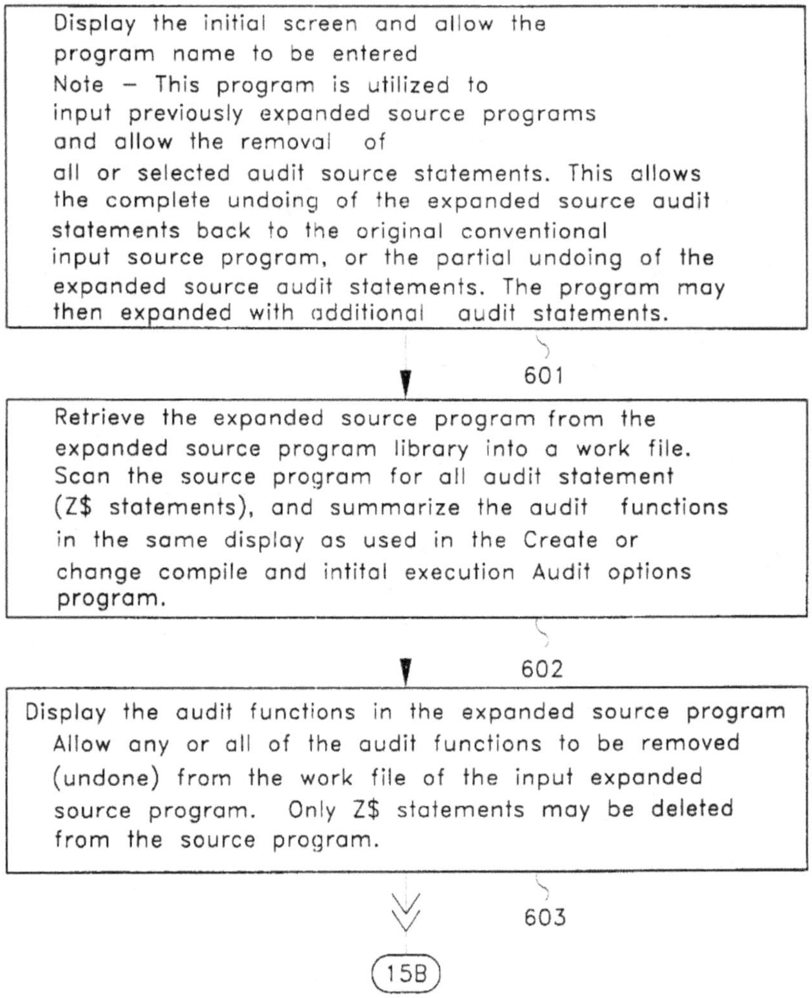

Display the initial screen and allow the
program name to be entered
Note — This program is utilized to
input previously expanded source programs
and allow the removal   of
all or selected audit source statements. This allows
the complete undoing of the expanded source audit
statements back to the original conventional
input source program, or the partial undoing of the
expanded source audit statements. The program may
then expanded with additional   audit statements.

601

Retrieve the expanded source program from the
expanded source program library into a work file.
Scan the source program for all audit statement
(Z$ statements), and summarize the audit functions
in the same display as used in the Create or
change compile and intital execution Audit options
program.

602

Display the audit functions in the expanded source program
Allow any or all of the audit functions to be removed
(undone) from the work file of the input expanded
source program.   Only Z$ statements may be deleted
from the source program.

603

15B

Fig.   15A

260

Retrieve and display the initial (current) execution
options for the expanded source program

from the Initial execution audit options file Z$AUDITO.
Allow any or all initial exection audit options to be
removed (undone) for the program

604

Provide a command key to allow exiting the
program without updates. Validate all selections,
and when there are no errors, provide a command
key to save the source program from the work file
back into the expanded source program library.
Update any changes to the initial execution

to the   initial execution audit options file Z$AUDITO.

605

Print a summary of the auditing options removed
and tthe audit options remaining in the expanded
source program. Print informational, warning,
and error messages as required, including counts of the
input and output source statements.

606

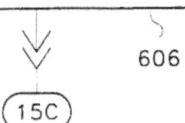

Fig. 15B

261

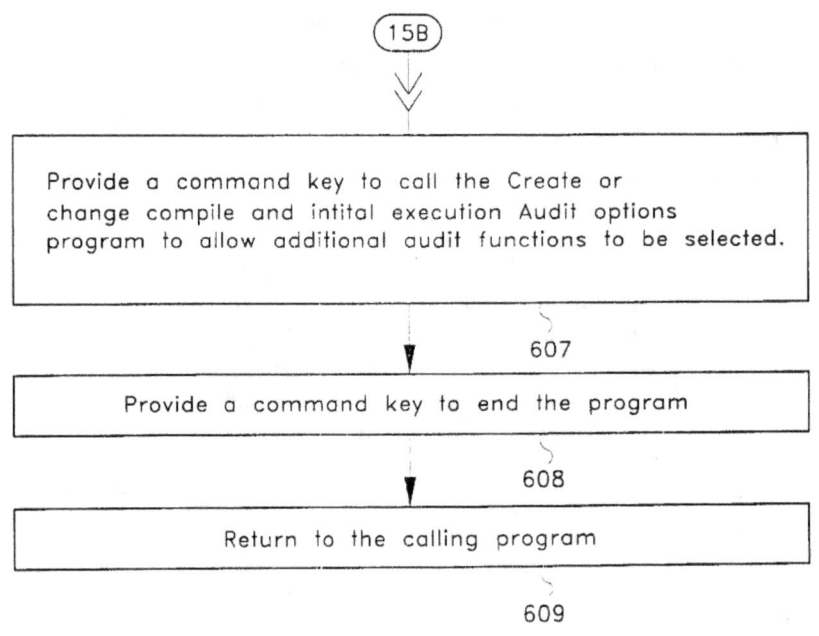

Fig. 15C

Appendix I U.S. Patent Application On-Demand Forensic Accounting Universal Program Auditing Language

U.S. Patent Application Number 61720706   Abandoned

The On-Demand Forensic Accounting Universal Program Auditing Language patent has been abandoned due to lack of funds.

Paul Houston Harkins

UNITED STATES PATENT AND TRADEMARK OFFICE

UNDER SECRETARY OF COMMERCE FOR INTELLECTUAL PROPERTY AND
DIRECTOR OF THE UNITED STATES PATENT AND TRADEMARK OFFICE

NOVEMBER 30, 2012

PTAS

PANITCH SCHWARZE BELISARIO & NADEL LLP
ONE COMMERCE SQUARE
2005 MARKET STREET, SUITE 2200
PHILADELPHIA, PA 19103

502143739

UNITED STATES PATENT AND TRADEMARK OFFICE
NOTICE OF RECORDATION OF ASSIGNMENT DOCUMENT

THE ENCLOSED DOCUMENT HAS BEEN RECORDED BY THE ASSIGNMENT RECORDATION BRANCH
OF THE U.S. PATENT AND TRADEMARK OFFICE. A COMPLETE COPY IS AVAILABLE AT THE
ASSIGNMENT SEARCH ROOM ON THE REEL AND FRAME NUMBER REFERENCED BELOW.

PLEASE REVIEW ALL INFORMATION CONTAINED ON THIS NOTICE. THE INFORMATION
CONTAINED ON THIS RECORDATION NOTICE REFLECTS THE DATA PRESENT IN THE PATENT
AND TRADEMARK ASSIGNMENT SYSTEM. IF YOU SHOULD FIND ANY ERRORS OR HAVE
QUESTIONS CONCERNING THIS NOTICE, YOU MAY CONTACT THE ASSIGNMENT RECORDATION
BRANCH AT 571-272-3350. PLEASE SEND REQUEST FOR CORRECTION TO: U.S. PATENT
AND TRADEMARK OFFICE, MAIL STOP: ASSIGNMENT RECORDATION BRANCH, P.O. BOX
1450, ALEXANDRIA, VA 22313.

RECORDATION DATE: 11/29/2012   REEL/FRAME: 029370/0877
                                  NUMBER OF PAGES: 3

BRIEF: ASSIGNMENT OF ASSIGNORS INTEREST (SEE DOCUMENT FOR DETAILS).

DOCKET NUMBER: 10849-7US/MES

ASSIGNOR:
  HARKINS, PAUL H.   DOC DATE: 11/22/2012

ASSIGNEE:
  HARKINS & ASSOCIATES, INC.
  816 DAISY LANE
  WEST CHESTER, PENNSYLVANIA 19382

APPLICATION NUMBER: 61720706   FILING DATE: 10/31/2012
PATENT NUMBER: ISSUE DATE:
TITLE: ON-TIME DEMAND FORENSIC ACCOUNTING UNIVERSAL PROGRAM AUDITING
        LANGUAGE

ASSIGNMENT RECORDATION BRANCH
PUBLIC RECORDS DIVISION

P.O. Box 1450, Alexandria, Virginia 22313-1450 - WWW.USPTO.GOV

264

Published Works by the Author

An Illustrative Comparison of five of the Most Common Computer
   Programming languages: Assembler, COBOL, Fortran, PL/I, RPG   Drexel   1969

How to Dramatically Increase Your Programming Capability,
Productivity, and Value…
in any Corporate Programming Language   McPress 2004

How to Become a Highly Paid Corporate Programmer   McPress 2004

How to Lead, Manage, and Motivate Corporate Programmers   McPress 2005

On-Demand Forensic Accounting and Analytics   KDP   2014

The Future of Corporate Computing   KDP   2015

Inventions and Patents

U.S. Patent No. 6,775,827 Real-Time Program Audit (RTPA) August 10, 2004
        Australian Patent No. 778165

Real-Time Program Audit (RTPA) software for the IBM i (AS/400) computer. Languages:
RPG, COBOL, CLP copyrighted 2002, 2007

Disk storage Volume Calculator software (VOLCAL) 1970

Sources, References and Permissions

Permissions for references obtained via the Internet have been sought and obtained from the following:

- Wikipedia
- **ITJungle** Reprinted with permission of Guild Companies, Inc., all rights reserved
- **copyright webopedia.com**
- Erik Larson

Other important background material on the Internet where permission has been sought and not obtained due to copyright, licensing considerations or legal constraints is not included in this book.

The interested reader may search the Internet for additional reference material with Google using searches including:

- Current Ponzi schemes
- IBM layoffs
- 10 Biggest Company Layoffs of All Time
- IBM roadmap 2015

www. Web links are included for the paperback print edition

References

Preface

Cognitive computing: A definition and some thoughts
http://www.kmworld.com/Articles/News/News-Analysis/Cognitive-computing-A-definition-and-some-thoughts-99956.aspx

Autonomic computing
http://en.wikipedia.org/wiki/Autonomic_computing

The Innovators - By Walter Isaacson
http://www.panoramatours.com/en/salzburg/salzburg-highlights/sights/getreidegasse/

Kidnapped, Beaten, Robbed While in Hawaii for Sony Open
http://bleacherreport.com/articles/2333621-robert-allenby-allegedly-kidnapped-beaten-robbed-while-in-hawaii-for-sony-open#articles/2333621-robert-allenby-allegedly-kidnapped-beaten-robbed-while-in-hawaii-for-sony-open

Indonesia investigators say no evidence of terrorism in AirAsia plane crash
http://www.aol.com/article/2015/01/19/indonesia-investigators-say-no-evidence-of-terrorism-in-airasia/21131673/

Real-Time Program Audit (RTPA)
http://www.harkinsaudit.com/

Chapter 1 The Future of Corporate Computing

Dr. Grace Murray Hopper
http://www.women-inventors.com/Dr-Grace-Murray-Hopper.asp

BASIC
http://en.wikipedia.org/wiki/BASIC

They Made America: From the Steam Engine to the Search Engine: Two Centuries of Innovators
http://www.amazon.com/They-Made-America-Centuries-Innovators/dp/0316013854

A Clean New Life for Grimy Gas Stations
http://www.nytimes.com/2012/07/11/realestate/commercial/a-clean-new-life-for-grimy-gas-stations.html?pagewanted=all&_r=0

Steve Jobs' 313 patents
http://fortune.com/2011/08/25/steve-jobs-313-patents/

Thomas Edison
http://en.wikipedia.org/wiki/Thomas_Edison

What hourly rate do you pay your offshore developers? India ...
http://www.quora.com/What-hourly-rate-do-you-pay-your-offshore-developers-India-Eastern-Europe-Vietnam

Average Salary for IBM Global Services Employees
http://www.payscale.com/research/US/Employer=IBM_Global_Services/Salary

ENIAC
http://en.wikipedia.org/wiki/ENIAC

Chapter 2 The End of the Corporate In-house Programmer

Cooperative Education | Drexel University

http://catalog.drexel.edu/undergraduate/coop/

253 million cars and trucks on U.S. roads; average age is 11.4 years
http://www.latimes.com/business/autos/la-fi-hy-ihs-automotive-average-age-car-20140609-story.html

General Information Manual IBM 1401 Data Processing System From Control Panel to Stored Program
http://bitsavers.trailing-edge.com/pdf/ibm/140x/F20-208_1401_GenInfo1959.pdf

"This may be an awkward time, but did he happen to mention source code?
https://books.google.com/books?id=mXEbp4U3AT8C&pg=PA3&lpg=PA3&dq=%22This+may+be+an+awkward+time,+but+did+he+happen+to+mention+source+code?&source=bl&ots=DjPD0Z-x1_&sig=s_dcQN0Y6FgK9qKA42EmJk-

IPiM&hl=en&sa=X&ei=g2GbVOCnHY2_sQSugoCYAg&ved=0CCEQ6AEwAQ#v=onepage&
q=%22This%20may%20be%20an%20awkward%20time%2C%20but%20did%20he%20happen
%20to%20mention%20source%20code%3F&f=false

Unit record equipment
http://en.wikipedia.org/wiki/Unit_record_equipment

Plugboards and petaflops
http://www-03.ibm.com/ibm/history/witexhibit/wit_definitions.html

ibm 80-column punched card

https://www.google.com/search?q=ibm+80-col-
umn+punched+card&biw=1464&bih=796&tbm=isch&tbo=u&source=univ&sa=X&ei=Gt2uVIe_I4b7sATltYGIA
Q&ved=0CC0QsAQ#tbm=isch&q=ibm+80-column+punched+card

Google's driverless car is now "fully functional"

http://www.dezeen.com/2014/12/23/google-fully-functional-driverless-car-headlights-steering-wheel-brake-pedal/

Audi, Mercedes Benz debut driverless cars

http://www.kcra.com/money/technology/audi-mercedes-benz-debut-driverless-cars/30569698

WordPress.org

https://wordpress.org/

BNSF moves toward allowing trains with 1 crew member

http://www.omaha.com/money/bnsf-moves-toward-allowing-trains-with-crew-member/article_c17ca655-40bf-5c59-
b837-912f6c083359.html

Run your entire business with QuickBooks

http://search2.quickbooksonline.com/qb-
online?gclid=CKXCyai2hcQCFW4Q7AodVlMAuQ&cid=ppc_g_Broad_US_QB_US_B_Online_Broad_Tier1_G_S
_quickbooksonline_txt&cvosrc=ppc.google.quickbooksonline&matchtype=b&adposition=1t2&creative=500809314
08&content=&cvo_search=1&mobile=&ef_id=VMWRcwAABFmt3R@w:20150228195729:s

Get your maximum refund Guaranteed

https://www.turbotax.com/lp/ty14/ppc/tmp2_2.jsp?srqs=null&cid=ppc_gg_b_stan_all_us_turbotax-main_ty14-bu2-
sb5&srid=sb8ZShHGb|pcrid|42808017708|pkw|turbotax|pmt|e|pdv|c|&skw=turbotax&adid=42808017708&kw={sea
rchQuery}&ven=gg&

SAP What the world needs now is simple

http://www.sap.com/index.html

Oracle CLOUD REVOLUTION

http://www.oracle.com/index.html

C Programming/Strings

http://en.wikibooks.org/wiki/C_Programming/Strings

John Deere S690 Combine with 616C 16 Row Corn Head ...
https://www.youtube.com/watch?v=uePjX09U7_c

Chapter 3 Corporate Executive Migration Path to Cloud computing

Cloud computing
http://en.wikipedia.org/wiki/Cloud_computing

cloud services
http://www.webopedia.com/TERM/C/cloud_services.html

cloud management services

http://www.webopedia.com/TERM/C/cloud_management.html

Executive Briefing Centers

http://www-03.ibm.com/systems/services/briefingcenter/rochester/

IBM Country Club in Poughkeepsie New York.

http://www.forbes.com/sites/work-in-progress/2010/12/13/mourning-the-ibm-country-club-and-end-of-the-corporate-family/

A Manufacturing Revolution (excerpt)

http://h2g2.com/approved_entry/A3488646

Wheaton Arts and Cultural Center

http://www.wheatonarts.org/artiststudios/glassstudio/rent

Chapter 4 Mailroom or Intern or Co-op to CEO in Today's Corporation

Philadelphia abandoned factories

https://www.flickr.com/search/?q=philadelphia+abandoned+factories&ct=0&mt=all&adv=1

From Mailroom to Boardroom: 10 Modern-Day Execs Who Started At The Bottom
http://www.youngupstarts.com/2012/06/05/from-mailroom-to-boardroom-10-modern-day-execs-who-started-at-the-bottom/

The One Minute Manager
http://www.amazon.com/One-Minute-Manager-Kenneth-Blanchard/dp/0688014291/ref=sr_1_1?s=books&ie=UTF8&qid=1421604037&sr=1-1&keywords=the+one-minute+manager

Internet
http://en.wikipedia.org/wiki/Internet

GoToMeeting
https://www4.gotomeeting.com/m/g2msem3.tmpl?Portal=www.gotomeeting.com&c_name=gget-d-c&c_mark=NAPPC&c_kwd=gotomeeting-Exact&c_prod=GTM&c_cmp=sf-70150000000adcs&c_date=CATnumber&c_cell=CPOMy6SsocMCFQQQ7AodIW4AUA&gclid=CPOMy6SsocMCFQQQ7AodIW4AUA&gclsrc=aw.ds

Screen Recording & Video Editing
http://www.techsmith.com/camtasia.html?gclid=CJb93dPej8QCFUojgQodzVEAew

Skype keeps the world talking. Call, message and share whatever you want for free
http://www.skype.com/en/

Chapter 5 The Road to Singapore

Singapore

http://www.world-finance-conference.com/sites/default/files/beautiful-singapore-cityscape-1600x1066_0.jpg

World's most expensive cities revealed
http://www.aol.com/article/2015/03/04/worlds-most-expensive-cities-revealed/21149616/?icid=maing-grid7%7Chtmlws-sb-bb%7Cdl20%7Csec1_lnk2%26pLid%3D622532

Chapter 6 The Bernie Madoff Case - The Forensic Accounting Investigation

Madoff investment scandal
http://en.wikipedia.org/wiki/Madoff_investment_scandal

No One Would Listen: A True Financial Thriller
http://www.amazon.com/No-One-Would-Listen-Financial/dp/0470919000/ref=sr_1_3?ie=UTF8&qid=1422122109&sr=8-3&keywords=Madoff+books

The Club No One Wanted To Join-Madoff Victims In Their Own Words

http://www.amazon.com/Wanted-Join-Madoff-Victims-Their-Words/dp/0982250932/ref=sr_1_1?ie=UTF8&qid=1422216300&sr=8-1&keywords=No+one+wanted+to+join+the+club

The Wizard of Lies: Bernie Madoff and the Death of Trust
http://www.amazon.com/Wizard-Lies-Bernie-Madoff-Death/dp/1250007437/ref=sr_1_1?ie=UTF8&qid=1422122109&sr=8-1&keywords=Madoff+books

Betrayal: The Life and Lies of Bernie Madoff
http://www.amazon.com/Betrayal-Life-Lies-Bernie-Madoff/dp/B0051BNW0S/ref=sr_1_4?ie=UTF8&qid=1422124970&sr=8-4&keywords=Madoff+books

Too Good to Be True: The Rise and Fall of Bernie Madoff
http://www.amazon.com/Too-Good-Be-True-Bernie/dp/1591842999/ref=sr_1_5?ie=UTF8&qid=1422124970&sr=8-5&keywords=Madoff+books

The Madoff Chronicles: Inside the Secret World of Bernie and Ruth
http://www.amazon.com/Madoff-Chronicles-Inside-Secret-Bernie/dp/140131029X/ref=sr_1_7?ie=UTF8&qid=1422124970&sr=8-7&keywords=Madoff+books

Lost and Found: One Woman's Story of Losing Her Money and Finding Her Life
http://www.amazon.com/Lost-Found-Womans-Losing-Finding/dp/0452297761/ref=sr_1_8?ie=UTF8&qid=1422124970&sr=8-8&keywords=Madoff+books

The End of Normal: A Wife's Anguish, A Widow's New Life
http://www.amazon.com/End-Normal-Wifes-Anguish-Widows/dp/0452298571/ref=sr_1_1?ie=UTF8&qid=1422738876&sr=8-1&keywords=madoff+wife

The almost daily reporting by Erik Larson of the recent more than five month trial of five Madoff employees, including two Madoff programmers provides fascinating detail of what the jury was told. Google: Erik Larson Madoff trial reporting

Madoff Ex-Employees' Jury Told of 'Smoke And Mirrors'
http://www.bloomberg.com/news/2013-10-28/madoff-ex-employees-jury-told-of-smoke-and-mirrors-.html

Ex-Madoff Employee Tells Jury of 'Cut And Paste' Trades
http://www.bloomberg.com/news/2013-10-24/ex-madoff-employee-tells-jury-of-cut-and-paste-trades.html

Madoff Ex-Aide Balances Almost $70 Million, Jury Told
http://www.bloomberg.com/news/2014-01-23/madoff-ex-aide-balances-almost-70-million-jury-told.html

Ex-Madoff Programmers Sought Pay in Diamonds, Jury Told
http://www.bloomberg.com/news/2013-12-10/ex-madoff-programmers-sought-pay-in-diamonds-jury-told.html

Madoff Case Is Paying Off for Trustee ($850 an Hour)
http://dealbook.nytimes.com/2012/05/28/madoff-case-is-paying-off-for-trustee-850-an-hour/?_r=0

Madoff Scorecard, in Billions: $17.5 Lost, $10 Recovered, $1 to Do It
http://www.bloomberg.com/news/2014-11-20/madoff-bankruptcy-costs-top-1-billion-six-years-later.html

Madoff Prosecutors Criticize Judge for Being Too Soft

http://www.bloomberg.com/news/2014-12-11/mercy-for-madoff-aides-fraud-seen-hindering-justice.html

Madoff's many brainstorms included fake trade platform
http://seattletimes.com/html/businesstechnology/2009651388_madoff13.html

An AS/400 was critical to Madoff's Ponzi scheme- The Inquirer
http://www.theinquirer.net/inquirer/news/1529209/an-as-400-critical-madoff-ponzi-scheme

Jerome O'Hara, George Perez arrested for allegedly creating computer programs for Madoff's scam
http://www.nydailynews.com/news/money/jerome-o-hara-george-perez-arrested-allegedly-creating-computer-programs-madoff-scam-article-1.414683

Bruce G. Dubinsky, MST, CPA, CVA, CFE, MAFF, CFF
https://www.linkedin.com/pub/bruce-g-dubinsky-mst-cpa-cva-cfe-maff-cff/a/688/859

IBM AS/400
https://www-03.ibm.com/ibm/history/exhibits/rochester/rochester_4010.html

IBM System i5 and i5/OS
V5R4https://www.flickr.com/search/?q=AS%2F400&l=comm&ct=0&mt=all&adv=1

Securities and Exchange Commission fy 2015 Budget request by program
https://www.sec.gov/about/reports/sec-fy2015-budget-request-by-program.pdf

House Committee OKs Smaller SEC Budget Raise Than Hoped For

http://www.thinkadvisor.com/2014/06/18/house-committee-oks-smaller-sec-budget-raise-than

Despite Exposure of Madoff Fraud, New Ponzi Schemes Emerge
http://dealbook.nytimes.com/2014/07/10/despite-exposure-of-madoff-fraud-new-ponzi-schemes-emerge/?_r=0

Big Four Audit Firms

http://en.wikipedia.org/wiki/Big_Four_(audit_firms)

Chapter 7 How IBM and SAP Can Succeed and Grow: A Revolutionary Strategy

Honeywell 200
http://en.wikipedia.org/wiki/Honeywell_200

Why Did IBM Survive?
http://www.forbes.com/sites/stevedenning/2011/07/10/why-did-ibm-survive/

IBM's $ 5000000000 Gamble

http://www.cedix.de/Literature/History/FiveMillGamble1.pdf

IBM System/360 Announcement
http://www-03.ibm.com/ibm/history/exhibits/mainframe/mainframe_PR360.html

548 F. 2d 1065 - International Business Machines Corporation v. Catamore Enterprises Inc
http://openjurist.org/548/f2d/1065/international-business-machines-corporation-v-catamore-enterprises-inc

BUNCH
http://en.wikipedia.org/wiki/BUNCH

New IBM Pricing Policy 1969
http://archive.computerhistory.org/resources/access/text/2014/06/102712825/102712825-05-01-acc.pdf

IBM System/3
https://www-03.ibm.com/ibm/history/exhibits/rochester/rochester_4008.htmlhttps://www-03.ibm.com/ibm/history/exhibits/rochester/rochester_4008.html

Essentials of Strategic Management - Page 110 - Google Books
https://books.google.com/books?id=VdG243upAqwC&pg=RA1-PA110&lpg=RA1-PA110&dq=john+opel+low-cost+producer&source=bl&ots=EQFmpL-YCi&sig=ODsamIPu8BeGGsOgPYFBMipnSA4&hl=en&sa=X&ei=L8z0VKmfKrDlsAShqYCwBw&ved=0CCQQ6AEwAQ#v=onepage&q=john%20opel%20low-cost%20producer&f=false

Inside the As/400 by Frank G. Soltis

http://www.amazon.com/Inside-As-400-Frank-Soltis/dp/1882419138/ref=sr_1_3?ie=UTF8&qid=1423150275&sr=8-3&keywords=Frank+soltis

Fortress Rochester: The Inside Story of the IBM iSeries

http://www.amazon.com/Fortress-Rochester-Inside-Story-iSeries/dp/1583040838/ref=sr_1_1?ie=UTF8&qid=1423948833&sr=8-1&keywords=fortress+rochester

SALES FORCE REALIGNED BY I.B.M.
http://www.nytimes.com/1981/10/02/business/sales-force-realigned-by-ibm.html

John Fellows Akers

http://en.wikipedia.org/wiki/John_Fellows_Akers

Louis Gerstner's vision for IBM: the customer is always right
http://jonathangifford.com/louis-gerstners-vision-for-ibm-the-customer-is-always-right/

IBM sales in 11th straight fall amid business revamp

http://www.ft.com/cms/s/0/7001724a-a0e6-11e4-8ad8-00144feab7de.html#axzz3QWXHyFN2

IBM in the midst of massive reorganization

http://www.businesscloudnews.com/2015/01/09/ibm-in-the-midst-of-massive-reorganisation/

Next Week's Bloodbath At IBM Won't Fix The Real Problem

http://www.forbes.com/sites/robertcringely/2015/01/22/next-weeks-bloodbath-at-ibm-wont-fix-the-real-problem/

As IBM reportedly cuts 50000 India jobs, CEO replaces Global

https://www.google.com/?gws_rd=ssl#q=ibm+job+cuts+today

Robots Replacing Human Factory Workers at Faster Pace
http://abcnews.go.com/Business/wireStory/robots-replacing-human-factory-workers-faster-pace-28849861

Human–computer interaction
http://en.wikipedia.org/wiki/Human%E2%80%93computer_interaction

IRS Says It Depends on Kennedy-Era Computing

http://www.dailyfinance.com/2015/02/04/irs-kennedy-era-computers-process-tax-returns/

Autonomic computing

http://en.wikipedia.org/wiki/Autonomic_computing

Big data

http://en.wikipedia.org/wiki/Big_data

Cognitive computing

http://en.wikipedia.org/wiki/Cognitive_computing

AirAsia Flight 8501: Captain Was Out Of His Seat When Co-Pilot Lost Control Of Plane, Sources Say

http://www.ibtimes.com/airasia-flight-8501-captain-was-out-his-seat-when-co-pilot-lost-control-plane-sources-1801348

On-Demand Forensic Accounting and Analytics

http://www.harkinsaudit.com/docs/On_Demand_Forensic_Accounting_and_Analytics_copyright.pdf

Chapter 8 My Conclusions (and my Opinion)

IBM System/360 computer

http://www-03.ibm.com/ibm/history/exhibits/mainframe/mainframe_PR360.html

new line of business computers

https://www-03.ibm.com/ibm/history/exhibits/rochester/rochester_4008.htmlhttps:/www-03.ibm.com/ibm/history/exhibits/rochester/rochester_4008.html

GSD division

http://www.amazon.com/Fortress-Rochester-Inside-Story-iSeries/dp/1583040838/ref=sr_1_1?ie=UTF8&qid=1423948833&sr=8-1&keywords=fortress+rochester

Run Simple with SAP - Technology Solutions from SAP

http://discover.sap.com/runsimple?campaigncode=CRM-XH15-POR-PPC-BRND&utm_source=google&utm_medium=PPC&utm_term=run%20simple%20+sap&utm_campaign=NA-NA-AC-Brand-General%20(Paid%20Search-%20Google%20-%20Br)

How Steve Jobs' Love of Simplicity Fueled A Design ...

http://www.smithsonianmag.com/arts-culture/how-steve-jobs-love-of-simplicity-fueled-a-design-revolution-23868877/?no-ist

KISS principle - Wikipedia, the free encyclopedia

http://en.wikipedia.org/wiki/KISS_principle

About the Author

Author Paul Houston Harkins has fifty-five years of experience in corporate information technology, working with hundreds of companies worldwide. The founder and CTO of Harkins & Associates Inc., he develops and implements audit and programming productivity software for high-profile corporations.

His extensive résumé also includes programming consultant, IT analyst, systems developer, expert forensic accounting investigator, and senior systems engineer at IBM in Philadelphia from 1962 to 1984. He is still actively consulting.

In his book *The Future of Corporate Computing*, Paul Houston Harkins offers his observations of corporate computing as a driver of change.